CHILD ABUSE AND NEGLECT
Biosocial Dimensions

CHILD ABUSE AND NEGLECT
Biosocial Dimensions

Edited by

Richard J. Gelles

Jane B. Lancaster

Sponsored by the
Social Science Research Council

ALDINE DE GRUYTER
New York

ABOUT THE EDITORS

Richard J. Gelles is Dean of the College of Arts and Sciences and Professor of Sociology and Anthropology at the University of Rhode Island. His previous publications include "The Violent Home," "Family Violence," "Behind Closed Doors: Violence in the American Family," and "International Perspectives on Family Violence."

Jane B. Lancaster is Professor of Anthropology, University of New Mexico. She chairs the Social Science Research Council's Committee on Biosocial Science Perspectives on Parent Behavior and Offspring Development as well as the General Anthropology Unit of the American Anthropological Association. She is the co-editor of "School-Age Pregnancy and Parenthood" and "Parenting Across the Life Span" and the co-author of "Eve and Adam: The Origins of Sex and the Family."

ALDINE DE GRUYTER
A Division of Walter de Gruyter, Inc.
200 Saw Mill River Road
Hawthorne, New York 10532

Library of Congress Cataloging-in-Publication Data

Child abuse and neglect.
  (Foundations of human behavior)
  Includes bibliographies.
  1. Child abuse.   2. Child abuse—Cross-cultural
studies.   I. Gelles, Richard J.   II. Lancaster, Jane
Beckman, 1935–   .   III. Social Science Research
Council (U.S.). Committee on Biosocial Perspectives
on Parent Behavior and Offspring Development.
IV. Series.   [DNLM: 1. Child Abuse.   WA 320 C534014]
HV6626.5.C485   1987   362.7'044   87-8999
ISBN 0-202-30333-0
ISBN 0-202-30334-9 (pbk.)

Printed in the United States of America
10 9 8 7 6 5 4 3 2 1

CONTENTS

v

ACKNOWLEDGMENTS

All aspects of the program of the Committee on Biosocial Perspectives on Parent Behavior and Offspring Development which have focused on child abuse and neglect have been funded by the Harry Frank Guggenheim Foundation (New York). The committee and the Council are very appreciative of the support provided by the Foundation. A previous grant to the Council from the National Institute of Child Health and Human Development provided funding for a series of planning workshops that led to the formation of the committee. The editors of the volume wish also to thank the Social Science Research Council for its support of the committee.

Among the early activities relating to the topic, Child Abuse and Neglect, the committee held a conference at the Breckenridge Conference Center, of Bowdoin College, in May of 1984. The committee wishes also to express its appreciation to the staff of the Center, particularly to Anne Underwood, the director.

⁓ During the several years of planning and preparation following this conference, that have resulted in the present volume, the editors were assisted by the members of the committee and the staff of the Social Science Research Council. A particular expression of appreciation is due Terry Ciatto at the SSRC who has handled all of the daily aspects of typing, mailing, distributing proofs, telephoning authors, and generally maintaining the progress of the volume. The management and staff at Aldine de Gruyter were of invaluable assistance throughout all phases of production of the volume.

LIST OF CONTRIBUTORS

J. Lawrence Aber
Department of Psychology
Barnard College
New York, New York 10027

Karen G. Braunwald
Department of Psychology &
Social Relations
Harvard University
Cambridge, Massachusetts 02138

Larry D. Byrd
Yerkes Regional Primate
    Research Center
Emory University
Atlanta, Georgia 30322

Vicki Carlson
Department of Psychology
Harvard University
Cambridge, Massachusetts 02138

John P. Capitanio
Department of Psychology
University of Massachusetts
Boston, Massachusetts 02125

Dante Cicchetti
Mt. Hope Family Center
Rochester, New York 14627

Martin Daly
Department of Psychology
McMaster University
Hamilton, Ontario L8S 4K1
Canada

Byron Egeland
Department of Psychology
University of Minnesota
Minneapolis, Minnesota 55455

James Garbarino
Erikson Institute
Chicago, Illinois 60610

Richard J. Gelles
College of Arts & Sciences
University of Rhode Island
Kingston, Rhode Island 02881

Sarah Blaffer Hrdy
Department of Anthropology
University of California, Davis
Davis, California 95616

Deborah Jacobvitz
Institute of Child Development
University of Minnesota
Minneapolis, Minnesota 55455

Sheila Ryan Johansson
Graduate Group in Demography
University of California
Berkeley, California 94303

Jill E. Korbin
Department of Anthropology
Case Western Reserve University
Cleveland, Ohio 44106

Jane B. Lancaster
Department of Anthropology
University of New Mexico
Albuquerque, New Mexico 87131

Carolyn Moore Newberger
Judge Baker Guidance Center
Boston, Massachusetts 02115

Kathleen Papatola
Institute of Child Development
University of Minnesota
Minneapolis, Minnesota 55455

Martin Reite
Department of Psychiatry
University of Colorado
School of Medicine
Denver, Colorado 60262

Euclid O. Smith
Department of Anthropology
    and Yerkes Regional Primate
    Research Center
Emory University
Atlanta, Georgia 30322

Margo Wilson
Department of Psychology
McMaster University
Hamilton, Ontario L8S 4K1
Canada

FOUNDATIONS OF HUMAN BEHAVIOR

An Aldine de Gruyter Series of Texts and Monographs

Edited by
Sarah Blaffer Hrdy, *University of California, Davis*
Richard W. Wrangham, *University of Michigan*

The Biology of Moral Systems
Richard D. Alexander

Child Abuse and Neglect: Biosocial Dimensions
Richard J. Gelles and Jane B. Lancaster, Editors

Parenting Across the Life Span: Biosocial Dimensions
Jane B. Lancaster, Jeanne Altmann, Alice S. Rossi, and Lonnie R. Sherrod, Editors

Primate Evolution and Human Origins
Russell L. Ciochon and John G. Fleagle, Editors

Human Birth: An Evolutionary Perspective
Wenda R. Trevathan

School-Age Pregnancy and Parenthood: Biosocial Dimensions
Jane B. Lancaster and Beatrix A. Hamburg, Editors

Despotism and Differential Reproduction: A Darwinian View of History
Laura L. Betzig

Sex and Friendship in Baboons
Barbara Boardman Smuts

Infanticide: Comparative and Evolutionary Perspectives
Glenn Hausfater and Sarah Blaffer Hrdy, Editors

Navajo Infancy: An Ethological Study of Child Development
James S. Chisholm

In Preparation

Homicide
Martin Daly and Margo Wilson

Human Ethology
Irenäus Eibl-Eibesfeldt

Brain and Behavior: Biosocial Dimensions
Kathleen Gibson and Anne Petersen, Editors

Early Hominid Activities at Olduvai
Richard B. Potts

Evolutionary History of the Robust Australopithecines
Frederick E. Grine, Editor

Inujjuamiut Foraging Strategies
Eric Alden Smith

Human Reproductive Ecology
James W. Wood

INTRODUCTION

part I

INTRODUCTION

Jane B. Lancaster
Richard J. Gelles

The Biosocial Perspective

This volume is the third in a series sponsored by the Social Science Research Council's Committee on Biosocial Perspectives on Parent Behavior and Offspring Development. The committee, formed in 1980, is a multidisciplinary group (including biological, behavioral, and social scientists). The committee seeks to promote an exchange of concepts, methods, and data across disciplines on a variety of substantive issues on which the group shares intellectual and policy concerns. The goals of the committee's program are: to develop conceptualizations of social phenomena relying on biosocial science, to explore the interface between biological and social phenomena, and to advance our understanding of human social behavior. The first volume of the series, *School-Age Pregnancy and Parenthood: Biosocial Dimensions,* edited by J. Lancaster and B. Hamburg (Aldine, 1986) focuses on a particular segment of the life span and the challenges, problems, and opportunities inherent in parenthood during such an early phase of the reproductive years. The second volume, *Parenting Across the Life Span: Biosocial Dimensions,* edited by J. Lancaster, J. Altmann, A.S. Rossi, and L.R. Sherrod (Aldine, 1987) sweeps across the life span, examining parenthood as a commitment involving the entire life course. Of particular concern is the impact of modern changes in the timing, distribution, and intensity of the commitment to parenthood for both parent and child behavior and experience. The current volume draws on a biosocial perspective to examine what has become a major concern of modern society, both for scientific inquiry and social policy formulation: child maltreatment.

Biosocial science is particularly relevant to research on human family systems and parent behavior because the family is the universal social institution within which the bearing and care of children has been

3

based. Family systems are where cultural traditions, beliefs, and values are transmitted to the young as individual actors fulfill their biological potential for reproduction, growth, and development. The biosocial perspective takes into account the biological substrate and the social and environmental contexts as determinants of patterns of behavior. The perspective also pinpoints areas in which contemporary human parental behavior exhibits continuities with, and departures from, patterns evident throughout human history. Unless discontinuities in family behaviors and their overall costs and benefits are examined, we are not able to assess them objectively in terms of modern circumstances. The biosocial perspective, therefore, extends our understanding of parent behavior by sensitizing us to the variety of patterns among current practices as well as by highlighting the full range of parent–child patterns that have been represented in the evolutionary and historical past. Both the spectrum of options and the basis for making judgments about these options are expanded.

The term "biosocial" was selected to emphasize the functional unity of both biological and socioenvironmental factors. The mutual influences of these factors are more than additive; indeed, they are interrelated through reciprocal processes that can significantly alter the characteristics of each. The potential for change and variation in biological attributes is less well understood than is the potential for human learning and behavioral change. There has been a misleading tendency to perceive biological behaviors as being unlearned, independent of the environment, and not readily susceptible to change. There also has been an expectation that there will be uniformity of biological response to a specific stimulus. For human beings especially, prior experience, motivation, and context will influence biological responses to all kinds of stimuli, whether they are pathogenic bacteria or social interactions. The recognition of the continuous, mutual, inseparable interaction between biology and the socioenvironmental factors is one of the critical foundations of the biosocial perspective.

The volume opens the way for a biosocial synthesis of perspectives on child abuse and neglect by presenting and integrating recent advances in biological and social science research on parental behavior and patterns of investment in young. The past decade witnessed the maturation of two separate foci of science dealing with offspring abuse and neglect. The biological sciences developed theories of kin selection and parental investment at the same time that the social sciences focused on the context and immediate causes of child maltreatment as well as the long-term developmental consequences. The value of applying a biosocial perspective to the problem of human child abuse lies in the wider dimension through time and space that it adds to modern studies. It takes the focus off abuse as a modern pathology by demonstrating its occurrence in nonhuman species, other cultures, and past history. It directs attention to questions about when and where a pattern of abuse is expectable at high frequencies because of the social and ecological contexts in which reproductive units are found. By emphasizing not only causation but also long-term consequences of child maltreatment through prospective studies following cohorts of parents and children through time, the recent research expands the focus of child abuse studies beyond the identification of abusive parents and the immediate short-term costs to the child. In this fashion, we develop a broader view of intergenerational effects and the factors which may ameliorate or enhance the impact of maltreatment on the development of children.

Armed with a commitment to a biosocial science perspective, 20 scientists from the disciplines of anthropology, evolutionary biology, history, human development, family studies, primatology, psychiatry, psychobiology, psychology, and sociology contributed chapters that discuss their own research and/or review the state of knowledge of their respective disciplines on offspring abuse and neglect. The collective body of work is interdisciplinary, biosocial, and comparative. The work provides new insights, explodes old fallacies, and charts a course for new models of research.

EVOLUTIONARY BIOLOGY AND PARENTAL INVESTMENT THEORY

Long-term, naturalistic field studies conducted in the last 10 years provided fresh perspectives on parenthood and the life span. As behavioral ecology advanced the concept of life history strategies and tactics and sociobiology modeled kin selection and parental investment theory, new theoretical models transformed evolutionary biology. Parental investment, defined as any investment by a parent in an offspring that increases the recipient's fitness at the cost of parental capacity to invest elsewhere, emphasizes the limited amount of parental resources (time, energy, attention) that can be apportioned to offspring over the course of the life spans of both parent and offspring (Clutton-Brock, in press; Daly and Wilson, 1983; Maynard Smith, 1977; Trivers, 1972). The fit between reproductive strategies and environmental resources and the shaping of the life course to optimize reproductive success in a given environment became a major focus of theoretical exploration. A common theme of such analysis, especially in regard to long-lived, intelligent mammals, is parenthood as a life span commitment and the sensitivity of parental investment patterns to availability of social and environmental resources.

The implications of parental investment theory for the understanding of variability in human parental behavior are profound. The evolutionary history of the human family and parent/offspring relations suggests that human parental investment patterns are a fundamental adaptation for the species (Lancaster, 1984; Lancaster and Lancaster, 1983). Human offspring are unusually vulnerable to deficits in parental investment because of their long period of development with a prolonged juvenile period and because of an unusual degree of brain growth after birth and during the first four years of life. Among monkeys and apes, our closest living relatives, female parents shoulder the responsibility of rearing single nutritionally dependent offspring at one time with minimal assistance from males. In contrast, humans, through the evolution of the division of labor and the role of husband/father, formed an adaptive pattern in which both male and female parents contribute to the feeding of infant and juvenile offspring. This pattern allows for the care of two or more nutritionally dependent young of differing ages at the same time. Among most mammals the juvenile period is the riskiest part of the life course because of the disadvantages such youngsters have in locating and competing for food to feed themselves. For humans, the collaboration of male and female parents in the feeding of juveniles was a pivotal step in the evolution of the species. It allowed for the expansion of the juvenile years as a protected phase of learning (Johnston, 1982) and increased survivorship to adulthood at the same time that it made human parental investment patterns unusually sensitive to the availability of both social and environmental resources (Lancaster and Lancaster, 1983).

Evolutionary theory would suggest that humans, because of the long commitment made by both parents or by an extended kin network to rearing infants to adulthood, should display strong facultative effects on offspring-rearing strategies and in discriminative parental solicitude according to parental assessment of resources. Humans should be able to "cut their losses" from a child with poor potential in preference to children, perhaps yet unborn, with more favorable chances for survival and reproduction. Wasser and Isenberg (1985) have applied this type of perspective to human fertility and argue that the course of conception and pregnancy for human women should be continuously sensitive to changing measures of fetal viability and to shifts in environmental resources and social support. They suggest that one way to look at medical pathologies such as low fertility, miscarriage, abortion, and premature delivery, is as "healthy infertility"—an evolved adaptation to cut investment when the conceptus or context shift negatively in characteristics. Other studies (Lamb and Hwang, 1982; Scheper-Hughes, 1985) follow similar reasoning about the facultative nature of mother–infant bonding. They find no special period for mother–infant attachment in humans. The once hoped for bonding during a critical period at birth (Klaus and Kennell, 1976) melts away in the face of complex contextual variables. Bonding is not the issue but rather maternal assessment of environmental support. For humans, there is no "quick fix" for problems of parent–child attachment because by nature the relationship will always have an at least partially facultative response to the social and environmental context. Such work raises the question that it may not be unnatural for a mother to miscarry or abort or for parents to neglect their children or even target a special child for abuse under particular sets of unfavorable contexts for parental behavior. Humans, with their greatly expanded intelligence, are in a position to reassess, at each step along the way of parenthood, the current and future prospects of each child. In the face of limited resources and unfavorable circumstances it is not surprising that they should use such capacity to discriminate their investment and allow context to aid in defining relative value of offspring.

Hrdy (this volume, Chapter 5) presents a single measure of parental discriminative solicitude, sex-biased parental investment among mammals (including humans). She discusses not only the variability and complexity of such behaviors across and within species, but also the difficulties inherent in testing theoretical propositions to explain them. The value of evolutionary theory in helping to understand differential investment in sons and daughters or even infanticide is not to suggest that adaptations of the past are equivalent to normatively "good" in the present. Rather such understanding is important in preparing modern society to recognize challenges posed by our evolutionary past to the adaptations of today—just as understanding the evolutionary history of appetite for fats and sugars helps with treatment of modern obesity and heart disease. Evolutionary theory does not justify—it explains and suggests mechanisms and pathways.

COMPARATIVE PERSPECTIVES: ACROSS SPECIES, CULTURES, AND HISTORY

A primary advantage of comparative data from other species, cultures, and history is the expanded dimension beyond the modern time and context. It shifts the focus away from child abuse and neglect as a pathology characteristic of modern society. To acknowledge that offspring abuse and neglect not only occurred in the history of western society but also in other cultures and even in animal species, is to shift the primary question from causes of pathology to one which asks under what conditions is offspring abuse predictable and who are most vulnerable as perpetrators and victims. For example, such an expanded perspective on infanticide indicates that although such behavior is predictable in a wide variety of species, humans are the only ones in which the most likely perpetrators are the parents themselves (Hausfater and

Blaffer Hrdy, 1984). The chapters in this volume by Gelles (Chapter 2), Hrdy (Chapter 5), Johansson (Chapter 4), and Korbin (Chapter 3), broaden the comparative dimension by exploring issues in human abuse and neglect of children across time and space. Their contributions underscore the facultative nature of human parental solicitude and emphasize differential investment in children according to assessment of both their costs and prospects as defined by the social and environmental context. Another striking feature of these chapters is the emergent fact that across time and space, childhood morbidity and mortality have been influenced much more by neglect than by outright abuse, the focus of so much societal concern today.

Comparisons across species, especially with the closest living relatives of humans, indicate some of the reasons why human parents are so unusual as perpetrators of both infanticide and abuse and neglect of offspring. For the most part, monkey and ape mothers rear their young more or less as only children. They do not have to face the implications of the feeding dependency of multiple young of differing ages with their capacity to maintain dependent young highly vulnerable to the withdrawal of social support from mate or kin as it is for human mothers (cf. Newberger, this volume, Chapter 10). There is also evidence that, in the course of human history, the wide 4- to 5-year birth spacing typical of the great apes and human, low-density, foraging, and horticultural societies, contracted down to 2 years or less (J.B. Lancaster and C.S. Lancaster, 1987). This historic contraction of the length of lactation and the time between successive births greatly increased dependence of human mothers on outside support for the rearing of children. Second, the cognitive tasks of parenthood for monkey and ape mothers appear far different from what are expected of human mothers, especially in the modern context. A good primate mother protects and nurtures an infant until it is weaned and promotes the social status and survival of her juvenile. She does so using a cognitive set which essentially defines her offspring as an extension of herself without empathy for them as independent sentient beings (Altmann, 1980). The criteria by which she is judged is the mortality and morbidity of her offspring not their social adjustment or cognitive well-being.

CAUSATION AND CONTEXT: THE PREDICTION OF RISK

In the past decade, social scientists have struggled to go past description and documentation to probe into the immediate causal mechanisms and social and ecological contexts most often associated with child maltreatment. The major goal of social science research has been to explode myths and develop theories beyond simple univariate causal statements. Reite and Capitanio (this volume, Chapter 6) summarize the similarities between the ecological and social environment of offspring abuse in human and nonhuman primates. The similarities suggest that there are aspects of offspring abuse that are defined by neither culture nor species but may rest on a deeper, higher-primate biological substrate. The authors identify two situations associated with physical abuse (but not neglect) in human and nonhuman primates: the first being an increase in the frequency of social and environmental stressors and the second being aberrant experience in infancy, particularly found with separation between mother and infant and a failure to establish the psychobiological synchrony associated with mother–infant attachment. Smith and Byrd (this volume, Chapter 7) similarly probe the psychobiological bases of attachment in monkeys by manipulation of neurochemistry. They too find indication of limbic-mediated brain mechanisms which involve the expression of attachment and aggression. Interestingly, they find that the frequency and target of aggression is affected by both brain neurochemistry and by social kin context. Their work underscores an important theme of the biosocial perspective: the multiple levels of mutual interaction between biological and social factors in determining social behavior.

Besides understanding the immediate brain mechanisms associated with abusive behavior, the profile of children and parents most at risk for such extremes of abuse as child homicide and reported maltreatment expands our theoretical understanding of offspring maltreatment. Daly and Wilson (this volume Chapters 8 and 9) examine the characteristics of parents who kill their own children indicating a very different age and mental status of mothers who commit infanticide and mothers who murder older children. They also note that, as predicted by evolutionary theory, the presence of a stepparent in a household increases risk to unrelated stepchildren but not to one's own children, irrespective of other socioeconomic factors. Newberger, Johansson, and Korbin (this volume, Chapters 3, 4, and 10) examine other risk factors associated with child maltreatment. These authors find that parental cognitive modes are significant in the production of quality child care. They point to mature levels of parental awareness or empathy and personal responsibility as critical to the task of parenthood among modern humans and note the varying expression of these traits in the cross-cultural and historic record. They concur that historic change away from the sib to a parent-care system of child rearing greatly altered childhood morbidity and mortality in the historic and contemporary cross-cultural record, which raises the question whether parent-care systems have higher or lower rates of child abuse.

The identification of risk associated with offspring maltreatment clearly involves multiple and interactive levels of analysis including biological (neurochemical substrate in the brain), social stress, and familial structure, and mature cognitive function in parents—the latter being a psychological potential of the human species but affected by culture differences, behavior, and values for completeness of their expression.

OUTCOMES AND CONSEQUENCES

The child maltreatment literature contains many assumptions and theories about the consequences of abuse and neglect. The immediate consequences are the obvious injuries and harm done by acts of commission or omission. Other possible impacts are more long term. Some researchers and clinicians believe that untreated abused children frequently grow up to be juvenile delinquents, murderers, and batterers of the next generation of children (Schmitt and Kempe, 1975). The literature consistently includes assumptions about how the abuse of children leads to violent behavior when the children grow up. As adults, maltreated children are thought to have higher rates of drug and alcohol abuse, criminal behavior, and psychiatric disturbances (Smith *et al.*, 1973). As children, victims of maltreatment are thought to suffer higher rates of developmental delays and more social and emotional difficulties (Galdston, 1975; Martin *et al.*, 1974).

Actual data which *both* meet the normal rules of empirical evidence and conclusively demonstrate the negative short- and long-term consequences of maltreatment are rare. The large majority of studies of the consequences of child maltreatment suffer from one or more significant methodological flaws, including failing to employ control groups, failing to obtain adequate base-line measures of both the independent and dependent variables, small sample sizes, and basing conclusions on cross-sectional retrospective research.

Chapter 11 (this volume) by Egeland, Jacobovitz, and Papatola and Chapter 12 (this volume) by Cicchetti, Carlson, Braunwald, and Aber are exceptions to the normally methodologically flawed examinations of the consequences of maltreatment. Both chapters report on research that employed a prospective longitudinal design, with appropriate comparison groups, and psychometrically sound measures. Both chapters also evidence the theoretical advantage of applying a biosocial perspective to examining the outcomes and consequences of maltreatment. Egeland and his colleagues have been able to pinpoint some of the factors that can lead to the intergenerational transmission of abuse. Mothers who did not repeat the pattern of abuse they had experienced as children shared stable home situations, and intact families, and supportive husbands (who are the fathers of the children). Clearly, environmental resources, support, and two available and willing caretakers play a significant role in lessening the risk of abuse. Cicchetti *et al.*'s project is at a much less advanced stage than Egeland *et al.*, but here, too, a broad-based examination of factors related to the consequences of maltreatment provides more insight than the traditional narrow and unilinear approaches which state that abuse leads to abuse.

Garbarino (this volume, Chapter 13) applies a biosocial perspective to assessing the development of abused children. Drawing on a biosocial and ecological framework, he assesses how maltreatment can affect human development and possibly raise the risk of later juvenile delinquency on the part of the victimized child. Garbarino forsakes the traditional univariate approach and considers a system of relevant biosocial and ecological forces that impact upon families and children.

The manifest advantage of a biosocial approach to studying outcomes and consequences of maltreatment is the initial exploding of the myth that all maltreated children are permanently damaged and doomed to grow up to be violent adults. In place of this "deterministic" model of the impact of maltreatment, investigators have developed a more realistic stochastic model which goes beyond individual considerations of abuser and victim and incorporates assessments of family systems, environmental factors, and developmental variables and constructs.

REFERENCES

Altmann, J. *Baboon mothers and infants.* Cambridge, MA: Harvard, 1980.

Betzig, L. L., Borgerhoff Mulder, M., and Turke, P. W. *Reproduction and parental investment in humans.* NY: Cambridge, in press.

Clutton-Brock, T. H. *Reproductive success.* Chicago, IL: Chicago University Press, in press.

Daly, M., and Wilson, M. *Evolution and behavior* (2nd Edition). Boston, MA: Willard Grant, 1983.

Galdston, R. Observations of children who have been physically abused by their parents. *American Journal of Psychiatry* 1975, 122(4):580–590.

Hausfater, G., and Blaffer Hrdy, S. (eds.) *Infanticide: Comparative and evolutionary perspectives.* NY: Aldine, 1984.

Johannson, S. R. Deferred infanticide: Excess female mortality during childhood. In G. Hausfater and S. Blaffer Hrdy (Eds.), *Infanticide: Comparative and evolutionary perspectives.* NY: Aldine, 1984, 463–486.

Johnston, T. D. Selective costs and benefits in the evolution of learning. *Advances in the Study of Behavior,* 1982, 12:65–106.

Klaus, M. H., and Kennell, J. H. *Maternal-infant bonding.* St. Louis, MO: C. V. Mosby, 1976.

Lamb, M. E. and Hwang, C. P. Maternal attachment and mother-neonate bonding: A critical review. In M. E. Lamb and A. L. Brown (Eds.), *Advances in developmental psychology,* Vol. 2. Hillsdale, NJ: Erlbaum, 1982, pp. 1–39.

Lancaster, J. B. Evolutionary perspectives on sex differences in the higher primates. In A. S. Rossi (Ed.), *Gender and the life course.* NY: Aldine, 1984, pp. 3–27.

Lancaster, J. B., and Lancaster, C. S. Parental investment: The hominid adaptation. In D. Ortner (Ed.), *How humans adapt: A biocultural odyssey.* Washington, D.C.: Smithsonian, 1983, pp. 33–65.

Lancaster, J. B., and Lancaster, C. S. The Watershed: Change in parental investment and family-formation strategies in the course of human evolution. *In* J. B. Lancaster, J. Altmann, A.S. Rossi, and L. R. Sherrod (Eds.), *Parenting across the life span: Biosocial dimensions.* NY: Aldine, 1987.

Martin, H. P., Beezley, P., Conway, E. G., and Kempe, C. H. The development of abused children. *In* I. Schulman (Ed.), *Advances in pediatrics,* Vol. 21. Chicago: Yearbook of Medical Publishers, 1974.

Maynard-Smith, J. Parental investment: A prospective analysis. *Animal Behavior,* 1977, *25*: 1–9.

Scheper-Hughes, N. Culture, scarcity, and maternal thinking: Maternal detachment and infant survival in a Brazilian shantytown. *Ethos,* 1985, *13*: 291–317.

Schmitt, B. and Kempe, C. H. Neglect and abuse of children. *In* V. Vaughan and R. McKay (Eds.), *Nelson textbook of pediatrics.* Philadelphia, PA: Saunders, 1975.

Scrimshaw, S. C. M. Infanticide in human populations: Societal and individual concerns. *In* G. Hausfater and S. Blaffer Hrdy (Eds.), *Infanticide: Comparative and evolutionary perspectives.* NY: Aldine, 1984, pp. 439–462.

Smith, S., Hansen, P., and Noble, S. Parents of battered babies: A controlled study. *British Medical Journal,* 1973, *5(5889)*: 388–391.

Trivers, R. L. Parental investment and sexual selection. *In* B. Campbell (Ed.), *Sexual selection and the descent of man.* Chicago: Aldine, 1972, pp. 136–179.

Wasser, S.L ., and Isenberg, D.Y . Reproductive failure among women: Pathology or adaptation? *Journal of Psychosomatic Obstetrics and Gynecology,* in press.

CHILD ABUSE: CROSS-CULTURAL, HISTORICAL, AND EVOLUTIONARY PERSPECTIVES

part

II

WHAT TO LEARN FROM CROSS-CULTURAL AND HISTORICAL RESEARCH ON CHILD ABUSE AND NEGLECT: AN OVERVIEW

Richard J. Gelles

Considerable research has been carried out over the past 25 years that attempts to explain the problem of child abuse and neglect. While scattered individual cases of abuse were known about and discussed by medical and social service professionals during the nineteenth century (Lynch, 1985) it was not until the latter half of the twentieth century that a previously apathetic and indifferent public and professional community devoted concentrated effort to the issue of abuse and neglect of children (Johnson, 1984; Nelson, 1984). Between 1962 and 1967, each of the 50 states enacted child abuse legislation which included provisions for the mandatory reporting of child abuse and neglect. The federal government enacted the Child Abuse Prevention and Treatment Act of 1974 (PL 93-247) and established the National Center for Child Abuse and Neglect. A handful of research efforts and publications quickly multiplied into hundreds of books and articles. Prior to 1960, abused and neglected children were virtually the missing persons of the medical, social work, social problem, and child welfare literature. Today, we have accumulated sufficient data to provide preliminary answers to the important questions pertaining to this field of inquiry. Nonetheless, many questions remain unanswered, and much research offers ambiguous or contradictory findings. The most recent reviews of the state of knowledge on child maltreatment agree that we still know little about the causes of child abuse or how to treat, predict, or prevent it. Moreover, little is known about the long-term consequences of child abuse and neglect (Gelles, 1980; Starr, 1979; Zigler, 1979).

CONVENTION WISDOM AND REVERSE ETHNOCENTRISM

Increased research on child maltreatment and widespread media attention to individual and often sensational cases of child abuse have resulted in the creation and dissemination of a number of conventional wisdoms about the extent, causes, and consequences of child abuse and neglect. Such conventional wisdoms, while often containing a grain of truth, tend to cloud present thinking and confuse future research efforts.

Myth 1: Child Abuse is Rare

Until the mid-1960s, most people considered abuse a rare phenomenon. There were few official statistics and no reliable and valid surveys on the incidence of child maltreatment. What data that did exist tended to paint abuse and neglect as a relatively unlikely event in the lives of most children (see, e.g., Gil, 1971). Today, experts still disagree over how extensive the abuse of children is; but most agree that it impacts upon at least 1 million children per year in the United States, and the true incidence may be three or four times higher (Straus, Gelles, and Steinmetz, 1980).

Myth 2: Child Maltreatment Is Confined to Mentally Ill or Disturbed People

The few cases of child abuse that were publically recognized tended to picture abusers as mentally deranged people inflicting inexplicable harm upon defenseless infants. Drowning, mutilating, raping, and disfiguring children were seen as acts only mentally disturbed people could commit. Since the most bizarre incidents were publicized, further fuel was added to the myth. Today, research carried out on child abuse concludes that the mental state of the caretaker, parent, or abuser explains only a fraction of the variance in child abuse. In fact, some experts argue that psychological factors explain little more than 10% of the variance (Straus, 1980; Steele, 1978).

Myth 3: Child Abuse Is Confined to Those of Low SES

Forsaking the mental illness model, some observers of child abuse have substituted a social determinism model. Since low income, limited education, and low SES families are overrepresented in the official statistics on child maltreatment, some have argued that abuse and neglect are "confined" to those of this class. Official statistics are far from adequate evidence in assessing causal linkages because low SES families are more likely to be accurately and falsely identified as abusers (Gelles, 1975; Newberger *et al.*, 1977). Middle-class children who appear in hospitals, schools, and physicians' offices with injuries are likely to be classified as victims of accidents and not inflicted injury (child abuse).

Myth 4: Children Who Have Been Abused Will Grow Up to Be Child Abusers

Another variation of the social determinism model of child maltreatment is the notion that children who are abused will always grow up to be abusers. Again, official report data and social surveys find an overrepresentation of abused children among reported and self-reported child abusers. However, as with social and economic factors, the relationship between being abused and becoming an abuser is stochastic and not deterministic.

Myth 5: The Problem of Child Maltreatment Is Worse Today in the United States Than at Other Times or in Other Countries

This last popular myth brings us to the point of this chapter. The explosion of scientific and popular attention paid to child abuse and neglect over the last 25 years has produced an unintentional "reverse ethnocentric" view of child maltreatment. Our society's willingness to examine child abuse, publicize it, collect statistics, and enact legislation has made it appear that the problem of child abuse and neglect is worse today than at any other time in our history, and that the problem is greater in the United States than in other countries. "Violence is as American as apple pie," the journalists tell us, and social scientists then supply evidence that the number of official cases of reported child abuse has grown every year for the last two decades. Since few other countries require the reporting of child abuse (Canada does, most European countries do not) and since maltreatment data have been collected only for the last 20 or so years, we have no "hard" evidence to deny the claim that today's families in the United States are the most abusive in the world. The "soft" data (see Johansson's, Chapter 4, this volume) and other ethnographic and historical evidence suggest that today's families are not the most abusive and the problem is not confined to the United States.

This chapter examines the issue of child abuse and neglect form a cross-cultural and historical perspective. The chapter does not answer questions about incidence, factors associated with maltreatment, or the causes and consequences of abuse and neglect. Rather, the chapter suggests what can be learned from a cross-cultural and historical perspective on child maltreatment. The chapter begins with a review of the stages societies go through in developing an awareness of child maltreatment. Next, the constraints and roadblocks that have limited cross-cultural and historical research on abuse and neglect are reviewed. The following section proposes some solutions to overcoming the constraints and roadblocks. Next, some propositions are presented that are suitable for testing with cross-cultural and historical data. It concludes with a brief discussion of what additions to the knowledge base we could achieve with programs of research that studied abuse and neglect over time and across societies.

THE SOCIAL TRANSFORMATION OF AN AWARENESS OF CHILD MALTREATMENT

In the 1980s, societies around the globe have begun to recognize that the family can be a potentially dangerous institution rather than the proverbial scene of love and tranquility.

The development of an awareness of child maltreatment and a professional literature on this subject in other countries frequently parallels the development of such awareness and knowledge in the United States. Kempe (1978) identified five developmental stages that all societies pass through in order to become aware of and address the various manifestations of child maltreatment.

In *Stage 1*, the problem is denied. The myth that child abuse is rare and confined to a few mentally disturbed individuals has hold during this stage. In *Stage 2*, the more sensational and lurid aspects of physical abuse are recognized. In *Stage 3*, physical abuse is dealt with effectively and attention is given to such issues as failure to thrive. In *Stage 4*, emotional abuse and neglect are recognized. Finally, in *Stage 5* sexual abuse is addressed. Perhaps the most difficult transition is from the denial stage, through the lurid stage, to better recognition and handling of physical abuse problems.

Awareness of child maltreatment presently varies between societies depending on the political, social, economic, and cultural milieu of the country. In underdeveloped and developing nations, changes in traditional ways of life, urbanization, and industrialization have led to the identification of increasing instances of physical abuse and neglect (Jinadu, 1980; Loening, 1981; Mahmood, 1978; Oyemade, 1980). In countries such as Sweden, norms that legitimized violence for centuries are now being questioned as these nations move out of the denial stage (Maroulis, 1979; Olmesdahl, 1978; Vinocur, 1980). Even in the developed nations of Western Europe denial still exists, and there are still heavy taboos on the subject of family violence and child maltreatment (Taylor and Newberger, 1979). Child abuse is presently recognized as a problem in Great Britain, Africa, the United States, Western Europe, Australia, and New Zealand. China, the USSR, Poland, and Japan claim that the abuse of children is either nonexistent or rare (Taylor and Newberger, 1979). Whether a country recognizes child abuse often depends on local definitions, traditions, and priorities. The actual definitions of what is abuse vary considerably from country to country, and this poses a problem for those who wish to pursue cross-cultural and historical research on the maltreatment of children.

CONSTRAINTS AND ROADBLOCKS TO CROSS-CULTURAL AND HISTORICAL RESEARCH

Defining Child Maltreatment

The single most important roadblock to carrying out cross-cultural and historical research on child abuse and neglect is the range and diversity of definitions of abuse, neglect, and maltreatment. The first widely disseminated article on child abuse in the United States established its first definition. Kempe and his colleagues (1962) identified and defined the problem of child abuse as the "battered child syndrome," which was seen as a clinical condition (with diagnosable physical and medical symptoms) caused by deliberate physical assault by a parent or caretaker. The term *battered child syndrome* quickly gave way to the terms *child abuse, child abuse and neglect,* and *child maltreatment.* Today in the United States, abuse is defined not only as physical assault but also as malnutrition, failure to thrive, sexual abuse, educational neglect, medical neglect, and mental abuse. While some definitions of abuse concern only violent acts of commission that result in diagnosable injury, other definitions include acts of commission such as failure to feed or clothe.

The problem of defining maltreatment in the United States is compounded by the fact that each state and the federal government has its own definition of what legally constitutes child abuse and neglect. The official federal definition of child abuse, stated in the federal Child Abuse Prevention and Treatment Act of 1974 (PL 93-237) is:

> The physical or mental injury, sexual abuse, negligent treatment, or maltreatment of a child under the age of eighteen by a person who is responsible for the child's welfare under circumstances which would indicate that the child's health or welfare is harmed or threatened thereby.

One would think that a federal definition of abuse might establish a national standard and eliminate the problem of varying definitions. This is not so because the federal (and state) definitions are only nominal definitions. They are operationalized by those who are charged with recognizing, identifying, and reporting official cases of child abuse. Individual definitions of what is considered maltreatment influence which children and caretakers are officially reported and will vary according to research, by profession, education, race, ethnicity, and culture (Gelles, 1982; Giovannoni and Becerra, 1979).

The current concept of child abuse in the United States is perhaps more political than scientific. It implies behavior that is considered immoral or improper but fails to provide a specific definition of the nature of that behavior, although it has been broadened considerably since

Kempe and his colleague's initial 1962 definition of the "battered child syndrome."

That 20 years of research have failed to produce a uniformly accepted and applied definition of abuse in the United States introduces us to the problems encountered in carrying out historical or cross-cultural research. As in the United States, there is little consensus about definitions of abuse and neglect among investigators studying the problem around the world. Korbin (1981 and Chapter 3, this volume) explains that the inability to arrive at a consensus about what constitutes abuse and neglect results from the fact that there is no universal standard for optimal child rearing. Without such a standard, it is nearly impossible to imagine that one for *incorrect* parenting can be developed.

The central problem with arriving at a cross-cultural and historical definition of child abuse is the same problem that has constrained the development of one for abuse and maltreatment in the United States over the last 20 years—definitions of what is abuse almost always rely on *value judgments*. If, in the United States, one was against all forms of hitting, spanking, and slapping, than by that person's definition, 90% of all Americans are abusive (Straus *et al.,* 1980). If malnutrition is a form of child maltreatment, than in the underdeveloped nations of the world, especially Third World nations, most children who live in poverty-stricken families would be considered maltreated.

There is considerable variation in values and norms from society to society, and these values and norms vary over time, thus further blurring the boundaries between abuse and normal parenting. For example, in the United States it would not be unusual to find a social worker arguing that if a family situation is such that a mother shares a bed with her three young children, this is evidence of a neglectful environment. Among parents in the United States, the normative sleeping arrangement for children is that they have their own beds and probably their own bedrooms (alone or with one or more siblings). Yet, among the !Kung, it would be unimaginable and even thought abusive if a parent were to put an infant into a bed and put the child to sleep in a dark, separate room. Even infanticide, considered by some the ultimate abusive act, is not easily or uniformly classified as abuse across cultures and situations.

Additional Problems in Defining Child Abuse and Neglect

Clearly, the core problem in developing applicable cross-cultural and historical definitions of child maltreatment are variable values and norms across and within cultures. There are other issues that also impinge on obtaining useful and uniform scientific characterizations of abuse and neglect.

First, there is evidence that definitions of abuse and neglect vary not only across cultures but over time. The experience in the United States has been that what constitutes child maltreatment tends to broaden as we have moved through the initial phases of the five stages of recognition and awareness identified by Kempe (1978). Whereas the United States first paid almost exclusive attention to physical abuse in the early 1960s, definitions of maltreatment now include emotional neglect, sexual abuse, and a variety of other behaviors viewed as harmful to a child's fulfilling his or her developmental potential (Gil, 1975).

Second, as we mentioned earlier, definitions of child maltreatment can be politicized. For example, an outgrowth of the current controversy over legalized abortion is that many groups argue that abortion is child abuse. Failure to treat a deformed or premature baby has also been viewed as abusive, and the reauthorization in 1984 of the Child Abuse Prevention and Treatment Act included failure to medically treat such deformed or premature neonates under the federal definition of child abuse and neglect.

Last, and again as mentioned earlier, the definition of child neglect poses major problems for those studying child maltreatment. If malnutrition is maltreatment, then the vast majority of families in Third World countries would be maltreators.

Constraints on Research Method

There are other constraints that impinge upon carrying out research on child abuse in a single culture, and these issues are even more important limitations in planning and carrying out cross-cultural research.

The first constraint is *denial*. Simply stated, if a society does not recognize the existence of forms of abuse or neglect, it will not invest in developing a definition, collecting official records, or carrying out research. Thus, a society may classify itself (or be classified) as having no abuse but in reality obscures and hides whatever problem may exist.

A second problem, typically resulting from the first, is that few countries have developed mechanisms to measure the existence of child maltreatment, either through the use of counting publically recognized instances of child maltreatment or by carrying out scientific research. Most societies have some form of record keeping of births and deaths, but few officially record forms of maltreatment. Official records of child maltreatment have been obtained in the United States only for the past 20 years. Among other nations, only Canada presently requires the official reporting of child abuse and neglect.

Even if we were able to obtain official data on child abuse for other countries, official report data are an imperfect and often biased means of counting the extent of child maltreatment and assessing patterns, correlates, and causes. There are four major limitations to existent official report data:

1. First, because of the continuation of a denial attitude about child maltreatment, maltreatment incidents are underreported in the United States. Estimates are that today only one out of three instances of child maltreatment are ever officially reported—even though all 50 states have mandatory reporting laws (Burgdorf, 1980).

2. Because we are more attuned to the problem of physical abuse (Stage 2 of the Kempe stages of recognition), neglect instances are dramatically underreported. Emotional maltreatment is difficult to define and thus, instances are rarely validated as official reports.

3. There are social, economic, racial, and psychological biases in who gets reported. Black, poor, and ethnic minorities with psychological disturbances tend to be more prone to be accurately and inaccurately reported to official agencies (Gelles, 1975; Newberger et al., 1977; Turbett and O'Toole, 1980). Thus, investigators who use official records to study the correlates of abuse and neglect often conclude that blacks, poor people, or mentally disturbed individuals are at risk of abusing their children. In all likelihood, they are indeed at risk, but they are overrepresented in the official statistics because of a selective labeling process that brings certain individuals and families to public attention.

4. As alluded to earlier, there are errors in who is reported and recognized as a child abuser. Thus, official report records are biased both by the social status of those who are "caught" and by the values of those charged with the "catching." Such biases can lead to errors in diagnosis. For instance, a Chinese woman was charged with abuse because a social worker thought that her practice of sticking needles into her child's arm was a form of torture. In fact, the mother was practicing acupuncture! (NOTE: this event occurred before there was a public understanding of acupuncture in the United States.)

Another constraint is the cost of cross-cultural research. Because only the United States has official child abuse data, investigators wishing to carry out cross-cultural research have to rely either on available historical documents (as did Johansson, Chapter 4, this volume), time-consuming ethnographic research (Korbin, 1981), or expensive social surveys.

The historical denial of child maltreatment and the variability of definitions of maltreatment across societies that actually recognize its existence limit the availability of historical data that can be used to compare rates, patterns, and causes of maltreatment across societies.

A final constraint is the ethical standards that limit the conduct of within and cross-cultural research. In the United States, students of maltreatment must conform to state reporting laws that require cases of suspected abuse to be reported to designated official agencies. Thus, a survey or field researcher who uncovers a suspected case of abuse would be obliged to report that case. For that reason, investigators are typically required to inform all research subjects of this possibility before data collection begins. As a result of the need to obtain informed consent, researchers may have to sacrifice some sample representativeness or validity of the study. Cross-cultural researchers do not typically have to concern themselves with the problem of mandatory reporting. They do have to face the ethical problem of applying their own definitions of appropriate child-rearing techniques to other cultures. Researchers may find themselves labeling child-rearing practices in another society as abuse or neglect, when, in fact, those practices are considered appropriate (or in the case of malnutrition, unavoidable) in that society.

OVERCOMING CONSTRAINTS AND ROADBLOCKS

That there are a variety of roadblocks to carrying out reliable and valid research on child maltreatment cross-culturally does not mean that conducting such research is impossible. A number of scholars have attempted to solve the major problems of definition and design.

The first technique has been to narrow the concept of maltreatment to a much more limited and objective concept. Straus, Gelles, and Steinmetz (1980) focus not on the wide range of acts that could be considered maltreatment, but on a limited number of acts of interpersonal violence. Violence is defined as "an act carried out with the intention, or perceived intention, of causing physical pain or injury to another person" (Straus et al., 1980:20). Abusive violence is those acts that have the high probability of causing an injury (pp. 21–22). Levinson (1981) has used this definition to study violence toward women and children cross-culturally. The advantage of focusing only on acts of physical violence is that the definition is objective and less subject to differing values than other, more inclusive definitions of maltreatment. Obviously, however, focusing only on acts of physical violence leaves out an extensive range of acts of commission and omission that harm the welfare of children.

A second solution is Korbin's (1981; see also Chapter 3, this volume). Korbin notes that those who seek to develop a cross-cultural definition of abuse face the dilemma of choosing between a culturally relative standard in which any behavior can be abusive or nonabusive depending on the cultural context or an idiosyncratic standard whereby abusive acts are those behaviors that are at variance with the normal cultural standards for raising children. Korbin and others have tended toward using the latter standard as they develop and carry out cross-cultural research (see Korbin, 1981).

The most innovative solution to the definitional constraint is Rohner's use of the concept of parental acceptance/rejection. Rather than try to use the value-laden concepts of abuse and neglect, and not content to limit himself to a limited number of harmful acts, Rohner sought a wider, more universalistic concept to test his theories about child development. Rohner (1984), noting the same problems with the nominal and operational definitions of child abuse and neglect that have been summarized in this chapter, states that abuse is often a specialized form of rejection. Rohner defines rejection as the absence or significant withdrawal of warmth and affection by parents toward children. Rejection can take the form either of hostility and aggression or indifference and neglect. Acceptance is defined as warmth, affection, and love (Rohner, 1984).

Method

There have been few cross-cultural or historical studies of child maltreatment. Korbin's (1981) anthology includes chapters that examine maltreatment in single societies (e.g., New Guinea, Sub-Saharan Africa, South America, India, Turkey, Japan, Taiwan, The People's Republic of China, and Polynesia).

There have been a small number of attempts to design suitable crosscultural comparisons of child abuse and neglect. Levinson (1981) employs a holocultural method of studying the physical punishment of children in relation to wife-beating. Levinson used the Human Relations Area Files Probability Sample Files and examined 60 well-described, small-scale, and folk societies that represented all major cultural regions of the world. The data had been collected from ethnographic reports included in the Human Relations Area Files data archive. Rohner (1984) has also used holocultural methods to study his parental acceptance–rejection theory.

A second approach was Edfelt's (1985) replication of Straus and his colleague's survey of family violence in the United States. Edfelt used the Conflict Tactics Scales for parent-to-child violence and surveyed a representative sample of households with children in Sweden.

Summary

The key to solving the problem of conducting cross-cultural and historical research on child maltreatment is adopting precise and replicable definitions of maltreatment. Thus far, although scholars have tried to develop a global, nominal definition of maltreatment, the only crosscultural studies carried out have employed narrow, precise, and crossculturally replicable definitions.

A second solution has been the use of replicable samples and replicable measures. Edfelt (1985) translated the Conflict Tactics Scales into Swedish and drew a similar representative sample to that drawn in the United States. Levinson used coded data based on ethnographic reports.

WHAT CAN BE GAINED FROM CROSS-CULTURAL AND HISTORICAL RESEARCH

There would be little point in struggling with the myriad of complex problems involved in studying child maltreatment over time and across societies if there were no major scientific payoff to be gained from such research. There are three major reasons for pursuing cross-cultural and historical research on abuse and neglect. First, such research offers the opportunity to test hypotheses that have not been tested. Second, such research is the only means of testing hypotheses operationalized at the societal level. Third, cross-cultural and historical research can test for the influence of cultural complexity on the likelihood of children being abused and neglected.

Propositions Suitable for Cross-Cultural and Historical Investigation

Other reviews have carefully analyzed the factors that have been found associated with the maltreatment of children in the United States (see, e.g., Maden and Wrench, 1977; Parke and Collmer, 1975; Gelles, 1980). The last two decades of research on the abuse and neglect of children are in agreement on one major point—there are a multitude of factors associated with abuse and neglect.

The unidimensional explanations of abuse and neglect that focused on the psychological characteristics of the abuser have been replaced with models that consider not only intraindividual factors, but sociopsychological, family structure, and social–cultural variables. The last three levels of analysis are the most amenable to cross-cultural analysis, and many of the relationships found in the United States should be examined by assessing families in other societies.

Certain Family Structures Are Related to the Maltreatment of Children. Students of child abuse and neglect in the United States have found that certain structural arrangements of families and caretakers increase the risk that children will be abused. Maltreatment tends to be found associated with marital instability, separation, and divorce. In addition, the degree of familial intergration into a network of kin and community is also related (inversely) to maltreatment. Theorists have also proposed that the purported high level of abuse and neglect in the United States is an outgrowth of the degree of privacy of the modern nuclear family—a high degree of privacy shields families from sources of social control that would limit parental deviance (Gelles, 1983).

Historical and cross-cultural evidence suggest that abuse and neglect would be less likely to occur in societies where the degree of family privacy is low (Laslett, 1973; Beatrice Whiting, personal communication). Korbin (1981) notes that families in the People's Republic of China are subject to preventive intervention before abuse and neglect occur primarily because of the lack of privacy in the Chinese community.

Levels of Societal Violence Are Related to Child Abuse. Straus and his colleagues (1980), at the conclusion of a major national survey of violence in the American family, summarize their study by noting that the high level of violence in the United States must inevitably be viewed as part of any causal model that attempts to explain violence toward children. That "Violence is as American as apple pie" is considered a significant causal factor by these and other students of child maltreatment (Gil, 1971; Zigler, 1979). Straus and his colleagues propose that the general level of violence in the United States, the high incidence of homicide, suicide, and violent crime, the easy availability of guns (especially handguns), and the public use of capital and corporal punishment are all factors that explain the widespread use of violence toward children that leads to physical injury. To this list of items, Straus and his colleagues also add the widespread portrayal of violence on television and in other popular media, which they see as both glorifying violent acts and raising the social approval for using violence expressively and instrumentally.

The notion that societal levels of violence are causally linked to physical violence toward children is compelling, but such a theory cannot be tested or validated in a study of a single society. Cross-cultural and historical research are essential if the propositions relating societal violence to abuse are to be tested.

Cultural Attitudes and Child Abuse. Scholars not only posit that societal violence is related to physical abuse, but they also propose that social and cultural attitudes about the acceptability of violence as both instrumental and expressive behavior are part of the causal chain leading to physical abuse. Cultural support for the physical punishment of children, support for the death penalty, attitudes about the acceptability of hitting wives and family members, and the acceptability of corporal punishment have been proposed as correlates of physical abuse. Researchers have found the various attitudinal measures of approval are correlated with one another (Owens and Straus, 1975). Nevertheless, the general proposition relating attitudes to behavior requires a cross-cultural test.

Presence of Other Forms of Family Violence. Given that scholars have proposed that attitudes and behaviors concerning violence are likely to be related to physical abuse of children, one would expect that other forms of family violence (e.g., wife-beating, sibling violence, and violence toward parents) would also be related to the abuse of children.

Levinson's (1981) holocultural research has found modest support for the claim that the physical punishment of children is correlated with the presence of wife-beating in the same society. The relationship, however, was complex and required more analysis than a simple correlation. Societies that had rare or infrequent physical punishment also had rare or infrequent wife-beating. But, frequent wife-beating was not related to the physical punishment of children.

Alcohol and Drugs and Child Abuse. Researchers in the United States have found consistent relationships between caretaker use and abuse of alcohol and drugs and the abuse and neglect of children. Quite a few professionals and most of the public see alcohol as some kind of superego solvent that precipitates violent and neglectful behavior. Cross-cultural analysis (see MacAndrew and Edgerton, 1969) finds that behavior among people who drink varies considerably. The variation is almost always explained by the social definition of alcohol and social expectations for those who drink. Thus, while individuals in one society may become violent and aggressive when drunk, in another society drunkenness may bring on withdrawal and depression. To date there appears to be no direct examination of the variation across societies of the likelihood of violent or neglectful behavior when individuals are using various amounts and types of drugs.

Child-Rearing Practices. One of the most obvious and fertile areas for research on child maltreatment is to assess varying child-rearing practices and their relation to abuse and neglect. Researchers in the United States have proposed that the use of physical punishment is a necessary precursor to physical abuse. Single-parent families have also been suggested as having higher than expected rates of maltreatment; but, in the United States, single parenthood is so closely linked to poverty that researchers have been unable to disentangle the relative contribution of each.

Poverty, Inequality, and Maltreatment. As we noted at the beginning of this chapter, the notion that child abuse was a classless phenomenon gave way to a social deterministic explanation that placed the blame for abuse on poverty. While maltreatment is found disproportionately among the poor, it is not confined to this group in the United States. To what extent is the degree of social inequality related to maltreatment across societies? Are rigid caste structures more likely to have high rates of abuse, or are class societies with degrees of social inequality abuse-prone? What is the effect of social mobility and the opportunities for social advancement on the rate of maltreatment? These and other propositions are important to test over time and across societies.

Degree of Cultural Complexity. Observers of child maltreatment in Third World countries have noted that maltreatment tends to increase with increasing modernization (Bhattacharyya, 1979; Jinadu, 1980; Loening, 1981; Maroulis, 1979; Oyemade, 1980). Beatrice Whiting (personal communication) notes that as soon as families moved from communal dwellings into separate residence, hitting among family members began. Observers have noted that they believe the phenomenon that we call "child abuse" did not occur within hunting–gathering societies (Konner, personal communication). Whether these are objective observations or nostalgic denials of abuse can only be determined through cross-cultural research and historical analysis.

Characteristics of Children at Risk. Handicapped, low-birth weight, developmentally delayed, premature, and unwanted children have been found to be at risk of maltreatment in the United States. These characteristics of children are consistent with a biosocial explanation of maltreatment that states that parents will not invest in children with low reproductive potential (Burgess and Garbarino, 1983; Burgess, 1979). Similarly, foster children and stepchildren are thought to be at risk of abuse and are indeed overrepresented in official child abuse reports. Cross-cultural and historical data would be of considerable value in further supporting, modifying, or rejecting the initial propositions of the biosocial explanation of maltreatment.

Household Composition. Data on household size, presence of extended family members, and the economic roles of family members (e.g., dual worker households) would also be of value in elaborating findings from research in the United States that find that large households and lack of extended kin are related to maltreatment.

CONCLUSION

To date, little attention has been devoted to the situation of child abuse in the United States compared to abuse in other societies, either as it existed in the past or at present. The long denial of the existence of child maltreatment, followed by an initial period of attention during which child maltreatment was conceptualized within either a psychodynamic, medical, or social stress model did not mandate a cross-cultural or historical perspective. If, in fact, abuse was caused by psychopathology, a disease, or social stress, there was little utility to pursuing expensive and time-consuming cross-cultural analysis.

The last two decades of research has revealed that abuse and neglect are neither explainable strictly by individual or sociopsychological variables and models. Moreover, what evidence there is shows that abuse is certainly not restricted to the U. S. or Western European countries.

A cross-cultural and historical perspective widens conceptualization of child maltreatment. Rather than viewing abuse as a rare event confined to only those households where there are mentally ill caretakers or massive social stress, the wider conceptualization afforded by analysis over time and across societies reveals abuse and neglect as regularly occurring patterns of parent–offspring behavior. Cross-cultural and historical analysis takes the focus off the parent, child, and the individual family and poses questions about under what societal and cultural conditions and in what ecological contexts rates of offspring maltreatment are highest or lowest.

Posing empirical questions at the cultural and societal level of analysis offers us a chance to expand our perspective on maltreatment and to more fully understand the generative sources of abuse and neglect.

REFERENCES

Bhattacharyya, A. K. Child abuse in India and nutritionally battered child. *Child Abuse and Neglect*, 1979, 3(2):607–614.

Burgdorf, K. *Recognition and reporting of child maltreatment*. Rockville, MD: Westat, Inc., 1980.

Burgess, R. L. Family violence: Some implications from evolutionary biology. Paper presented at the annual meetings of the American Society of Criminology, Philadelphia, 1979.

Burgess, R. L., and Garbarino, J. Doing what comes naturally? An evolutionary perspective on child abuse. In D. Finkelhor, R. Gelles, M. Straus, and G. Hotaling, Eds., *The dark side of the family: Current family violence research*. Beverly Hills, CA: Sage, 1983, pp. 88–101.

Daly, M., and Wilson, M. Discriminative parental solicitude: A biological perspective. *Journal of Marriage and the Family*, 1980, 42:277–288.

Daly, M., and Wilson, M. Child maltreatment from a sociobiological perspective. *New Directions for Child Development*, 1981, 11:93–112.

Edfeldt, A. Research and theory on violence towards children in Sweden. Paper presented at the Swedish/American Symposium on Physical and Sexual Abuse of Children, Satra Bruk, Sweden, 1985.

Gelles, R. The social construction of child abuse. *American Journal of Orthopsychiatry*, 1975, 45:363–371.

Gelles, R. Violence in the family: A review of research in the seventies. *Journal of Marriage and the Family*, 1980, 42:873–885.

Gelles, R. Applying research on family violence to clinical practice. *Journal of Marriage and the Family*, 1982, 44:9–20.

Gelles, R. J. An exchange/social control theory. In D. Finkelhor, R. Gelles, M. Straus, and G. Hotaling, Eds., *The dark side of the family: Current family violence research*. Beverly Hills, CA: Sage, 1983, pp. 151–165.

Gil, D. Violence against children. *Journal of Marriage and the Family*, 1971, 33:637–648.

Gil, D. G. Unraveling child abuse. *American Journal of Orthopsychiatry*, 1975, 45:346–358.

Giovannoni, J. M., and Becerra, R. M. *Defining child abuse*. NY: Free Press, 1979.

Jinadu, M. K. The role of neglect in the aetiology of protein-energy malnutrition in urban communities of Nigeria. *Child Abuse and Neglect*, 1980, 4(4):233–245.

Johnson, J. Symbolic salvation: The changing meanings of the child maltreatment movement. *Studies in Symbolic Interaction*, 1984, 6.

Kempe, C. H. Recent developments in the field of child abuse. *Child Abuse and Neglect*, 1978, 2(4):261–267.

Kempe, C. H., Silverman, F. N., Steele, B. F., Droegemueller, W., and Silver, H. K. The battered child syndrome. *Journal of the American Medical Association*, 1962, 181:107–112.

Korbin, J., Ed. *Child abuse and neglect: Cross-cultural perspectives.* Berkeley, CA: University of California Press, 1981.

Laslett, B. The family as a public and private institution: A historical perspective. *Journal of Marriage and the Family,* 1973, *35*:480–492.

Levinson, D. Physical punishment of children and wifebeating in cross-cultural perspective. *Child Abuse and Neglect,* 1981, *5*(4):193–196.

Loening, W. E. K. Child abuse among the Zulus: A people in transition. *Child Abuse and Neglect,* 1981, *5*(1):3–7.

Lynch, M. Child abuse before Kempe: An historical review. *Child Abuse and Neglect,* 1985, *9*(1):7–15.

MacAndrew, C. and Edgerton, R. B. *Drunken comportment: A social explanation.* NY: Aldine, 1969.

Maden, M. F. and Wrench, D. F. Significant findings in child abuse research. *Victimology,* 1977, *2*:196–224.

Mahmood, T. Child abuse in Arabia, India and the West–comparative legal aspects. *In* J. Eekelaar and S. Katz, Eds., *Family violence: An international and interdisciplinary study.* Toronto: Butterworth, 1978, pp. 281–289.

Maroulis, H. Child abuse: The Greek scene. *Child Abuse and Neglect,* 1979, *3*(1):185–190.

Nelson, B. J. *Making and issue of child abuse: Political agenda setting for social problems.* Chicago, IL: University of Chicago Press, 1984.

Newberger, E. *et al.* Pediatric social illness: Toward an etiologic classification. *Pediatrics,* 1977, *60*:178–185.

Olmesdahl, M. C. Parental power and child abuse: An historical and cross-cultural study. In J. M. Eekelarr and S. N. Katz, Eds., *Family violence: An international and interdisciplinary study.* Toronto: Butterworth, 1978, pp. 253–268.

Oyemade, A. Child care practices in Nigeria-An urgent plea for social workers. *Child Abuse and Neglect,* 1980, *4*(2):101–103.

Owens, D. M., and Straus, A. The social structure of violence in childhood and approval of violence as an adult. *Aggressive Behavior,* 1975, *1*:193–211.

Parke, R. D., and Collmer, C. W. Child abuse: an interdisciplinary analysis. *In* M. Hetherington, Ed., *Review of child development research,* vol 5. Chicago, IL: University of Chicago Press, 1975, pp. 1–102.

Rohner, R. Foundations of parental acceptance-rejection theory. Mimeographed, 1984.

Starr, R. Child abuse. *American Psychologist,* 1979, *34*(10):872–878.

Steele, B. F. The child abuser. *In* I. Kutash, S. Kutash, and L. Schlesinger Eds., *Violence: Perspectives on murder and aggression.* San Francisco, CA: Jossey Bass, 1978, pp. 285–300.

Straus, M. A sociological perspective on the causes of family violence. *In* M. R. Green, Ed., *Violence and the family.* Boulder, CO: Westview, 1980, pp. 7–31.

Straus, M. A., Gelles, R. J., and Steinmetz, S. K. *Behind closed doors: Violence in the American family.* Garden City, NY: Anchor/Doubleday, 1980.

Taylor, L., and Newberger, E. H., Child abuse in the International Year of the Child. *New England Journal of Medicine,* 1979, *301*:1205–1212.

Turbett, J. P., and O'Toole, R. Physician's recognition of child abuse. Paper presented at the annual meetings of the American Sociological Association, New York, 1980.

Vinocur, J. Sweden's antispanking law is something of a hit. The New York Times, Sunday, 19 October, 1980, p. 22.

Zigler, E. Controlling child abuse in America: An effort doomed to failure? *In* R. Bourne and E. H. Newberger Eds., *Critical perspectives on child abuse.* Lexington, MA: Lexington, 1979, pp. 171–213.

CHILD MALTREATMENT IN CROSS-CULTURAL PERSPECTIVE: VULNERABLE CHILDREN AND CIRCUMSTANCES

Jill E. Korbin

Children throughout the world suffer an array of threats to their development, well-being, and survival. They suffer from poverty, famine, disease, and war. They suffer as they navigate the child-rearing practices and rites of their diverse cultures. And, they suffer from acts of omission or commission by their individual parents and caretakers. Parental behavior that compromises the development and survival of their offspring seems to contradict the biological and cultural dictates of rearing the next generation. This enigma of human behavior demands consideration from a wider range of human cultural adaptation than that afforded by Western societies alone. This chapter will consider definitional issues that have been an impediment to cross-cultural research on child maltreatment. It will then turn to a review of current knowledge concerning categories of children vulnerable to abuse, the relationship of kinship and social networks to child maltreatment, and the impact of urbanization and social change.

"Child abuse" arose as a label of consequence in the United States in the early 1960s. Children with inflicted injuries emerged from an obscure radiological diagnosis (Caffey, 1946) to a matter of public and professional concern (Adelson, 1961; Elmer, 1960; Kempe, Silverman, Steele, Droegmueller, and Silver, 1962; Nelson, 1984; Pfofl, 1977). Questions inevitably arose as to whether child abuse was universal or unique to the United States. Attention first focused on societies most similar to the United States as European nations underwent similar transformations from initial denial that child maltreatment existed within their boundaries to a recognition of its multiple manifestations (Kempe, 1978). Repeated experience with nations that first denied the existence of child abuse only to "discover" it, promoted skepticism that child abuse and neglect could be absent anywhere and stimulated interest in a broader cross-cultural investigation.

A growing international literature on child abuse and neglect has

31

emerged since the late 1970s. Child advocates, social workers, health care providers, researchers, and educators in diverse nations have sought to demonstrate the existence of child maltreatment in their own nations as a first step in combatting the problem.[1] Multiple forms of child maltreatment are considered in this literature, including physical abuse and neglect, sexual molestation, nutritional deprivation, emotional maltreatment, and institutional abuse. While infectious disease, diarrhea, and malnutrition dwarf the magnitude of child maltreatment in developing nations, it nevertheless has arisen as a problem of concern. This literature primarily has a single-nation focus and establishes that the spectrum of child maltreatment is recognized in both industrialized and developing nations. Causal factors, when suggested, most often echo etiological formulations from Euro–American clinical and research experience. There has been an exporting not only of techniques for identifying and treating child abuse and neglect, but also of factors postulated to be responsible for its occurrence.

A second cross-cultural literature encompasses social and medical research, predominantly from the United States. This literature has sought to delineate the parameters and assess the patterns of child abuse across diverse cultural and ethnic groups (Cohn, 1982; Dubanoski, 1981; Dubanoski and Snyder, 1980; Eisenberg, 1981; Garbarino and Ebata, 1983; Gelles and Pedrick-Cornell, 1983; Giovannoni and Becerra, 1979; Green, 1978; Kammerman, 1975; Korbin, 1977, 1979, 1980, 1981a; Lauderdale, Vallinuas, and Anderson, 1980; Levinson, 1981; Spearly and Lauderdale, 1983; Taylor and Newberger, 1979). While this literature is constrained by definitional and methodological problems and a lack of systematic data, it nevertheless underlines the importance of a cultural perspective in practice and theory. Anthropologists have also addressed questions of infanticide (e.g., Colishaw, 1978; Dickeman, 1975, 1984; Divale and Harris, 1976; Hausfater and Hrdy, 1984; Scrimshaw, 1983, 1984), differential child treatment and selective neglect (e.g., Levine, 1985; McKee, 1984; Miller, 1981; Scheper-Hughes, 1984; Scrimshaw, 1978, 1983), and parental investment (e.g. Lancaster and Lancaster, 1983).

Anthropological research on child maltreatment, as with other forms

---

[1]For a sampling of this growing literature, the reader is referred to: Agathanos (1983); Agathanos et al. (1982); Arnold (1982); Bhattacharya (1979); de Silva (1981); Fergusson et al. (1972); Haditono (1981); Ikeda (1982); Jinadu (1980); Kellerman (1979); Loening (1981); Mehra (1982); Mehta (1982); Mehta, Prabhu, and Mistry (1985); Nathan and Hwang (1981); Nwako (1974); Okeahialam (1984); Oyemade (1980); Semiawan (1981); Sereewat (1983); Tauber, Meda, and Vitro (1977); Tevoedjre (1981); Van Staden (1979).

of deviant and negatively sanctioned behavior, has been slow to develop. Attention has focused on regularities of culture rather than on departures from normative behavior (Edgerton, 1976, 1978). Further, as low base rate behaviors, child abuse and neglect are difficult to submit to cross-cultural analysis. In small populations, child maltreatment may not be observed during the traditional year-long period of ethnographic fieldwork, or there may be so few cases that they are difficult to assess and interpret within the cultural framework. These cases, then, do not find their way into the literature. Graburn, in studying the Canadian Inuit, documented cases of severe child abuse. However, the rarity of such cases, and their seeming contradiction to his and others' observations of nurturant and indulgent Inuit parenting made him hesitant to publish these accounts (Graburn, 1984). Similarly, cases of child maltreatment in my fieldwork among rural Hawaiians seemed aberrant from the cultural pattern (Korbin, 1976). One can only speculate on the number and content of cases of child maltreatment noted by cross-cultural researchers about which the literature is silent. This severely limits the data base and thus the ability of the cross-cultural record to contribute to knowledge about child maltreatment.

Current cross-cultural knowledge about child maltreatment is largely suggestive and anecdotal. There has been a lack of systematic cross-cultural comparisons. Documentation of child maltreatment in one society does not necessarily mean that such behavior is absent in neighboring groups. Nevertheless, despite the formative stage of cross-cultural research on child maltreatment, a cross-cultural perspective is critical to understanding parental aggression and neglect of children as within the repertoire of human behavior. Western industrialized societies, on which most of the research on child maltreatment has been based, do not constitute a sufficient sample from which to draw conclusions about all of human behavior.

DEFINITIONAL ISSUES

Definitional ambiguity is a major impediment to cross-cultural research on child maltreatment. In Euro–American nations, imprecision and variability in definitions have hampered research and precluded valid and reliable comparisons. While this issue has received considerable attention in the literature, solutions remain to be found (Aber and Zigler, 1981; Besharov, 1981; Cicchetti and Rizley, 1981; Gelles, 1973, 1982; Giovannoni and Becerra, 1979). Definitional problems are exacerbated in cross-cultural comparisons. The necessity for cultural equivalence creates difficulties in validly and reliably defining behaviors across diverse contexts. Two definitional problems, the homogeneity with which the term "child abuse and neglect" is employed and the lack of precise operational criteria, have important implications for cross-cultural research.

The label, "the battered child syndrome," was intentionally chosen to grasp public, professional, and legislative attention. It referred to a "clinical condition in young children who have received serious physical abuse . . . " (Kempe *et al.*, 1962:17). In 25 years, definitions of child abuse and neglect have expanded to include a range of caretaker behaviors and child outcomes as exemplified by the definition employed by the most recent incidence study in the United States:

> A child maltreatment situation is one where, through purposive acts or marked inattention to the child's basic needs, behavior of a parent/substitute or other adult caretaker caused foreseeable and avoidable injury or impairment to a child or materially contributed to unreasonable prolongation or worsening of an existing injury or impairment (National Center on Child Abuse and Neglect, 1981).

In a sense, then, "child abuse and neglect" has come to be used in the singular, encompassing anything deemed "bad" for children for which parents or caretakers can be deemed accountable. The dynamics involved in various forms of maltreatment do not justify the homogeneous use of the term (Besharov, 1981; Cicchetti and Rizley, 1981; Giovannoni and Becerra, 1979; Jason, Williams, Burton, and Rochat, 1982; Polansky, Chalmers, Buttenweiser, and Williams, 1981). Further, of critical importance, conceptions of "badness" are culturally bound. Behaviors considered acceptable in one culture may be viewed as detrimental to children in another (Korbin, 1981a).

Three levels have been suggested for culturally informed definitions of child maltreatment: (1) cultural practices that are viewed as abusive or neglectful by other cultures, but not by the culture in question; (2) idiosyncratic departure from one's cultural continuum of acceptable behavior; and (3) societally induced harm to children beyond the control of individual parents and caretakers (Korbin, 1980, 1981a). Literature from developing nations supports distinguishing traditional practices that involve pain and suffering from idiosyncratic forms of maltreatment that more recently have been identified in urban centers (e.g., Okeahialam, 1984).

Definitional ambiguity in the cross-cultural literature has arisen from confusing these three levels. In the absence of an adequate data base, cross-cultural comparisons largely have been limited to a listing of the harms to which children come in different contexts. What often ensues is a cataloguing of practices that appear abusive when viewed from outside the cultural context, but not when viewed from within. Such comparisons were a necessary first step in alerting the international community to cultural variability in definitions of child maltreatment. Cross-cultural comparisons of such practices, however, obscure the issue. In this light, it is instructive to view Euro–American child-care practices through the eyes of other cultures. Many Euro–American child-care practices, even those as seemingly benign as sleeping arrangements in which infants have separate beds and rooms, are seen as ill-informed at best and uncaring and abusive at worst by many of the world's societies (Korbin, 1981a).

Definitions of child abuse and neglect in the United States have been based upon identifiable harm to a child that can be attributed to caretaker commission or omission. Neither parental action nor physical injury are adequate in themselves as critical defining elements of child maltreatment cross-culturally. Since determinations of maltreatment depend on the interaction of consequences to a child and caretaker action or inaction, the issue is complex. The same parental behavior may have different meanings and interpretations in different cultural contexts. For example, continual physical contact with an infant increases chances of survival in societies with high infant mortality while the same behavior in societies with low infant mortality carries a meaning of indulgence (LeVine, 1977; Super, 1984). Similarly, child outcomes may have different meanings. It does not make sense to equate bruises inflicted on a child by angry parents in the United States with a child who is bruised in the process of the Vietnamese curing practice of "coin rubbing" (Yeatman, Shaw, Barlow, and Bartlett, 1976).

Definitions of child abuse have many grey areas, both within and between cultures, that rely on careful consideration of sociocultural context before being identified as abuse or neglect. A working definition of child maltreatment as "the portion of harm to children that results from human action that is proscribed, proximate, and preventable" (Finkelhor and Korbin, 1985) fills two criteria for culturally informed definitions. It distinguishes child abuse from other circumstances that have detrimental consequences for children, and it is flexible enough to encompass a range of cultural contexts.

Efforts must be made to operationalize caretaker behavior resulting in harm to children that falls within the parameters of child maltreatment. As the field matures, it would be well to work toward reserving the terms "maltreatment," "abuse," and "neglect" for situations defined *emically*, by the culture in question, as proscribed and negatively sanctioned behaviors for which specific caretakers can be held culpable. At present, it should be recognized that these terms are used as a shorthand. Research should move toward use of terms more amenable to operationalization, such as nonaccidentally inflicted trauma or failure to thrive, that can be employed more validly and reliably across cultural boundaries.

The Cultural Context

The most promising contribution of a cross-cultural perspective is an enhanced understanding of the conditions under which child maltreatment is more or less likely to occur. It is more useful to look for factors that promote or prevent child maltreatment than to grasp for comparisons of incidence and prevalence statistics that are unreliable even in nations with legally mandated reporting systems (e.g., Gelles, 1973).

Since regularities in the antecedents and consequences of child-rearing practices can be identified cross-culturally (Minturn and Lambert, 1964; Whiting and Whiting, 1975), regularities in the antecedents and consequences of child maltreatment similarly should be amenable to cross-cultural research (Korbin, 1981a; Rohner, 1975). The sparseness of data on child maltreatment in the cross-cultural record, makes postulated causal and outcome factors difficult to identify and analyze. Nevertheless, despite this scarcity of data specifically on child maltreatment, the cross-cultural record on parenting and child care patterns affords an important perspective on human behavior and suggests future research directions.

Since intracultural variability can be equal to or greater than intercultural variation, both within and between culture analyses will be necessary. Peer aggression, for example, is more likely to be negatively sanctioned in extended households than in nuclear households, regardless of the culture in which the family resides (Minturn and Lambert, 1964). For any factor, such as household composition to be implicated in the etiology of child abuse and neglect, it must have explanatory power both within any society and between societies.

The emerging literature from developing nations indicates that children are subjected to the spectrum of types of maltreatment that have been identified in industrialized nations. Severely abused and neglected children look sadly similar across cultural boundaries.

Selective neglect, or underinvestment, appears to be more frequent in the cross-cultural literature than deliberate killing, even if the end result is frequently the same. Selective neglect is defined as "any combination of medical, nutritional, physical, or emotional neglect of an infant or young child in comparison to other children in the family or to children of families in similar socioeconomic and educational circumstances" (Scrimshaw, 1983:716). Importantly, the definition of selective neglect is relative to other children in the family and community so that pervasive detrimental social and environmental conditions are not confounded with individual parental behavior (Scrimshaw, 1983). Categories of children at risk of deliberate infanticide are also at risk of these less overt mechanisms (Dickeman, 1975; Scrimshaw, 1984; Scheper-Hughes, 1984).

Nondeliberate and covert mechanisms for dealing with disvalued and unwanted children diminish parental feelings of culpability. Under usual circumstances in many societies, some highly valued and well cared for infants die while some disvalued and ill cared for infants survive. This empirical "evidence" allows parental neglect of unwanted children without societal or self blame for the consequences. Some groups of Tibetans, for example, acknowledged that certain children, particularly girls and later borns, received a lesser standard of care (Levine, 1985). If the child survived, this was viewed fatalistically and also indicated a hearty child. In Japanese society, abandonment of an unwanted infant rather than infanticide diminished parental feelings of responsibility for harm to the child and allowed parents to harbor the hope that an altruistic individual would rescue and rear their child (Wagatsuma, 1981).

The emotional content and psychological costs of deliberate harm to a child are not usually accessible to researchers. Such behavior is generally stigmatized and not openly discussed. Only anecdotal information exists on the emotional impact, for example, of deliberate infanticide. Bugos and McCarthy (1984) found women unwilling to talk about their own infanticidal behavior, even though they would talk about that of other individuals. The presence of others during the birth process may be necessary to enforce rules concerning deliberate infanticide. Among the Bariba of West Africa, "witches" are believed to identify themselves at birth and must be killed or sold to neighboring groups. Women who give birth alone may conceal signs identifying the newborn as a "witch," thereby saving their child (Sargent, 1984).

In societies that permit infanticide, cultural rules define the parameters of such behavior. Among the Machiguenga, for example, once a mother began nursing her infant, after approximately 1 day, she has made a commitment to rear the child. Prior to nursing, an infant could be deliberately killed, exposed to the elements, or given to another family (Johnson, 1981). Among the Japanese, the first birth cry signalled safety for the infant. Delivery of unwanted infants often was accompanied by a cloth to smother the first cries before they could be uttered, thereby sparing the infant (Wagatsuma, 1981).

Cessation of parental investment immediately at birth or shortly thereafter through deliberate infanticide is one matter, while killing a child years or months later is another. Infanticide is a relatively early cessation of parental investment, even after the metabolic costs of pregnancy. Once a child has survived past a culturally defined critical point or is old enough to contribute to the household economy, the costs and benefits of child rearing are more easily perceived by individual parents and the group. There is no necessary selective advantage to later parental disinvestment (Scrimshaw, 1984). Clinical experience in Euro–American nations suggests that abusive parents do not wish to terminate investment in their child. Rather, consciously or unconsciously, the abusive parent is seeking to enhance investment by securing improved behavior from the child.

Scant attention has been directed toward normative child-rearing practices that "function[s] to selectively reduce the probability of survival" (McKee, 1984:91). In Sierra Leonne, for example, the Temne bathed their infants in cold streams and held them in the air to dry, despite a relatively high rate of infant mortality due to pneumonia (Dorjahn, 1976). Folk medicines have been known to contain substances toxic to children (Trotter, Ackerman, Rodman, Martinez, and Sorvillo, 1983). Before being too quick to assign a label of abuse, such cultural practices generally persist because parents believe that they will enhance their children's well-being. If some children do not fare well, it is considered beyond parental culpability.

Vulnerable Children

The cross-cultural literature suggests that child maltreatment is less likely in cultures in which children are highly valued for their economic utility, for perpetuating family lines and the cultural heritage, or as sources of emotional pleasure and satisfaction. Nevertheless, generalized cultural values on children are not sufficient to prevent maltreatment. Most of the world's cultures would espouse a value on children and a disvalue on their deliberate harm. However, certain cultural values on children may place some children in jeopardy. If, for example, children primarily are valued for their economic contributions, those who fail to be useful are at increased risk of maltreatment. In Turkey (Olson, 1981) and among the Machiguenga of Peru (Johnson, 1981), for example, the welfare of orphans who are taken in as economic helpers is dependent on their continued utility. If children are valued to perpetuate family lines and cultural traditions, in societies that require males to perform requisite ceremonies, daughters are less valued and at greater risk of maltreatment (Wolf, 1974; Wu, 1981). Further, if children are expected to be sources of psychological and emotional satisfaction, they may fail parental expectations making them vulnerable to abuse. This has been an important dynamic contributing to child abuse in the United States (Steele, 1980).

Even in cultures that place a high value on children in general, some children are less valued than others. This disvalue or undervalue may be expressed in a range of behaviors. Such children may be subjected to deliberate infanticide, physical abuse and neglect, sexual misuse, psychological maltreatment, or economic exploitation.

The cross-cultural record suggests categories of children who are at greater risk of maltreatment. Some of these categories can be identified through demographic analyses of differential mortality patterns (Johansson, 1984; Scrimshaw, 1978, 1984), while other categories can be identified only with a thorough understanding of the cultural context. Undervalued and disvalued children may be broadly grouped as follows.

Health Status. While the direction of cause and effect is difficult to determine, children whose health status is inferior to that of their siblings or peers are more likely to be accorded a lesser standard of care. In societies with high infant and child mortality, the stronger child is likely to receive preferential treatment over the weaker. This is in direct contrast to the resources allocated to an ill infant in industrialized societies (LeVine, 1977). The active involvement of a child is necessary for attachment and elicitation of parental care but may be precluded in children who are ill and/or malnourished (Ainsworth, 1967).

Scheper-Hughes found that Brazilian shantytown mothers identified categories of sickly children whose survival was considered too risky for maternal investment. These children were poorly cared for and often died unattended. "The expansiveness and flexibility of the folk diagnosis allows Alto mothers a great deal of latitude in deciding which of their children are not favored for normal development and from which she may withdraw her attentions. The woman does not hold herself responsible for the death nor is she blamed by the immediate female community (men seem to have little knowledge of the matter) . . . " (Scheper-Hughes, 1985: 305).

Malnourished children also are vulnerable to maltreatment. The quality of maternal care and feeding patterns vary among siblings, and only one child in a family may be malnourished (Chavez, Martines, and Yaschine, 1975; Latham, 1974). Apathetic, anorexic, and unresponsive behaviors of malnourished children may fail to elicit the parental solicitiousness that would improve their health status and thereby their behavior. Cultural beliefs may further compromise an already malnourished child. Kwashiorkor, a word from the Ga tribe, means "the sickness one child gets when the next one is born" (Foster and Anderson, 1978; Werner, 1979). In areas of Mexico and Central America, a child displaying behaviors indicative of malnourishment may instead be perceived as "chipil," or angry at the mother during weaning and envious of the new sibling. The child is punished or ignored for perceived bad behavior instead of being fed to ameliorate the underlying cause.

Deformed and Handicapped Children. Related to health status, the treatment of deformed or handicapped children varies within and between cultures. Deformed or handicapped children may be regarded as supernatural gifts and accorded special status and care. More usually, deformed or handicapped children are regarded as a burden, an ill-omen, or nonhuman, thus falling outside of the usual protections generally afforded children.

Perception of physical handicaps and deformities often are culture-bound. Chinese peasants regarded extra digits as a sign of incorrigible behavior. Even if the extra digit was surgically removed, the stigma remained with the child who was more likely to be ill-treated (Galston and Savage, 1973).

As has been suggested by research in industrialized nations, children with minor handicaps, such as mild central nervous system dysfunction, may be at greater risk of maltreatment than more obviously handicapped or deformed children. While these mildly dysfunctional children are at odds with parental expectations, many go undiagnosed, increasing parental frustration and potential for abuse (Martin, 1976).

Sex. Cultural beliefs about proper care of sons versus daughters can compromise health and survival without conscious malintent. In a Mestizo community in Ecuador, mothers follow customary beliefs that males must be breast-fed until a later age than females, thereby compromising the well-being and survival of daughters (McKee, 1984).

In societies with a strong son preference, such as India and China, female children are at greater risk of maltreatment. In India, a strong son preference acts against the survival and well-being of female children. Regional variation in differential sex ratios and female infanticide has been linked to women's economic participation and rights of land inheritance (Miller, 1981). Selective neglect of female children in terms of access to food and medical resources contributes powerfully to increased morbidity and mortality of females. Contrary to the nursery rhyme in the United States that little girls are made of "sugar, spice, and everything nice" while boys are made of "snakes, snails, and puppy dog tails," parents in India liken little boys to flowers, who must be carefully tended while girls are likened to stones, who can survive any treatment (Poffenberger, 1981). Girls are less likely to be fed as well as their brothers or to receive the same standard of medical care. Nevertheless daughters who survive are more likely to be treated warmly by their mothers in later childhood than are sons (Poffenberger, 1981).

Female infanticide in China illustrates the relationship between sex preference and the larger cultural context. Prior to the Revolution in 1949, female infanticide was reported to be widespread. Unwanted female infants were drowned in wells or exposed to the elements. The Marriage and Family Law of 1950 specifically prohibited female infanticide. Economic and educational reforms stressed the equality of women in the work force, and thereby the value of daughters. Recognizing that son preference was a deeply held value, family planning programs, particularly in rural areas, in effect subsidized a number of daughters while couples continued to try to have a son (Potter, 1984). While there is an absence of statistical data, it appeared that female infanticide had abated somewhat (Korbin, 1981b). However, with increasing government pressures for compliance with a one-child policy, families tried to ensure a son. Folk diagnostic techniques that predicted a female fetus were more likely to result in a voluntary abortion (Potter, 1984). Parents who give birth to a daughter are under particular pressure from family planning workers to be sterilized or to sign a pledge that they will not have a second child, hoping for a son. There are reports of a resurgence of female infanticide, despite government efforts to the contrary, particularly in the rural areas where a traditional value on sons persists most strongly.

The cultural context determines the impact of sex on child maltreatment. In Greece, for example, males are more likely to be physically abused. Higher cultural expectations of sons translates into harsher punishments for boys that has the potential for spilling over into abuse (Agathanos, Stathacouooulou, Adam, and Nakou, 1982).

Developmental Stage. Children may be more vulnerable to maltreatment at different developmental stages. In industrialized nations, developmental stages have been suggested as placing children at increased risk of maltreatment. Toddlers and adolescents, both of whom display oppositional behaviors, may be at greater risk for abuse (Straus, Gelles, and Steinmetz, 1980). Toddlers who have accidents in the course of toilet training are at increased risk of abuse, including burns inflicted by dunking in hot water (Feldman, 1980). In societies where children are not expected to understand, and thereby follow, the rules of proper behavior until a given age, there is little justification for parental anger.

Unusual or Difficult Births. Circumstances surrounding a child's birth may predict subsequent maltreatment. Among the Machiguenga, infants resulting from a difficult birth are thought to be excessively angry. Since anger is disvalued, these infants are more likely to be killed, abandoned, or given to another family. Among the Bariba of West Africa, infants who are born face down or with the appearance of a smile or teeth are thought to be witches. A "witch baby" is subject to deliberate infanticide or sale as a slave to a neighboring group. Stigma attached at birth may be considered immutable. Even if these infants undergo a ceremony to remove their "witch" status, they continue to be regarded as suspect. After selling children into slavery became prohibited by law, parents were likely to dispose of unwanted "witch babies" by giving them to Christian missionaries (Sargent, 1984).

Multiple births are considered a good omen in some cultures, whereas in others they bode evil. Multiple offspring may be likened to animal litters rather than human reproduction. In societies that disvalue or are ambivalent about multiple births, one or all of the infants may be subject to deliberate infanticide. Even if the infants are not killed at birth, they may be subjected to later maltreatment. Among tha Navajo, Levy (1964) documented a case of repetitive and fatal maltreatment of one twin attributable to cultural ambivalence about twins.

Excess Children. Children who stress and tax family resources may also be subject to maltreatment. Demographic analyses indicate that later born children, second children of the same sex, particularly females, and children too closely spaced may be less likely to survive (Scrimshaw, 1978).

Behavioral and Personality Characteristics. Categories of undervalued children cannot necessarily be identified by evident characteristics but vary with cultural values on personality and physical attributes. A characteristic valued in one society may be disvalued in others. Among the Machiguenga of the Peruvian Amazon, anger is disvalued. Toddlers who have frequent tantrums are thought to be excessively angry and are subjected to scalding baths (Johnson, 1981). Yet, among the Yanomamo of Venezuela, aggressiveness is highly valued in young male children who are encouraged to be "fierce," even to to the extent of striking their fathers (Chagnon, 1968). In another South American culture, infants who cry excessively are thought to be upset by multiple men's semen due to the mother's infidelity during pregnancy. Mothers are under considerable social pressure to keep their infants from excessive crying by whatever means necessary (Wilbert n.d., cited in Johnson, 1981).

Diminished Social Supports. The cross-cultural record strongly suggests that children with diminished social support networks are vulnerable to maltreatment. In the LeVine's work in East Africa, children from broken homes or out-of-wedlock births accounted for 2.5% of the population, but 25% of malnourished children. Five of the eight deaths of children under 5 years of age during the 2 years of their study were born of illegitimate unions (LeVine and LeVine, 1981). Fraser and Kilbride (1981) similarly found that children from intertribal marriages among the Samia of East Africa were at increased risk of neglect. If the marriage floundered and the children were not well cared for, neither the kin of the mother nor of the father felt that the children necessarily fell under their protection. Illegitimate children among the Chambri of the Sepik could be sold as victims to neighboring groups whose boys were required to commit a homicide to enter manhood (Gewertz, 1977).

Stepchildren are at increased risk of maltreatment in a number of societies. In the United States and European nations, stepchildren are more vulnerable to abuse (Daly and Wilson, 1985) and sexual molestation (Finkelhor, 1980; Russell, 1984). In China, the Marriage Law of

1950 specifically protected stepchildren who, in prerevolutionary China, were subject to a range of abuses and who the Chinese continue to view as vulnerable to maltreatment (Korbin, 1981b).

Orphans also are at risk of maltreatment unless they become re-established in a network of individuals concerned for their welfare. In Turkish society, for example, female orphans are vulnerable to sexual assault, after which they have little option but prostitution (Olson, 1981).

A case of neglect in a rural Hawaiian community underlined the problems of a child who did not have a network of concerned kin. The child was not well-liked by his stepfather, and the mother's parents and kin did not live in the community. Unrelated community adults were kind to the child, watched out for him when they could, and fed him when he appeared in their yards. However, he was frequently found wandering about the community well after dark when the rest of the small children had been gathered up and taken home. He frequently complained of stomachaches and often had a distended belly from gorging himself at the many households in which his requests for food would be met. The child was viewed as neglected by the adults in the community. However, since most were unrelated to the parents, they did not feel that they could actively intervene on behalf of the child. All they could do was feed him and treat him kindly when they stumbled upon him. The child's plight was viewed as unacceptable and the parents culpable (Korbin, 1976).

Embeddedness of Child Rearing in Social Networks

Even if categories of vulnerable children can be delineated cross-culturally, the potential for maltreatment can be mitigated by social networks. Communities vary in the degree of risk for child maltreatment according to the balance of social supports and stresses (Garbarino and Sherman, 1980). When child rearing is a shared concern within a supportive network, the consequences of having an inadequate or aggressive parent are diminished.

Social networks serve multiple protective functions for children. First, they provide assistance to parents with child-care tasks and responsibilities. Second, networks provide options for the temporary and/or permanent redistribution of children. And third, networks afford the context for collective standards and, therefore, for the scrutiny and enforcement of child-care standards. Embeddedness of child rearing in kin and community acts against the social isolation that has been linked with child maltreatment in industrialized nations (Garbarino and Crouter, 1978; Garbarino and Sherman, 1980; Gelles, 1973).

Assistance. Social networks provide options for assistance with child care. This may take the form of alternative caretakers that provide relief from unremitting responsibility for child care. It also may take the form of temporary or permanent fosterage or adoption that allow redistribution of children who would otherwise be unwanted and vulnerable to maltreatment.

Shared responsibility for children's welfare provides sources of alternative caretakers. Alternative caretakers may be other adults or older household children. If alternative caretakers are older household children, this assistance with caretaking serves the additional function of providing experience in child care that acts against the ignorance of child development and age-inappropriate expectations associated with child maltreatment in industrialized nations.

Cross-culturally, mothers who are isolated in child-care tasks, with little periodic relief or assistance, are the most likely to be harsh and rejecting toward their children (Minturn and Lambert, 1964; Rohner, 1975). In some societies, solidarity among females is the critical variable for determining how children will be treated. In times of domestic stress among the Machiguenga, for example, women must rely on their female relatives to help them and their children. If these other women are unavailable or unsupportive, the woman is more likely to take out her stress on her children (Johnson, 1981).

The importance of paternal investment to children's welfare is evident in the cross-cultural record. Urban Colombian women are more likely to report the couvade (male pregnancy symptoms) if they have weak social networks and feel that paternal investment in their pregnancy is tenuous (Browner, 1983). Among subsistence-based groups, women are more likely to kill or dispose of an infant if there is no male to hunt and provide meat for the child (e.g., Johnson, 1981).

Redistribution. Social networks with shared responsibility for children and their care also allow redistribution of children, some of whom might be at risk of abuse or neglect with their biological parents. Children who are not wanted by their parents can be absorbed into other households where they are wanted for their economic or emotional contributions. Mechanisms such as child lending, fostering, and informal adoption allow redistribution of children on a temporary or permanent basis.

Informal child lending may ease the stress of children who tax scarce family resources. In some black communities in the United States, children are regularly redistributed among a network of households depending on the need for child helpers and the available resources. If one family is low on its food stamps, for example, the children may go to live for a few weeks with an "aunt" who has a better supply (Stack, 1974).

As already discussed, children exhibiting troublesome behaviors or who are at difficult developmental stages are at increased risk of maltreatment. However, the presence of a network in which children can

be redistributed reduces the risk of maltreatment. Children whose behavior is regarded as recalcitrant or disobedient are particularly likely
to be sent as economic helpers to other households where presumably
the child will be treated more strictly and forced to behave (Johnson,
1981). Children undergoing developmental tasks that might cause difficulties for their parents can be redistributed in larger networks. Among
the Baganda, children were regularly sent to live with their grand-
mothers during weaning (Ainsworth, 1967). Since the child's behavior
was expected to be difficult during the transition away from unrestricted
access to the breast, the mother's burden was eased and the potential
for problems disarmed. Among the Gonja, boys of 7 or 8 were cus-
tomarily sent away from their parental homes to live with relatives for
an extensive period of fosterage during which they were taught rules
of proper behavior and economic skills (Goody, 1970). Indulgent and
warm relations could be maintained with the biological parents while
the frustrations and burdens of socialization were transferred to other
adults.

The impact of redistribution of children on maltreatment is inex-
tricably linked to the cultural context. While promoting survival for
children who might otherwise be subject to abuse or neglect, redistribution does not necessarily ensure an absence of subsequent maltreatment. Some cultures are quite explicit regarding the lack of rewards
for rearing another's child. A proverb among the Gusii of East Africa
likens raising someone else's child to caring for "cold mucus" (LeVine
and LeVine, 1981). In Taiwan, while adopted daughters were legally
protected, their actual treatment could be dismal. Young girls could
be adopted into households as little better than slaves. For some, their
years as adopted daughters were a painful apprenticeship in preparation
for marriage to one of the household sons and a life serving their adoptive mother who would later become their mother-in-law. Maltreatment
of adopted daughters accounted for a substantial portion of the skewed
sex ratio that previously had been explained as due to female infanticide
(Wolf, 1974; Wu, 1981).

Among Polynesians, in contrast, the care of adopted children tends
to be warm and loving (Caroll, 1970; Gallimore, Boggs, and Jordan,
1974; Howard, 1974). *Hanai,* the Hawaiian term for informal adoption,
literally means "to feed." Children are frequently adopted because of
the emotional value attached to children. Hawaiians believe that "a
house without children is a house without life" (Young, 1980:12).
Adopted children are thought to have an advantage because of having
two sets of parents, biological and adoptive, who will care about their
welfare. Further, adopted children in Polynesia are likely to be relatives,
thus providing an additional impetus for good care and survival (Silk,
1980).

Children who are redistributed to other households for their economic contributions are at risk of maltreatment if they fail to be useful. However, adoptive parents have reason to treat their charges well or they may be unable to secure others in the future (Silk, 1980).

Consensus, Scrutiny, and Enforcement. If child care is shared in a community, greater consensus is likely concerning the acceptable boundaries of child socialization methods and goals. Standards are more likely to be enforced and departures more noticeable. If others are regularly involved in child care, intervention across families is less likely to be viewed as unduly intrusive or a strategy of last resort.

While physical discipline, or threats thereof, may be well accepted by a community, the presence of networks provides safeguards against excess. If child-care tasks and children are shared, rather than considered the property of one or two biological parents, a situation is more likely in which "no one needs an invitation to intervene in the case of an overly severe spanking" (Olson, 1981). Hawaiian parents prefer physical discipline to other measures because it is thought to be swift, quickly forgotten, and therefore less disruptive to the parent–child relationship than scolding and harsh words (Dubanoski, 1982). Hawaiian parents more frequently express concern that hitting a child too often or too hard will cause resentment rather than concern that the parent will physically harm the child (Korbin, 1976). Among rural Hawaiians, relatives do not hesitate to yell from one house to the next that a spanking has gone on long enough or is too severe for the child's misbehavior. Children are quite open about calling for help more quickly and loudly than a spanking warrants as an effective strategy for disarming an angry parent (Korbin, 1976).

Only one episode of physical battering of an infant was recounted in the Hawaiian community where I conducted fieldwork. The father had been drinking, became angry when the baby would not stop crying, and hit the infant with a closed fist. The grandmother took immediate custody of the child and stated her intention to permanently adopt and rear the child. Her rights to do so were supported by the community since the infant was considered a part of the larger kin group and not the exclusive property of his biological parents. The parents pleaded with the grandmother to return their child and, after several weeks, the grandmother relented. As far as anyone in the community knew, the child was not subsequently mistreated (Korbin, 1976).

The distribution of socialization responsibilities beyond the biological parents can also involve supernatural agents. Among rural Hawaiians, if neighbors and kin do not intervene, ancestral spirits will. One mother in the same Hawaiian community beat her 10-year-old daughter severely and often. She was contrite and ashamed that she bruised the child. She also was fearful that the ancestors for whom her daughter was named would become angry at her maltreatment of the child and take the girl back to their realm where she would fare better (Korbin, 1976).

Collective child rearing, however, also can contribute to harsh treatment. Among the Hopi, parents rarely punished their children. However, representations of dieties, the katchinas, inflicted severe pain on children in the context of rituals during which children were to learn cultural lore and rules of behavior (Simmons, 1942). Children who have been disobedient and poorly behaved may be subject to harsher treatment than their peers during initiation rituals in the Highlands of Papua New Guinea when there is a collective context for remonstration that cannot be exhibited by individual parents (Langness, 1981).

Situations of Change

Socioeconomic and sociocultural change have been linked in the literature with an increase in child maltreatment (Gelles and Pedrick-Cornell, 1983; Korbin, 1981; Okeahialam, 1984). Even modest environmental change can alter child-care patterns. Some Native American groups initiated harsher and more demanding toilet-training practices following a change from dirt floors that were easily swept and cleaned to wooden floors that required more care (Honigman, 1967). However, the impact of change on child treatment is a complex issue. Most often, the literature attributes an increase in child maltreatment to a breakdown in traditional patterns and practices. Change has been associated too readily with a range of social and individual ills, including child maltreatment. This is due, in large part, to a continued reliance on the folk–urban continuum that assumes an absence of deviance in traditional, smaller scale societies. While this assumption of a lack of deviance is not supported by empirical evidence (Edgerton, 1976, 1978), the cross-cultural literature suggests that sociocultural and socioeconomic change have an impact on parent–child relationships and interaction, including the potential for maltreatment.

Immigrant and urbanizing families face unique problems that have a potential effect on child maltreatment. In the change from an agrarian to an urban economy, children become consumers rather than producers and an economic liability rather than an asset (LeVine and LeVine, 1985; Logan, 1979; Olson, 1981). Through formal schooling, immigrant children acquire more knowledge of the new environment and society than do their parents. They become less obedient and compliant (LeVine and LeVine, 1985), providing greater opportunity for parent–child conflict. Children's behaviors in urban areas are more aggressive and disruptive (Weisner, 1979), and mothers who move to urbanizing areas and come into situations of culture contact are less confident of their efficacy in child rearing (Graves, 1972). These potential problems are exacerbated by increased isolation of families from traditional kin and social networks and diminished availability of sources for assistance with child care.

Normative child-rearing practices may be adaptive in one setting but potentially harmful in changed circumstances. Among Polynesians sibling caretaking is highly valued as crucial for child development (Gallimore et al., 1974; Korbin, 1978; Ritchie and Ritchie, 1981a). In traditional rural settings, sibling caretaking not only was embedded in multiage groups of children with adults nearby to call upon for help, but also occurred in an environment relatively free of physical hazards. As New Zealand Maoris moved to urban areas, however, sibling caretaking placed both sibling caretakers and their young charges in potentially dangerous situations. Substandard urban housing increased the risk of accidents, and isolation of families decreased the likelihood that there would be others to call upon for assistance in an emergency (Ritchie and Ritchie, 1981a). In addition to an increase in hazards associated with sibling caretaking, cultural misunderstandings of the practice by New Zealand whites contributed to increased and disproportionate child-protection reports. While Maori children accounted for 12% of the population, they represented 51% of neglect cases and 54% of children not being "under proper control" (Fergusson, Flemming, and O'Neill, 1972).

Importantly, change also can be in a positive direction. In a 20-year perspective on an Indian community, Minturn (1982) found that improvements in locally available medical care promoted the survival and health of female children, thereby diminishing the previous imbalance in the sex ratio. While parents still favor sons and are less willing to transport daughters equally long distances for medical care, if a clinic is readily accessible, daughters are more likely to receive care than in the past.

Change also may eradicate traditional cultural practices perceived as abusive from outside the culture in question, but an increase of idiosyncratic abuse. Children may no longer be subjected to harsh initiation rites, footbinding, or a variety of collective practices, but in the absence of protective networks, they may be more vulnerable to nonaccidental inflicted injury or sexual misuse (Korbin, 1981a). The costs and benefits remain to be assessed.

FUTURE DIRECTIONS

Definitional validity and reliability are critical for future cross-cultural research on child maltreatment. While this seems a basic requirement for research, it has not yet been accomplished either in nations that have been dealing with child maltreatment for over 25 years or in the developing cross-cultural literature. This is a major impediment for research both within and between cultures. While "child abuse and neglect" tends to be used as a singular concept, it encompasses a range of child outcomes, caretaker behaviors, and societal processes for determining culpability. This is problematic within a single cultural context but becomes even more so when applied cross-culturally.

Cross-cultural research on child maltreatment has been sparse. Nevertheless, the cross-cultural record indicates that child maltreatment, in its various manifestations, is not restricted to a single society or type of culture. Available data is suggestive and points toward the need for systematic cross-cultural research on the magnitude and circumstances of the multiple manifestations of child maltreatment and their antecedents and consequences. Current models based primarily on research and clinical experience in Euro-American nations have proved inadequate for exploring the complexity of child maltreatment. Etiological models must be developed that encompass the range of human cultural adapatation. The cross-cultural record provides an invaluable resource as well as a challenge in unravelling the circumstances under which children are vulnerable to maltreatment.

ACKNOWLEDGMENT

I would like to thank the participants at the Social Science Research Council Conference on "Biosocial Perspectives on Child Abuse and Neglect" held in York, Maine in May 1984. I benefitted a great deal from their presentations and helpful comments. Special thanks are due to Lonnie Sherrod for his organization of the conference and to Richard Gelles and Jane Lancaster for their patience and helpful comments on the manuscript. I would also like to thank J. Amster for his comments on several drafts of the chapter.

REFERENCES

Aber, L., and Zigler, E. Developmental considerations in the definition of child maltreatment. *In* R. Rizley and D. Cicchetti, Eds., *Developmental perspectives on child maltreatment*. San Francisco: Jossey-Bass, 1981, pp. 1–29.

Adelson, L. Slaughter of the innocents: A study of forty-six homicides in which the victims were children. *New England Journal of Medicine,* 1961, 264:1345–1349.

Agathanos, H. Institutional child abuse in Greece: Some preliminary findings: *Child Abuse and Neglect: The International Journal,* 1983, 7(1):71–74.

Agathanos, H., Stathacoupoulou, N., Adam, H., and Nakou, S. Child abuse and neglect in Greece: Sociomedical aspects. *Child Abuse and Neglect: The International Journal,* 1982, 6(3):307–311.

Ainsworth, M. *Infancy in Uganda. Infant care and the growth of love.* Baltimore, MD: Johns Hopkins Press, 1967.

Arnold, E. The use of corporal punishment in child rearing in the West Indies. *Child Abuse and Neglect: The International Journal,* 1982, 6(2):141–145.

Besharov, D. Toward better research on child abuse and neglect: Making definitional issues an explicit methodological concern. *Child Abuse and Neglect: The International Journal,* 1981, 5(4):383–390.

Bhattacharya, A. Child abuse in India and the nutritionally battered child. *Child Abuse and Neglect: The International Journal,* 1979, *3*(2):607–614.

Browner, C. Male pregnancy symptoms in urban Colombia. *American Ethnologist,* 1983, *10*(3):494–510.

Bugos, P., and McCarthy, L. Ayoreo infanticide: A case study. *In* G. Hausfater and S. Hrdy, Eds., *Infanticide: Comparative and evolutionary perspectives.* NY: Aldine, 1984, pp. 503–520.

Caffey, J. Multiple fractures in the long bones of infants suffering from chronic subdural hematoma. *American Journal of Roentgenology* 1946, *56*(2):163–173.

Caroll, V., Ed. *Adoption in Eastern Oceania.* Honolulu: University of Hawaii Press, 1970.

Chagnon, N. *Yanomamo: The fierce people,* NY: Holt, Rinehart and Winston, 1968.

Chavez, A., Martines, C., and Yaschine, T. Nutrition, behavioral development, and mother–child interaction in young rural children. *Federation Proceedings,* 1975, *34*(7):1574–1582.

Cicchetti, D., and Rizley, R. Developmental perspectives on the etiology, intergenerational transmission, and sequelae of child maltreatment. *In* R. Rizley and D. Cicchetti, Eds., *Developmental perspectives on child maltreatment.* San Francisco, CA: Jossey-Bass, 1981, pp. 31–55.

Cohn, A. Stopping abuse before it occurs: Different solutions for different population groups. *Child Abuse and Neglect: The International Journal,* 1982, *6*(4):473–483.

Colishaw, G. Infanticide in aboriginal Australia. *Oceania,* 1978, *68*(4):262–283.

Daly, M., and Wilson, M. A sociobiological analysis of human infanticide. *In* G. Hausfater and S. Hrdy, Eds., *Infanticide: Comparative and evolutionary perspectives.* NY: Aldine, 1984, pp. 487–502.

Daly, M., and Wilson, M. Child abuse and other risks of not living with both parents. *Ethnology and Sociobiology,* 1985, *6*:197–210.

de Silva, W. Some cultural and economic factors leading to neglect, abuse and violence in respect of children within the family in Sri Lanka. *Child Abuse and Neglect: The International Journal,* 1981, *5*(4):391–504.

Dickeman, M. Demographic consequences of infanticide in man. *Annual Review of Ecology and Systematics,* 1975, *6*:100–132.

Dickeman, M. Concepts and classification in the study of human infanticide: Sectional introduction and some cautionary notes. *In* G. Hausfater and S. Hrdy, Eds., *Infanticide: Comparative and evolutionary perspectives.* NY: Aldine, 1984, pp. 427–437.

Divale, W., and Harris, M. Population, warfare, and the male supremacist complex. *American Anthropologist,* 1976, *78*:521–538.

Dorjahn, V. Rural–urban differences in infant and child mortality among the Temne of Kolifa. *Journal of Anthropological Research,* 1976, *32*:1.

Dubanoski, R. Child maltreatment in European– and Hawaiian–Americans. *Child Abuse and Neglect: The International Journal,* 1981, *5*:457–465.

Dubanoski, R., and Snyder, K. Patterns of child abuse and neglect in Japanese– and Samoan–Americans. *Child Abuse and Neglect: The International Journal,* 1982, *4*:217–225.

Edgerton, R. B. *Deviance: A cross-cultural perspective.* Menlo Park, CA: Cummings, 1976.

Edgerton, R. B. The study of deviance—Marginal man or everyman? *In* G. Spindler, Ed., *The Making of psychological anthropology.* Berkeley, CA: University of California Press, 1978, pp. 442–478.

Eisenberg, L. Cross-cultural and historic perspectives on child abuse and neglect. *Child Abuse and Neglect: The International Journal*, 1981, 5(3):299–308.

Elmer, E. Abused young children seen in hospitals. *Social Work*, 1960, 5(4):98–102.

Feldman, K. Child abuse by burning. *In* C. H. Kempe and R. E. Helfer, Eds., *The battered child*, 3rd ed. Chicago, IL: University of Chicago Press, 1980, pp. 147–162.

Fergusson, D., Flemming, J., and O'Neill, D. *Child abuse in New Zealand*. Wellington, Government Press, 1972.

Finkelhor, D. Risk factors in the sexual victimization of children. *Child Abuse and Neglect: The International Journal*, 1980, 4(4):265–273.

Finkelhor, D., and Korbin, J. Child maltreatment in global perspective. UNICEF Working Paper, 1985.

Foster, G., and Anderson, B. *Medical anthropology*. NY: Wiley, 1978.

Fraser, G., and Kilbride, P. Child abuse and neglect—Rare but perhaps increasing phenomena among the Samia of Kenya. *Child Abuse and Neglect: The International Journal*, 1981, 4(4):227–232.

Gallimore, R., Boggs, J., and Jordan, C. *Culture, behavior and education. A study of Hawaiian–Americans*. Beverly Hills, CA: Sage Publications, 1974.

Galston, A., and Savage, J. *Daily life in People's China*. NY: Thomas Y. Crowell, 1973.

Garbarino, J., and Crouter, A. Defining the community context for parent–child relations: The correlates of child maltreatment. *Child Development*, 1978, 49:604–616.

Garbarino, J., and Ebata, A. On the significance of ethnic and cultural differences in child maltreatment. *Journal of Marriage and the Family*, 1983, 45(4):773–783.

Garbarino, J., and Sherman, D. High risk neighborhoods and high risk families: The human ecology of child maltreatment. *Child Development*, 1980, 51:188–198.

Gelles, R. J. Child abuse as psychopathology: A sociological critique and reformulation. *American Journal of Orthopsychiatry*, 1973, 43(4):611–621.

Gelles, R. J. Toward better research on child abuse and neglect: A response to Besharov. *Child Abuse and Neglect: The International Journal*, 1982, 6(4):495–496.

Gelles, R. J., and Pedrick-Cornell, C., Eds. *International perspectives on family violence*. Lexington, MA: Lexington Books, 1983.

Gewertz, D. From sago suppliers to entrepreneurs: Marketing and migration in the Middle Sepik. *Oceania*, 1977, 48(2):126–140.

Giovannoni, J., and Becerra, R. *Defining child abuse*. NY: Free Press, 1979.

Goody, E. Kinship and fostering in Gonja: Deprivation or advantage? *In* P. Mayer, Ed., *Socialization: The approach from social anthropology*. London: Tavistock, 1970, pp. 51–74.

Graburn, N. Severe child abuse among the Canadian Inuit. Paper presented at the Annual Meeting of the American Anthropological Association, Denver, 1984.

Graves, N. City, country, and child rearing: A tricultural study of mother–child relationships in varying environments. Ph.D. dissertation, University of Colorado, 1972.

Green, J. The role of cultural anthropology in the education of social service personnel. *Journal of Sociology and Social Welfare*, 1978, 5(2):214–229.

Haditono, S. Prevention and treatment of child abuse and neglect among children under five years of age in Indonesia. *Child Abuse and Neglect: The International Journal*, 1981, 5(2):97–101.

Hausfater, G., and Hrdy, S., Eds., *Infanticide: Comparative and evolutionary perspectives*. NY: Aldine, 1984.

Honigman, J. *Personality in Culture*. New York: Harper and Row, 1967.

Howard, A. *Ain't no big thing: Coping strategies in a Hawaiian–American community*. Honolulu: University of Hawaii Press, 1974.

Ikeda, Y. A short introduction to child abuse in Japan. *Child Abuse and Neglect: The International Journal*, 1982, 6(4):487–490.

Jason, J., Williams, S., Burton, A., and Rochat, R. Epidemiological differences between sexual and physical abuse. *Journal of the American Medical Association*, 1982, 247(24):3344–3345.

Jinadu, M. The role of neglect in the aetiology of protein–energy malnutrition in urban communities of Nigeria. *Child Abuse and Neglect: The International Journal*, 1980, 4(4):233–245.

Johansson, S. Deferred infanticide: Excess female mortality during childhood. *In* G. Hausfater and S. Hrdy, Eds., *Infanticide: Comparative and evolutionary perspectives*. NY: Aldine, 1984, pp. 463–486.

Johnson, O. The socioeconomic context of child abuse and neglect in native South America. *In* J. Korbin, Ed., *Child abuse and neglect: Cross-cultural perspectives*. Berkeley, CA: University of California Press, 1981, pp. 56–70.

Kammerman, S. Eight countries: Cross-national perspectives on child abuse and neglect. *Children Today*, 1975, 4(3):34–37.

Keesing, R. Introduction. *In* G. Herdt, Ed., *Rituals of manhood: Male initiation in Papua New Guinea*. Berkeley, CA: University of California Press, 1982, pp. 1–43.

Kellerman, F. *Child battering*. Pretoria: Department of Social Welfare and Pensions, 1979.

Kempe, C. H. Recent developments in the field of child abuse. *Child Abuse and Neglect: The International Journal*, 1978, 2(4):261–267.

Kempe, C. H. Silverman, F. N., Steele, B. F., Droegmueller, W., and Silver, H. K. The battered child syndrome. *Journal of the American Medical Association*, 1962, 181:17–24.

Korbin, J. Fieldnotes. 1976.

Korbin, J. Anthropological contributions to the study of child abuse. *Child Abuse and Neglect: The International Journal*, 1977, 1(1):7–24.

Korbin, J. Caretaking patterns in a rural Hawaiian community: Congruence of child and observer reports. Ph.D. Dissertation, University of California, Los Angeles, 1978.

Korbin, J. A cross-cultural perspective on the role of the community in child abuse and neglect. *Child Abuse and Neglect: The International Journal*, 1979, 3(1):9–18.

Korbin, J. The cultural context of child abuse and neglect. *In* C. H. Kempe and R. E. Helfer, Eds., *The battered child*, 3rd ed. Chicago, IL: University of Chicago Press, 1980, pp. 21–35.

Korbin, J., Ed. *Child abuse and neglect: Cross-cultural perspectives*. Berkeley, CA: University of California Press, 1981.(a)

Korbin, J. "Very few cases": Child abuse and neglect in the People's Republic of China. *In* J. Korbin, Ed., *Child abuse and neglect: Cross-cultural perspectives*. Berkeley, CA: University of California Press, 1981, pp. 166–187.(b)

Lancaster, J., and Lancaster, C. Parental investment: The hominid adaptation. *In* D. Ortner, Ed., *How humans adapt: A biocultural odyssey*. Washington, D.C.: Smithsonian Institution Press, 1983.

Langness, L. L. Child abuse and cultural values: The case of New Guinea. *In* J. Korbin, Ed., *Child abuse and neglect: Cross-cultural perspectives*. Berkeley, CA: University of California Press, 1981, pp. 13–34.

Latham, M. C. Protein-calorie malnutrition in children and its relation to psychological development and behavior. *Psychological Reviews,* 1974, *54*:541–565.

Lauderdale, M., Vallinuas, A., and Anderson, R. Race, ethnicity, and child maltreatment: An empirical analysis. *Child Abuse and Neglect: The International Journal,* 1980, *4*(3):163–169.

Levine, N. Differential value, differential care: Family planning and child neglect in three Tibetan societies. Paper presented at the Annual Meeting of the American Anthropological Association, Washington, D.C., 1985.

LeVine, R. Child rearing as cultural adaptation. *In* P. H. Leiderman *et al.,* Eds., *Culture and infancy. Variations in the human experience.* NY: Academic Press, 1977, pp. 15–27.

LeVine, S., and LeVine, R. Child abuse and neglect in sub-Saharan Africa. *In* J. Korbin, Ed., *Child abuse and neglect: Cross-cultural perspectives.* Berkeley, CA: University of California Press, 1981, pp. 35–55.

LeVine, S., and LeVine, R. Age, gender, and the demographic transition: The life course in agrarian societies. *In* A. Rossi, Ed., *Gender and the life course.* NY: Aldine, 1985, pp. 29–42.

Levinson, D. Physical punishment of children and wife beating in cross-cultural perspective. *Child Abuse and Neglect: The International Journal,* 1981, *5*(2):193–195.

Levy, J. The fate of Navajo twins. *American Anthropologist,* 1964, *66*(4):883–886.

Loening, W. Child abuse among the Zulus: A people in transition. *Child Abuse and Neglect: The International Journal,* 1981, *5*(1):3–7.

Logan, R. Socio-cultural change and the perception of children as burdens. *Child Abuse and Neglect: The International Journal,* 1979, *3*:657–662.

McKee, L. Sex differentials in survivorship and customary treatment of infants and children, *Medical Anthropology,* 1984, *8*(2):91–108.

Martin, H., Ed. *The abused child: A multidisciplinary approach to developmental issues and treatment.* Cambridge, MA: Ballinger, 1976.

Mehra, B. Highlights on abuse in education: A view from India. *Child Abuse and Neglect: The International Journal,* 1982, *6*(2):225–228.

Mehta, M. Physical abuse of abandoned children in India. *Child Abuse and Neglect: The International Journal,* 1982, *6*(2):171–175.

Mehta, M., Prabhu, S., and Mistry, H. Child labor in Bombay. *Child Abuse and Neglect: The International Journal,* 1985, *9*(1):107–111.

Miller, B. *The endangered sex: Neglect of female children in rural North India.* Ithaca, NY: Cornell University Press, 1981.

Minturn, L. Changes in the differential treatment of Rajput girls and boys. *Behavior Science Research,* 1982, *17*(1–2):70–90.

Minturn, L., and Lambert, W. *Mothers of six cultures. Antecedents of child-rearing.* NY: Wiley, 1964.

Nathan, L., and Hwang, W. Child abuse in an urban centre in Malaysia. *Child Abuse and Neglect: The International Journal,* 1981, *5*(3):241–248.

National Center on Child Abuse and Neglect. *Study findings: National study of incidence and severity of child abuse and neglect.* Washington, D.C.: DHEW, 1981.

Nelson, B. *Making an issue of child abuse. Political agenda setting for social problems.* Chicago, IL: University of Chicago Press, 1984.

Nwako, F. The child abuse syndrome in Nigeria. *International Surgery,* 1974, *59*:613–616.

Okeahialam, T. C. Child abuse in Nigeria. *Child Abuse and Neglect: The International Journal,* 1984, *8*(1):69–74.

Olson, E. Socioeconomic and psycho-cultural contexts of child abuse and neglect in Turkey. *In* J. Korbin, Ed., *Child abuse and neglect: Cross-cultural perspectives.* Berkeley, CA: University of California Press, 1981, pp. 96–119.

Oyemade, A. Child care practices in Nigeria—An urgent plea for social workers. *Child Abuse and Neglect: The International Journal,* 1980, 4(2):101–103.

Pfofl, S. J. The "discovery" of child abuse. *Social Problems,* 1977, 24(3):310–323.

Poffenberger, T. Child rearing and social structure in rural India: Toward a cross-cultural definition of child abuse and neglect. *In* J. Korbin, Ed., *Child abuse and neglect: Cross-cultural perspectives.* Berkeley: University of California Press, 1981, pp. 71–95.

Polansky, N., Chalmers, M., Buttenwieser, E. and Williams, D. *Damaged Parents. An Anatomy of Child Neglect.* Chicago: University of Chicago Press, 1981.

Potter, S. China's rural family planning program. Paper presented at the Annual Meeting of the American Anthropological Association, Denver, 1984.

Ritchie, J., and Ritchie, J. Child rearing and child abuse: The Polynesian context. *In* J. Korbin, Ed., *Child abuse and neglect: Cross-cultural perspectives.* Berkeley, CA: University of California Press, 1981, pp. 186–204.(a)

Ritchie, J., and Ritchie, J. *Spare the rod.* Sydney: Allen and Unwin, 1981.(b)

Rohner, R. *They love me, they love me not: A worldwide study of the effects of parental acceptance and rejection.* New Haven, CT: HRAF Press, 1975.

Russell, D. The prevalence and seriousness of incestuous abuse: Step-fathers versus biological fathers. *Child Abuse and Neglect: The International Journal,* 1984, 7:133–146.

Sargent, C. Born to die. The fate of extraordinary children in Bariba culture. Paper presented at the Annual Meeting of the American Anthropological Association, Denver, 1984.

Scheper-Hughes, N. Infant mortality and infant care: Cultural and economic constraints on nurturing in northeast Brazil. *Social Science and Medicine,* 1984, 5:535–546.

Scheper-Hughes, N. Culture, scarcity, and maternal thinking: Maternal detachment and infant survival in a Brazilian shantytown. *Ethos,* 1985, 13(4):291–317.

Scrimshaw S. Infant mortality and behavior in the regulation of family size. *Population and Development Review,* 1978, 4(3):383–403.

Scrimshaw, S. Infanticide as deliberate fertility regulation. *In* R. Lee and R. Bulatao, Eds., *Determinants of fertility in developing countries: A summary of knowledge.* NY: Academic Press, 1983, pp. 714–731.

Scrimshaw, S. Infanticide in human populations: Societal and individual concerns. *In* G. Hausfater and S. Hrdy, Eds., *Infanticide: Comparative and evolutionary perspectives,* NY: Aldine, 1984, pp. 439–462.

Semiawan, C. An invitational environment to treat and prevent emotional deprivation: A meaningful approach to increase psychological development. *Child Abuse and Neglect: The International Journal,* 1981, 5(4):481–486.

Sereewat, S. The work of the foundation for children in Thailand. *Child Abuse and Neglect: The International Journal,* 1983, 7(3):359–361.

Silk, J. Adoption and kinship in Oceania. *American Anthropologist,* 1980, 82(4):799–820.

Simmons, L. *Sun chief.* New Haven, CT: Yale University Press, 1942.

Spearly, J., and Lauderdale, M. Community characteristics and ethnicity in the prediction of child maltreatment rates. *Child Abuse and Neglect: The International Journal,* 1983, 7(1):91–105.

Stack, C. *All our kin. Strategies for survival in a black community.* NY: Harper and Row, 1974.

Steele, B. Psychodynamic factors in child abuse. *In* C. H. Kempe and R. E. Helfer, Eds., *The battered child,* 3rd ed. Chicago, IL: University of Chicago Press, 1980, pp. 49–85.

Straus, M., Gelles, R., and Steinmetz, S. *Behind closed doors: Violence in the American family.* NY: Anchor, 1980.

Super, C. Sex differences in infant care and vulnerability. *Medical Anthropology,* 1984, *8*(2):84–90.

Tauber, E., Meda, C., and Vitro, V. Child ill-treatment as considered by the Italian criminal and civil codes. *Child Abuse and Neglect: The International Journal,* 1977, *1*(1):149–152.

Taylor, L., and Newberger, E. Child abuse in the International year of the child. *New England Journal of Medicine,* 1979, *301*:1205–1212.

Tevoedjre, I. Violence and the child in the adult world in Africa. *Child Abuse and Neglect: The International Journal,* 1981, *5*(4):495–498.

Trotter, R., Ackerman, A., Rodman, D., Martinez, A., and Sorvillo, F. "Azarcon" and "Greta": Ethnomedical solution to epidemiological mystery. *Medical Anthropology Quarterly,* 1983, *14*(3):3,18.

Van Staden, J. The mental development of abused children in South Africa. *Child Abuse and Neglect: The International Journal,* 1979, *3*:997–1000.

Wagatsuma, H. Child abandonment and infanticide: A Japanese case. *In* J. Korbin, Ed., *Child abuse and neglect: Cross-cultural perspectives,* Berkeley, CA: University of California Press, 1981, pp. 120–138.

Weisner, T. Urban-rural differences in sociable and disruptive behavior of Kenya children. *Ethnology,* 1979, *18*(2):153–172.

Werner, E. *Cross-cultural child development. A view from the planet Earth.* Monterey, CA: Wadsworth, 1979.

Whiting, B. B., and Whiting, J. W. M. *Children of six cultures. A psychocultural analysis.* Cambridge, MA: Harvard University Press, 1975.

Wolf, A. Marriage and adoption in northern Taiwan. *In* R. Smith, Ed., *Social organization and the applications of anthropology.* Ithaca, NY: Cornell University Press, 1974, pp. 128–160.

Wu, D. Y. H. Child abuse in Taiwan. *In* J. Korbin, Ed., *Child abuse and neglect: Cross-cultural perspectives.* Berkeley, CA: University of California Press, 1981, pp. 139–165.

Yeatman, G., Shaw, C., Barlow, M., and Bartlett, G. Pseudobattering in Vietnamese children. *Pediatrics,* 1976, *58*:616.

Young, B. The Hawaiians. *In* J. McDermott, W. S. Tseng, and T. Maretzki, Eds., *People and cultures of Hawaii: A psychocultural profile.* Honolulu: University of Hawaii Press, 1980, pp. 5–24.

NEGLECT, ABUSE, AND AVOIDABLE DEATH: PARENTAL INVESTMENT AND THE MORTALITY OF INFANTS AND CHILDREN IN THE EUROPEAN TRADITION

S. R. Johansson

chapter

4

"Rock-(or hush) a- by baby" is one of the most famous nursery rhymes in *Mother Goose*. But what is it really about? An infant, with no parent nearby, is in its cradle in a tree. When the wind blows, the cradle sways back and forth until the wind breaks the branch and the baby falls down, "cradle and all." It would be a miracle if the infant were to survive such an accident. Why would a nursery rhyme about a deserted infant who suffers an awful accident ever become part of an oral (later literary) tradition directed at children?

Most historians of childhood would find in this rhyme yet another indication that the neglect and abuse of infants and children was once the norm in preindustrial Europe. Thus far, only a few historians have disagreed with this pessimistic outlook on past parenting. Those historians who are more optimistic about the history of childhood and parenting would either find a sunnier interpretation of the lullabye or point out that most nursery songs for babies involve expressions of parental solicitude.

The disagreements between historians have left us with this question: Is the history of childhood a nightmare from which we have only begun to awaken in the twentieth century (DeMause, 1974:1) or is it yet another demonstration that certain aspects of human behavior are immune to social and economic change? (Pollock, 1983:vii).

At present, the history of childhood and parenting is an active field of research with much to offer contemporaries who deal with threats to the health and welfare of children. It is also intellectually relevant to debate over whether or not human reproductive behavior remains deeply rooted in our evolutionary past or is primarily influenced by individual preferences, social norms, and economic constraints, all of which are inherently shifting and unstable.

From whatever angle the study of childhood and parenting is approached certain problems inevitably arise. The attempt to prove that there was more, less, or the same amount of child maltreatment in the past as in the present, or in our own culture as opposed to a foreign culture, or in this subculture rather than that, always presumes that child maltreatment is an objective phenomena that exists apart from the observer–judge's preferences and/or cultural biases (Giovannoni and Becerra, 1979; Korbin, 1981). But culture-free forms of child abuse or neglect have not proved easy to isolate. Neither is it easy to obtain data on the sorts of behaviors identified as abusive or neglectful (Gelles, 1978). Historians are at an even greater disadvantage than contemporary researchers in this respect, because no government or church, prior to the nineteenth century even tried to estimate the extent to which children were neglected or abused by their parents.

But from the sixteenth century onward many European governments put a great deal of effort into gathering data on the baptisms and burials of their citizens. This data has been used by demographic historians to reconstruct estimates of infant and child mortality. The purpose of this chapter is to use historical data on the extent to which children survived infancy and childhood in premodern Europe in order to explore what it can tell us about past parenting in the cultures ancestral to our own.

The connection between mortality and parenting is far from obvious. Descriptive historians who make parenting the focus of their research generally refer to mortality in passing which sometimes leads them to make ill-considered and unfounded assertions. Demographic historians, on the other hand, have given little or no consideration to what their data might show about the extent of malparenting in the past. Thus there has grown up two related disciplines that have so far remained isolated. This chapter builds a much needed bridge between the qualitative and quantitative aspects of the history of childhood and past parenting.

First, this bridge requires a justification for postulating a connection between neglect, abuse, and "avoidable" death. Second, it necessitates a review of theories of past parenting that explain why most parents either did or did not maltreat their infants and children. Third, it analyzes infant mortality in terms of its component parts—estimating what fraction of observed deaths may, in fact, have been "avoidable"—by selecting and reviewing some of the quantitative data available. The methodology used to do this is, in all fairness, highly eclectic. The resulting estimates should be judged as much for their imaginative content as their potential objectivity. But where angels have feared to tread, the less inhibited will rush in. The only justification for their rashness is the possibility of bringing new perspectives to important problems.

AVOIDABLE DEATH

Parental Investment, Abuse, and Neglect

Parental investment is crucial to the survival of the young in many different species, but none more so than among humans. Total maternal rejection will lead to infant death within hours or days. But there are many forms of lowered biological, social, and emotional support that will not kill an infant so soon; instead the infant will be placed in a category that renders it more vulnerable to the risk of dying from disease, accidents, or violence. Infanticide can take as many forms as there are reasons for it (Hrdy and Hausfater, 1984), and it can be deferred from the first year of life to later childhood (Johansson, 1984). But, in general, the poorer the environment the more dependent on parental investment infants and children become for their survival. Where resources are few, pathogens abundant, and sanitation a luxury, the fact that any newborn survives through childhood is dependent on the fact that one or both parents have invested a considerable amount of energy in keeping it alive.

In most premodern societies, where medical technology was either nonexistent or even dangerous, it was inevitable that infant mortality would be higher than it is at present. But if a premodern infant died because of parental neglect while giving more to a favored child, we can speak of that death as if it were an avoidable one caused by neglect (Lancaster, 1983; Scrimshaw, 1984). What about avoidable deaths caused by "abuse" rather than neglect?

For the sake of conceptual symmetry, we will define "abuse" as a form of parental overinvestment. At first the idea that parents could overinvest in a child, and therefore harm or even kill it, may seem jarring or absurd. (Most biologists regard both neglect and abuse as forms of underinvestment.) But that is what is implied in the ordinary use of terms like "spoiling children" or "overprotection." For infants and children protection is a very important form of parental investment; but protection carried to extremes will distort the normal maturation process. Similarly, when parents train children to behave in socially acceptable ways, they must use some form of discipline. Normal discipline is a beneficial form of investment. But discipline can be carried to life-threatening extremes, and in that sense it becomes a form of overinvestment, especially when the violent parent thinks he or she is using force in order to ensure compliance on the part of the child in the pursuit of some socially desirable goal. (Violence administered randomly or in response to stress can be thought of as a failure to protect, hence a form of neglect.) Even sexual abuse can be regarded as a perverse amplification of a normally desirable form of parental investment (touching, hugging, physical closeness).

Any form of abuse or neglect causes stress which can either lower the efficiency of the body's immune system (Laudenslager and Reite, 1984) or provoke a child to run away or adopt some other high-risk life style. In any case, parents do not have to be conscious of what they are doing to their children. Only an outside observer can render the judgment that abuse or neglect led to an avoidable infant or child death.

The concept of avoidable death is far from new. It has appeared in the ideas of European theologians, moralists, doctors, and reporters for many centuries. One such example can be found in the writings of Dr. Ashby, an early twentieth century English physician who practiced in Manchester, England. Dr. Ashby wrote *Infant Mortality* in 1915, which was based on his long experience treating ordinary working-class patients in that city. In the book, Ashby distinguished between levels of parental investment among two subpopulations, Jewish parents and non-Jewish parents, both of whom had approximately the same income levels (the Jewish parents were primarily recent immigrants from Eastern Europe) and both of whom lived in the same slum and semislum conditions. Ashby knew that registered infant mortality rates published for the working-class districts of Manchester by the Registrar-General indicated that for every 1000 live born infants, 150 died in their first year of life. In the working-class district inhabited primarily by Jewish families, infant mortality was only 110. Ashby attributed the difference to the fact the Jewish fathers turned over their entire incomes to their wives, who in turn spared no effort to maximize the welfare of their children. Gentile fathers, in contrast, reserved a hefty proportion of their income for themselves (some of which they spent at the pub), and their wives were not so collectively committed to maintaining high standards of cleanliness or medical care as were the Jewish mothers. Ashby stated that he had never seen a dirty or ragged child among the working-class Jewish families.

The quantitative implications of his argument were that as a result of differential parental investment something like 40/1000 of those infants born to non-Jewish working-class families died otherwise avoidable deaths. This was almost one-third of all newborns dying and 4% of all those born. Ashby did not assert that Gentile parents actively sought these deaths (although this possibility was not precluded) but only that infant survival was not the first priority among the ordinary members of this subculture, whereas among Jewish working-class families it was.

What saves Ashby's use of the concept "avoidable death" from being the result of simple ethnocentrism (his preferences for clean faces, neat clothing, and intensive mothering are obviously "middle class") is the fact that he tied his preferences to an estimate of excess infant deaths given a common set of material constraints (which included low incomes and an unsanitary environment). Unless one is willing to turn a blind eye to infant death on a fairly substantial scale, the forms of parental underinvestment that he indicts do not deserve to fall into the realm of culturally neutral choices that deserve to be respected by the nonchauvinistic. A mortality-based standard for evaluating parental behavior may be the closest we can get to "culture-free" definitions of neglect and abuse. At any rate it provides a good basis, or a promising basis, for attempting to estimate how parental investment influences the overall level of infant and child survival in a specific population, at a specific economic level, in a specific time, etc.

Parental Investment, Choice, and Ideology

One could question and even reject the reports of Dr. Ashby, but if he is accepted as a knowledgeable and unbiased observed (which he might not be if he were a religious man writing for a religious audience) we must ask why two populations, subject to the same or very similar material constraints, in the same place and at the same time would choose to differentially invest in the welfare of their children. Ashby's description points us in the direction of "ideology." The Jewish parents he observed were under the influence of a powerful set of ideas justly famous for inculcating the importance of good parenting as well as institutionalizing that preference in many aspects of daily life. All parents, unless they find themselves in a very atypically extreme environment, will have a certain amount of choice with respect to whether or not they channel the resources at their disposal toward minimizing or maximizing the welfare of their children. Under the influence of their religious beliefs the Jewish parents used their available resources to do the latter; the non-Jewish parents were not under the influence of such ideas and did not make the welfare of their children their first priority.

Accepting this explanation requires a prior commitment to a theory of behavior that awards dominance to cultural rather than instinctual forces in the determination of the form and intensity of parental investment. In the "culture counts" theory of parenting the brain is conceived of as a computer that is mentally programmed by those who raise and educate children and ultimately by those who control information streams, including information about what is good, right, just, or best for children. The cultural "software" of parenting is believed to be strong enough to override any instinctual preprogramming (if it exists) and to generate the patterns of collective behavior that enable observers to distinguish one culture or subculture of parenting from another, whether in working-class Manchester or anywhere.

Diametrically opposed to such learning-dominated theories of pa-

rental behavior are those that embody some form of biological determinism and that claim that human parenting, like parenting among the
higher mammals, is a function of genetically rooted programs "entered"
into the brain by nature in the course of evolution. The function of
these hard-wired (instinctual) programs is to produce forms of behavior
that promote reproductive success. Sociobiologists do not agree on
the implications of this belief. Some argue that the drive toward reproductive success will instinctually lead parents to do their utmost to
ensure the survival of *all* of their offspring (except under extremely
stressful conditions); while others propose more sophisticated forms
of programming that require parents to differentially invest in those of
their offspring most likely to succeed as parents in the future. Both
versions imply that parental behavior will be relatively invariant in those
aspects that directly involve the health and welfare of all or most infants
and children. It follows from this that intergroup differences in infant
mortality rates are largely the result of factors exogenous to parental
behavior.

These theories of parenting have played an active role in shaping
current historical debates about past parenting and their relation to
infant and child survival. Thus Pollock believes she is defending sociobiological theories when she argues that the pessimists have erred
in ignoring the instinctual basis of parental behavior and supposing
that many or most parents in traditional Europe were abusive or neglectful of their offspring (Pollock, 1983: 36). She goes so far as to assert
that parental solicitude kept infant mortality rates "low" in premodern
Europe, not "high" as Stone (1977) and other pessimists have argued.
The empirical implications of this are discussed later.

Analyzing Infant and Child Mortality Rates

For the moment it is sufficient to note that both intellectual orientations toward the interpretation of parental behavior allow for the
possibility that there are two basic components of any infant mortality
rate. One component includes those infant deaths that were beyond
human control (no amount of parental solicitude would have helped)
and those that were the result of some failure of potential parental
investment, either through neglect or abuse. It is this category that
contains the *avoidable* infant deaths. Pessimists have been arguing that
in the past, infant mortality rates were artificially inflated by a large
number of avoidable deaths in all or most years. Optimists, influenced
by their understanding of sociobiological theories, generally deny this,
unless they are dealing with populations under great stress.

There is another form of avoidable death that both camps often neglect to consider. In stratified societies parents often have differential
access to resources of the kind necessary to invest in the survival of

offspring. Even within simple societies material environments differ sufficiently to effect the survival chances of those born to the least advantaged parents. In the Manchester example both sets of parents shared a disadvantageous environment because of their social class. Had the resources of the privileged been available to either group and levels of parental investment kept constant, the improved environment alone would have resulted in fewer infant deaths in both groups. Thus some of the avoidable deaths due to inadequate parental investment were *socially avoidable*. Assuming that it would be possible to distinguish socially avoidable deaths as a separate category (and this is not at all clear since environmental stress effects both parental behavior and biological resiliance) how would we estimate the contribution of socially avoidable death to the Manchester case?

Let us *imagine* that the Jewish working-class parents were suddenly transferred to one of London's most privileged urban districts and given a substantial increase in their collective income. If their infant mortality rate dropped to those of such a district it would have been between 60 and 80 in 1915. If we take 70 as the new value for infant mortality and subtract it from 110 (which is the rate the Jewish parents achieved in an unfavorable environment) then the socially avoidable infant death rate could be said to equal 40. If we assume in turn that there were no socially avoidable deaths in the new privileged environment and none due to parentally avoidable deaths, then the biologically unavoidable residual would be around 70/1000 live births. This is probably still too high, since peerage families had already achieved an infant mortality rate of 50/1000 by 1900. The rate of 70/1000 achieved by privileged urban families may still reflect 20/1000 deaths that are due to urban disamenities.

We now have the following two "equations" in which three unknowns have been estimated through controlled comparisons:

Infant mortality	=	Parentally avoidable deaths	+	Socially avoidable deaths	+	Biologically unavoidable deaths

Example 1: Manchester working classes (1915):

Infant mortality 150	=	40	+	40	+	70

Example 2: Manchester working classes (1915) (Jewish parents):

Infant mortality 110	=	0	+	40	+	70

Trisecting infant mortality in this fashion is very crude. (See Winter, 1979, and Yankauer, 1959, for similar approaches to the same problem.)

It would be more realistic to imagine infant deaths distributed along a continuum in which biological factors dominated one end and parental investment the other. In between there would be a category of infant deaths in which specific environments either enhanced or diminished the efficiency of a given level of parental investment applied to babies of average biological robustness. At no point is individual choice fully separable from biology or the environment from either. But the question remains—if we were perfectly knowledgeable observers of premodern European parenting who had completely accurate data on infant mortality, how large a fraction of the observed deaths in a specific time period would we say were "caused" by the reluctance/unwillingness of any set of parents to invest to the limits of their capacity in the survival of their infants?

No historians have access to such observers or such data, but if we were optimistic historians we could appeal to informal but explicit theories about the importance of parental investment to infant survival (and therefore the probability that parental behavior is insured by the strength of evolutionarily selected instincts) and argue that "few" such deaths ever took place. If we are pessimistic historians we cannot appeal to theories at all but only to the large number of knowledgeable and semiknowledgeable observers and authorities who over and over asserted and acted as if they believed that preindustrial Europeans treated their children very badly and their infants even worse. If we are to look for the fire of avoidable death behind the smoke of moralizing rhetoric we must understand in greater detail what the pessimists are arguing and why it does in fact make a great deal of sense to believe that avoidable infant death was endemic in preindustrial Europe, much more widespread than even the foregoing example would suggest.

THE PESSIMISTS AND PAST PARENTING

Theoretical Perspectives

The importance of knowledgeable observers and reformers to the darker interpretation of the quality of past parenting in Europe cannot be exaggerated. Pollock (1983) rejected such sources when she attempted to "disprove" the pessimist case by arguing for the superiority of first person materials—accounts of parenting generated by parents themselves or by their children. In surveying hundreds of such accounts she found little evidence for abuse or neglect of any sort, let alone widespread neglect and abuse. Of course most of her self-reported data came from parents or children who were moderately privileged or very well off. Moreover, most of her sample accounts are from eighteenth- and nineteenth-century families, many of whom had already started to artificially restrict their fertility (a fact of great importance to the pessimist case). This set of families was never even remotely typical of the average preindustrial European family; it was from their ranks that many of the pessimistic moralizers were drawn. Outside of the unrepresentative character of her self-reporters, she fails to take seriously the issue of whether or not her sources would have reported themselves or their parents as neglectful and abusive or have taken pen in hand in the first place if they had come from traumatic backgrounds.

In the modern era the problem of child abuse ("the battered child syndrome") was *not* discovered because abusing parents or their child victims identified themselves, publicized their problem, and sought help. Instead it was brought to light by doctors and social workers—knowledgeable observers of the kind that pessimists have always relied on in doing historical research. Even more serious is the problem of survivorship in the preindustrial era. When mortality in general was so much higher than now, how likely is it that infants and children targeted for elimination would have in fact survived to write at all?

Pessimistic historians may object to Pollock's optimism on the basis of her approach to source materials and their characteristics. But on what ground can they recommend their own case except a similar willingness to believe in the implications of their own preferred source materials? Pessimistic historians do not appeal to any one theory of malparenting. They do not believe that malparenting was in fact caused by any one factor operating with undiminished intensity over time. They do not even deal with human parenting per se, but with parenting among specific sets of Europeans who lived at specific times in specific places in the preindustrial era. The essays collected by DeMause in *The History of Childhood* (1974) are not unified along any other dimension except the belief that abuse, neglect, and avoidable death were once widespread but highly variable as well. Pessimists determine how widespread (as well as the specific forms that malparenting took) by closely examining the details of each case, and by practicing what has been called "dense description,"[1] a time-intensive form of analysis that piles detail upon detail until a coherent picture emerges—one that may in fact be unique to a specific case.

In effect, pessimists practice on historical data the kind of approach to analysis that a modern therapist brings to the treatment of a currently abusive or neglectful parent. Although the field of child abuse and neglect was once dominated by researchers who looked for the single

---

[1]Dense description is also called "thick description." Both refer to the process whereby a storyteller keeps filling in his narration with more and more detail until all questions are answered and understanding is achieved.

cause of malparenting, recently theorizing has taken an "ecological" or "interactive" turn. Interactive theories assert that to explain any act of malparenting it is necessary to understand the individual character- istics of the parent(s), the characteristics of the maltreated child, the social and economic status of the family, the neighborhood in which they live, etc. (Newberger, Newberger, and Hampton, 1983). In this the- oretical perspective it is quite respectable to take seriously the ideas that the offending parent has about how he or she should parent and whether or not these ideas represent personal preferences or a set of traditional beliefs transmitted intergenerationally. Changing someone's ideas becomes an important part of the therapy intended to change behavior.

Empirically oriented historians, however much they might protest, have all along been operating in the ecological or "interactive" theo- retical framework. They do not appeal to general theories to justify their analyses, because they do not think that ahistorical theories of parenting have any intellectual validity. Instead they argue that one can only understand parenting behavior in a specific (very particularistic) environment in which many factors are interacting, sometimes resulting in "unique" patterns.

Whatever legitimacy one grants or refuses to such claims, it never- theless becomes obvious that summarizing the beliefs of the pessimist school in a brief form is difficult, even intellectually unacceptable. In this chapter we are concerned with patterns of parenting in Western Europe in the centuries antecedant to industrialization and urbanization, but even this restricted time period and limited geographical area would seem a vast tapestry to most ecological historians that one could not "summarize" in any meaningful fashion. Nevertheless such an attempt is made in the next section.

The Pessimist Theory for Preindustrial Europe

With the understanding that pessimistic historians are a very diverse lot who place far more importance on the particular than the general, the gist of their approach to understanding the plight of children in preindustrial Europe is as follows: In preindustrial Europe most/many parents had more children than they would have wanted under ideal circumstances. Pervasive malparenting was one of many complex re- sponses to this "excess" fertility, and some of it had as its purpose the attempt to covertly or overtly eliminate unwanted children (Langer, 1974). That parents found themselves burdened with too many children in the first place was a result of the rise and institutionalization of Christianity which forbade all forms of fertility control, particularly in- fanticide at or near the time of birth (Flandrin, 1976). Despite the in- stitutionalization of Christian precepts many/most/some parents kept trying to restrict the numbers of surviving children by selectively investing in wanted children more than others. Those targeted for suboptimal levels of parental investment were those in categories familiar today—high parity births, girls (especially those in girl-loaded families), weak or deformed infants, or infants born too closely after an earlier sibling. (In the very lowest economic strata all children might be regarded as equally burdensome.) Ultimately, in all social strata, the malparenting given to unwanted children may have become pervasively institutionalized and extended by default even to wanted children as the quality of parenting in Europe was driven downward by the pressure of uncontrolled or inefficiently controlled fertility.

The pessimist "model" has never been specified in any but the most general verbal fashion, although individual historians sometimes given casual estimates of how many children is "too many" by discussing how expensive children were in the preindustrial world.

Economic Constraints on Reproduction in Early Modern Europe

When pessimists argue that most/many preindustrial Europeans did not want all the children they were in fact producing, they often begin by discussing the "costs" of children, broadly construed to include everything from food, clothing, and shelter to the expenses involved in arranging marriages for daughters and establishing sons in a way that would preserve their family's social status. In between were the costs of educating and training children (if any) and the possible costs involved in removing wives from the labor force (or reducing their participation in the family economy) so that they could breast-feed and care for young dependents. Those infants whom the family could not ever hope to establish properly were automatically consigned to second-class citizenship within the family.

Different social classes experienced the relative costs of children differentially. Peasants could hope to recover some of the costs of child rearing through child labor for the family farm and possibly through support in old age; but the truly impoverished and the genuinely privileged had no economic use for children at all. If children were valued among the rich it was in connection with their potential for enhancing the status of their families, and this was a costly gamble connected with child rearing.

In most preindustrial western European societies those who were privileged enough to own property in any substantial amount were a minority of the population. The majority (the "propertyless" urban and rural proletariat) lived on the margin of subsistence in good times, while in bad times they were driven into destitution, including starvation or prolonged malnutrition. Children, unless they were employable, were truly a luxury that poor could ill afford. Pessimists sympathetic with the extremely hard lot of the poor argue that if the dispossessed appear in the available source material to have neglected, abandoned, exposed, sold, rented-out, or otherwise dispensed with some/many of their children, it was a result of the traumatizing effects of extreme poverty compounded by the endemic instability of most preindustrial economies (McLaughlin, 1974).

There is nothing at all surprising in a connection between a high level of malparenting and a high level of stress in the context of resource-poor environments. Some animal parents faced with harsh environmental conditions are prompted by instinct to cease investment and restrict reproduction until conditions improve. But the fact that the poor and propertyless of preindustrial Europe composed 30–50% of the total population ought to predispose us to accept that malparenting in the form of extreme parental neglect (or even abuse) must have been very widespread. (Pollock acknowledges that human population can be driven to collective malparenting through stress. She cites Turnbull's (1973) classic study of the Ik without realizing that many more European parents lived like the Ik than like the privileged writers with whom she deals.)

Among the propertied classes conditions varied so much that an equally sweeping generalization is difficult. As stated earlier peasants valued children for their labor, but raising laborers involved a reduction in the wife's economic contribution to the family economy (at least in the short run) wherever family structure was basically nuclear. Peasants also had to bear the high costs connected with establishing at least some of their children in a manner that reaffirmed or improved family status. Too many surviving children meant too many claims on a limited patrimony. Optimal family size might mean as few as three survivors, and as many as five, if land or other economic opportunities were abundant.

For related reasons the titled and privileged families who dominated the social and political landscape of preindustrial Europe might have wanted as few or even fewer children. The basic costs of feeding, clothing, and sheltering children were easily met, but the costs of marrying off daughters and establishing sons were often staggering. Daughters were particularly expensive and grew more so throughout the entire preindustrial period as dowries spiraled to unprecedented heights (Stone, 1977). As the costs of daughters escalated, the price of establishing sons dropped somewhat. But all sons had some kind of claim against the family's estate. In those areas where estates were passed on intact to one male heir, each surplus son was an additional burden that threatened the integrity of the estate and the status of the family.

In addition, the life styles led by most premodern aristocrats were not such to encourage titled husbands and wives to value the emotional aspects of parenting. The aristocratic couple was a "two-career" marriage in which each partner had attractive, high-status alternatives to parenting. They used their material resources to totally "buy-out" of the drudgery of child care and dealt with their children through surrogates. The fact that titled mothers are frequently described as having little or no emotional commitment to their children was paralleled by the fact that they often had little or no emotional commitment to their husbands, and vice versa. Aristocratic wives were "hired" to provide heirs and to perform certain essential social functions. They were not chosen, nor did they choose, spouses in order to maximize emotional or even sexual utilities. This coldness carried over into the realm of parenting.

Middle-class families, most of whom were city dwellers, were in one of the most constrained positions of all with respect to the costs of raising and establishing children. Like aristocrats, middle-class parents had no economic "use" for their children, but unlike the truly privileged the middle class could not totally insulate themselves from the time-intensive emotional aspects of child rearing. Moreover, middle-class families found it less easy to feed, clothe, and shelter children in the manner necessary to affirm the family's status, just as it was more difficult to marry off daughters and establish sons. Thus middle-class mothers and fathers (who were often more emotionally involved with each other than were aristocratic spouses) had a more personal relationship with their children that made them want to do as much as possible for each with the limited resources available. Of all the preindustrial Europeans, middle-class families had the greatest incentives to avoid large families.

Consider the following lines from a French play written in 1706: "All excesses are fatal to us bourgeoisie. We must on occasion from pleasure abstain, having only those children we well can maintain. Tis better to nurture with care just one child, than produce half a dozen and let 'em run wild." (Flinn, 1981: 45). Here is an explicit, economically, and socially constrained concept of "reproductive success" that seems to be saying that fertility below replacement is better than producing a large number of children who have not been raised properly.

The aristocracy and the middle classes dominated societies politically and culturally, but the demography of preindustrial Europe was dominated by peasants and proletarians who constituted more than 80–90% of a typical population.

Sexual Constraints on Reproduction in Early Modern Europe

Pessimistic historians do not believe that the costs of children were limited to the economic realm alone. If we return to the poor bourgeoise gentlemen, even if he and his wife had preferred to have six living children who carried their genes as opposed to one who was properly raised, trained, and established, he and his wife would still have had to give up a certain amount of pleasure in order to ensure the survival of their numerous brood.

Throughout human history down to the invention of cheap, sanitary substitutes for mother's milk, the most crucial form of parental investment has been prolonged breast-feeding. But prolonged breast-feeding was widely believed to preclude sexual activity for its duration. Even where the taboo was not strong, European midwives and physicians often noted that breast-feeding women were reluctant to resume sexual relations for health reasons (their own or the newborn's) or simple disinclination. For whatever reason there was a certain tension which was caused by one instinct (sexuality) pitted against another (breast-feeding).

In the tug-of-war between sexual, social, and economic aspirations, on the one hand, and parental protectiveness, on the other, the latter came off badly all to often. Many ordinary premodern women chose not to nurse and instead hired a surrogate (a wet nurse). Some nursed only for the first few months. Some mothers nursed very infrequently and had substitutes (who were not wet nurses) feed extremely young babies liquids or solids of one sort or another. All these choices moved infants into a category of higher death risk, as was well known at the time. Those infants who survived to early childhood could be placed at risk by minimizing the amount or kind of care given during their repeated bouts of illness, or by the failure to quarantine during epidemics, or by patterns of feeding that left them poorly nourished, even by standards of the time. Historians have uncovered some evidence that seems to support the fact that parents selectively underinvested in older children to a degree which now seems shocking (Flandrin, 1976).

Why did the parents of unwanted children keep them alive for a sufficiently long period to necessitate maltreatment for years after their birth. Why did they not prevent their birth, or, failing that, withdraw the necessary forms of life-sustaining investment as close as possible to the birth of an unwanted child? Infanticide at or shortly after birth has been practiced by most peoples at one time or another and was certainly practiced by the barbarian, pagan, ancestors of sixteenth- and seventeenth-century Europeans. It is at this point that one begins to understand the important role religion plays in the pessimistic analysis of parenthood in Christian Europe.

Religious Constraints on Reproduction in Early Modern Europe

In their collective writings, historical pessimists of past parenting stress the differential contributions of three great ideologies to the reproductive behavior of premodern Europeans. The first and for many centuries the most powerful was traditional Catholic Christianity, whose intellectual monopoly was shattered in the sixteenth and seventeenth centuries by the rise of Protestantism. Subsequently, both Christianities were challenged by the rise of various "enlightened" philosophies of parenting promulgated by the seventeenth- and eighteenth-century secular humanists.

None of these ideologies should be thought of as mental programs that individuals were free to choose. Throughout the premodern period, although the software of parenting programs was written by a small body of specialists, their ideas were taken up and enforced by both religious and secular authorities who were appointed to positions in various institutions where they proceeded to instruct (program), observe, admonish, investigate, and punish deviance among the masses. Parish registration systems were one arm of this vast system designed to impose cultural uniformity with respect to reproduction, regardless of personal preferences or economic constraints.

The reproductive ideals of traditional Christianity (later Catholicism) were first brought to Western Europe in the centuries after the fall of Rome. For hundreds of years missionaries and priests worked with secular authorities to transform a sexually active, polygynous population that believed in free-and-easy divorce and the rational limitation of fertility through whatever means were available (including infanticide at birth) into a Christian culture that confined sexual expression to monogamous marriages that could only be broken by death. Within these marriages parents were free to limit their fertility only by practicing mutually agreed upon sexual abstinence. If they chose to remain sexually active, a husband and wife had to accept as many children, of whatever sex and condition God chose to send them. All forms of contraception, abortion, and overt infanticide were explicitly forbidden. The campaigns against the latter were particularly fierce.

The Church was so determined to wipe out the deliberate elimination of unwanted children that it began to discourage the previously widespread custom of bed-sharing, whereby fathers and mothers (or mothers) shared a bed with a baby and even older children. In the eyes of Church authorities too many infants were "accidently" smothered in the middle of the night. It is from these campaigns that the Western custom of sleeping separately from infants originates. Ironically, the peoples of many non-Western developing countries regard the habit that Westerners have of putting an infant in a bed by itself to sleep alone as a form of child abuse/neglect (Korbin, 1981).

The Catholic Church, despite its dedication, was never entirely successful in eliminating either the old forms of sexual self-expression or reproductive rationality. But it raised the costs of "deviance" through guilt, fear of detection, and the public punishment of guilty parties.

The penalty for infanticide was often death, sometimes involving forms of torture prior to execution. Individuals unwilling to bear the increased costs of reproductive rationality could very well find themselves forced to bring into the world children they did not want and did not dare eliminate at birth. "Speaking in general terms" says Flandrin, the great historian of Catholic family life and reproduction, "the inability to control births multiplied the unwanted children" (1976:153).

There were several ways out of reproductive fatalism all of which involved forms of malparenting. For example the Church taught that if a woman's husband was unable to remain chaste during the breastfeeding period following the birth of a child, it was morally better for the woman to avoid or abbreviate breast-feeding and quickly resume sexual relations. This extreme callousness toward the needs of the vulnerable infant (an infant that may have been unwanted) was fostered by the belief that God's will was the sole determinant of whether or not a child survived or died after birth, provided, of course, that its parents did not murder it outright.

To all infants and children God assigned guardian spirits who watched after them, so that mothers and fathers could in good conscience leave small children unattended or in the care of their siblings. If a child fell into a river or well, or out of its cradle, or into a fire, or was eaten by the family pig, or attacked by a dog or some other child and died, this was the will of God. If God had not wished to recall the infant or child, it would have survived. Catholic parents, in good faith, could thus engage in several lethal forms of underinvestment that practically assured higher mortality levels for their infants and children, especially those who were not wanted in the first place. Flandrin reports that in propertied families the first son (the presumed heir) was often extensively nursed by its mother, whereas younger sons were sent to a wet nurse who might live far away—too far to allow much parental visitation. Daughters were particularly subject to selective forms of underinvestment because they were so costly to dower for a marriage.

Selective or even indiscriminate neglect may have characterized the upbringing of children among the landless poor and the marginal peasants whose wives were so hard-working. Hanawalt reports that in late medieval England (still a Catholic country) accidental death among children appeared to be a common form of death. Of all those dying in accidents, 70% were infants or small children who had obviously been left alone (Hanawalt, 1977). Today under 10% of those who die in accidents are infants and small children. No amount of "adjustment" will eliminate those startling differentials.

If outright infanticide was a capital crime (and local authorities were instructed to investigate all suspicious deaths) (Piers, 1978) poor parenting was not even socially reprehensible. It was, in short, costless to parents, although it inflicted much suffering and trauma on children. Not all of those targeted for elimination died; some survived as the resentful victims of malparenting. Flandrin (1976), Badinter (1980), and others have found examples of these survivors in the French tradition.

The first ideology strong enough to break the power of Catholic Christianity was Protestant Christianity. There were many doctrinal differences between them, but those that concern us involved the greatly enhanced emphasis on good parenting found in most Protestant creeds. Indeed the reformation and upgrading of parenting was one of the central achievements of the rise of Protestantism (Hardymut, 1983). As part of the reform of family life, most Protestants stressed the doctrine of stewardship—God sent children to parents, and they must be accepted in whatever form they came (the ban against fertility control continued unabated). Once born mothers and fathers had the duty to do everything that could be done to ensure their survival. Guardian spirits were deemphasized or banished to the realm of superstition. Breast-feeding became a mandatory maternal duty that could not be set aside lightly. Godly parenting required vigilence, but vigilence meant that someone had to be there. Mostly, this meant mother. But if mother was no longer allowed to leave children unattended, neither could she work as efficiently in the fields or in the family business. The economic role played by women in the premodern Protestant economy often contracted as the number and nature of maternal duties expanded. The Protestant father was not excused from parenting; his role was also upgraded and expanded with the emphasis on home religious instruction and the need for proper, often severe, discipline (Ozment, 1984).

Parenting became much less severe and even more altruistic with the expanding influence of enlightened doctrines of child rearing from the eighteenth century onward (Hardymut, 1983). The enlightened philosophers who laid the groundwork for attitudes that currently dominate parenting in the developed countries did not found a religion or take over any particular state. However, they did give impetus to the movement for mass and higher education which has become so much a part of modern culture. Schools were the churches of the enlightenment, and it was there that mental programs dominated by reason fought the older ideologies, ultimately undermining the religious basis for reproductive fatalism based on formal resignation to God's will.

Enlightened parenting, like Protestant parenting, was supposed to be time-intensive. In addition it was supposed to be loving. Enlightened parents had as one of their principle charges getting to know a child as an individual and striving to make it possible for that child to achieve his (later her) individual potential. Advanced education was an intrinsic part of this program. It was not the heavenly future of the child that concerned enlightened parents but its future on earth. The point of advanced education was to improve one's condition and to see to it that future generations could improve their own prospects. In this sense enlightened parenting was altruistic, but in reality the child was expected to justify the high level of parental investment in it by succeeding in worldly terms. This pressure to succeed could become as abusive as severe discipline practiced by Protestants.

If both Protestant and Enlightened parenting had as their aim the reduction of child neglect, one of the costs of this reduction may have been the spread of psychologically "abusive" forms of parenting that did their own forms of damage but did not cause excessive mortality.

The most important achievement of the Enlightenment as it spread through Europe from the privileged classes to the peasants and urban workers was that it removed the basis for guilt connected with reproductive rationality. As fertility control reemerged in developing Europe (but not in the form of infanticide) the underlying need for malparenting was reduced. As Flandrin (1976) and others have argued, fertility control and the treatment of children cannot be separated, but their causal relationships are not simple or uniform. If parents could be talked out of malparenting by a religious or intellectual revolution, they or their children would be pushed into the adoption of fertility control sooner or later in order to reduce the increased number of survivors that better parenting would produce. On the other hand, if a traditional population adopted fertility control, the forms of malparenting that had been institutionalized in their cultures would no longer be functional and would thus disappear sooner or later.

Meanwhile, between 1600 and 1800 Europe became an increasingly diversified patchwork of subcultures divided by profound economic and cultural differences. Economic diversity was generated by the differential pace with which economies were transformed by agricultural commercialization and early industrialization. Cultural diversity was generated by the Protestant Reformation and the Catholic Counter Reformation (which slowly adopted some of the newer ideas about parenting) and finally by the rise of the secular Enlightenment. The landless masses in some areas were becoming protoindustrial. The peasantry was split along religious and economic lines. The privileged classes were as privileged as ever, but their collective mentalities were exceptionally diversified according to whether or not they had been influenced by religious reform or the rise of secular humanism with its emphasis on reason.

Implications for Preindustrial Infant and Child Mortality

The demographic implications of increasing economic and cultural diversity have not been systematically considered by any of the qualitatively oriented historians. Pessimists often speak of infant mortality as if it were "high" and invariant until the nineteenth or twentieth century (DeMause, 1974; Stone, 1977). This generalization might be called the simple pessimistic hypothesis about the impact of parenting on infant mortality. Its optimistic counterpart is the simple assertion that infant mortality was "low" and invariant in premodern Europe (as elsewhere) because of the moderating effect of instinctual protectiveness (Pollock, 1983:51).

Both these hypotheses have their complex counterparts: A pessimist aware of the great underlying diversity of economic and cultural forces in premodern Europe would expect to find a great deal of variation in infant mortality rates, variation that was not correlated in any obvious way with simple material conditions. The optimistic counterpart, however, would expect that observed variations in the level of infant mortality at the local level should have obvious social or economic causes that had relatively little to do with individual-level parental behavior.

In the next section we explore what demographic historians have in fact discovered about levels of infant mortality at the national and local level in Europe in the 200–300 years before life was dramatically transformed by the rise of urbanization, industrialization, and mass education.

Infant Mortality in the Premodern Era

The Range of Variation

Of all the demographic parameters in preindustrial Europe that we can measure, none is more variable than infant mortality. This alone forces us to reject both "simple" versions of the optimistic or pessimistic hypotheses.

If we were to consider the whole set of European villages for which data on infant mortality (infancy being equal to the first 12 months of life) exists for at least one 50-year period during the sixteenth, seventeenth, and nineteenth centuries we would find them arrayed in a distribution that approximated a normal form. At one end of the distribution would be a small set of villages that had infant mortality rates (hereafter IMR) that fell below 100 per thousand; to their right would be a larger set of villages that had IMRs between 100 and 199; further right a still larger set of villages would have IMRs between 200 and 299; to the right of these villages one would find a smaller set characterized by stable rates between 300 and 399; and, finally, the extreme right end of the distribution would contain a few areas (some urban but some rural in character) in which IMRs were persistently above 400 per

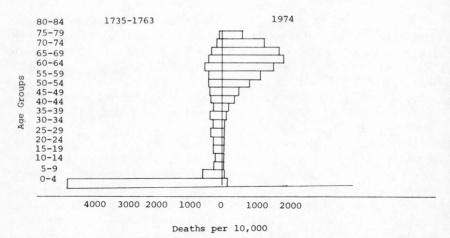

FIGURE 4.1. The age profile of deaths in Sweden, 1755–1763 and 1974. (Dupaquier, 1979:83).

thousand (Flinn, 1981:130–131).[2] On average, a stable preindustrial IMR was around 250 per thousand, a rate much higher than the 150 per thousand that Pollock asserts is both universal and "low."

Generally, judgments of "high" or "low" depend on a standard of some sort. If we take as our standard rates in the developed countries today (where stable IMRs are usually between 15 and 30 per thousand) all the preindustrial rates are high, some staggeringly so. But if we judge high and low by preindustrial averages, then any rate much below 200 would be low and any above 300 would be high. Let us look closely at Figure 4.1, an age-profile of deaths in a preindustrial, premodern country where stable levels of IMR were in the 200s. The society selected is Sweden, the European country for which we have the most abundant and highest quality data.

What Fig. 4.1 shows is that in an average year in an average European society before the nineteenth century 40% of all the deaths occurring in any one year involved infants and young children, and over 50% involved children under 10. In a modern developed country most deaths have been postponed to old age, still biologically unavoidable.

In Table 4.1 we get some idea of what higher than average, average, and lower than average levels of infant mortality imply for both life expectancy and survivorship in premodern Europe. Generally, where something like 300 per thousand infants die in their first year of life,

[2]At the present time the local level data available does not yet constitute anything like a random sample of European or Western European villages. The villages of Catholic France dominate historical research thus far.

TABLE 4.1. Survivorship at Different Levels of Life Expectancy at Birth[a,b]

Age	$e_0 = 25$	$e_0 = 35$	$e_0 = 45$
0	100	100	100
1	69	79	85
5	54	67	77
10	51	64	75
20	46	60	72

[a]From Coale and Demeny (1983:42-47) (females, West).
[b]The table is to be read in the following fashion: If the overall life expectancy at birth (e_0) equals 25, for every 100 babies born in a given year, 69 will survive to the age of 1, 54 to the age of 5, etc.

life expectancy at birth will be around 25, and less than one-half of those babies born in a typical year will survive through the age of 20. When 200 per thousand infants die in their first year of life (a value that approximates the eighteenth century Swedish experience), life expectancy at birth will be around 35, and 60% of those infants born will survive to the threshold of adulthood. At lower than average levels of infant mortality (where only 150 per thousand babies die in their first year of life) almost three-quarters of those ever born will survive to the age of 20. (Since these are values derived from model life tables they do not necessarily faithfully reflect the actual experience of any real population, but they give us a rough approximation of the range of experience in premodern Europe.)

The question remains—to what is this enormous range of variation in infant mortality life expectancy, and survivorship due? The extreme range of variation in IMR has attracted a good deal of attention from demographic historians and others interested in the nondemographic determinants of mortality in preindustrial Europe. Thus far those efforts have involved the exploration of environmental and economic factors—climate and standard-of-living variables (like the real wage) have received most attention. In summarizing the results of this research effort, Flinn (1981) says: "There is no clear pattern in the local or regional variations in the level of infant mortality; high and low rates were fairly randomly distributed and seem not to be characteristic of any particular type of region or economy" (p. 17). There are some density effects—preindustrial cities are generally at the higher end of the IMR spectrum, although even in this regard there are puzzling anomalies.

The failure to find any obvious materialist logic in preindustrial European IMR does not mean that there was none. One can always attribute the failure to systematically explain variation in IMRs to defects in the data (whether demographic, economic, or climatological, etc.). Because appeals to defective or inadequate data provide one with so many potential "outs," the failure to find obvious or strong correlations between IMRs and material variables has not lead researchers to suspect that ideological factors might be at work. At present, it is even fashionable among some demographic historians to argue that mortality in the preindustrial period was totally driven by exogeneous fluctuations in the number and strength of disease-linked pathogens, phenomena that must forever remain unobserved and unobservable for past centuries. Less mechanistic historians will attribute importance to social controls over mortality (Mielke, 1984), but few have believed that human choice at the individual level has played a major role in mortality patterns among any age group. In this way the complex optimistic hypothesis cannot be rejected so easily as its simple counterpart. But the current state of research leaves just as much room for the possibility that at least some of the variation in IMRs before industrialization had something to do with ideological influences on parental behavior.

However interesting it would be to use religion as an independent variable in a real regression analysis of the determinants of infant mortality, it would be unwise to expect much in the way of a definitive proof of the importance of religion. The strength and effectiveness of religious or secular ideologies in centuries past cannot be observed any more directly than can the virulence of pathogens. Between communities classified as Catholic or Protestant there is bound to be some temporal and regional variation in the degree to which each creed influenced the behavior of its adherents. Even within a Protestant sect as strongly internalized as Quakerism in the eighteenth and nineteenth centuries, variations in infant mortality could be found between groups living in different places, although all had rates lower than average for their time and region (Vann and Eversley, in manuscript).

But it is not impossible to detect the probable influence of religious or secular ideologies on parental behavior. If we confine the analytic framework to small populations who shared the same space and time and for which we have surviving accounts written by knowledgeable observers, it is possible to do the same kind of controlled comparisons that were done earlier for sections of Manchester.

Preindustrial German Peasants

One set of preindustrial populations for which we have an abundance of data on IMR as well as descriptive accounts of parenting practices comes from early and mid-nineteenth century Germany. Although these populations existed after the eighteenth century, they were still largely composed of peasants who were living in a rural, preindustrial world.

In mid-nineteenth century Germany infant mortality levels covered an even wider range of life expectancies at birth than displayed in Table 4.1. Infant mortality at the village level varied from extremely low (by premodern standards) to extremely high. These stark differences at the local level attracted the attention of nineteenth-century Germany physicians who observed and analyzed the possible causes of such large differences. They also acted as reformers, for they initially believed that in the high mortality villages, people would be very receptive to the gospel of vaccination and sanitary reform out of a "natural" desire to reduce their excessively high death rates. The medical topographies that were produced by the nineteenth-century observer—physicians— provided a wealth of detail on how the peasants in different villages lived, worked, earned, married, and died; but above all they provide us with a rich source of information about the attitudes and beliefs of the ordinary premodern men and women who lived under starkly different demographic regimes.

Arthur Imhof has devoted a great deal of time and effort to studying the medical topographies, the descriptive information they contain, and the patterns of vital rates that appear to be associated with different local economic and cultural conditions. It is of great interest and importance that he finds himself agreeing with a belief widespread among the doctors themselves—that attitudes and beliefs made more impact on demographic patterns at the village level than material (geographical or economic) conditions. As in Flinn (1981), Imhof's research indicates that infant mortality rates were not systematically related to geographical, biological, or major economic differences. What mattered most was whether or not the peasants of a village were dominated by a pervasive fatalism he termed an overall "indifference to life" or a much more activist philosophy, which he labeled a respect for the "conservation of life."

The "indifference to life" mentality was always found in the villages where infant mortality was very high (over 300–450 deaths per thousand live births). It was here that the doctors met with most resistance in their well-intentioned efforts to improve sanitation, introduce vaccination, and reform parental behavior, particularly the reluctance and unwillingness of mothers with newborns to nurse their own babies, either at all or beyond very short time periods. In explaining why they did not breast-feed, the fatalistic peasant mothers said that God was very prone to recall infants to their heavenly homeland. Once "back home" the infants acted as intercessors for their earthly families: thus dead babies continued to play an active role in their family's fortunes on earth, an earth they were lucky to have left. In general, the mothers did not admit that their actions had much impact on whether or not an infant or child survived to adolescence. Survival was God's doing. Imhof argues that areas characterized by "indifference to life" in the nineteenth century were those that were once traumatized by widespread violence and destruction during the religious wars of the seventeenth century (a view that implies a transmission-of-behavior rate that seems unrealistically immune to changed social conditions). More interesting, perhaps, is the fact that most high infant mortality rate areas were still Catholic, and that the malparenting that doctors found so shocking may have been part of a rational strategy aimed at preserving the family farm from excessive subdivision in areas that still rejected any other form of fertility control.

This is the gist of Edward Shorter's analysis of the medical topographies from high infant mortality regions. According to Shorter (1982) peasants there were extremely conscious of the need to keep down the number of surviving claimants to family property, and in the pursuit of this end, openly and quite consciously practiced forms of parental underinvestment that they knew were very likely to bring about an infant's death. The high infant death rate was caused primarily by the extremely high death rates of third and higher parity children. Parents were so conscious of the harmful nature of their infanticidal practices that they could stop and totally reverse their behavior patterns in situations involving the birth of wanted children.

In any case those areas of Germany where infant mortality rates were "low" by traditional standards were generally the Protestant-dominated areas of the north. While villages in this area were not any wealthier than their southern counterparts, infant mortality rates rarely exceeded 150 per thousand. Some had rates that were much lower. They were generally characterized by a willingness to adopt health reforms that were beneficial to the survival of infants and children.

We can assume, that in a model Protestant village (where conservation of life attitudes prevailed, and IMRs were between 120–150 per thousand), all of these deaths (or almost all) would have been due to biological and social factors. Therefore, in an economically similar village dominated by the indifference-to-life complex, any excess above this range would have to be attributed to the reluctance of parents to fully invest in all or some offspring. If the IMR here were 350–400 per thousand, roughly 200–280 per thousand deaths would have been parentally avoidable. This is over one-half of all those dying and about one-quarter of all those born.

That this is not so farfetched is demonstrated by further detailed analysis carried out by Imhof (1981a). In the low mortality villages there seems to be little or no birth-order effect—that is, IMRs do not rise with parity until values reach eight or more. (In the high infant mortality villages IMR rates rise with parity, starting from the second birth.) Thus, the supposedly "fatalistic" mentality proves under close analysis to be progressively reducing the chances that additional children will survive.

In the end both types of villages tended to produce approximately the same number of survivors to adulthood from any given cohort. In the high mortality/high fertility villages women who gave birth on average to 9 or 10 infants produced 4 or 5 survivors to approximately age

20. In the low mortality/low fertility villages women who gave birth to 6 or 7 infants also saw 4 or 5 survive past adolescence.

According to mechanistic–biological analyses, infant mortality levels would be said to have "caused" fertility rates in both areas by determining the length of interbirth intervals. Where infant death was frequent women would resume ovulation much faster than in the low mortality villages where infant survival (accompanied by breast-feeding) would delay the onset of biological susceptibility to a new conception. Where no artificial means are used to block conception or gestation this biological relationship is self-evident. But historians like Flandrin, Imhof and Knodel regard it as more illuminating to start from the factors that promote or suppress universal, prolonged breast-feeding. In France, Flandrin regards the widespread rejection of breast-feeding as having cultural roots, and it is these nonbiological forces that drove the cycle of frequent infant death, short birth intervals, and high fertility. In preindustrial Germany Imhof sees the same thing for a slightly different mix of cultural factors. For both it is human choice that is giving a specific pattern form to human biology, and the choices made are being influenced by material and religious values (Knodel and VandeWalle, 1967).

If we accept this perspective we might be led to argue that IMRs around 150 per thousand in preindustrial Europe represent something like a "natural" level of peasant infant mortality (in which there is little or no human interference in the form of deliberately withheld parental investment). But even at this "low" level there seems to be evidence that the level of parentally avoidable death should not be set at zero.

English Villages in the Seventeenth Century

It is in the study of English infant mortality in the preindustrial period that one gains a more realistic appreciation for the limited role of strictly biological factors in the determination of overall levels of infant mortality. Seventeenth-century England has long been considered an anomaly by demographic historians since it represents an entire country in which national average IMRs were around 150 per thousand at a time when 250 per thousand was characteristic of its European neighbors, especially France. These "low" English rates are all the more puzzling in that England had a higher than average percentage of its population living in cities and a higher than average rate of proletarianization both of which almost surely should have driven IMRs upward, not downward.

But England was also a Protestant country, one in which the power of Protestantism over social life gained ground from the fifteenth century to the civil war of the mid-seventeenth century, in which extreme Protestants eventually seized control of the government after executing the king (1640s). It was at in the course of this religious transformation that England's system of parish registration was established (1530s) and gradually secured across the 10,000 or so parishes of preindustrial England. In the massive reconstruction of English population history recently completed by Wrigley and Schofield (1981) data from a set of "reconstituted" English parishes was published showing how remarkably stable infant mortality levels were for those families in the reconstituted parishes.

The data in Table 4.2 displays the experience of ordinary English families (agriculture laborers, tenant farmers and some small owners, along with a few rural and urban craftsmen) who were typical of the entire population at the time, except for the fact that they were less mobil than their compatriots, and they lived in villages where record keeping was exceptionally good. Their economic circumstances were representative, but they were exceptionally well integrated into their communities and hence under the close supervision of the ever watchful authorities.

The women of the families in the reconstituted villages had exceptionally low age-specific fertility rates and exceptionally small completed families. Seven births was the norm. According to Wilson (1981) they achieved this "low" fertility by practicing universal, prolonged breast-feeding. That they did so should not be surprising. According to Protestant propaganda, breast-feeding was a duty from which a woman could not lightly be excused. Only the inability to lactate or some other form of severe health problem could justify the use of substitutes. If it was Protestantism that kept breast-feeding the norm, then, once more, we would have to argue that cultural forces determined the expression of human biology in the form of fewer births through longer birth intervals. Since fewer children were born to ordinary families fewer would have fallen into the unwanted category, and this, in turn, would have supported the adoption of reformed parenting norms and their extension to all children.

TABLE 4.2. Age-Specific Death Rates for Infants and Children, England, 1550–1699[a]

	Period					
	1550–1599		1600–1649		1650–1699	
Age group	Males	Females	Males	Females	Males	Females
0–1	142	127	142	123	154	133
1–4	65	59	88	81	96	102
5–9	29	30	42	37	38	45

[a]From Wrigley and Schofield (1981: 249). Based on simple means from 12 reconstituted English parishes varying markedly in the social and economic characteristics, but all supposedly characterized by excellent data.

But were all the unwanted children eliminated before birth in Protestant England? A second look at Table 4.2 shows that the IMRs are not constant through the entire period; they rise in the very last set of 50-year averages. This in itself need not rouse our suspicions. The last half of the seventeenth century was a poor one for mortality throughout Europe. Everywhere average death rates tended to rise in response, most probably, to factors beyond human control. In England, however, dowries were especially inflated and marriage markets were exceptionally tight, meaning that it was both difficult and expensive to marry off daughters. Worst still the growing reluctance of the employers of agricultural labor to use women in hard, heavy field work, combined with the increasing reluctance of women to be thus used (another side effect of Protestant values about what was appropriate for women) meant that females were becoming relatively less valuable to the ordinary family economy of the rural world. Is this relevant to the fact that although there appears to be no sign of female infanticide in infancy, child mortality rates for girls rose much faster than those for boys, so that by the end of the seventeenth century there is a clear pattern of excess female mortality among young children? This pattern of "deferred infanticide" is one which, I have argued elsewhere, is common among historical rural populations where the economic value of females deteriorates relative to that of males (Johansson, 1984). If parents did not eliminate unwanted females at birth it was because they were unwilling or afraid to do so for fear of detection and punishment. But they were not afraid or reluctant to distribute resources unequally according to whether or not a child was wanted, relatively unwanted, or not wanted at all. Nevertheless, there is some evidence that a few parents were still willing to eliminate unwanted infants close to the time of their birth.

In these seventeenth-century English families around 50% of all infant deaths were concentrated in the first month of life and most of those in the first week of life (Wilson, 1981).[3] These values for "neonatal" infant mortality are intermediate between those observed for traditionally infanticidal populations (where even today neonatal mortality is above 60% of all first-year deaths) and those population that do not have infanticidal traditions (where neonatal infant deaths usually involve under 40% of all first-year deaths).

The couples in Table 4.2 who experienced an infant's death in the first week of its life had birth intervals that were longer by 3 months or so than couples who experienced the death of a 3-month-old infant.

[3]A different set of parish level data from seventeenth to eighteenth century England shows an even greater concentration of infant deaths in the first month (see Wrigley, 1977).

Wilson (1981) attributes this strange effect to the possibility that all the early infant deaths involved very difficult births from which it took the mother an exceptionally long time to recover. But if some of these deaths were the result of traditional infanticide (with the guilt and fear that such an act must have engendered) couples driven to this eventuality might have modified their behavior in other ways as well so as to delay the birth of the next unwanted child. The interpretation of the data, as always, involves a theoretical perspective. Mechanistic demographers will go to great lengths to avoid seeing human choice in the English mortality experience, and, since there are always rational, plausible, biological, or data-related explanations that can account for any premodern demographic patterns there are not many definite cases that force the choice of one theory over the other. It is to two subpopulations, which come as close as any to being definitive, that we will now turn.

Aristocrats and Expatriots in Seventeenth-Century England

It is among the English aristocracy and those English Protestant extremists who fled England to colonize the New World that we find the most compelling evidence that culture drove biology in the seventeenth century. Both groups violated the "natural" relationship between infant mortality and fertility. The aristocracy had lower than average fertility and higher than average infant mortality; while the religiously motivated colonists who settled in New England in the seventeenth century had higher than average fertility and lower than average infant mortality.

By definition the set of titled families who controlled a vastly disproportionate amount of England's power and wealth in the preindustrial period could not have had any infant deaths that we would be willing to attribute to involuntary relative deprivation. Their socially avoidable infant death rate must be set at zero. Similarly we would expect that since their women should have been in better health than the average woman who produced the births in Table 4.2, we would expect them to have a biologically unavoidable death rate lower than average.

By all rights then, aristocratic infants should have enjoyed a substantial mortality advantage over those of the common people. But as Fig. 4.2 shows, aristocratic IMRs were either equal to or above those for the general population through the sixteenth and seventeenth centuries. Only in the eighteenth century did privileged babies gain a decided mortality advantage over their ordinary counterparts. In the first 50-year period (1550–1599) aristocratic babies have a very similar pattern of infant mortality to common babies (although we would not expect

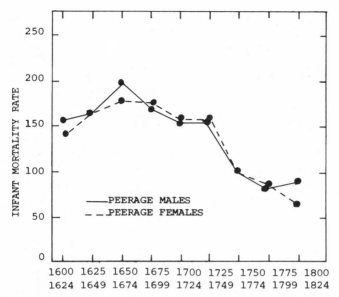

FIGURE 4.2. Infant mortality in British peerage families, 1550–1899 (Hollingsworth, 1977:327).

this to be the case). But in the second period (1600–1649) the rise of the female infant mortality (unaccompanied by a rise in the male rate) is very suspicious. This is the period when female dowries began to rise in response to very tight marriage markets.

By 1650–1699 IMRs for both sexes rose. It would be unwise to attribute this solely to choice, since the last half of the seventeenth century was a generally unhealthy period. Nevertheless it is hard to believe that the aristocracy was somehow more vulnerable to a difficult environment than the ordinary people. At any rate by 1650–1699 both male and female infants had a poorer chance of surviving their first year than the sons and daughters of agricultural laborers and small farmers (see Table 4.2). Subsequently, throughout the eighteenth century things improved dramatically for the infants of both sexes (although aristocratic females continued to do worse or no better than aristocratic males).

This dramatic fall of aristocratic IMRs has attracted the attention of Trumbach (1978), who exhaustively researched the possible causes of such a startling transformation. According to Trumbach the great improvement in the first year survival chances of privileged infants can only be explained by a transformation of the marriage, family, and parenting among the titled upper classes, which in itself was related to the growing influence of both religious and enlightenment-derived ideas among them. Privileged families did not experience a rise in their already fabulous standard of living, nor did they benefit from any non-existent revolution in medical technology. But their parenting goals and behavior changed and very dramatically—so dramatically that even breastfeeding came back into fashion after having been banished for centuries as something "animalistic" and "unseemly." By the late eighteenth century it was fashionable among aristocrats to care about one's own children and to give them the benefit of the vast resources at the disposal of their wealthy and privileged families. This more than halved the IMR of the seventeenth century and finally gave privileged infants the mortality advantage they should have enjoyed all along.

But intensive parenting and improved infant survival had a disruptive effect on aristocratic family life; it appeared to increase the number of survivors above some desired maximum. Hollingsworth's (1965) data on peerage fertility shows that from the Middle Ages to modern times, privileged wives gave birth to an average of no more than three children. The generation that first adopted marriage and parenting "reforms" (1700–1749) produced an unprecedented five births per woman. This must have disrupted the aristocratic reproduction equilibrium so severely that the children of the "large" families of 1700–1749 were driven to adopt fertility control in 1750–1799. If the privileged parents who allowed themselves to be "reformed" away from malparenting wanted to neither deal with the increased numbers of survivors nor return to malparenting, then fertility control in some form or another was their only option.

In the meanwhile if we take the late eighteenth century mortality rate for aristocratic infants as our biological baseline (the IMR the privileged could have achieved all along had they wished to make the survival of their infants top priority) than we have the following estimate of parentally avoidable death for the late seventeenth century.

Infant mortality rate = Parental + Social + Biological
(Peers, England, 1650–1699)
175   105   0   70

Seventy is probably still too high for the "biological" estimate, because girls were still stripped of any mortality advantage in infancy. But in this breakdown it is still the case that well over one-half of the deaths to babies born to aristocratic families were "avoidable" in the seventeenth century.

If we return to the estimates of avoidable death among the ordinary English families in the seventeenth century, we must assume that biologically avoidable death was either equal to or somewhat higher than the figure assigned to the aristocracy (it could not be lower). If biologically unavoidable deaths were as high as 100 per thousand, then the remainder, 50, must be subdivided between the other two categories. Even an equal division would leave parentally avoidable death at a fairly low level—25 per thousand—confirming the generally high level of parenting that a successfully internalized and institutionally enforced Protestant revolution might well have brought about.

Such a revolution would nevertheless leave the aristocracy in a position to continue infanticidal practices (if they failed to incorporate the new norms) because "deviance" among the powerful would not be observed by the "authorities" (many of whom would have been appointed by the aristocracy) nor investigated and punished.

There is one remaining subpopulation of Englishmen and women that gives us not only another perspective on infant mortality in the preindustrial era but also an understanding of its relation to fertility. Those colonists, who left old England for New England in order to set up Godly societies dominated by true religious principles, achieved their goal by the late seventeenth century. On the whole, their colonies (once established) were characterized by relatively high standards of living, an unusual degree of social homogeneity, and an exceptionally well ordered and supervised social life which included the enforcement of parenting norms. Although sect-specific philosophies of parenting differed in some respects, all the seventeenth century Puritan New England colonies were committed to intensive parenting, including prolonged breast-feeding (Moran and Vinovskis, 1983). Nevertheless, their women had exceptionally high fertility rates (even when age of marriage is controlled) and often shorter birth intervals than those common in England. Average completed family sizes of 8–10 were not uncommon. But this high fertility was not accompanied by high infant mortality. Quite the contrary, infant mortality rates in colonial New England were usually at or below 100 per thousand. Special subpopulations, like Demos' founding families of Plymouth, where seventeenth-century women colonists and their daughters completed fertility with eight births, appear to have lost fewer than one child (on average) from birth to age 21 (1970:192).

These low seventeenth-century colonial New England rates seem unbelievable (in fact they are often "adjusted" upward to achieve more acceptable values) but from the pessimistic perspective they are to be expected rather than adjusted. Since one would assign very few infant deaths to the category "parental underinvestment" and few to socially avoidable death (there was initially very little inequality) most infant deaths would have been caused by biologically unavoidable factors, and hence one would expect IMRs below 100 per thousand. Economic constraints would not work against the desire to parent efficiently because the labor of children was needed, and the land available to endow grown children seemed abundant, at first.

The Decline of Widespread Malparenting

The major implication of the pessimistic perspective is that (other things being equal) infant mortality in preindustrial Europe was a function of malparenting—the lower the infant mortality, the lower the level of malparenting and vice versa. From this follows a theory of the relationship between infant mortality, malparenting, and fertility during the demographic transition. If a population traditionally using malparenting to eliminate some or all of its unwanted infants could be "reformed" (while remaining in a static economy), it would in all probability be forced to adopt some kind of fertility control that operated before rather than after birth. Flandrin implies this is what happened in France. By implication a parental revolution that took place in the context of an industrial revolution (or something else that relaxed economic constraints for most people by providing extra employment or extra land for their offspring) would not necessarily reduce fertility until something else raised the costs of children and forced the adoption of fertility control. This, of course, would fit the English case where a small eighteenth-century decline in infant mortality (related to the development of better parenting among the less privileged classes) was not accompanied by a sustained decline of fertility until the latter part of the nineteenth century. The American case (in New England) would begin with the absence of malparenting in the context of land abundance and labor shortage. Fertility would not decline until land shortages raised the cost of establishing children or ideological developments independently acted to reduce desired family size. At any rate one way or another throughout the nineteenth century both economic development and its absence were working with ideologically driven improvements in parenting (itself correlated with the increase of literacy and schooling) and declining infant and child mortality.

Ultimately with the decline of fertility, pessimists get optimistic about the improved quality of parenting and describe the modern era as one in which child neglect and abuse has been greatly reduced from traditional levels (although it may be the case that subtle forms of abuse like overdiscipline and impossible expectations accompany the decline of child neglect).

One indirect piece of evidence for this new found optimism can be found in Fig. 4.3. At levels of life expectancy below 45 (when fertility in the countries whose statistics contributed to the table were most likely to have been high) the death rate from accidents and violence (not related to automobile accidents) was also high. As life expectancy rose and fertility declined, the accidental death rate dropped off rather sharply and then proceeded to decline slowly. The pessimistic interpretation of this would be that accidental deaths were simply the tip

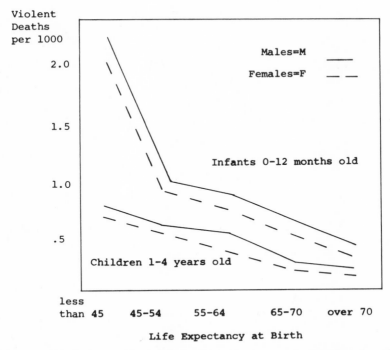

FIGURE 4.3. Deaths caused by "violence" (accidents, murders) with automobile-
          related fatalities excluded. Death rates per 1000 infants, 0–1 year;
          children 1–4 years (Preston, 1976:91–94).

of the iceberg of all deaths related to malparenting (although some of
the accidental deaths would have been genuinely unavoidable), many
of which were assigned to other causes. But the fact that nonautomobile
fatalities continued to decline as life expectancy rose indicated the
continuing decline of malparenting.

Does the pessimistic story of parenting ultimately have a happy end-
ing in the modern developed countries? We know that it does not, as
the chapters in this volume all bear witness. Child abuse and neglect
is once again believed to be a major social problem by the knowledgeable observers who have devoted much time to its study.

But how is it possible that in wealthy societies, where contraception
is cheap, easily available, and where there are very few truly unwanted
babies born, that child neglect and abuse should even appear to be
widespread.

This is an extremely complex problem, one which deserves a chapter
unto itself. But I would argue that any answer must involve a detailed
investigation of the matter of "transmission rates"—the probability that

a child who is abused or neglected will grow up to abuse or neglect a child of its own independent of the social and economic circumstances in which he/she finds him/herself. Experts do not agree on how common this form of learned behavior is; estimates range from 50% to nearly 100%. These high estimates raise the frightening possibility that in modern societies the stock of children who have been subjected to abuse and neglect will simply build upon its own, because mortality rates for infants and children are now so low that being placed in a high-risk-of-dying category by malparenting is no longer an important phenomena (demographically at least). Parental investment has been partially disassociated from death rates by the extremely high level of investment in public health in modern societies and by increasingly sophisticated medical techniques for saving the child victims of severe traumas, some of which are still related to malparenting.

Compounding the situation is the "fact" or possibility that those parents most likely to malparent are also those most likely to have higher than average fertility. If modern societies contain a core of parents who malparent because they were abused or neglected as children, and if such parents in fact have more children than parents who do not abuse or neglect their children, and if the vast majority of the malparented children survive to adulthood, and if transmission rates are as high as generally thought, then a stock of abused and neglected children will in fact build up independent of high standards of living. The only way to stop this process from continuing is to break the cycle by using the force of ideology (in one form or another) to change behavior. That is, of course, what therapists try to do.

The very existence of high transmission rates (if verified) would point again to the dominance of cultural forces relating to learned parenting behavior over biological forces relating to hard-wired instincts. (If instinctual responses dominated parenting behavior one would expect transmission rates to be fairly low—much less than 50%.)

In order to correct the build up of abused and neglected children and their strong tendency to transmit this form of learned behavior we would have to invest time and energy into teaching them and their children new forms of behavior. This in turn requires that those who are in a position to do such reprogramming would themselves have some ideas of what desirable parental behavior was and, hence, were not overly tolerant and relativistic about what constituted child neglect and abuse.

In the meanwhile the survival of badly treated children may be generating more and more bizarre forms of "psychic" death in response to maltreatment. Recently, a newspaper article appeared about researchers who are studying the relationship between severe child abuse (in the form of relentless beatings) and the emergence of multiple personalities in children. The article gave descriptions of several cases in which the abused children were able to have their main personality "die" temporarily when severe abuse began, while a second personality emerged who effectively absorbed the abuse, leaving the first personality "untouched," other than that it now shared one body with two selves.

But this rare "modern" form of child "death" relating to malparenting exists alongside the much more traditional form of real death. Most of the accidental deaths among children today are still related to neglect, not abuse. This point is made forcefully in Long (1983) concerning "latchkey" children (children left alone at home because one or both parents are at work and cannot find or pay for day care). This book contains statistics and warnings that early premodern parents would not have found irrelevant to their own lives.

REFERENCES

Ashby, H. (Dr.). *Infant mortality.* London: Arnold & Co., 1915.

Badinter, E. *Mother love: Myth and reality.* NY: Macmillan, 1980.

Boulanger, P., and Tabutin, D. *La mortalite des infants dans le monde and dans l'histoire.* Liege, Belgium: Ordina Editions, 1979.

Coale, A.J., and Demeny, P. *Regional model life table and stable populations,* 2d ed. NY: Academic Press, 1983.

DeMause, L., Ed. *The history of childhood.* NY: Harper Torchbooks, 1974.

Demos, J. *A little commonwealth.* London: Oxford University Press, 1970.

Dupaquier, J. Population. *In* P. Burke, Ed., *The Cambridge modern history,* Vol. XIII. Cambridge: Cambridge University Press, 1979.

Flandrin, J. *Families in former times.* Cambridge: Cambridge University Press, 1976.

Flinn, M. *The European demographic system: 1500–1820.* Baltimore, MD: Johns Hopkins University Press, 1981.

Garbarino, J. The human ecology of child maltreatment: A conceptual model for research. *Journal of Marriage and the Family,* 1977, *39*:721–727.

Gelles, R. Violence towards children in the United States. *American Journal of Orthopsychiatry,* 1978, *48*:580–592.

Giovannoni, J., and Becerra, R. *Defining child abuse.* NY: Free Press, 1979.

Given, J.B. *Society and homicide in 13th century England.* Stanford, CA: Stanford University Press, 1977.

Hanawalt, B. Childrearing among the lower classes of late medieval England. *Journal of Interdisciplinary History,* 1977, *8* (1):1–22.

Hardymut, Christine. *Dream babies: Child care from Locke to Spock.* London, 1983.

Hoffer, P.C., and Hull, N.E.H. *Murdering mothers: Infanticide in England and New England 1558–1803.* NY: New York University Press, 1981.

Hofstede, G. *Culture's consequences' international differences in work related values.* Beverly Hills, CA: Sage, 1984.

Hollingsworth, T.H. A Demographic study of the British ducal families. *In*

D. Glass and D. Eversley, Eds., *Population in history*. Chicago: Aldine Publishing Company, 1965.

Hollingsworth, T.H. Mortality in the British peerage families since 1600. *Population*, Numero Special (September 1977):323–352.

Houdaille, J. La Mortalite des infants en Europe avant le XIXe siecle. *In* P. Boulanger and D. Tabuin, Eds., *La Mortalite des infants dans le monde et dans l'histoire*. Liege, Belgium: Ordina Editions, 1979.

Hrdy, S., and Hausfater, G. Comparative and evolutionary perspectives on Infanticide: Introduction and overview. *In* G. Hausfater and S. Hrdy, Eds., *Infanticide: Comparative and evolutionary perspectives*. NY: Aldine, 1984, pp. xiii–xxxviii.

Imhof, A. Unterschiedliche Sauglingssterblichkeit in Deutschland, 18 bis 20 Jahrhundert—Warum? *Zeitschrift fur Bevolkerungswissenschaft*, 1981, *7*:343–382. (a)

Imhof, A. The amazing Simultaneousness of the big differences and the boom in the 19th century: Some facts and hypotheses about infant and maternal mortality in Germany, 18th to the 20th centuries. Paper presented to the International Symposium on Mortality Decline, June 22–26, 1981, Lund, Sweden. (b)

Johansson, S. Deferred infanticide: Excess female mortality during childhood. *In* G. Hausfater and S. Hrdy, Eds., *Infanticide: Comparative and Evolutionary Perspectives*. NY: Aldine, 1984.

Knodel, John, and Van de Walle, E. Breastfeeding, fertility and infant mortality. *Population Studies*, 1967, *21*:109–131.

Korbin, J. Introduction. *In* J. Korbin, Ed., *Child abuse and neglect: Cross-cultural perspectives*, Berkeley, CA: University of California, 1981.

Lancaster, J., and Lancaster, C. Parental investment: The hominid adaptation. *In* Donald Ortner, Ed., *A biocultural odyssey*. Washington, D.C.: Smithsonian Institution Press, 1983.

Langer, W. Forward. *In* L. DeMause, Ed., *The history of childhood*. NY: Harper Torchbooks, 1974, pp. vii–xii.

Laudenslager, M., and Reite, M. Losses and separations: Immunological consequences and health implications. *In* P. Shaver, Ed., *Review of personality and social psychology: Relationships and health*. (Special issue). Beverly Hills, CA: Sage, 1984.

Long, Lynette, and Long, Thomas. *The handbook for latchkey children and their parents*. NY: Arbor House, 1983.

McLaughlin, M. Survivors and surrogates: Children and parents from the ninth to the thirteenth centuries. *In* L. DeMause, Ed., *The history of childhood*. NY: Harper, 1974, pp. 102–131.

Mielke, J., Jorde, L., Trapp, P., *et al.* Historical epidemiology of smallpox in Aland, Finland: 1751–1890. *Demography*, 1984, *3*(21):271–296.

Moran, G., and Vinovskis, M. The great care of Godly parents: Early childhood in New England. Paper prepared for the Biennial Meeting of the Puritan Society of Research in Child Development, Detroit, April 23, 1983.

Newberger, E., *et al.* "Child abuse, the current theory base and future research needs." *American Journal of Child Psychiatry*, 1983, *22*(3):262–268.

Ozment, S. *When fathers ruled: Family life in Reformation Europe*. Cambridge, MA: Harvard University Press, 1984.

Perrenoud, A. La mortalite a Geneve de 1625 a 1825. *Annales de Demographie Historique*, 1978, pp. 209–233.

Piers, M. *Infanticide*. NY: Norton, 1978.

Pollock, L. *The forgotten children.* Cambridge: Cambridge University Press, 1983.

Preston, S.H., *Mortality patterns in national populations.* NY: Academic Press, 1976.

Preston, S.H., Keyfitz, N., and Schoen, R. *Cause of death patterns for national populations.* NY: Seminar Press, 1972.

Shorter, E.S. The great transformation of mother–infant relations, eighteenth to twentieth centuries. Paper presented to the conference Sozialization des Kindes, Bielefeld, Germany, September, 1982.

Skinner, G.W. Infanticide in Tokugawa Japan. Manuscript, in preparation.

Stone, L. *The family, sex and marriage in England 1500–1800.* London: Weidenfield and Nicholson, 1977.

Trumbach, R. *The rise of the egalitarian family.* NY: Academic Press, 1978.

Turnbull, C. *The mountain people.* London: Johnathan Cape, 1973.

Vann, R.T., and Eversley, D.E.C. The Demography of the British and Irish Quakers. Manuscript, 1985.

Wilson, C. Marital Fertility in Pre-Industrial England, 1550–1840. Ph.D. dissertation, Trinity College, Cambridge, England, 1981.

Winter, J. Infant mortality, maternal morality and public health in Britain in the 1930s. *Journal of European Economic History,* 1979, *10*:458–460.

Wrigley, E.A. Births and baptisms: The use of Anglican baptism registers as a source of information about the numbers of births in England before the beginning of civil registration. *Populations Studies,* 1977, *31*:281–312.

Wrigley, E.A., and Schofield, R.S. *The population history of England, 1541–1871.* Cambridge, MA: Harvard University Press, 1981.

Yankauer, A. An approach to the cultural base of infant mortality in India. *Population Review,* 1959, *3*(2):39–51.

EXPLAINING CHILD ABUSE AND NEGLECT

part

III

SEX-BIASED PARENTAL INVESTMENT AMONG PRIMATES AND OTHER MAMMALS: A CRITICAL EVALUATION OF THE TRIVERS–WILLARD HYPOTHESIS

Sarah Blaffer Hrdy

chapter

5

INTRODUCTION: INFANTICIDE, CHILD NEGLECT, AND THE CONCEPT OF PARENTAL INVESTMENT

Infanticide, either by a parent, by another relative, or by an unrelated individual of either sex is a widespread and very variable phenomenon in nature whose comprehension requires multiple explanatory frameworks. To date, the most widely reported form of infanticide among animals involves the killing of infants by unrelated males (e.g., in many species of nonhuman primates and cats and in certain strains of mice and lemmings) or by females with varying degrees of relatedness to the mother (e.g., species of ground squirrels and prairie dogs) (Hausfater and Hrdy, 1984; Hoogland, 1985). Although abandonment of infants or litters is not uncommon, animals in their natural habitats virtually never physically attack or directly destroy their own offspring. Humans, in this respect, are quite unusual among mammals in that across cultures parents themselves are the most likely perpetrators of infanticide through abandonment or even direct killing (these issues are discussed at length in Hausfater and Hrdy, 1984).

The decision to terminate further investment in a particular infant is typically made at birth or shortly after, and the mother is party to the decision (Dickemann, 1975; Minturn and Stashak, 1982; Daly and Wilson, 1984; Scrimshaw, 1984). Infanticide in such instances is probably usefully viewed as a very late form of abortion. From a sociobiological perspective, such parents are viewed as strategists whose ultimate goal is to increase the survival and lifetime breeding prospects of their entire lineage, even if it means a temporary setback in the form of a lost infant. It is assumed that each family has only limited resources to channel into reproduction. Since the time frame at issue is long term, a particular infant may be sacrificed if there is a chance that termination of in-

97

vestment in a particular infant would, on average, eventually enhance opportunities to perpetuate the lineage. The classic example involves killing the youngest of two closely spaced children, withholding investment from a new infant in order to invest in a healthy, older child already past the perilous first years of life.

Theoretically then, family resources should be allocated according to the degree of relatedness of the parent or stepparent to the infant, how likely a candidate the offspring is for translating parental investment into subsequent reproduction (i.e., offspring quality), as well as according to what other options the parents have for using available resources (Alexander, 1974; Daly and Wilson, 1984 and Chapter 8, this volume). According to this perspective, parents perpetually monitor both the "worth" of particular infants and their probable future demands on family resources (including demands long after weaning, such as marriage dowries), weighing these in the context of current socio-ecological conditions (e.g., anticipated investment from the father or other family members; family economic status; probable food availability) and invest in offspring accordingly (for an illustrative case study, see Bugos and McCarthy, 1984). Along the same lines, several authors have suggested that in some cases, offspring neglect in societies where infanticide is not an option may be a consequence of the same "decision-making" process which reduces parental motivations to invest in a particular infant. Should this happen, additional demands for nurture made on the parent by the infant (or other parties) may result in abuse of the infant.

This conceptual framework derives from a particular model, a hypothetical continuum of parental investment beginning at conception and continuing through weaning and beyond where parents are (at some level) thought to be continuously monitoring the costs and benefits of additional investment. This model is both new and speculative but has already begun to attract attention from researchers in anthropology, biology, and public health (e.g., Hausfater and Hrdy, 1984). Even those subscribing to the model, however, differ in their assessment of how much of contemporary infanticide and child abuse such a conceptual framework is likely to explain (compare, for example, Daly and Wilson, 1980 with Lenington, 1981). In my own opinion the model has the widest explanatory scope at low levels of subsistence (e.g., as among societies like the Ayoreo [Bugos and McCarthy, 1984]) and the narrowest in societies like our own which are (at least temporarily) characterized by a state of "ecological release." Starvation is uncommon, and parents virtually never benefit from killing an infant. In other words, I believe the model addresses itself to only a subset of contemporary western cases, a point dealt with elsewhere (Hrdy and Hausfater, 1984). The model remains relatively untested (see Daly and Wilson,

Chapter 9 this volume, for an exception and for a slightly different perspective that stresses psychological motivations rather than outcomes), and the fact is we do not yet know to what extent child neglect and infanticide can be explained by such a model.

Cross-culturally, there appears to be little doubt that most cases of human infanticide seem directly related to parental perceptions of either offspring quality or of the probable quality of the subsistence base in the near future. However, in a small portion of cases, sex of the infant rather than quality per se turns out to be the significant variable. Sex preferential infanticide is uncommon but is reported to occur in nearly 9% of the world's cultures (Minturn and Stashak, 1982). In some extreme North Indian cases, all daughters born in certain groups are killed at birth, and wives for sons must be recruited from outside of the group (Miller, 1981; Dickemann, 1979).

Traditional preferences for sons in some Indian communities is currently manifested in parental decisions to retain a fetus diagnosed as male or female. Of 700 prenatal diagnoses undertaken at one hospital in Western India between 1976 and 1977, 100% of fetuses diagnosed male contrasted to 5% of fetuses diagnosed female were carried to term (Ramanamma and Bambawale, 1980). We can not know how typical the sample for this controversial study is, but it does clearly document a continuing and drastic preference for sons in some parts of the world. The incidence of preferential male infanticide is certainly low, and its practice has been reported for 1–4% of human cultures (Minturn and Stashak, 1982; Whyte, 1978).

Even where parents do not practice outright infanticide, other forms of sex-biased investment by parents are widespread. As Johansson (this volume, Chapter 4) points out, differential provisioning of sons and daughters is one of the primary modes of biasing parental investment. Reports of one sex or the other being nursed longer are common in the ethnographic and historical literature, and such phenomena are almost certainly underestimated. Among the Wolof of West Africa, for example, females are said to be breast-fed up to 24 months, while males are nursed 18 months (Falade, 1971; cf. Burrows and Spiro, 1957, for the Ifaluk case; Orent, 1975, for the Kafa of Southwest Nigeria; Miller, 1981:90, for various Moslem Middle Eastern examples). The most widely spread bias, however, particularly in Asia, parts of Latin America, and occasionally Europe, appears to be in favor of feeding males more. For a sample of 422 Lebanese infants from the Middle East in a culture where sons are regarded with greater "warmth" than daughters, Prothro reports: "In every group [studied] there were more girls than boys breastfed for less than five months and more boys than girls for more than fourteen months"; these trends were statistically significant (Prothro, 1961:74; see also Tekçe and Shorter, 1984, for Jordan). The

nursing ideal for ninth-century France closely resembles that for contemporary Ecuador: Daughters should be nursed an average of 1 year,
boys twice that long (McKee, 1982; Coleman, 1976; see also Margery
Wolf for Taiwan, cited in McKee, 1982; Gessain, 1963, for Guinea; Khan,
1973, for Northern India). Similar biases are suggested by data on birth
spacing where the span of time until the next infant is born is longer
after a son than after a daughter (Haldar and Bhattacharyya, 1969; Khan,
1973).

The connection between early weaning and mortality is indirect and
therefore difficult to prove. In my opinion, however, there can be little
doubt that early curtailment of breast-feeding and the double loss of
both nutritional and immunological benefits of mother's milk renders
infants more susceptible to rotavirus and other sources of diarrhea,
the world's major mortality threat to infants in undeveloped countries
(Blacklow and Cukor, 1981). Preferential feeding of sons can be viewed
as potentially lethal discrimination against daughters. At the same time
the alternative possibility, that parents are merely trying to compensate
for the greater vulnerability of males by feeding them better or feeding
them longer, must also be kept in mind, a point that will be returned
to.

Traditional explanations for parental sex preferences, particularly the
widespread preference for sons in many cultures (Coombs, 1977; Miller,
1981; Park, 1983) stress: (1) the greater strength of males and their essential contributions to hunting and heavy agricultural work; (2) their
importance as warriors and in local disputes; (3) male roles in rituals
and in transmission of family names; (4) high cost of dowries in those
societies that have dowries (at a bare minimum, 8% of human cultures);
and (5) high value placed on males for "ideological" reasons.

There can be little doubt that such factors do indeed play a role.
Strong arguments can be marshalled to explain preferential female infanticide among groups like the Copper Eskimo in terms of the importance of hunting by males or female infanticide among the Yanomamo in terms of the importance of sons needed to wage war and to
successfully raid for wives (Balikci, 1967; Chagnon, 1968; see also Divale
and Harris, 1976). The ideological arguments, and especially arguments
based on male roles in rituals, and dowries, are more problematic simply because one suspects that a strong preference for sons preceded
the establishment of these institutions. Similarly the hypothesis that
female infanticide can be attributed to low female participation in subsistence (e.g., Miller, 1981) leaves much to be explained, particularly
its occurrence in areas where females work very hard and its absence
in some areas where women work little.

The failure of traditional explanations to explain a large portion of
the known cases of sex bias have led some authors (e.g., Hartung,

1983; Dickemann, 1979a) to consider a sixth explanation, essentially a sociobiological explanation that focuses on the probable reproductive contribution of sons versus daughters under different socioecological conditions. In this realm, the most logically powerful tool to date has been what is now known in evolutionary biology as the "Trivers–Willard hypothesis."

It should be noted that the Trivers–Willard hypothesis is a very broad one insofar as it applies across species, to many animals as well as to humans; it is also narrow in that it applies only under specialized conditions (detailed in the next section). Even if valid, the Trivers–Willard hypothesis is not going to provide an explanation for all sex-biased investment by parents. Nevertheless, I would contend that to explain even a portion of cases in which parents terminate investment in one sort of offspring while investing in another represents a significant advance in an area where general theories have not previously been used. For the most part, the Trivers–Willard hypothesis has been ignored out of hand by most or else cited as a proved "theory" by a very few. This chapter provides a critical and comprehensive examination and evaluation of the success this hypothesis has had in explaining sex-biased parental investment by parents in primates (including humans) and other mammals.

THE TRIVERS–WILLARD HYPOTHESIS

An offhand remark by evolutionary biologist Robert Trivers has turned out to be a prophetic one: "Even if I'm wrong, it will take them years to find out." Shortly afterward, in January 1973, *Science* published a brief paper by Trivers and his fellow graduate student (from mathematics), Dan Willard. They proposed that "natural selection should favor parental ability to adjust the sex ratio of offspring produced according to parental ability to invest" so that "under certain well-defined conditions, natural selection favors deviations from a 50/50 sex ratio at conception . . ." (1973:90). Specifically, Trivers and Willard thought their model should apply whenever the variance in male reproductive success is greater than that for females (as it is in many polygynous species) and when maternal condition is correlated with subsequent reproductive success of her offspring. Under these conditions, mothers in good condition should bias parental investment toward the sex where it would make the most difference (typically males). Efforts either to refute or validate this hypothesis have resulted in a vast and frequently contradictory literature (reviewed by Williams, 1979; Burley, 1982; Clutton-Brock and Albon, 1982; Charnov, 1982). In addition to these specific models, "Trivers–Willard" has also come to be used as a synonomous term with any sex-biased parental investment—whether before or after birth—that results on average in increased reproductive success for a lineage. In this chapter all three forms of the Trivers–Willard hypothesis are discussed, but it is this more general proposition that will primarily concern us.

The specific hypothesis that parents were facultatively adjusting sex ratios at conception in line with parental ability to invest in offspring has been beset by theoretical problems, by the dearth of information concerning possible mechanisms for facultative adjustment of the sex ratio at conception, and by serious difficulties in documentation. Thirteen years later, opinions about the hypothesis vary. What to some was a triumph for the power of evolutionary logic, with the correct theoretical solution achieved well in advance of any data to support it, has struck others as a foolhardy diversion of energies when it would have been wiser to follow Darwin's example of delaying judgment on the matter of sex ratios: "I formerly thought that when a tendency to produce the two sexes in equal numbers was advantageous to the species it would follow from natural selection," Darwin wrote in the revised, second edition 1871/1974:256) of *The Descent of Man*, "But I now see that the whole problem is so intricate that it is safer to leave its solution to the future." Darwin's sentiments have, I suspect, rung a chord in virtually every researcher who has tried to make sense of the exasperating literature concerning the adaptiveness for parents of biasing sex ratios toward either sons or daughters.

BIASING SEX RATIOS PRIOR TO BIRTH

Theoretical Difficulties

Some 50 years ago it occurred to R.A. Fisher (1930), as it had also occurred in a more general way to Darwin before him (1871/1974), that powerful selective forces would lead parents in panmictic (randomly mating) populations to invest equally in their sons and daughters. Since, in most cases, sons and daughters are about equally costly, equal investment would in most cases lead to equal production of both sexes. If ever a subset of parents began to specialize in the production of one sex at the expense of the other, natural selection would quickly reward the idiosyncracy of parents producing the other, rarer sex with a disproportionate number of grandchildren. This balance of opposing trends has become known as "Fisher's principle of the sex ratio."

Fisher's argument is based on an equilibrium model. Deviants who veer toward either extreme are eventually penalized with lower than average reproductive success. This may be the first discussion in the biological literature of what Maynard Smith was later to term "an evolutionary stable strategy" (formalized by Shaw and Mohler, 1953, and discussed at length in Charnov's excellent 1982 monograph on *The Theory of Sex Allocation,* p. 13 ff.). As Fisher's principle became dogma, innovative investigators began to examine exceptions to the rule. In 1967 W.D. Hamilton published a paper entitled "Extraordinary sex ratios." His primary focus was on the predominantly female broods produced by many species of mites and insects.

The fig wasps, among whom mothers produce up to ten times as many daughters as sons, are typical of this group. Fig wasps are typical, too, in that each mother lays her eggs in an isolated and confined place (inside of a fig) where the subsequent mating of her offspring will be anything but random since a male—who does not even have wings— never leaves the fig of his birth, and his most likely sexual partners will be his sisters. The extraordinary level of inbreeding typically dictated by this life style—the fact that competition for mates is nonrandom and strictly local—means that mothers producing predominantly female broods are no longer in competition with mothers who do not, so the equilibrating pendulum conceptualized by Fisher never has a chance to swing.

Such "local mate competition" is widespread among small arthropods and, as Hamilton noted, a most economical phenomenon since each mother produces only as many sons as are needed to fertilize her many daughters (Werren, 1980). However, it can only be maintained when clutches are so widely dispersed and isolated that competition for mates is only between same-sex sibs, an improbable precondition among most migrating birds and mammals.

In addition to Fisher's principle of the sex ratio, there are other processes that would promote the production of equal numbers of males and females among higher vertebrates, in particular, the cytological machinery for reproduction found in many birds and mammals (Williams, 1979). At conception each individual is allocated a combination of sex-determining chromosomes that are either XX or XY. The situation is quite different from that among many reptiles or fish where sex is determined after birth or where sex may change during the course of the individual's life span (cases of temperature-determined sex in turtles and alligators, and size and socially determined sex in fish, etc., are reviewed in Charnov, 1982). Among other higher vertebrates, by contrast, the XX individual becomes a lifelong female, the XY a male (except among birds, where the homogametic ZZ individual becomes a male, the heterogametic ZW a female). Mendelian segregation of the chromosomes means that at conception, each individual should have an equal chance of receiving from the father either an X or a Y chromosome. Sex is determined by chance—a flip of the coin yields an X or a Y, and the result should accordingly be random. Hence, as Williams notes, among pairs of dizygotic human twins one would expect a binominal distribution with 25% both boys, 25% both girls, and 50% one of each sex.

Production of biased sex ratios then is no easy task among the higher vertebrates. At least two sorts of natural barriers must be surmounted: forces selecting for an equilibrium (Fisher's principle) and the more fundamental condition of Mendelian segregation of the sex chromosomes. Both processes oppose any deviation from equality. Hence there is considerable reason to expect balanced sex ratios to be the norm in mammals.

Wood lemmings provide one of the few known mammalian exceptions to this general expectation: Three to four times more females than males are produced in this species (Frank, cited in Fredga, Gropp, Winking, and Frank, 1977). Williams (1979) suggests that wood lemmings may represent one of the rare cases of "local mate competition" among mammals (see also Maynard Smith and Stenseth, 1978). Lemming populations are characterized by large fluctuations in numbers, with the result that brother–sister matings might prevail during periods when the population is low, and families of wood lemmings are widely separated. Although many rodent species share this "boom or bust" population ecology, not all would also possess a mechanism permitting them to bias production of offspring toward daughters. In the wood lemming case, biased sex ratios are made feasible by the presence of a mutant form of the X chromosome with peculiar powers to overwhelm expression of the Y chromosomes. When linked to a Y chromosome the peculiar X chromosome produces a daughter instead of the expected son. Furthermore, the gametes produced by these XY females mostly contain the X rather than Y chromosome (Fredga et al., 1977). According to this hypothetical reconstruction, both selection for a departure from 50/50 and a chance mutation leading to the wood lemming's "imperialistic" version of the X chromosome had to be present to maintain this unusual reproductive system in the wood lemming.

Stringent conditions must be met in order to permit parents to skew their production of offspring in favor of one sex or the other. Even commercial animal breeders (who have invested far more time and money toward this end than have scientists) have met with little success. So far no one has produced a line of hen-producing hens. (For a review of the history of such efforts, see Hohenboken, 1981.) This situation has led more than one eminent theoretician to question the presence of sex ratio adaptations in outbred species where there are two separate sexes: "I find no support for any theory of adaptive sex ratio (in outcrossed vertebrates), . . ." writes evolutionary biologist George Williams. "Sex seems to be just another Mendelian unit character" (1979:577). Similar doubts have been expressed by John Maynard Smith:

I feel a certain uneasiness about sex ratio theory as it applies to diploids with genetic sex-determining mechanisms. This uneasiness arises because some of the most extensive data sets reveal little or no evidence for any genetic variance of the primary sex ratio. Clearly, if there is no genetic variance, evolutionary adaptation is not to be expected. Now there are some examples (usually based on rather small numbers) in which observed sex ratios have been found to vary strikingly in the direction predicted by theory. This suggests that the frequent failure to find evidence of genetic variance is misleading, and this may indeed be the case. However, I would be happier if I thought that investigators, and referees, were as keen to publish negative evidence as positive—i.e., evidence that the sex ratio in some populations does *not* show a theoretically predicted bias . . . (1983:873).

Yet there is tension and puzzlement behind these disclaimers, for neither scientist can deny the logic of the Trivers–Willard argument. As Williams puts it:

I find it rather mysterious that adaptive control of progeny sex ratio seems not to have evolved. In particular, the conformity of human progeny sex ratios to binominal distributions seems to contradict evolutionary theory. Either the physiological advantage of adjusting offspring sex to maternal capabilities, or the demographic advantage of decreasing competition for mates ought to produce noteworthy effects. Instead, deviations from random sex determination are trivial at best (1979:578).

Difficulties in Documentation

From the outset, the Trivers–Willard hypothesis was plagued by serious difficulties in documentation. The "trivial" magnitude of the difference in the sex ratios of most mammals was indeed a problem. The fact that 106 males are born for every 100 females in human populations is typically regarded as a small difference, explained by the need to compensate for higher male mortality. Even where significant differences could be detected, it could not be proved that such differences were in fact adaptive. Problems now evident in the original article by Trivers and Willard are in many ways illustrative of the problems encountered in sex ratio research generally and merit a closer look.

Trivers and Willard began by inviting us to imagine a population of animals in which "the condition of adult females varies from good to poor" and to assume that a female in good condition is better able to bear and nurse her progeny than is a female in poor condition, so that at the end of the period of parental investment, the offspring of females in good condition will tend to be "the healthiest, strongest, and heaviest." If we also assume that these advantages extend into adult life, and that "such adult differences in condition affect male reproductive success more strongly than they affect female reproductive success" (because males are competing with one another for access to females) then it follows that a female in good condition should, ideally, bias production of offspring toward sons. By the same reasoning, the offspring of mothers in poor conditions would be at a disadvantage; to make the best of their poor lot, they should produce daughters who in contrast to males in poor condition would at least be able to breed. In support of their argument, Trivers and Willard cited data for deer collected by Robinette, Gashwiler, Low, and Jones (1957).

These data were to prove very controversial. In an influential critique of the Trivers–Willard article Judith Myers pointed out that the difference in the proportion of male fawns born to these deer after mild winters (57% males, $N=399$) was only slightly greater (3%) than the percentage of male fawns born after harsh winters (54% males, $N=164$) and not statistically significant (1978:382). In the deer study with the greatest differences, the results deviated in a direction opposite to that predicted by the theory (Myers, 1978:282).

Trivers and Willard had also cited the classic, early study of red deer by Fraser Darling (1964): "Adult red deer who fail to breed the preceding year (and therefore are presumably in better than normal condition during the present year) appear to produce a much higher sex ratio than do adult females who bred the preceding year" (Trivers and Willard, 1973:91). Commenting on that evidence, Myers (1978:383) noted that:

> While Darling mentions two studies, one with a sample size of six and another with a sample size of 13, which indicates a trend consistent with this interpretation, the major study cited by him is work by Miller (1932). Females which had offspring 2 years in a row produced 62.3% sons (total young = 79), while the sex ratio of offspring of "yield" or previously barren females was 57.8% males (total young = 192). Sex ratios of offspring from these two types of female deer are not significantly different, and in fact the trend goes in the direction opposite that predicted by Trivers and Willard (1978:383).

Nor could Myers resist adding that "another reference cited to show that pigs support the predictions of the hypothesis . . . turns out to be a study of rabbits. . . ."

There is a certain irony to this problematic use of the red deer data. Some of the most solid support of the Trivers–Willard hypothesis was eventually to come from precisely this species.

Support for the Hypothesis

A year after Trivers and Willard published their hypothesis, Rivers and Crawford reported that when laboratory mice are fed a low-fat diet, subsequent litter sizes were reduced and the incidence of still-births and cannibalism increased—all findings that had been reported before. What struck them as unusual was that the marked reduction in litter size was almost entirely due to a reduction in the number of male births so that the sex ratios of litters born to the poorly nourished mothers were 32.2 compared to 101.5 (males per 100 females) in the controls (1974:Table 1). The finding that food-stressed mothers produce proportionally fewer males has been replicated now in several studies (McClure, 1981, for wood rats; Labov, Huck, Vaswani, and Lisk, 1984 and in press, for hamsters). These findings could be interpreted either as evidence that male fetuses are more sensitive to stress *in utero* (e.g., McMillen, 1979; Golovachev, 1978) or they could be interpreted as support for the Trivers–Willard hypothesis. Predictions generated by the two hypotheses, "Greater Male Vulnerability" and Trivers–Willard, are very similar, and it is difficult to compare them. Indeed, it is possible that greater male vulnerability could be a proximate cause for a phenomenon ultimately best explained by the Trivers–Willard hypothesis, or it could be that male vulnerability is an independent phenomenon, a physiological "given" that parents adaptively allocating investment to sons and daughters have to cope with.

Data for multiple births raise similar problems. In the case of human twins and triplets, where one might expect reduced maternal investment in each embryo, parents either skew investment away from sons or perhaps sons are less viable when competing with a twin. In any event, twin births tend to be female-biased (Wyshak, 1978; Imaizumi, 1982; James, 1983a). A recent study of coypu (or "nutria") revealed that large litters are typical, but when mothers do produce small litters, there is apparently greater maternal investment available for each embryo. It was just such mothers with small litters that selectively aborted daughters through an unknown mechanism while continuing the pregnancy if the small litter was primarily male (Gosling, 1983). Gosling hypothesizes that maternal condition and larger male body size are more important for male than female reproductive success, but what is missing from this, as in other studies, is the relevant information on the reproductive performance of males and females born to poorly fed (or low-investing) mothers compared to well-fed (high-investing) mothers.

A recent study of a free-ranging population of red deer *(Cervus elaphus)* on the isle of Rhum off the Scottish coast provides us with some of the best data to date concerning lifetime reproductive success of males and females (Clutton-Brock, Albon, and Guinness, 1982) and permits us to address these issues. Searching for indications that the sex ratio of fawns varied adaptively with maternal condition, Clutton-Brock and his associates found no correlation between sex ratio and quality of mother's range, between sex ratio and the number of competing herd members, or between sex ratio and whether or not the mother had bred the preceding year. Hence they initially concluded that the sex ratio varied "very little" with maternal condition (1982:162).

It was only when, several years later, Clutton-Brock, Albon, and Guinness (1984) began to look at the relationship between female dominance rank and sex ratio that they found significant differences that were in line with predictions generated by the Trivers–Willard hypothesis.[1] In this paper, Clutton-Brock *et al.* show that "dominant mothers produce significantly more sons than subordinates and that maternal rank has a greater effèct on the breeding success of males than of females."

Records collected for some 200 hinds and 150 stags between 1971 and 1983 were analyzed, revealing that the sex ratio of offspring born to high-ranking females was significantly male biased (60.6% male offspring, $N = 149$, $p < .01$). Furthermore, while there was no consistent relationship between maternal rank and the reproductive success of daughters, the breeding success of sons did turn out to be positively correlated with their mother's rank, suggesting that the male-biased sex ratios might indeed be adaptive. It is also possible however, as Clutton-Brock *et al.* point out in a later paper, that the differential mortality of sons born to low-ranking females might be "a consequence of a greater susceptibility of males to food shortage associated with their faster growth rates and increased nutritional requirements" (1985:13). Once again then, we encounter the possibility that parents compensate for "greater male vulnerability" by investing more in the production of sons.

Long-term data for rhesus macaques collected on the island of La Parguera off Puerto Rico have been similarly interpreted in support of Trivers–Willard. In an ambitious study undertaken by Meikle, Tilford, and Vessey (1984), the authors argue that sex ratios varied with both the rank of social groups (with high-ranking groups producing relatively more sons than daughters) as well as with genealogical rank of females (i.e., dominant matrilines overproduced sons). One of their most striking findings was that when a formerly very high-ranking group that previously had produced 54% male offspring each year fell in rank relative to other groups, the proportion of males produced decreased to 35% in the succeeding birth season. During the same period, the formerly second-ranking troop that had produced 52–53% males in the

[1]Why this delay in recognizing the importance of female dominance hierarchies occurred is a separate issue that can only be understood in the context of the general intellectual climate that characterized the early years of sociobiological research of mammals. The emphasis was almost entirely on competition between males, and the amount of competition between females as well as variance in female reproductive success were both widely underestimated (Hrdy, 1981; Wasser and Waterhouse, 1983).

two previous birth seasons began to produce 62–65% males in successive birth seasons as the troop began to rise from second to first-ranking position in the hierarchy of troops (Meikle et al., 1984:Table 2). Looking at individual females, they found that in 719 births, high-ranking females produced 54% sons, low-ranking females 49% sons; these differences were statistically significant (1984:Table 1B).

These findings are so striking that it is important to keep in mind several cautionary reminders, namely that the interpretation of these data is based on certain as yet unproven assumptions. First, it is taken as a given that maternal rank influences the reproductive success of sons just as it is known to do for daughters in this population (Drickamer, 1974). But, the case for maternal influence on the rank of cercopithecine daughters and on these daughters' ability to successfully rear offspring is far stronger than is the case for maternal influence on the reproductive success of sons. Second, the crucial assumption that variance in reproductive success is greater for male than for female rhesus is supported by estimates of the lifetime reproductive success for 42 males and 44 females born between 1964 and 1968 rather than by actual numbers of surviving offspring that were sired or borne by these individuals. Using such estimates Meikle et al. (1984) found that the variance in the reproductive success of males was nearly three times that of females. In assessing the validity of these estimates as actual measures of the relative variance in reproductive success of males and females, we need to keep in mind that La Parguera is a provisioned, predator-free breeding colony with relatively high infant survival rates. Approximately 82% of all rhesus infants born on the Puerto Rican Island colonies survive to weaning (Drickamer, 1974) compared to some 42% survival for infants of the related toque macaque species in a nonprovisioned population studied by Dittus (1979). Furthermore, methods of estimating male reproductive success do not take into account the possibility that females might occasionally copulate "adulterously" with males outside of their troop. Whereas the high survival rate of infants would lead to an underestimation of potential variance in female reproductive success since even the most harassed or poorly fed offspring would still survive (discussed in Hrdy, 1981:131–134), the assumption that females only mate with males in their own troop would lead to overestimations of the variance in male reproductive success since males in troops with a large number of females receive inflated scores for reproductive success while other males might receive undeservedly low ones. It is also possible that female reproductive careers extend over a longer time-span than do males'. Finally, it should be kept in mind that behind every wildly reproductively successful male, there must also be, one generation back, a mother (Hartung 1983 and in press).

The data presented by Meikle *et al.* (1984) suggest that rhesus macaque mothers belonging to high-ranking troops bias production of
progeny toward sons, precisely as the Trivers–Willard hypothesis predicts. A comparison of high- and low-ranking genealogies, however,
showed only a slightly greater proportion of sons born to high-ranking
mothers (54%) compared to low-ranking mothers (49%). Furthermore,
as Meikle *et al.* point out, it must be kept in mind that these findings
could also be explained by higher wastage of male fetuses (as in
McMillen, 1979) among low-ranking and presumably socially stressed
mothers. Higher sex ratios in dominant lineages could also be a function
of demography if high-ranking lineages reproduce faster and hence
tend to contain more young females and if (as is true in humans) mothers are more likely to produce sons at lower birth orders (see p. 117).
Several recent studies, however, suggest that maternal age and parity
will not have much effect on sex ratios in rhesus macaques (Rawlins
and Kessler, 1986; Small and Hrdy, 1986).

Maternal Condition and the Reproductive Success of Daughters—A Variation on Trivers–Willard

Nine studies of wild and captive monkey groups where the sex ratio
of offspring has been analyzed by maternal rank yielded very mixed
results. The lack of consistent patterns among closely related species
is striking and make earlier conclusions about the existence of biased
sex ratios in primates (e.g., Hrdy, 1981:113) seem premature. Two of
the studies, that by Meikle *et al.* (1984) and a second, smaller study by
Paul and Thommen (1984), based on a colony of Barbary macaques
(Macaca sylvana) in Germany, document a tendency for high-ranking
females to overproduce sons compared to the underproduction of
daughters by low-ranking females.

These results are considered consistent with the Trivers–Willard hypothesis. By contrast, additional studies, two of Japanese macaques
(Macaca fuscata) by Noyes (1982) and Wolfe (1984) and one of rhesus
macaques *(Macaca mulatta)* reported by Berman and Rawlins (1985; see
also Rawlins and Kessler, 1986) found no clear trends associated with
high rank. For example, in the more extensive of these two studies,
Berman and Rawlins analyzed 11 years of data for 322 births for the
Cayo Santiago population of rhesus, a population living under conditions very similar to those of the macaques Meikle *et al.* studied on
La Parguera.

Although Berman and Rawlins found a significant relationship between fecundity and the proportion of daughters produced, this was
not clearly related to rank. Indeed, their data indicated that middle-
ranking females were both more fecund and more prone to produce
daughters than were high-ranking females. Though these are the only

three published accounts reporting no effect of mother's rank, I suspect the existence of other such data where, because the results were "negative," such findings remained unpublished or else are mentioned only in passing (e.g., Small and Smith, 1984).

Despite very contradictory findings in different studies, the reports that are most frequently cited in connection with primate sex ratios are the three influential studies by Altmann (1980), Simpson and Simpson (1982), and Silk (1983). Recently, a fourth study (Small and Hrdy, 1986) reports similar results. These four studies, involving thousands of person-hours of observation, including birth records spanning 21 years for one colony of captive rhesus macaques *(Macaca mulatta)* and 9 years for another; 10 years of records for captive bonnet macaques *(Macaca radiata);* and 13 years of data collected for wild, unprovisioned savana baboons *(Papio cynocephalus)* at Amboseli all report the same pattern: low-ranking females overproduce sons (Silk, 1983; Small and Hrdy, 1986). Furthermore, these studies can be interpreted as the "exception" that would support the general proposition underlying the Trivers–Willard hypothesis, namely that parents invest in offspring in line with probable reproductive returns. In this instance, it is argued that because high maternal rank benefits daughters more than sons in baboon and macaque breeding systems, high-ranking mothers should preferentially produce daughters and low-ranking mothers sons (Altmann, 1980), what might be referred to as "the advantaged daughter" model.

At first glance, of course, the fact that four out of eight studies show high-ranking females producing a higher proportion of daughters than low-ranking females (Table 5.1) would seem to contradict the specific predictions of the Trivers–Willard hypothesis, but as Altmann stresses, a basic assumption of the hypothesis that high-ranking females should overproduce sons may not be met in the case of cercopithecine monkeys, namely the assumption that sons benefit more from good maternal condition than do daughters. This is an area of disagreement between Altmann and Silk, on the one hand, and Meikle *et al.,* on the other, who contend that high maternal rank benefits sons more than daughters. This disagreement can not be resolved on the basis of current information.

All researchers in this area agree that macaques and baboons are matrilineal and highly nepotistic, and that mothers, daughters, and sons assist their kin in competing with other matrilineages (e.g., Kurland, 1977). All accept also Kawamura's and Sade's early findings on matrilineal inheritance of rank and younger sister ascendancy (at about the time she begins to breed, a younger daughter will often rise in rank above her older sisters) (discussed in Sade, 1967; Hausfater, Altmann, and Altmann, 1982). Furthermore all agree that whereas most sons will migrate from their natal troop to breed elsewhere, daughters will remain

TABLE 5.1. Different Patterns in the Relationship between Maternal Rank and Sex Ratio of Progeny Reported for Eight Studies of Cercopithecine Monkeys

Species (study location)	Rank	Proportion of male offspring	Statistical test of rank differences (Chi square)	Sources
A. Overproduction of sons by low-ranking mothers				
Papio cynocephalus (Amboseli, Africa)	High	.34 ($N=29$ infants)	$p<.05$	Altmann, 1980[a]
	Low	.68 (22)		
Macaca radiata (California Primate Center, Davis)	High	.52 ($N=83$)	N.S.	Silk, 1983
	Low	.63 (120)		
Macaca mulatta (Madingley Colony, England)	High	.28 ($N=53$)	$p<.0005$	Simpson and Simpson, 1982
	Low	.63 (86)		
Macaca mulatta (California Primate Center, Davis)	High	.46 ($N=193$)	N.S.	Small and Hrdy, 1986
	Low	.54 (181)		
B. Overproduction of sons by high-ranking mothers				
Macaca mulatta (La Parguera Puerto Rico Colony)	High	.54 ($N=388$)	$p<.005$	Meikle *et al.*, 1984
	Low	.49 (352)		
Macaca sylvana (Salem, FRG Colony)	High	.58 ($N=33$)	N.S.	Paul and Thommen, 1984
	Mid	.47 (49)		
	Low	.38 (34)		

C. No effect of maternal rank

		Mean dominance rank				
Macaca mulatta (Cayo Santiago, Puerto Rico Colony)	High Mid Low	.51 ($N = 145$) .32 (59) .52 (87)			N.S.	Berman and Rawlins, 1985
Macaca fuscata (Arashiyama West Colony, Texas)		28.8[b] ($N = 45$) 27.8 (65)	Sons Daughters	No apparent difference		Noyes, 1982[b]
Macaca fuscata (Arashiyama, Japan) 1976 birth season 1977 birth season 1978 birth season		19.63 ($N = 16$) 16.38 (16) 20.72 (18) 18.40 (20) 16.28 (18) 12.91 (11)	Sons Daughters Sons Daughters Sons Daughters	No significant differences		Wolfe, 1984

---

[a]These data are for the 7 years 1971–1978. Data presented for 80 births over 10 years in Altmann *et al.* (in press) follow the same pattern.

[b]Study published in abstract form only.

113

in the troop of their birth, not only assisting the mother and other matrilineal kin in their perpetual feuding, but also competing with kin for scarce local resources, a point stressed by Silk (1983). Where they disagree is over which sex a high-ranking mother can help most, and this has to do in large part with how these researchers interpret the reproductive consequences of female–female competition.

The "local resource competition" hypothesis was first suggested by Clark (1978). Clark had noticed that among the galagos—small, nocturnal African prosimians—that she studied, mothers seemed to produce more sons than daughters (cf. Foerg, 1982, for a similar male bias among infants born to *Cheirogaleus medius*, another fairly solitary nocturnal prosimian). Checking zoo records and museum specimens, she found a similar trend. (Note, however, that such sources are scarcely ideal for information on sex ratios since we know so little about the methodology of sexing, what happened in the "undecided" cases, etc. This is especially a problem in the case of a male bias since it may be easier to obtain a positive result, that is, the presence of a penis, when sexing a male.) To explain this apparent preponderance of male births, Clark proposed that because daughters should remain in the mother's territory, competing with her for resources, mothers would "prefer" to produce sons who would scatter to breed, leaving the mother with her own larder intact.[2]

Silk (1983) reformulated this hypothesis for cercopithecine monkeys by suggesting that daughters who would be future competitors for troop resources would be targeted for far more aggression than sons. If immature females receive more aggression than immature males, mothers would then be forced to provide more care and protection for daughters than sons if the daughters were to survive (see also similar arguments presented by van Schaik and van Noordwijk, 1983). Van Schaik and van Noordwijk concur that given the poor survival prospects of daughters born to low-ranking females, stressed mothers would reduce their losses by terminating investment in daughters at the earliest possible point. While Silk emphasizes selection pressures for facultative adjustment of sex ratios by the mother, van Schaik and van Noordwijk emphasize selection pressures on other females to curtail the survival of daughters born to competitors; this is essentially a variant of Clark's "local resource competition" model.

One prediction from Clark's model would be that in species where males rather than females remain in their natal area, sons would be

[2]Note that this model assumes a very low mortality among adult females. If mother galagos were likely to die from predation or old age it would behoove them to produce daughters rather than sons to inherit their territories. I know of no data on life expectancy for wild female galagos that would permit us to assess this assumption.

the target of more attacks by conspecifics. Interestingly, the only non-human case of possibly sex-biased infanticide I know of for primates involves differential attacks on chimp infants; 8 of 9 victims of infanticidal attacks by adult males were male infants (Nishida, 1985). Since chimps are a species where males are philopatric while females transfer, this preliminary and still small data set are in line with predictions generated by the local resource competition hypothesis.

Like van Schaik and van Noordwijk, Silk argues that in female-philopatric species (where females remain in their natal troop, as in macaques), daughters born to low-ranking mothers are the victims of intense harassment. Indeed, she cites data suggesting that this process begins even before daughters are born. Data indicating that macaque mothers pregnant with daughters receive more attacks have been presented by both Sackett (1981) and by Simpson et al. (1981). These attacks begin only after midterm, a timing that correlates with the onset of sexual differentiation and differential secretion of testosterone into the mother's blood by the fetus. Mothers are not disproportionately attacked before this—an important point.

In summary, Silk is suggesting that competition for local resources combined with the tendency of daughters to remain in their natal groups while males migrate leads to intense competition among females for reproductive opportunities. She proposes that "females limit the number of females born and raised in their groups through the effective harassment of females carrying female fetuses and immature females. In response to such harassment, females appear to invest more in their daughters than sons, and to adjust the sex ratio of their progeny in relation to the expected reproductive success of their sons and daughters" (1981:63). In line with Silk's hypothesis, evidence for wild Amboseli baboons and captive rhesus (Altmann, Altmann, and Hausfater, in press; Simpson and Simpson, 1985) suggest that daughters are indeed more costly to produce in that birth intervals are longer after daughters are born than after sons; whether or not the longer birth intervals after daughters is related to greater harassment by other females and the mother's need to protect her daughter is not yet known.

Insofar as Silk proposes that parents are adjusting the sex ratio of progeny in accordance with the expected reproductive success of sons versus daughters, her model is a variant of the generalized Trivers–Willard hypothesis (cf. Altmann, 1980:39); the local resource competition hypothesis however remains quite distinct. Finally, like Altmann (1980), Small and Hrdy (1986) stress the benefits for high-ranking mothers who produce daughters ("the advantaged daughter" hypothesis). Such daughters not only benefit from inheriting the mother's advantaged position but remain in the troop as useful allies for the mother and her lineage. Currently, primatologists are directing a great deal of attention toward refining and testing these complex hypotheses.

The Evidence for Sex-Ratio Adaptations among Humans

There appears to be a strong tendency among human populations for sex ratios to fall between 104 and 107. In an analysis of birth registrations from all over the world, Visaria (1967) found that 50 of 80 values reported for 76 territories fell within this range. A few countries, notably Korea, yielded surprisingly high sex ratios (116.9 in a sample of 11,131 births registered from 10 hospitals; 113 for over 5 million births in a national register; Visaria, 1967). Park (1983) has recently suggested that Korean parents may have contributed to such high sex ratios by practicing birth control after one or more sons have been born but continuing to bear children if the family contains only or mostly daughters, but it is difficult to see how, mathematically, this could work. The alternative hypothesis is that Koreans are genetically predisposed to produce sons. Offering preliminary support for this hypothesis, Morton, Chung, and Mi (1967) found slightly higher than average sex ratios among Hawaiian children whose fathers were of Korean descent. At present, it is difficult to know what to make of the perplexingly high Korean secondary sex ratios beyond noting the need for further research.

Of 23 territories or countries that yielded sex ratios below 104, 15 contained substantial numbers of people of African descent, leading Visaria to suggest that "negroid populations might have a somewhat lower masculinity at birth . . . ." (1967:137), an effect now thought to be due to the father rather than the mother (Khoury, Erickson, and James, 1984). This hypothesis is supported by much data for North American blacks (with sex ratios around 102) but interestingly, sex ratios recorded for a Nigerian population were not significantly different from those reported for European and North American whites (both around 106) (Ayeni, 1975). Another sample containing over 1 million Hausa children yields a sex ratio as high as 107 (Rehan, 1982). Such variation raises the possibility that the low sex ratios at birth for blacks in America and other countries might be related to their generally low socioeconomic status, a clear prediction of the Trivers–Willard hypothesis and, in fact, an association that was assumed to be true in Trivers' and Willard's original article (1973:91).

Trivers and Willard acknowledged that "the application of the model to humans is complicated by the tendency for males to invest parental effort in their young (which reduces variance in male RS), and by the importance of kin interactions among adults" (1973:91). Nevertheless, they argued that their model would apply so long as the reproductive success of a brother at the higher end of the socioeconomic scale exceeded his sister's and so long as the sister's reproductive success exceeded that of her brother at the lower end of the socioeconomic scale.

Oddly given the number of earlier studies that have claimed a correlation between sex ratio and socioeconomic status, Trivers and Willard cited only one (Schapiro *et al.*, 1978), apparently unaware until later (Trivers, 1985) of the definitive study up to that time (Teitelbaum and Mantel, 1971). Teitelbaum and Mantel analyzed 40,000 births for which comprehensive data on the socioeconomic status of each subject had also been recorded. In that study, children born to families in the lowest socioeconomic class had a sex ratio approximately 8–9% lower than that of the highest two classes. These results, then, are surprisingly strong and in line with the Trivers–Willard hypothesis. However, subsequent studies make it questionable whether or not this relationship between socioeconomic status and sex ratios is as clear as originally supposed.

The primary impetus for reassessing the correlation came from the analysis of a major sample of over 1 million Scottish births that had been classified by sex, maternal age, birth order, and class (Rostron and James, 1977). The sample happened to be almost completely homogeneous for race. Rostron and James found that sex ratio declined with birth order and maternal age (and in fact, appeared to do so independently) but could detect no meaningful association between sex ratio and class. Several recent analyses utilizing much smaller American samples have similarly failed to find any association between status or wealth and sex ratio (cf. Essock-Vitale, 1984; Christopher, 1984).

Rostron and James (1977) suggested that the earlier analyses of American census data by Teitelbaum and others may have been confounded by the tendency for low socioeconomic groups in the United States to contain a large black component as well as a tendency for low socioeconomic families to be large. The first point is only relevant if sex ratios for blacks are indeed low (e.g., see Table 5.2), but as suggested earlier, low sex ratios among blacks in America may themselves be an artifact of something else (such as poor maternal condition). Even more clear was the tendency for offspring born in large families to have a low sex ratio (cf. Novitski and Kimball, 1958; and especially Teitelbaum, Mantel, and Stark, 1971; and Erickson, 1976). There is a highly significant rise in the proportion of male births among low birth orders (i.e., small families), although it should be noted that the difference between the two extremes is less than 2% and that birth order accounts for less than 10% of the variation in sex ratios (Erickson, 1976, for a sample of more than 5 million births).

Confirmation of what once seemed like a clearcut association between high socioeconomic status and high sex ratios at birth turns out, upon closer inspection, to be elusive. Furthermore, we are left to wonder whether the most consistently detected significant trends (such as lower sex ratios at high birth orders) are themselves adaptations or artifacts. Whichever way it turns out, we must consider how tendencies such as the birth-order effect are going to affect our interpretations.

TABLE 5.2. Inverse Relationship between Secondary Sex Ratio and Birth Order for White and Black Births from a Large Sample[a]

Birth order:	1	2	3	4	5	6	7	8	Not reported
White births	1,648,310	1,207,913	710,317	393,008	215,424	118,716	67,198	99,070	49,218
Sex ratio	1.064	1.058	1.057	1.052	1.050	1.042	1.044	1.038	1.064
Black births	296,767	188,652	116,218	74,016	49,148	32,735	22,679	49,510	10,544
Sex ratio	1.04	1.029	1.016	1.019	1.007	1.012	1.006	1.019	1.026

[a]Adapted from Erickson, 1976.

118

For example, Meikle *et al.* (1984) argue that high sex ratios among high-ranking macaques are an adaptation in line with the Trivers–Willard hypothesis. But if high-ranking lineages in expanding populations contain more young females (and the provisioned La Parguera population is expanding) how do we know that the slightly higher sex ratios among high-ranking lineages is not in part a birth-order effect—assuming such effects apply to monkeys as well as humans? We know almost nothing about the factors influencing sex ratios among nonhuman primates, far less than we do in the human case. Without such information, it is exceedingly risky to attribute high or low sex ratios to any single factor (like mother's rank).

Facultative Adjustment of the Sex Ratio and the Guerrero Model

Even if facultative adjustment of sex ratios does occur, we do not yet know what sort of mechanisms might be involved. As discussed earlier (p. 104) there is unlikely to be any widely spread genetic trait that predisposes its possessors to produce one sex or the other. Stern (1960:440) mentions two extraordinary examples of sex-biased family pedigrees, one English pedigree showing 35 births over 10 generations only 2 of which were female, and a second French kindred in which 72 births over 3 generations were exclusively female. Stern himself (personal communication to J. Lancaster) was uncertain of the mechanisms involved and given the extraordinary rarity of such sex-biased lineages was unwilling to rule out chance.

Other investigators have focused on more situation-dependent factors such as differential mobility of male and female sperm within the vagina (Clutton-Brock and Albon, 1982) or stress on the mother which leads to greater attrition among supposedly more vulnerable male zygotes (Meikle *et al.*, 1984). There is anecdotal evidence that paternal condition may affect the sex ratio of his offspring (e.g., men who fly high-performance aircraft are thought to disproportionately sire daughters [Snyder, 1961]; as are fathers with lean body build [Damon and Nuttall, 1965]), as well as two studies indicating that father's race may affect the sex ratio at birth (Morton *et al.*, 1967; Khoury *et al.*, 1984). However there are no theoretical grounds for expecting fathers to be implicated unless it can be shown that paternal condition affects subsequent reproductive success of sons and daughters. For example, Burley's studies of zebra finches indicate that sex ratio of offspring may be biased toward the sex of the parent that has been experimentally rendered more attractive to mates by the addition of more or less attractively colored leg bands (1981 and personal communication). If confirmed, these studies would provide us with one of the few documented instances where a paternal trait affects reproductive success of one sex of offspring more than the other. (Cases where paternal rank, territory, or wealth may be correlated with maternal condition as well as subsequent survival of young, as among humans, are discussed later.)

There are several reasons then why researchers have tended to focus on maternal rather than paternal condition (see Clutton-Brock and Albon, 1982; Charnov, 1982, and references therein). In fact, the only study specifically aimed at testing the possibility of facultative adjustment of sex ratios by fathers among rhesus macaques revealed no significant effect of paternal rank (Small and Smith, 1986).

Given the constraints, is it possible to design a system that would permit facultative determination of sex ratios by mothers? The answer is yes. As an example one could turn to models such as that proposed for humans by Guerrero (1974). Although far from conclusively proven, Guerrero's model seems promising, compatible not only with various human studies (reviewed in James, 1983b) but also with data from an array of mammals. In particular, the Guerrero model provides an example of a mechanism that would permit mothers to respond to current local conditions, altering sex ratios at conception by altering behavior.

Guerrero's orientation is primarily that of a medical and public health professional, and he focuses on human populations. He compiled data on 1318 pregnancies in the United States, France, Canada, and Mauritius for which time of insemination was known in relation to the shift in basal body temperature. (This slight elevation in temperature at the time that the ovum is released is a more reliable indicator of ovulation than is calendar date indicating the fourteenth day of the menstrual cycle.) Guerrero found that the proportion of male births rises significantly for conceptions that occurred on either side of the temperature shift: 9 to 6 days before the shift, .683 males were born; the proportion of males sinks as low as .435 right at the temperature shift (probable time of ovulation), and then rises again to .534 on the second and third days after the shift.

Essentially then, the Guerrero model predicts peaks in the production of males when insemination occurs either early or late in the fertile period, and a depression in the production of males (i.e., a peak in production of females) right at midcycle. Interestingly, Guerrero found almost exactly the opposite pattern for mothers who had been artificially inseminated. Since sperm in such cases would not encounter the same vaginal environment, one interpretation is that the presumed greater survival of Y-bearing sperm early and late in the fertile period is mediated by variations in vaginal and intracervical conditions.

Guerrero's findings have been substantiated in part by a recent study in Israel by Susan Harlap (1979; see also James, 1980).[3] Many Jewish women still follow Talmudic injunctions concerning a period of abstinence during menstruation and for 7 "clean days" following known as the "niddah." In the words of the Talmud, "when any daughter of Israel has a flow, even if it is a drop no larger than a mustard seed, she should upon the cessation of the flow count for herself seven days of cleanness . . . and must then immerse herself on the eighth day . . . thereafter she is permitted her husband" (cited in Guttentag and Secord, 1983:98). At the end of 7 clean days the woman takes a ritual bath ("Mikvah") followed by a resumption of intercourse with her husband. Harlap studied 3658 births born to Jewish mothers who practiced the niddah. She found a slight peak in the proportion of boys conceived 2 days prior to ovulation and a significant peak (65.5% boys) 2 days after ovulation.[4] Because of the period of abstinence, however, no data were collected for the earliest days of the fertile period when Guerrero found the highest proportion of boys conceived. It has been suggested that Guerrero's and Harlap's findings might be relevant to understanding the curiously high sex ratios (up to 146 males born per 100 females) known to characterize Orthodox Jewish populations in nineteenth-century Russia (Guttentag and Secord, 1983:98).

Given the range of variation documented by Guerrero and Harlap, it does seem possible for humans to vary the sex ratio by resorting to periods of ritualized abstinence, by concentrating copulations at particular times of the month, or in the case of preferential production of sons, simply by frequent intercourse that makes it likely that a woman will conceive earlier rather than later in the month. That is, high sex ratios do not necessarily mean a genetically determined tendency to produce sons; cultural practices (such as the "niddah") may explain biased sex ratios in a population.

Whether or not the Guerrero model could apply to experimental animals where the precise date of all matings is known is only beginning to be investigated (Small and Hrdy, 1986). However, there are several lines of evidence suggesting that there do exist mechanisms by which mothers could behaviorally influence sex ratio of their offspring. For

[3]As James and others have noted a model such as Guerrero's could explain why sex ratios tend to be higher under conditions when intercourse is particularly frequent (e.g., early in marriages; when soldiers return from war). This is a far more convincing explanation for the widely reported increases in sex ratios after wars (Bernstein, 1958) than a somewhat earlier explanation that the population was compensating for men killed in war.

[4]Day of ovulation was estimated from the characteristics of each woman's menstrual cycle.

example, a study of 850 rhesus fetuses produced from timed matings (i.e., the mother was permitted to mate for only 48 hours at midcycle) produced female-biased conceptions; prior to 149 days of gestation the sex ratio was 89 males per 100 females (Di Giacomo and Shaughnessy, 1979). This finding is just what the Guerrero model would predict, although it should be noted that near term, the sex ratio rose inexplicably to 106. Such a finding, which suggests greater female mortality *in utero,* is completely at odds with the usual notion that male fetuses are more vulnerable. Interpretation of this puzzle depends on what the sex ratio at conception normally is among macaques, and we simply do not know the answer. If one assumes (as do most human geneticists) that the sex ratio at conception is normally male-biased, the finding that circumscribed midcycle matings among rhesus monkeys yield female-biased primary sex ratios provides a striking confirmation of Guerreros' model. In fact though, we do not know—even for humans—that primary sex ratios are typically male-biased.

Primary sex ratio estimates as high as 170 males per 100 females are frequently cited in genetics text books (Stern, 1960), but close examination of the literature reveals extraordinarily variable results from researchers using a range of techniques to obtain estimates of the sex ratio at conception. Even in large samples of incompleted pregnancies, sex ratio estimates for the first trimester of pregnancy may fall anywhere between 60 and 232 (Mikamo, 1969; Lee and Takano, 1970; Kellokumpu-Lehtinen and Pelliniemi, 1984). The only sensible course at this stage is to leave open the possibility that primary sex ratios could be either equal or biased in favor of either males or females! There may also exist interpopulation or interspecific variation. In short, no conclusion about sex ratios at conception is warranted at this time.

In addition to the single case cited previously of a female-biased fetal sex ratio following timed mating among rhesus, another line of evidence that suggests that something like the Guerrero effect might also apply to other mammals comes from studies of mothers who bred early versus late during a restricted breeding season. Among Norway rats, red deer, and possibly cattle, limited evidence suggests that offspring conceived early in the cycle may be more likely to be male. Data for Norway rats suggests that females who mate early in the 24-hour estrous period tend to produce sons (Hedricks and McClintock, 1982), but it is not yet clear that these early breeders are in fact socially dominant animals, and further analyses are ongoing (personal communication from M. McClintock). Similarly, the tendency of red deer to produce more sons early in the season approached statistical significance (Clutton-Brock *et al.,* 1982:164). There are also limited data for cattle that showed that calves conceived in the first 2 weeks of a 12-week breeding period contained 85 males and 59 females (a sex ratio of 144);

in weeks 3 and 4, there were 93 males and 80 females (116). Thereafter, there were slightly more females than males born (sex ratios were between 92 and 96) (Wells, 1980:Table 1).

BIASING INVESTMENT AFTER BIRTH

The Trivers–Willard need not apply only to parental manipulation of sex ratios at conception or *in utero*. Broadly interpreted, the model also applies to parental investment after birth. Evidence is accumulating for many species of mammals that sons and daughters are treated differently in early life. Such evidence tends to be much stronger than the scattered and often controversial evidence suggesting that parents bias investment prior to birth by producing different numbers of male and female offspring. Some of the evidence for biased investment in humans was discussed in the Introduction; the next section, focuses primarily on the animal evidence before returning, in the last section, to case studies that specifically seek to apply the Trivers–Willard hypothesis to human populations.

Differential Treatment of Sons and Daughters

Among wild primates, both mothers and other group members exhibit an intense interest in inspecting and smelling the genitals of newborn infants (Figure 5.1), and there is a growing body of quantitative data indicating that males weigh more at birth (e.g., Rasmussen, Ausman, and Hayes, 1980, for squirrel monkeys, Small and Smith, 1986, for rhesus) as well as anecdotal information suggesting other forms of contact between mother and offspring are patterned differently according to sex (e.g., Fairbanks and McGuire, 1985, for vervets; Berman, 1984, for macaques). For most of these species, however, we do not know exactly how mothers are discriminating between sons and daughters, even when observers are fairly confident that they are doing so.

Studies of laboratory rats provide a particularly detailed picture of the mechanisms of maternal discrimination in this species. Moore and Morelli (1979) found that Norway rat mothers licked male pups more than female pups. However, this effect could be obliterated through the application of a plastic coating of collodion on the anogenital area of pups. Dabs of perfume also interfered with sex discrimination (Moore, 1981). These results suggest that olfaction is involved in maternal discrimination between male and female pups, and it also seems likely that hormones in the urine are primary cues. Hence Moore found that if the anogenital region of a female pup is coated with the urine of a male pup (Moore, 1981) or if a female pup is injected with testos-

FIGURE 5.1. A langur mother with different-sexed twins aggressively rejects
her daughter while permitting her son to continue suckling; the
daughter complains accordingly.

terone neonatally (Moore, 1982), mothers will provide the treated
daughter with the same amount of licking as she would a male pup.
Even more important, it is increasingly clear that the amount of anogenital licking a pup receives does have long-term consequences. Licking not only facilitates urination and defecation of the pup, but also
appears to affect subsequent reproductive performance. Male offspring
born to mothers whose ability to smell them was experimentally blocked
received less licking as pups, and subsequently, as adults, displayed
longer latencies to ejaculation than did offspring of control mothers
(Moore, 1984). However, exactly what (if anything) such data mean in
any adaptive sense remains unclear.

Turning to studies of free-ranging animals, a number of cases of
biased parental investment are now documented, and several of these
can be plausibly explained in terms of the Trivers–Willard hypothesis
(Clutton-Brock and Albon, 1982). Among the highly polygynous elephant seals that breed off the California Coast, male pups are heavier

at birth (with a mean weight of 44.8 kg at birth compared to 35.2 for daughters; Reiter, Panken, and Le Boeuf, 1981) and were permitted by their mothers to nurse 1 full day longer on average than are daughters (27.8 versus 26.6 days) (Reiter, Stinson, and Le Boeuf, 1978). Given that elephant seal infants suckle infrequently and that the milk is tremendously rich, even 1 extra day would be biologically very significant. (See also Figure 5.1 for a primate example.) These data then are consistent with the Trivers–Willard hypothesis, but we have no data on the reproductive success of such "privileged" males relative to males not so well fed which would permit us to exclude various competing hypotheses. For example, mothers might be compensating for the oft cited "greater vulnerability of males" by gestating them longer. Similarly, the greater access to milk enjoyed by male pups might be an artifact of their greater size at birth, or else a by-product of more aggressive or persistent temperaments. Data showing that sons were more successful than daughters at converting mother's milk into subsequent reproductive success would be necessary in order to demonstrate convincingly that the bias in favor of males was an adaptive strategy on the part of mothers.

Clutton-Brock *et al.* (1984) suggest that we already have such data in the case of the similarly polygynous red deer (but see also Clutton-Brock *et al.*, 1985 for a caution!). As among the elephant seals, male fawns weigh more at birth, and grow faster. Young males suckle from their mothers significantly more often than do daughters. This additional investment in sons is evidently costly to the mother since hinds who have given birth to males calve later the following year than do those hinds who gave birth to daughters (Clutton-Brock *et al.*, 1984).

Whereas in the foregoing cases mothers apparently "favored" their sons, in the third case, involving eastern wood rats, mothers stressed by reduction of food (i.e., in the parlance of Trivers and Willard, mothers in "poor condition") actively discriminated against sons by ignoring them or physically rejecting them, while retrieving daughters and permitting daughters to nurse (McClure, 1981). Such reduced investment produced "higher nestling mortality and reduced growth in male nestlings" so that by day 20 after birth the surviving males in the food-restricted group had significantly smaller body mass than their female littermates and were much smaller than sons whose mothers received normal amounts of food (McClure, 1981:1059). In contrast to the food-restricted groups where more daughters than sons survived, in the control groups mothers (who were presumed to be in good condition) produced and reared equal numbers of sons and daughters. McClure interpreted her results as an adaptation by wood rats to fluctuating resources which was broadly in accord with the Trivers–Willard hypothesis.

Data for several species of monkeys are more difficult to interpret for "the advantaged daughter hypothesis," although many of them are quite compatible with the idea that in species with matrilineal inheritance of rank, high-ranking mothers invest preferentially in daughters. As discussed earlier, these findings conform to predictions of the Trivers–Willard hypothesis provided that maternal condition is more important for the reproductive success of daughters than it is for sons.

In a recent review of the evidence for captive colonies of *Macaca mulatta*, *M. fascicularis*, and *M. nemestrina*, Carol Berman (1984) notes that in most of these studies male infants are rejected sooner than female infants and spend more time off the mother by about 3 months of age (see also Figure 5.2). However some laboratories have reported results in exactly the opposite direction for these same species. Such contradictions may be due to differences in the social environments at the different colonies or to small sample sizes. Berman's own, unusually rigorous data for free-ranging rhesus macaques *(M. mulatta)* on Cayo Santiago revealed that among the mothers belonging to high-ranking lineages the amount of contact between mothers and their daughters was significantly greater than between mothers and sons, but that there was no significant difference in the treatment of sons and daughters among low-ranking mothers (1984:Table 1). Furthermore, Berman notes: "Mothers of females in the whole sample initiated significantly larger proportions of the nipple contacts with their infants than did mothers of males (Table IV). Although differences in other measures were not significant, pairs with male infants tended to spend less time on the ventrum, their mothers tended to reject them more, and the infants tended to play larger roles in maintaining proximity with them. To this limited extent, mothers of males could be described as more rejecting and more encouraging of independence than mothers of females. No trends related to infant's age were found" (1984:pp. 26–27). Fairbanks and McGuire (1985) report a similar trend toward greater proximity for mothers and daughters among colony-dwelling vervet monkeys *(Cercopithecus aethiops)*. Mothers approached daughters more than sons and groomed daughters more. Similarly, female juveniles approached their mothers more, groomed them more, and supported their mothers more during agonistic encounters than did sons.

The only comparably quantitative mother–infant studies among wild primates, those for baboons at Amboseli and Gilgil (Altmann, 1980; Nicolson, 1982), failed to reveal any significant differences in the treatment of sons and daughters, although Nicolson reported that mothers discouraged sons from riding on their backs sooner than they rejected daughters. However in a demographic study of the toque macaques *(Macaca sinica)* Wolfgang Dittus reported that high-ranking mothers produced far more daughters than sons that survived to reproduce. Of the surviving offspring born to 15 high-ranking mothers, 15 were daughters, 4 were sons. By contrast, 14 low-ranking mothers produced

FIGURE 5.2. A multiparous allomother holds a newborn langur infant upside-
down by its tail in order to inspect its genitals.

4 surviving daughters and no sons (Dittus 1979:Table 5). One could
interpret such findings to mean that there exists a widely spread tendency among macaques and other cercopithecine monkeys (characterized by both sedentary females and migrating males and by matrilineal inheritance of rank) for mothers, perhaps especially high-ranking

mothers, to maintain close contact with their daughters and to protect daughters more than sons.

Interestingly, these observations parallel in some respects findings from studies of abusive "motherless" mothers (usually rhesus macaques). Such mothers are apparently more harshly rejecting of male than female offspring, especially firstborn male offspring. Among rhesus monkeys, sons born to mothers who had been reared in the absence of their own mothers were four times as likely to be abused as were the daughters of such mothers (Ruppenthal, Arling, Harlow, Sackett, and Suomi, 1976; discussed further in Suomi and Ripp, 1983). However, the utterly unnatural conditions of rearing mothers used in such studies and the fact that under natural conditions a motherless mother could never exist, makes the apparent parallel difficult to interpret. It is worth noting however that as in the Ruppenthal *et al.* study of "motherless" mothers, recent studies of captive rhesus using normal (mother-reared) mothers also found that firstborn sons were peculiarly vulnerable (Simpson and Simpson, 1985). In the "motherless mother" study, primiparae cared for only 3 of 24 male babies compared to 7 of 18 female offspring (Ruppenthal *et al.*, 1976:344). The mortality figures for mother-reared mothers suggest a similar pattern: 4 of 16 male and 1 of 18 female neonates born to primiparae died (Simpson and Simpson, 1985:84).

Under natural conditions a female infant without another female to nurture her could not possibly survive, much less be the object of selection pressures. Hence any "adaptive" behaviors at issue in the "motherless mother" studies would have to be vestiges from selection pressures that once operated on ancestors living under quite different conditions. Furthermore, in the wild, it is exceedingly uncommon to witness a monkey or ape mother attack her own offspring even though she rather commonly may deal harshly with some other female's infant (Hrdy, 1977; Silk, Clark-Wheatley, Rodman, and Samuels, 1981; Fossey, 1984; Goodall, 1986) or abandon or neglect her own. (For an exceptional case of a wildborn, subsequently captive, Japanese macaque mother who lethally abuses her own offspring with direct attacks on them, see Troisi, D'Amato, Fuccillo, and Scucchi, 1982.)

"Difficult Males," "Vulnerable Males," and "Parental Manipulation": Alternative Hypotheses or Confounding Variables?

Infant male macaques appear to be at greater risk from maternal rejection than are daughters. Under some conditions sons may also be more likely than daughters to be abused or neglected by the mother. Similar findings have been reported for humans in studies reporting that little boys are at slightly greater risk from abuse than are little girls. For example, in a summary of findings on child abuse from five separate American populations, the incidence of abuse was highest for young male children born to poor families (Lenington, 1981:17). At present it is impossible to know if these various strands of evidence are related. However, assuming for the momentary purpose of this discussion that they are related, how can we explain an apparent pattern?

Young males are often described as more active, more difficult to pacify, more abrasive, and more aggressive than young females. Hence they are "more difficult." Males are sometimes described as having higher metabolic rates, growing faster, and needing to suckle more. That is they are more "costly." The "difficult male hypothesis," then, provides a widely cited rationale for the disproportionate ill-treatment of male infants (e.g., "It is well known that, in macaques at least, male infants in mother–infant dyads are more active. They also pester the mother, even bite her more . . ." cited in Schapiro and Mitchell, 1983:43). Because the female infant stays closer and is "calmer" she may be less likely to elicit punishment (e.g., in the unusual case of the abusive wildborn Japanese macaque mother "Okame" studied at the Rome zoo, Okame's infants of both sexes attempted to move away from her which precipitated her savage attacks; see Troisi et al., 1982). Does a mother macaque who invests differentially in daughters do so because daughters will ultimately be more likely to translate maternal investment into reproductive success or simply because on a day to day (proximate) level daughters are less irritating?[5] The "difficult" temperament and greater wanderlust of males has sometimes been attributed to some of the same physiological causes (such as high metabolic rates) as the hypothesis that males are more "vulnerable" than females. The greater aggressiveness of males and the fact that they grow faster and bigger than females—particularly in polygynous species where males will compete for females—are also attributed to the same ultimate evolutionary causes (e.g., Clutton-Brock et al., 1985).

Recently scientists trying to explain greater male mortality among the offspring of mothers in poor condition have used "the vulnerable

[5]Assuming that the "difficult male" hypothesis is actually an alternative hypothesis mutually exclusive with the Trivers–Willard hypothesis, species differences among the primates might allow a way to test different predictions of the two hypotheses. On the basis of what we know about chimpanzee breeding systems, daughters migrate away from their birthplace while males remain in the same area with their mothers and brothers. Male–male alliances among brothers are critical not only for attaining an advantageous dominance status but also for reproductive success (Nishida, 1983). Furthermore, in the case of particularly powerful male alliances one band of males may sometimes eliminate another (Goodall, 1986). According to the Trivers–Willard hypothesis, then, mothers in good conditions should be biasing investment toward sons in this sort of breeding system. Hence the finding that chimpanzee mothers, like macaque mothers, were also more rejecting of sons would be strong support for the "difficult male" hypothesis. Results in the opposite direction (i.e., if unlike macaques, chimp mothers were more solicitous of sons than daughters) would support the hypothesis that chimp mothers were biasing maternal investment in line with expected returns in reproductive success.

male" hypothesis as if it were a mutually exclusive alternative to the Trivers–Willard hypothesis (Clutton-Brock *et al.*, 1985; Labov, Huck, Vaswani, and Lisk, in press). In 1985, Clutton-Brock *et al.* argued that if reduced viability of males in suboptimal conditions is due to the greater requirements of faster growing males rather than to parental manipulation (i.e., Trivers–Willard) then (1) sex differences in mortality should not be confined to the early stages of parental investment and should be expected throughout the period when males grew faster or larger than females; (2) sex differences in mortality should not be associated with reduction in parental investment in juveniles of one sex; and (3) mortality differences should persist even if offspring are reared apart from their parents. Since all three of these predictions were confirmed for a sample of red deer, Clutton-Brock *et al.* favored the greater male needs hypothesis over the "competing" parental manipulation (Trivers–Willard) hypothesis. However, in a related study using golden hamsters Labov *et al.* (in press) arrive at the opposite conclusion, dismissing the greater-needs hypothesis in favor of Trivers–Willard.

In their study, Labov *et al.* subjected pregnant female hamsters to three different experimental treatments: females were malnourished during both pregnancy and lactation, malnourished during lactation only, or else, in their control group, fed ad libitum throughout both pregnancy and lactation. As mentioned earlier, the sex ratios of the litters born to females malnourished during pregnancy were significantly lower than for other mothers—a finding compatible with either hypothesis. However the differentially greater mortality of males was only apparent during the periods when mothers were still investing in offspring. After weaning, male hamsters, regardless of nutritional status, survived or died at the same rate as females. Labov *et al.* interpreted these findings as support for Trivers and Willard's hypothesis that parental manipulation rather than greater male vulnerability was at issue.

Each of these authors is assuming here that Trivers–Willard and "male vulnerability" are alternative competing hypotheses to explain the same phenomena. It needs to be kept in mind, however, that this approach might be overly simple. It could be that we are dealing with outcomes of independent factors. That is, greater male vulnerability could be a physiological "given" or constraint. Parents biasing investment toward male or female offspring either compensate for or aggravate the greater tendency of males to die. Looked at from this perspective the finding that the male offspring of low-ranking cercopithecine female monkeys are more likely to survive than are daughters of similarly low-ranking females is even more remarkable. Assume for a moment that the "dominant females favor daughters" pattern reported by Altmann, Silk, and the Simpsons (discussed earlier) is characteristic for cercopithecine monkeys under some conditions. High-ranking mothers bias investment toward daughters, low-ranking mothers toward sons in line with greater "anticipated" reproductive gains from this allocation of maternal investment. The fact that the sons of low-ranking, stressed females have higher survival rates than daughters does suggest that selection pressures for biased investment in sons by stressed mothers (Altmann, Altmann, and Hausfater, in press) have been so strong that the results more than compensate for greater male vulnerability in cercopithecine monkeys (e.g., Small and Smith, 1986). Similarly variables other than anticipated reproductive gains could override greater male mortality, so that in some rural societies (e.g., nineteenth-century Sweden) girls die at higher rates than boys because female labor is little valued and parents divert food and other resources toward sons, rendering daughters more vulnerable to disease (Johansson, 1984). That is, the situation here might well demonstrate the sort of interactional complexity Stephen Gould had in mind in writing about the need for "hierarchical models" for explaining natural phenomena. Gould stresses that "selection works simultaneously and differently upon individuals at a variety of levels" so that "negative interaction between levels might be an important principle in maintaining stability or holding rates of change within reasonable bounds" (Gould, 1982).

Trivers–Willard and Biased Investment after Birth among Humans

It can be argued that the importance of culture and history and the rapidity with which changes in marriage and inheritance systems can occur make prenatal determination of offspring sex impractical in the human case. For example, a family might shift from paternally to maternally inherited status in a matter of a few generations. A mother who invested preferentially in offspring of one sex or the other on the basis of her biological "condition" such as good nutrition and low stress would be wrong as often as she was right (Hrdy and Coleman, 1982). Under such circumstances we might expect the Trivers–Willard hypothesis to be most applicable to investment after birth where human parents can make the decision on the basis of current conditions, and indeed, this is what we find. Whereas there is little evidence for sex bias at conception (see earlier) there is a great deal of evidence that parents discriminate against one sex or the other in terms of provisioning, medical attention, legacies, and simply time spent in association, and where these biases have been examined with the Trivers–Willard hypothesis in mind, they often appear to conform to specific predictions from the hypothesis (discussed later).

However inefficient, infanticide or reduced investment after birth would appear to be more advantageous than the less flexible system of biasing investment at conception. Hence, despite a widespread preference for sons in many cultures, particularly in polygynous and patrilineal societies (Barry, Josephson, Lauer, and Marshall, 1973; Ayres, n.d.), human secondary sex ratios tend to be quite conservative, with only a slight male bias. (Obviously the recent possibility of determining sex before birth through amniocentesis or through analysis involving chorionic biopsy, combined with the ability to perform safe abortions, alters this picture for the future.)

There already exists a large literature on parental sex preferences, but it is unusual for data on this topic to be broken down by parental condition or socioeconomic status. One study that does present information in this way reveals a trend opposite to that predicted by the Trivers–Willard hypothesis (Coombs, 1977). In the Coombs survey of American mothers, poor mothers exhibited stronger son preference than mothers in wealthier families with incomes greater than $15,000 per year. Nevertheless, despite such reported preferences, one recent study of actual legacies—how much investment the parent left after death to sons versus daughters—revealed that even though poorer families may say they prefer sons, they may actually invest more in daughters.

In an innovative recent study by Smith, Kish, and Crawford (1984), researchers reviewed 1000 wills probated in Vancouver, Canada. If the estate were larger than $110,850 the greatest proportion was left to sons; if less than $20,350, the greatest proportion to daughters. These results were highly significant ($p<.01$) and in the direction predicted by Trivers–Willard. Nevertheless, as stressed by Smith et al., it should be kept in mind that the findings from this single study still remain to be replicated. More attention also needs to be directed at alternative explanations (e.g., perhaps those with legacies less than $20,000 are leaving primarily household possessions to daughters). Additional data on family composition (e.g., were there sons around in poor families to inherit?) as well as interview data to establish the ethnographic context are going to be essential to interpret Smith et al.'s findings.

Similarly, Betzig and Turke (1985) have also investigated predictions of the Trivers–Willard hypothesis among the inhabitants of Ifaluk Atoll in the Western Caroline Islands of the Pacific. Based on scan samples of human activity on Ifaluk, Betzig and Turke found that there was a strong bias in the frequency of parent–child interaction according to the status of the parent. Fathers of high status (i.e., traditional chiefs and cash-earners) spent a significantly higher proportion of observed parent–child interactions with their sons than did low-status fathers, and the same trend could be detected among the wives of high-status males who also spent more time with sons than daughters. The reverse was true for the low-status parents (Betzig and Turke, 1985). As in the Smith et al. study, however, we need much more information concerning the relationship between parental investment (if, indeed, time spent with the child can be considered investment) and subsequent reproductive performance of sons and daughters.

In all such studies, great caution is needed in interpreting differences in the time that parents spend interacting with same-sex offspring. From the relatively primitive little South American marmoset (Hoage, 1978:299–300) to higher primates such as humans, fathers are reported to spend more time with sons than daughters, to watch them more, feed and diaper them more frequently, and so forth (reviewed in Lamb, 1984:418–420). Hence (as with almost all the tests of the Trivers–Willard hypothesis) the more interesting side of the equation is documenting greater paternal interest in daughters among families in relatively "poor" reproductive condition. It is far more surprising and noteworthy when fathers can be shown to invest more in their daughters than they do in their sons.

By far the most convincing applications to date of the Trivers–Willard hypothesis to human societies are the three studies by (1) Dickemann (1979a) dealing primarily with female-preferential infanticide among a variety of high- and middle-caste groups in precolonial Northern India (including Brahmins, Jareja Rajputs, Khatris, Jats, Gujars, Ahirs, Sikhs, and Muslims); (2) Voland (1984) for eighteenth-century German peasants; and (3) Boone (1984; 1986) for medieval Portugal. In this last case, as in Clutton-Brock's red deer, the data actually permit us to compare the outcomes of biased investment in terms of the relatively greater reproductive success of high-status sons versus daughters. Available data also suggest that lower status daughters leave more offspring than of comparable low status.

For the North Indian case, Dickemann argues convincingly that female infanticide leading to sex ratios as high as 400 or more males per 100 females were common in the highest caste (read "good condition") groups while the killing of daughters was relatively uncommon or absent in the lower caste groups from which the high-caste groups took wives (see also Miller, 1981). Underlying female infanticide in this form, Dickemann sees a stratified, hypergynous (i.e., women marry up) society in which successful, high-ranking males are typically polygynous (apparently more true prior to the nineteenth century than it is today). At the lower level, families vie among themselves to place their daughters in high-ranking families by paying large dowries. At the upper level, daughters have few marriage options and become a liability so that it was apparently widely believed that "the father who preserves a daughter will never live to see her suitably married, or that the family into which she does marry, will perish and be ruined" (from an early British interview with a landholder from Uttar Pradesh, cited in Miller, 1981:49).

Dickemann takes as given the assumption that high status improves the reproductive success of both men and the women that they marry. Although quantitative data are hard to come by, she points to the relationship through history between possession of property and survival of family lines (1979b). She also notes the extreme vulnerability of the dispossessed, particularly during times of famine (cf. also Hufton, 1974; Greenough, 1982). For this reason, the focus on stratified societies is critical for it allows Dickemann to assume that a properly hypergynous marriage benefits not only the bride herself but her entire family. Her family can look forward to grandsons born into a world of improved opportunities. Large dowries can be understood as the price paid for these high-status grandsons whose prospects include good health, longevity, multiple wives or concubines, and crucially, many sons of their own. Along the way, granddaughters are sacrificed to maintain that status that benefits the lineage as a whole. This pattern conforms to predictions of the Trivers–Willard hypothesis far more closely than it does to predictions of the main competing hypothesis to explain female infanticide in North India which argues that women are devalued in North India because of their relatively low contribution to subsistence combined with the high dowry costs (Miller, 1981). In particular the "contribution to subsistence" idea does not explain why infanticide should be more marked in higher than in lower castes, since if anything the female labor argument should weigh heaviest on the classes actually doing labor. At present then, the Trivers–Willard hypothesis as applied by Dickemann remains the single most powerful explanation for the differential investment in sons in such stratified societies as feudal North India, imperial China, and medieval Europe, where many noble women were cloistered in convents to avoid marriage costs rather than killed at birth. (Note that the perpetual alternative, parental compensation for "greater male vulnerability" appears very implausible here in the face of sex ratios as high as 400:1.)

Quantitative demographic support for Dickemann's model have been gleaned from the *Peditura lusitana,* a seventeenth-century manuscript containing extraordinarily complete genealogies for medieval and early modern Portuguese families from which Boone (1984; 1986) has compiled a computerized registry of some 3700 individuals. The population consists of male and female patrilineal descendants of the top 25 lineages in Portugal who were born in the two centuries between 1380 and 1580. There are two limitations to this otherwise remarkably complete data set. First, a considerable number of women married outside of Portugal (typically into the Castillian, Burgundian, or Austrian courts) and were lost from this data set; hence, reproductive performance is recorded for only 32% of all women who married. Second, and typically, there are no written records for the poorest classes.

Based on the genealogies, Boone is able to show a clear correlation between male status and reproductive success. Whereas ever-married men in the primary nobility at the top of the hierarchy (including the royal family, dukes, counts, as well as the families of those holding the highest military positions) left on average 4.75 legitimate surviving offspring, ever-married men of the untitled or military classes at the bottom of the elite ranks (mostly cavaleiros who spent their lives warring overseas and some pensioned members of religious and military orders) left an average of 2.33 surviving recorded offspring—roughly one-half as many. Female reproductive success also increases with rank, but the range of increase is much smaller than among the males so, for example, a woman who married into the top class would leave on average 3.78 offspring compared to 3.32 offspring among women in the lowest class record. Many of these mothers had actually been born into some lower class and married up. A substantial proportion of women, mostly from the highest class (between 10 and 40% depending on time period), entered convents. Indeed, when Boone examined the proportion of men and women who married, he found that daughters from the lower, untitled classes were far more likely to marry than daughters of the primary nobility. Most importantly, the reproductive success of women from the lowest-status families was higher than that of same-status males, whereas in the highest class the opposite was true.

A pattern similar to that for Portugal can also be found in the breeding patterns of German peasants as revealed in parish records for the period between 1720 and 1869, but the focus is on the marriage potential of sons and daughters rather than on the greater variance in male reproductive success among sons born at high ranks (Voland, 1984). In any event, Voland (drawing on data collected and analyzed by Rolf Gehrmann) describes a society in which land-owning farmers have the highest status, farm laborers the lowest. Nevertheless, the land-owning class provided the only social circumstances in which girls were at higher risk of dying (a likelihood of 13.6%) than boys (12.6%) (Voland, 1984:102). By contrast, infants born to the laboring class, at the bottom of the social scale, suffered higher mortality if they were male (20.8%) and lower (14.6%) if female. (Voland's sample contained over 3000 infants, including infants born to small landholders and tradespeople. For brevity, I only discuss the extreme ends of the spectrum here, that is, large landholders and laborers, but the general trends are the same with the preference for daughters inversely correlated with status.) A reversal in male and female vulnerability as one moves from the highest to the lowest classes argues against any inherent vulnerability being responsible for the sex differences in mortality in the first 27 days after birth; males are indeed more vulnerable in both high and low classes. The most marked mortality difference between classes, in fact, is apparent between 27 and 180 days of life, in line with Voland's suggestion that parental neglect of one sex or the other is responsible for the differential mortality in high and low classes.

The Trivers–Willard hypothesis is a new one to the field of historical demography, and the human applications of this model have only recently begun to be considered (Alexander, 1974). Much of the progress in this area can be attributed to Dickemann's pioneering reformulation of the original Trivers–Willard hypothesis (1979). Hence, alternative explanations for the patterns that higher ranks or castes might prefer sons, lower ranks daughters, have scarcely been considered. Voland, for example, does not discuss possible differences in the labor potential of sons versus daughters, though in fact such a consideration would strengthen his case since at first glance one would expect rural laboring classes to prefer sons for work in the fields (see also Johannson, chapter 4, this volume). Instead, Voland focuses almost exclusively on the marriage potential of sons versus daughters among land-owning and laboring groups. In the highest ranking, land-holding class, only 34.4% of daughters manage to marry at the same rank as themselves (marrying up was, of course, not an option). The other daughters either did not marry or married beneath their social rank. Those daughters that married down did nevertheless reproduce, but at a lower rate characterized by longer birth intervals and higher infant mortality than would have been the case had they married at their own level (Voland, 1984:105). Nevertheless, the absence of data on the reproductive success of sons versus daughters in these different cases makes the German case less conclusive than that for medieval Portugal.

The outstanding question of course is whether parents are facultatively responding to good versus poor socioecological conditions at the time their children are born in some way that is ultimately determined by biology (e.g., Dickemann, 1979) or whether the similarity in the patterning of parental investment exhibited by some animal and human parents is actually due to conscious calculation by the human parents who long ago mastered the logic underlying the Trivers–Willard hypothesis. In the one case natural selection is envisioned to have produced a facultative biological response, in the other, humans consciously calculate the costs and benefits of sons and daughters in line with culturally constructed ideals of family honor and lineage survival.

On one point, however, there can be little doubt: Human minds are superbly equipped to devise subtle "strategies of heirship" (Bourdieu, 1976; Goody, 1976, 1983). However, I believe Dickemann would argue that this capacity is itself a naturally selected adaptation. At this arcane level of discussion "Trivers–Willard" becomes a code word for differential investment in sons and daughters that serves reproductive ends, but consideration of the issue of "adaptation" is postponed. Instead "Trivers–Willard" is removed from the realm of genes and evolution and is transformed into a logical proposition: In stratified partrilineal societies, elite parents bent on perpetuating a socially defined lineage do better by channeling investment into sons, often one, particular, older son. Poorer families enhance lineage survival and may even contribute to improved conditions for selected members of the lineage by investing in the daughters. Issues raised here about what, if anything, is adaptive in an evolutionary sense will not soon be resolved.

Gaps in the relevant data and many difficulties in analysis remain. Too little is known about the attitudes and values of the protagonists in these dramas, the parents who for whatever reasons either murdered their offspring outright (as in the North Indian case) or else promoted the survival of infants of one sex more diligently than they did offspring of the other sex (the German case). Nevertheless, the peculiar patterning of preferences for sons versus daughters found in precolonial North India, medieval Portugal, in one population of eighteenth-century German peasants, and possibly in a contemporary North American case as well is presently predicted by no model other than the Trivers–Willard hypothesis in its most general form. This, of course, does not make the model right. But in the world of historical demography, and indeed, in the social sciences generally, there have been so very few general theoretical models with predictive powers that this state of affairs is sufficiently strong to merit the scrutiny of psychologists, sociologists, and historians as well as those biologists and anthropologists who are already intrigued by an evolutionary hypothesis that is at once so logically coherent and so difficult to prove.

SUMMARY

Whereas a handful of evolutionary biologists treat the Trivers–Willard hypothesis as a proven theory, most social scientists have never heard of it at all. In between are the many researchers who are familiar with the theory, but perplexed by the poor quality of the data cited in support of the hypothesis and by the tremendous amount of contradictory data that also exist. A number of recent studies fail to confirm predictions of the Trivers–Willard hypothesis. More often, specific predictions of the hypothesis have been confirmed, but gaps in the data leave critical assumptions for the model untested. In particular, it has been difficult to prove that biased investment by parents actually affects the subsequent reproductive careers of male versus female offspring.

According to a broad interpretation of the hypothesis, natural selection should favor parental ability to adjust investment in male and female offspring in line with anticipated returns from the reproductive success of sons versus daughters. More specifically, Trivers and Willard proposed that where parents are in good condition, and where parental condition affects subsequent competitive ability of offspring, sons should typically be favored when the variance in the reproductive success of males exceeds that of females, as it would in polygynous societies or in monogamous societies where a substantial number of males never breed and others marry sequentially more than once. Where parents are in poor condition, daughters should be favored if daughters in poor condition do better on average than sons in poor condition. So far, only two studies, one of red deer and one involving medieval Portuguese genealogies, have actually been able to demonstrate that greater investment by high-status parents in sons is correlated with greater relative reproductive success for sons compared to that expected for daughters. Exceptions to this general pattern of son preference by parents in good condition may be expected in societies where rank is inherited matrilineally, and where mother's rank influences the reproductive success of daughters more than it affects the reproductive success of sons, as may be the case among cercopithecine monkeys. Under these circumstances, high-ranking mothers would be expected to invest differentially in daughters rather than sons. Whether or not high-ranking cercopithecine mothers overproduce daughters remains controversial, though it seems increasingly clear that mothers do spend more time in close association with daughters after birth. Documentation of daughter-preference is a particularly critical area of enquiry because, unlike son-preference, it cannot be explained as compensation for the supposed "greater vulnerability" of males, one of the main hypotheses competing to explain underproduction of sons by mothers in poor condition.

Although Trivers and Willard initially focused primarily on the ability to bias the sex ratio at conception, a far more common pattern—especially in humans—appears to be the biasing of investment after birth. In fact, the correlation between high socioeconomic status and high secondary sex ratios initially presumed to exist by Trivers and Willard is now in some doubt, even though we have good reason to suppose that such facultative adjustment of sex ratios at conception might actually be mechanically feasible for human and other mammalian mothers. At the same time, there is growing support for the observation that human parents invest differentially in sons versus daughters after birth, and at least some of this differential investment is precisely in line with predictions of the Trivers–Willard hypothesis. A variety of data concerned with many aspects of human existence in stratified societies (sex-preferential infanticide, cloistering of women in convents, time spent with children, legacies, and inheritance of lands and titles) conform in general outline to predictions derived from the Trivers–Willard hypothesis. Whether such convergence is due to a biologically based facultative response to socioenvironmental conditions or to conscious calculations by parents is a question that has never been explored.

ACKNOWLEDGMENTS

This review would not have been possible without the generous assistance of many people. In particular I thank Jeanne Altmann, Barbara Ayres, Steve Bartz, Laura Betzig, James Boone, Nancy Burley, Tim Clutton-Brock, Steven Christopher, Morris Gosling, John Hartung, Bill Huck, Jay Labov, Doug Meikle, Celia Moore, Martha McClintock, Joan Silk, Meredith Small, David Glenn Smith, Martin Smith, Bob Trivers, and John Whiting for discussion and for providing references, unpublished information, or manuscripts that were in press. Discussions with Paul Bugos, Emily Coleman, Carol Ember, Sarah Pomeroy, Paul Secord, George Sussman, Richard Trexler, and George Williams in connection with earlier projects provided me with material on sex-preferential infanticide (or the absence thereof), which has been very useful in my interpretations of the cross-cultural and historical literature, and I remain grateful to them. I thank also the staffs of the Museum of Comparative Zoology, Countway and Tozzer libraries, Yongmi Han, and Nancy McLaughlin for assistance. Steve Bartz, William Bennett, Martin Daly, Mildred Dickemann, Daniel Hrdy, Jim Moore, David Olmsted, and Margo Wilson criticized portions of the manuscript and made many valuable suggestions. Finally, I thank Jane Lancaster for encouraging me to write this chapter. My work on this subject has benefitted also by support from the Wenner–Gren Foundation and the Rockefeller Foundation Gender-Roles Program.

References

Alexander, R. D. The evolution of social behavior. *Annual Review of Ecology and Systematics*, 1974, 5:325–383.

Altmann, Jeanne. *Baboon mothers and infants*. Cambridge, MA: Harvard University Press, 1980.

Altmann, Jeanne, Altmann, S., and Hausfater, G. Determinants of reproductive success in savannah baboons *(Papio cynocephalus)*. *In* T. Clutton-Brock, Ed., *Reproductive success*. Chicago, IL: Chicago University Press, in press.

Ayeni, O. Sex ratio of live births in south-western Nigeria. *Annals of Human Biology*, 1975, 2:137–141.

Ayres, Barbara. Unpublished data, n.d.

Balikci, A. Female infanticide on the Arctic coast. *Man*, 1967, 2:615–625.

Barry, H., III, Josephson, L., Lauer, E., and Marshall, C. Agents and techniques for child training: Cross-cultural codes 6. *Ethnology*, 1977, 16(2):191–230.

Berman, Carol. Variation in mother–infant relationships: Traditional and nontraditional factors. *In* M. Small, Ed., *Female primates*. NY: Alan Liss, 1984.

Berman, Carol, and Rawlins, Richard G. Maternal dominance, sex ratio and fecundity in one social group on Cayo Santiago, 1974–1984. Paper presented to the American Society of Primatologists Annual Meeting, Niagra Falls, 1985.

Bernstein, Marianne. Studies in the human sex ratio: 5. A genetic explanation of the wartime increase in the secondary sex ratio. *American Journal of Human Genetics*, 1958, 10:68–70.

Betzig, L. L., and Turke, P. W. Parental investment by sex on Ifaluk. Paper presented to the symposium on Evolution and Human Behavior, University of Michigan, Ann Arbor, 1985.

Blacklow, N. R., and Cukor, G. Viral gastroenteritis. *New England Journal of Medicine*, 1981, 304:397–406.

Boone, James. The demographic structure of pre-industrial states. Paper presented to the 83rd Meeting of the American Anthropological Association, Denver, 1984.

Boone, James. Parental investment and elite family structure in preindustrial states: A case study of late medieval-early modern Portuguese genealogies. *American Anthropologist,* 1986, in press.

Bourdieu, Pierre. Marriage strategies as strategies of social reproduction. *In* R. Foster and O. Ranum, Eds., *Family and society.* Baltimore, MD: Johns Hopkins University Press, 1976.

Bugos, Paul, and McCarthy, Lorraine M. Ayoreo infanticide: A case study. *In* G. Hausfater and S. Blaffer Hrdy, Eds., *Infanticide: Comparative and evolutionary perspectives.* NY: Aldine, 1984.

Burley, Nancy. Sex ratio manipulation and selection for attractiveness. *Science,* 1981, *211:*721–722.

Burley, Nancy. Facultative sex ratio manipulation. *American Naturalist,* 1982, *120*(1):81–107.

Burrows, E. G., and Spiro, M. E. *An atoll culture, ethnography of Ifaluk in the Central Carolines.* New Haven, CT: HRAF, 1957.

Burton, M. L., and White, D. R. Sexual division of labor in agriculture. *American Anthropologist,* 1984, *86*(3):568–583.

Chagnon, N. *Yanomamo: The fierce people.* NY: Holt, Rinehart, and Winston, 1968.

Charnov, Eric. *The theory of sex allocation.* Princeton, NJ: Princeton University Press, 1982.

Christopher, Stevan. A test of the Trivers–Willard hypothesis of parental ability to adaptively vary the sex ratio in a large human population. Paper presented to the Animal Behavior Society Meetings, Cheney, Washington, 1984.

Clark, A. B. Sex ratio and local resource competition in a prosimian primate. *Science,* 1978, *201:*163–165.

Clutton-Brock, T., and Albon, S. D. Parental investment in male and female offspring in mammals. *Current problems in sociobiology.* Cambridge: Cambridge University Press, 1982.

Clutton-Brock, T., Albon, S. D., and Guinness, F. *Red deer: Behavior and ecology of two sexes.* Chicago, IL: University of Chicago Press, 1982.

Clutton-Brock, T., Albon, S. D., and Guinness, F. Maternal dominance, breeding, success, and birth sex ratios in red deer. *Nature (London),* 1984, *308:*358–360.

Clutton-Brock, T., Albon, S. D., and Guinness, F. Parental investment and sex differences in juvenile mortality in birds and mammals. *Nature (London),* 1985, *313:*131–133.

Coleman, E. Infanticide in the early middle ages. *In* S. Stuard, Ed., *Women in medieval society.* Philadelphia, PA: University of Pennsylvania Press, 1976.

Coombs, L. C. Preferences for sex of children among U.S. couples. *Family Planning Perspectives,* 1977, *9*(6):259–265.

Cowgill, U., and Hutchinson, G. E. Sex ratio in childhood and the depopulation of the Peten, Guatemala. *Human Biology,* 1963, *35:*91–103.

Daly, Martin, and Wilson, Margo. Discriminative parental solitude: A biological perspective. *Journal of Marriage and Family,* 1980, *42:*277–278.

Daly, M., and Wilson, M. A sociobiological analysis of human infanticide. *In* G. Hausfater and S. Blaffer Hrdy, Eds., *Infanticide: Comparative and evolutionary perspectives,* NY: Aldine, 1984.

Damon, A., and Nuttall, R. L. Ponderal index of fathers and sex ratio of children. *Human Biology,* 1965, *37:*23–28.

Darling, F. *A herd of red deer*. NY: Doubleday and Co., 1964.

Darwin, C. *The descent of man and selection in relation to sex*. London: John Murray, 1871.

Dickemann, M. Demographic consequences of infanticide in man. *Annual Review of Ecology and Systematics*, 1975, *6:*107–137.

Dickemann, M. Female infanticide and reproductive strategies of stratified human societies. *In* N. Chagnon and W. Irons, Eds., *Evolutionary biology and human social behavior*. North Scituate: Duxbury, 1979. (a)

Dickemann, M. The ecology of mating systems in hypergynous-dowry societies. *Social Sciences Information*, 1979, *18*(2):163–195. (b)

Di Giacomo, R. F., and Shaughnessy, P. W. Fetal sex ratio in the rhesus *(Macaca mulatta)*. *Folia Primatologica*, 1979, *31:*246–250.

Dittus, W. P. J. The evolution of behaviors regulating density and age specific sex ratios in a primate population. *Behaviour*, 1979, *69:*265–302.

Divale, W. T., and M. Harris. Population, warfare and the male supremacist complex. *American Anthropologist*, 1976, *78:*521–538.

Drickamer, L. C. A ten-year summary of reproductive data for free-ranging *Macaca mulatta*. *Folia Primatologica*, 1974, *21:*61–80.

Erickson, J. D. The secondary sex ratio in the United States, 1969–1971: Association with race, parental ages, birth order, paternal education and legitimacy. *Annals of Human Genetics*, 1976, *40:*205–212.

Erwin, J. Infant mortality in *Macaca fascicularis:* Neonatal and post-natal mortality at the Regional Primate Research Center Field Station, University of Washington, 1967–1976. *Theriogenology*, 1977, *7:*357–366.

Essock-Vitale, S. M. The reproductive success of wealthy Americans. *Ethology and Sociobiology*, 1984, *5:*45–49.

Fairbanks, L. A., and McGuire, M. T. Relationships of vervet mothers with sons and daughters from one through three years of age. *Animal Behaviour*, 1985, *33:*40–50.

Falade, S. Women of Dakar and the surrounding area. *In* D. Paulme, Ed., *Women of tropical Africa*. London: Routledge, Kegan, and Paul, 1971, pp. 217–229.

Fisher, R. A. *The genetical theory of natural selection*. Oxford: Oxford University Press, 1930.

Foerg, Renate. Reproduction in *Cheirogaleus medius*. *Folia Primatologica*, 1982, *39:*49–62.

Fossey, D. Infanticide in mountain gorillas with comparative notes on chimpanzees. *In* G. Hausfater and S. Blaffer Hrdy, Eds., *Infanticide: Comparative and evolutionary perspectives*. NY: Aldine, 1984.

Fredga, K., Gropp, A., Winking, H., and Frank, F. A hypothesis explaining the exceptional sex ratio in the wood lemming *(Myopus schisticolor)*. *Hereditas*, 1977, *85:*101–104.

Freed, Stanley. A preference for sons. *Natural History Magazine*, 1982, *91*(5):27.

Gessain, M. Coniaqui women, Guinea. *In* D. Pauline, Ed., *Women in Tropical Africa*. Berkeley, CA: University of California Press, 1963.

Golovachev, G. D. Human sex ratio and sex-related selection at birth. *Geneticka*, 1978, November *14*(11):2043–2045.

Goodall, J. *The chimpanzees of Gombe*. Cambridge: Harvard University Press, 1986.

Goody, Jack. *Production and reproduction*. Cambridge: Cambridge University Press, 1976.

Goody, J. *The development of the family and marriage in early modern Europe*. Cambridge: Cambridge University Press, 1983.

Gosling, M. Adaptive control of offspring sex ratio by female coypu. Paper presented to the Animal Behavior Society Meetings, Philadelphia, December 27–30, 1983.

Gould, Stephen. Darwinism and the expansion of evolutionary theory. *Science*, 1982, *216*:380–386.

Greenough, Paul R. *Prosperity and misery in modern Bengal*. Oxford: Oxford University Press, 1982.

Guerrero, R. Association of the type and time of insemination within the menstrual cycle with the human sex ratio at birth. *New England Journal of Medicine*, 1974, *291*(20):1056–1059.

Guttentag, M., and Secord, P. *Too many women: The sex ratio question*. Beverly Hills, CA: Sage Publications, 1983.

Haldar, A. K., and Bhattacharyya, N. Fertility and sex sequence of Indian children. *Sankhya*, 1969, B*31*:144.

Hamilton, W. D. Extraordinary sex ratios. *Science*, 1967, *156*:477–488.

Harlap, S. Gender of infants conceived on different days of menstrual cycle. *New England Journal of Medicine*, 1979, *300*(26):1445–1448.

Hartung, J. Daughter inheritance as a paternity strategy. Paper presented to the 82nd Annual Meeting of the American Anthropological Association Meetings, Chicago, November 16–20, 1983.

Hartung, J. *Matrilineal inheritance: New theory and analysis*. In press.

Hausfater, G., and Hrdy, S. Blaffer, Eds. *Infanticide: Comparative and evolutionary perspectives*. NY: Aldine, 1984.

Hausfater, G., Altmann, J., and Altmann, S. Long-term consistency of dominance relations among female baboons *(Papio cynocephalus)*. *Science*, 1982, *217*:752–755.

Hedricks, C., and McClintock, M. Regulation of mating and sex ratios during postpartum estrus. Paper presented to the Annual Meeting of Animal Behavior Society, 1982.

Hoage, R. J. Parental care in *Leontopithecus rosalia rosalia:* Sex and age differences in carrying behavior and the role of prior experience. *In* D. Kleiman, Ed., *The biology and conservation of the Callitrichidae*. Washington, D.C.: Smithsonian Institution Press, 1978.

Hoogland, John. Infanticide in prairie dogs: Lactating females kill offspring of close kin. *Science*, 1985, *230*:1037–1040.

Hohenboken, W. D. Possibilities for genetic manipulation of sex ratio in livestock. *Journal of Animal Science*, 1981, *52*(2):265–275.

Hrdy, S. Blaffer Infanticide among animals: A review, classification and examination of the implications for the reproductive strategies of females. *Ethology and Sociobiology*, 1979, *1*:13–40.

Hrdy, S. Blaffer. *The woman that never evolved*. Cambridge, MA: Harvard University Press, 1981.

Hrdy, S. Blaffer, and Coleman, E. Why are human secondary sex ratios so conservative? Prepared for "Infanticide in Animals and Man," Wenner-Gren Symposium No. 88, Ithaca, New York, August 16–22, 1982.

Hrdy, S. Blaffer, and G. Hausfater. Comparative and evolutionary perspectives on infanticide: Introduction and overview. *In* G. Hausfater and S. Blaffer Hrdy, Eds., *Infanticide: Comparative and evolutionary perspectives*. NY: Aldine, 1984.

Huck, U. W., Labov, J. B., Vaswani, P., and Lisk, D. Effects of pre- and postnatal undernutrition on manipulation of offspring sex ratio in golden hamsters. *American Zoologist*, 1983 (Abstr.), *23*:935.

Hufton, Olwen. *The poor in eighteenth-century France, 1750–1789*. Oxford: Clarendon Press, 1974.

Imaizumi, Y. Sex ratio of triplet births in Japan. *Human Heredity*, 1982, *32*(2):114–120.

James, W. H. Time of fertilization and sex of infants. *The Lancet*, May 24, 1980, 1124–1126.

James, W. H. The sex ratio of Japanese twins. *Human Heredity*, 1983, *33*(2):109–111. (a)

James, W. H. Timing of fertilization and the sex ratio of human offspring. *In* N. Bennett, Ed. *Sex selection of children*. NY: Academic Press, 1983. (b)

Johansson, S. Deferred infanticide: Excess female mortality during childhood. *In* G. Hausfater and S. Blaffer Hrdy, Eds., *Infanticide: Comparative and evolutionary perspectives*. NY: Aldine, 1984.

Kellokumpu-Lehtinen, and Pelliniemi, L. J. Sex ratio of human conceptuses. *Obstetrics and Gynecology*, 1984, *64*:220–222.

Khan, M. E. Factors affecting spacing of births. *Journal of Family Welfare*, 1973, *20*:54–67.

Khoury, M. J., Erickson, J. D., and James, L. M. Paternal effects on the human sex ratio at birth: Evidence from interracial crosses. *American Journal of Human Genetics*, 1984, *36*:1103–1111.

Kurland, J. Kin selection in the Japanese monkey. *Contribution to Primatology* 1977, *12*.

Labov, J., Huck, U. W., Elwood, R. W., and Brooks, R. Proximate and ultimate causes of infanticidal behavior in rodents. *Quarterly Review of biology*, 1985, *60*(1):1–20.

Labov, J., Huck, U. W., Vaswani, P., and Lisk, Robert. Effects of maternal pre- and postnatal undernutrition on pup growth and sex ratio in hamsters *(Mesocricetus auratus)*. Paper presented to the 20th Annual Meeting of Animal Behavior Society, Cheney, Washington, 1984.

Labov, J., Huck, U. W., Vaswani, P., and Lisk, R. D. Sex ratio manipulation and decreased growth of male offspring of prenatally and postnatally nourished golden hamsters *(Mesocricetus auratus)*. *Behavioral Ecology and Sociobiology*, in press.

Lamb, M. Observational studies of father–child relationships in humans. *In* D. Taub, Ed., *Primate paternalism*. NY: Van Nostrand Reinhold, 1984.

Lee, Sung, and Takano, Kiichi. Sex ratio in human embryo obtained from induced abortion: Historical examination of the gonad in 1,452 cases. *American Journal of Obstetrics and Gynecology*, 1970, *108*(8):1294–1297.

Lenington, S. Child abuse: The limits of sociobiology. *Ethology and Sociobiology*, 1981, *2*:17–29.

McClintock, M. Group mating in the domestic rat as a context for sexual selection: Consequences for the analysis of sexual behavior and neuroendocrine responses. *Advances in the Study of Behavior*, 1984, *14*:1–50.

McClure, P. Sex-biased litter reduction in food-restricted wood rats *(Neotomoa floridana)*. *Science*, 1981, *211*:1058–1060.

McKee, Lauris. Preferential care and mortality differentials. In *Indirect infanticide and sex differentials in children's treatment*. Symposium presented to the 81st Annual Meeting of the American Anthropological Association, Washington, D.C., December 3–7, 1982.

McMillen, M. M. Differential mortality by sex and neonatal death. *Science*, 1979, *204*(6):89–90.

Maynard Smith, J. The economics of sex (review of E. Charnov's *The theory of sex allocation)*. *Evolution*, 1983, *37*(4):872–873.

Maynard Smith, J., and Stenseth, N. C. On the evolutionary stability of the female-biased sex ratio in the wood lemming *(Myopus schisticolor):* The effect of inbreeding. *Heredity*, 1978, *41*:205–214.

Meikle, D. B., and Phyllis, R. W. *Social dominance rank and infant sex-biased maternal investment in free-ranging rhesus monkeys.* Submitted for publication, n.d.

Meikle, D. B., Tilford, B. L., and Vessey, S. H. Dominance rank, secondary sex ratio, and reproduction of offspring in polygynous primates. *American Naturalist*, 1984, *124*(2):173–187.

Meikle, D. B., and Vessey, S. H. Nepotism among rhesus monkey brothers. *Nature (London)*, 1981, *294*(5837):160–161.

Mikamo, Kazuya. Female preponderance in the sex ratio during early uterine development: A sex chromatin study. *Japanese Journal of Genetics*, 1969, *13*(4):272–277.

Miller, B. *The endangered sex: Neglect of female children in rural north India.* Cornell, NY: Cornell University Press, 1981.

Minturn, L., and Stashak, J. Infanticide as a terminal abortion procedure. *Behavior Science Research*, 1982, *17*(1,2):70–90.

Moore, C. L. An olfactory basis for maternal discrimination of sex of offspring in rats *(Rattus norvegicus)*. *Animal Behavior*, 1981, *29*:383–386.

Moore, C. L. Maternal behavior of rats is affected by hormonal condition of pups. *Journal of Comparative Physiological Psychology*, 1982, *96*(1):123–129.

Moore, C. L. Maternal contribution to the development of masculine sexual behavior in laboratory rats. *Developmental Psychobiology*, 1984, *17:* in press.

Moore, C. L., and Morelli, Gilda A. Mother rats interact differently with male and female offspring. *Journal of Comparative and Physiological Psychology*, 1979, *93*(4):677–684.

Morton, N. E., Chung, C. S., and Mi, M. P. Genetics of interracial crosses in Hawaii. Monograph in *Human Genetics*, 1967, *3*. NY: S. Karger.

Myers, J. Sex ratio adjustment under food stress: Maximization of quality or numbers of offspring? *American Naturalist*, 1978, *112*:381–388.

Nicolson, N. Weaning and the development of independence in olive baboons. Ph.D. Thesis, Harvard University, 1982.

Nishida, T. Alpha status and agonistic·alliance in wild chimpanzee *(Pan troglodytes schweiinfurthii)*. *Primates*, 1983, *24*(3):318–336.

Nishida, T. Within-group cannibalism by adult male chimpanzees. *Primates* 1985, *26*(3):274–284.

Novitski, E., and Kimball, A. W. Birth order, parental ages, and sex of offspring. *American Journal of Human Genetics* 1958, *10*:268–275.

Noyes, M. J. S. The association of maternal tributes with infant gender in a group of Japanese monkeys. *International Journal of Primatology*, 1982, *3*:320.

Orent, A. Cultural factors inhibiting population growth among the Kafa of South-west Ethiopia. *In* Moni Nag, Ed., *Population and social organization*. The Hague: Mouton, 1975.

Park, Chai Bin. Preference for sons, family size, and sex ratio: An empirical study in Korea. *Demography*, 1983, *209*(3):333–352.

Paul, A., and Thommen, Dieter. Timing of birth, female reproductive success and infant sex ratio in semifree-ranging barbary macaques *(Macaca sylvana)*. *Folia Primatologica*, 1984, *42*:2–16.

Prothro, Edwin T. *Child rearing in the Lebanon.* Harvard Middle Eastern monographs VIII. Cambridge: Center for Middle Eastern Studies, 1961.

Ramanamma, A., and Bambawale, U. The mania for sons: An analysis of social values in South Asia. *Social Science and Medicine*, 1980, *14B:*107–110.

Rasmussen, K. M., Ausman, L. M., and Hayes, K. C. Vital statistics from a laboratory breeding colony of squirrel monkeys *(Saimiri sciureus)*. *Laboratory Animal Science*, 1980, *30*(1):99–106.

Rawlins, R. and Kessler, M. Secondary sex ratio variation in the Cayo Santiago macaque population. *American Journal of Primatology*, 1986, *10*:9–23.

Rehan, N. E. Sex ratio of live-born Hausa infants. *British Journal of Obstetrics and Gynecology*, 1982, *89*(2):136–141.

Reiter, J., Panken, K., and Le Boeuf, B. J. Female competition and reproductive success in Northern elephant seals. *Animal Behavior*, 1981, *29*(3):670–687.

Reiter, J., Stinson, N. L., and Le Boeuf, B. J. Northern elephant seal development: The transition from weaning to development. *Behavioral Ecology and Sociobiology*, 1978, *3*:337–367.

Rivers, J. P. W., and Crawford, M. A. Maternal nutrition and the sex ratio at birth. *Nature (London)*, 1974, *252*:297–298.

Robinette, W. L., Gashwiler, J. S., Low, J. B., and Jones, D. A. Differential mortality by sex and age among mule deer. *Journal of Wildlife Management*, 1957, *21*:1–16.

Rostron, J., and James, W. H. Maternal age, parity, social class, and sex ratio. *Annals of Human Genetics*, 1977, *41*:205–217.

Ruppenthal, G. C., Arling, G. L., Harlow, H. F., Sackett, G. P., and Suomi, S. J. A ten-year perspective of motherless mother monkey behavior. *Journal of Abnormal Psychology*, 1976, *84*:341–349.

Sackett, Gene P. Receiving severe aggression correlates with fetal gender in pregnant pigtailed monkeys. *Developmental Psychobiology*, 1981, *14*(3):267–272.

Sackett, Gene P., Holm, R., and Landesman-Dwyer, S. Vulnerability for abnormal development: Pregnancy outcomes and differences in macaque monkeys. *In* N. R. Ellis, Ed., *Aberrant development of infancy: Human and animal studies*. NY: Halsted Press, 1975, pp. 59–76.

Sade, D. S. Determinants of dominance in a group of free-ranging rhesus monkeys. *In* Stuart A. Altmann, Ed., *Social communication among primates*. Chicago, IL: University of Chicago Press, 1967.

Schaik, C. P. van and van Noordwijk, M. A. Social stress and the sex ratio of neonates and infants among non-human primates. *Netherlands Journal of Zoology*, 1983, *33*(3):249–265.

Schapiro, Steven J., and Mitchell, G. Infant-directed abuse in seminatural environment: Precipitating factors. *In* Martin Reite and Nancy G. Caine, Eds., *Child abuse: The non-human primate data*. NY: Alan Liss, 1983.

Scrimshaw, S. C. M. Infanticide in human population: Societal and individual concerns. *In* G. Hausfater and S. Blaffer Hrdy, Eds., *Infanticide: Comparative and evolutionary perspectives*. NY: Aldine, 1984.

Shapiro, S., Schlesinger, E. R., and Nesbitt, R. E. L., Jr. *Infant, perinatal, maternal, and childhood mortality in the United States*. Cambridge, MA: Harvard University Press, 1968.

Shaw, R. F., and Mohler, J. D. The selective advantage of the sex ratio. *American Naturalist*, 1953, *87*:337–342.

Silk, Joan B. Local resource competition and facultative adjustment of sex ratios in relation to competitive abilities. *American Naturalist*, 1983, *121*(1):56–64.

Silk, J. B. Local resource competition and the evolution of male-biased sex ratios. *Journal of Theoretical Biology*, 1984, *108*:203–213.

Silk, Joan B., Clark-Wheatley, A. C. B., Rodman, P. S., and Samuels, A. Differential reproductive success and facultative adjustment of sex ratios among captive female bonnet macaques *(Macaca radiata)*. *Animal Behavior*, 1981, *29*:162–187.

Simpson, A. E., and Simpson, M. J. A. Short-term consequences of different breeding histories for captive rhesus macaque mothers and young. *Behavioral Ecology and Sociobiology*, 1985, *18*:83–89.

Simpson, M. J. A., and Simpson, A. E. Birth sex ratios and social rank in rhesus monkey mothers. *Nature (London)*, 1982, *300*:440–441.

Simpson M. J .A. *et al.* Infant-related influences on birth intervals in rhesus monkeys. *Nature (London)*, 1981, *290*:49–51.

Small, M. Sex differences in maternal investment by *Macaca mulatta*. *Behavioral Ecology and Sociobiology*, 1984, *14*:313–314.

Small, M., and Hrdy, S. Blaffer. Secondary sex ratios by maternal rank, parity and age in captive rhesus macaques *(Macaca mulatta)*. *American Journal of Primatology*, 1986, *11*:359–365.

Small, M., and Smith, D. G. Sex ratio of infants produced by male rhesus macaques. *American Naturalist*, 1984, *126*(3):354–361.

Small, M., and Smith, D. G. The influence of birth timing upon infant growth and survival in captive rhesus monkeys *(Macaca mulatta)*. *International Journal of Primatology*, 1986, *7*(3):289–304.

Smith, Martin, S., Kish, B. J., and Crawford, C. B. Inheritance of wealth as human kin investment. Paper presented to the Animal Behavior Society Meetings, August 13–17, 1984, Cheney, Washington.

Snyder, Richard. The sex ratio of offspring of high performance aircraft. *Human Biology*, 1961, *33*:1–10.

Suomi, Stephen J., and Ripp, Chris. A history of motherless mother monkey mothering at the University of Wisconsin laboratory. *In* Martin Reite and Nance G. Caine, Eds., *Child abuse: The non-human primate data*. NY: Alan Liss, 1983.

Stern, Curt. *The principles of human genetics*, 2d ed. San Francisco, CA: Freeman, 1960.

Teitelbaum, M. Factors affecting the sex ratio in large populations. *Journal of Biological Sciences Suppl.* 1970, *2*:61–71.

Teitelbaum, M., and Mantel, N. Socio-economic factors and the sex ratio at birth. *Journal of Biosocial Science*, 1971, *3*:23–41.

Teitelbaum, M., Mantel, N., and Stark, C. R. Limited dependence of the human sex ratio on birth order and parental ages. *American Journal of Human Genetics*, 1971, *23*:271–280.

Tekçe, Belgin, and Shorter, F. C. Determinants of child mortality: A study of squatter settlements in Jordan. *In* W. H. Mosley and L. C. Chen, Eds., *Child survival: Strategies for research*. Cambridge: Cambridge University Press, 1984.

Trivers, R. L. Parental investment and sexual selection. *In* B. Campbell, Ed., *Sexual selection and the descent of man*. Chicago, IL: Aldine, 1972.

Trivers, R. L. *Social evolution*. Menlo Park, CA: Benjamin Cummings, 1985.

Trivers, R. L., and Willard, D. E. Natural selection of parental ability to vary the sex ratio of offspring. *Science*, 1973, *179*:90–91.

Troisi, Alfonso, D'Amato, F. R., Fuccillo, Roberto, and Scucchi, Stefano. Infant abuse by a wild-born group-living Japanese macaque mother. *Journal of Abnormal Psychology*, 1982, *91*(6):451–456.

Visaria, Pravin. Sex ratio at birth in territories with a relatively complete registration. *Eugenics Quarterly*, 1967, *14*:132–142.

Voland, Eckart. Human sex-ratio manipulation: Historical data from a German parish. *Journal of Human Evolution*, 1984, *13*:99–107.

Wasser, Samuel K., and Barash, D. Reproductive suppression among female mammals: Implications for biomedicine and sexual selection theory. *Quarterly Review of Biology*, 1983, *58*(4):513–538.

Wasser, Samuel K., and Waterhouse, Mary. The establishment and maintenance of sex biases. *In* S. K. Wasser, Ed., *Social behavior of female vertebrates.* NY: Academic Press, 1983.

Wells, R. Increasing the proportion of heifer calves. Letter in *Veterinary Record,* 1980, *107*(6):139.

Werren, J. H. Sex ratio adaptations to local mate competition in a parasitic wasp. *Science,* 1980, *208:*1157–1159.

Whiting, J., Bailey, R. C., Hartung, J., and De Zalduondo, B. Sex ratio: Cross-cultural evidence. Paper presented to the Meeting of Society for Cross Cultural Research, East Lansing, Michigan, 1977.

Whyte, M. K. Cross-cultural codes dealing with the relative status of women. *Ethnology,* 1978, *17*(2):211–237.

Williams, G. C. The question of adaptive sex ratios in outcrossed vertebrates. *Proceedings of the Royal Society, London,* 1979, *B205:*567–580.

Wolfe, Linda D. Female rank and reproductive success among Arashiyama B Japanese Macaques *(Macaca fuscata). International Journal of Primatology* 1984, *5*(2):133–143.

Wrangham, Richard W. Apes as archetypes for human behavior. Paper presented to the 82nd Annual Meeting of the American Anthropological Association, Chicago, November 16–20, 1983.

Wyshak, Grace. Fertility and longevity in twins, sibs and parents of twins. *Social Biology,* 1978, *25:*315–330.

CHILD ABUSE: A COMPARATIVE AND PSYCHOBIOLOGICAL PERSPECTIVE*

Martin Reite
John P. Capitanio

INTRODUCTION

Child abuse has received increasing attention in the recent past, but with few exceptions the problem has been viewed from an essentially parochial perspective that is limited by time, species, and culture. While ultimately not the most productive strategy, initially such a strategy is reasonable and consonant with the fact that interest in and concerns about abuse arose from the clinic, where traditions and procedures are dictated by clinical need. In such cases it is customary for the identification of a new syndrome to be followed first by efforts to treat those afflicted, then to intervene in such a manner in order to quickly decrease risk and/or incidence, and finally, to do the research necessary to understand the etiology and pathophysiology of the phenomena. In the area of child abuse, only the first two strategies have been pursued with vigor. Optimal treatment of the individual case, and tertiary prevention generally, is facilitated by recognition of the syndrome (i.e., that certain injuries are likely to be the result of abuse) at first contact. Secondary prevention is facilitated by early case recognition, which in turn is facilitated by identifying those infants and children at greatest risk and, where possible, removing them from the source of risk prior to injury (e.g., protective custody). Such operations involve issues of epidemiology and correlating risk with certain environmental or other factors on a statistical basis, which can, and probably have been, easily misinterpreted or misconstrued as representing true etiological variables.

*This work was supported by USPHS Grants No. MH19514 and MH 31846. M. Reite was supported by NIMH Research Scientist Award No. 5K02 46335. J.P. Capitanio was supported by Institutional Postdoctoral Training Grant No. MH15442.

Having come this far, we find that although those cases that come to our attention are perhaps better treated, and certain children at risk are recognized and protected earlier, the problem has not disappeared, and we really do not understand it that much better. Previously it was hoped that with early identification of children at risk the problem could be largely resolved. These hopes, however, have not been fulfilled. Indeed, Lealman, Haigh, Phillips, Stone, and Ord-Smith recently stated: "Although prediction of child abuse may be possible, to suggest that prevention is straightforward is to underestimate the complexity of this difficult social and medical phenomenon" (1983:1424).

It is clearly time, therefore, for efforts on the third front, that is, the research necessary to understand the basic causes of the problem. Here the problems will be substantial, for child abuse is a complicated symptom complex, with a similar outcome (the abused child) likely resulting from the complex interplay of a number of separable and identifiable causal factors or etiological agents. It is necessary to examine the problem from a number of vantage points, including the historical, cross-cultural, comparative, and psychobiological. The historical vantage point permits us to view how infants and children are treated now compared to the past. The cross-cultural permits us to view the extent to which such behaviors are culture specific, and how they evolve with changes in cultural forces and patterns. The comparative viewpoint examines the treatment of offspring across species and permits inferences about evolutionary and phylogenetic considerations, which in turn implicate more basic biological issues. The latter avenues of investigation are somewhat more demanding from the standpoint that they require us to recognize that humans are first and foremost higher primates, and that certain of our behaviors may still be significantly influenced by forces long hoped by many to be inoperative, or at least under volitional control. This issue has never been one of major concern in the general area of pathophysiology, where, for example, little emotion is generated by suggesting that human kidneys may operate in a very similar fashion to other mammalian kidneys. In the area of behavior and behavioral pathology similar analogies have not met with an equally benign reception. It is likely, however, that, especially in the area of rearing of offspring, it will be necessary at least to maintain the necessary flexibility to consider such viewpoints, for it is likely that certain basic answers are to be found in the biology of the organism.

The rationale for such a viewpoint is rather simple. There is no more important function in the behavioral biology of higher organisms than that of proper parenting. In the case of our species, lack of viable offspring for a period of 50 years would result in extinction of the species. The implications of this observation are quite simple: parenting is too important to be left completely to the whim of a particular code of learning, or sociocultural environment, or to the vagaries of one type of stress or another. Parenting, at least in its broad outlines, must be in large part built into the organism as an intrinsic part of its genetic heritage. A corollary of this is that offspring must also be able to tolerate considerable variability in parenting styles to survive.

In this chapter we will present evidence pointing out certain similarities, from an ecological and environmental standpoint, in infant and "child" abuse in human and nonhuman primates. We will then examine relevant experimental data, primarily from nonhuman primates, suggesting how effective parenting is influenced by specific types of alterations in early experience. Finally, we will examine evidence suggesting that certain behavioral systems thought to be important for effective parenting are possibly determined to a significant degree by biological substrates.

PRIMATE PERSPECTIVES

Abusive Parenting in Nonhuman Primates

It was pointed out by Horenstein (1977) that students of child abuse would do well to consider the problem from a broader and comparative perspective. Horenstein reviewed earlier data from Harlow's laboratory in which monkey mothers who had not themselves been mothered (by monkey mothers) often appeared incapable of mothering their first born infants, frequently subjecting them to a variety of abusive behaviors. He felt that such information was relevant in developing more effective treatment and intervention strategies in cases of human child abuse and would improve our understanding of possible etiological mechanisms. Specifically, he suggested mothers "be given the opportunity to learn normal maternal behavior and motherliness through supervised experiences with their children in a therapeutic nursery setting . . . " (1977:564). A subsequent paper by Nadler (1980) pointed out that similar relevant data existed for chimpanzees, where the studies of Rogers and Davenport (1970) and Davenport (1979) found that early social deprivation led to subsequent impairment in maternal behavior. Drawing on additional data from rhesus monkeys and gorillas, Nadler found significant commonalities between certain factors (e.g., social withdrawal and psychological isolation) in infant abuse in human and nonhuman primates.

A subsequent volume examined in more detail similarities in patterns of infant abuse in human and nonhuman primates (Reite and Caine, 1983). These data were primarily archival in nature, since abuse is not intentionally created or accentuated in the laboratory; nevertheless, certain similarities to human child abuse were unmistakeable. Examples from this volume will be used to illustrate such similarities.

A chapter by Suomi and Ripp (1983) reviewed the data from the Wisconsin laboratory on mothering behavior of motherless mothers, including the summary by Ruppenthal, Arling, Harlow, Sackett, and Suomi (1976). The early work from Harry Harlow's laboratory was revolutionary for its time and still provides a body of work on basic aspects of primate mothering behavior that has profound implications for our understanding of child abuse. In 1962, Harlow reported the rather remarkable findings that monkeys who had not themselves been mothered had a great deal of difficulty becoming mothers themselves. Females who had been raised on inanimate surrogates or in wire cages, ignored, threatened, rebuffed, or even cruelly attacked their own infants, exhibiting virtually no evidence of maternal behavior (Harlow and Harlow, 1962). These findings implicated early experience as very important to the initial establishment of normal mothering behavior in primates. Subsequent studies established that monkey mothers who had exhibited no maternal behavior with their first born would, if they had sufficient contact with the first born, do much better with their second offspring. In general, the quality of mothering increased with increased exposure to offspring, with later offspring receiving much improved care. It was also noted that male infants were likely to be abused with greater frequency than female infants. Several important qualifications were also observed. First, age per se of the motherless mother at the time her first infant was born was an important variable. Mothers over 8 years old at the time of their first delivery rarely abused their infants, mothers under 8 did so with some frequency. Second, some motherless monkey mothers exhibited normal maternal behavior with their first born despite the fact that they themselves had not experienced mothering. This observation was most important, for it suggested that the capacity for normal mothering was present in all females. In some animals it required the experience of being mothered (or of having an infant) to become activated, whereas in some females it would appear in any case. While the mechanisms underlying this rather remarkable individual variability are not clear, biological variables stand to figure prominently, for they would be expected to affect behavior in this manner.

Suomi and Ripp (1983) also made the interesting observation that among mothers who had been raised with peers and who had at some earlier time experienced an experimental separation from her peers, those who had reacted to the separation with a behavioral depressive reaction were at greater risk to subsequently become abusive mothers than those who had not become depressed in response to separation. Thus it seemed that equally important as the nature of the mother's early experience was how she, individually, responded to that experience.

Examining data from pigtail monkeys living in social groups in a laboratory environment, Caine and Reite (1983) found several areas of commonality between abuse in humans and monkeys. Mothers who themselves had experienced disturbances in early attachment, effected by experimental separation from their own mothers in infancy, appeared to be at greater risk for subsequently abusing their own infants. Animals who themselves had been abused as infants also appeared at greater risk to abuse their own offspring. Evidence was also found indicating that temporary social isolation promoted abusive behavior in some mothers, as did overcrowding in social groups. Male infants tended to be abused with greater frequency than female, and some evidence was found supporting the concept of "abuse prone" immatures, with some infants seeming to attract more abusive behavior for no apparent reason. These similarities to the human condition, unless entirely fortuitous, clearly suggest that structures or mechanisms common to *Homo* and *Macaca* may interact with various environmental variables to exert a strong influence on how offspring are treated.

Schapiro and Mitchell (1983) examined abusive behavior in three species of macaques living in a seminatural outdoor environment. These authors found an abuse rate of 11% during the first 2 years of life for all infants born into outdoor field cages. Abuse was much more common in rhesus *(M. mulatta)* than in bonnet *(M. radiata)* social groups. External stress, as well as impaired health on the part of the mother, was noted to accentuate the frequency of abuse; no significant sex difference was noted in abused infants, however. These authors commented upon the differences observed in abusive behavior in animals housed as mother–infant pairs compared to those housed in seminatural environments. They suggested the social setting of a large field cage might be more similar to a human extended family, where responsibility for child care tends to be somewhat more dissipated, and where the incidence of abuse seems to be lessened.

Erwin (1983) described incidents of sudden major abuse to infants by pigtail monkeys in the face of external threat, not infrequently resulting in death of the infant. He suggested such phenomena might be interpretable within the framework of sociobiological models of infanticide and represent a special case of early parental divestment in the face of overwhelming threat. Similar sociobiological models have been thought to have ultimate explanatory value for other situations in which the takeover of monkey groups by new males is accompanied by the killing of infants not their own (Hrdy, 1977; Clarke, 1983). And, of course, similar phenomena are seen in the human situation, where unrelated males abuse the children of women with whom they are living

(Lightcap, Kurland, and Burgess, 1982). Whether the underlying proximate mechanisms are similar is uncertain, but it seems reasonable to
maintain an openness to considering such to be the case.

Plimpton and Rosenblum (1983) presented evidence that in bonnet
monkey social groups mothering behavior can be compromised in a
high foraging–demand environment and, further, that infants from a
high foraging–demand environment had a greater risk of becoming
depressed following separation from their mothers compared to those
from a low foraging–demand environment. They suggested that such
high foraging–demand infants have created "insecurely attached" infants (after Ainsworth, Blehar, Waters and Wall, 1978). Gaensbauer and
Harmon (1982) found evidence of less than optimal (or "insecure") parent–infant attachment in infants and children who had been abused
or neglected.

Maple and Warren-Leubecker (1983) presented evidence obtained
from gorilla, orangutan, and chimpanzee implicating parenting deficits
as stemming from early deficits in socialization, effects of prior parental
experience, and environmental or social stress. Similarly, Nadler (1983)
commented on the importance of social support at the time of delivery
and thereafter as important to the development and maintenance of
proper maternal behavior in gorillas as well as several other nonhuman
primate species.

Thus considerable data have been accumulated that document similarities between infant and child abuse in human and nonhuman primates, primarily from an environmental and ecological viewpoint. A
common thread running through the primate literature is that the incidence of abusive behavior on the part of adults is increased by various
forms of social stress that are also frequently implicated as increasing
the risk of frequency of abuse in human populations. The mechanisms
that underlie such commonalities are not yet clear, but taken as a sum
the evidence suggests that the human situation is not unique and that
there may be much to learn by studying comparative data.

A second major theme in the comparative primate data is that aberrant experience in early infancy may result in subsequent skewed development, including aberrant parenting behavior. Among the early
experiences that seem to figure prominently in this regard are disturbances in the early mother–infant attachment relationship. We have
mentioned the major aberrations in mothering (at least of the firstborn infant) seen in mothers who themselves have been raised without
mothers and have alluded to evidence suggesting that separations from
mother in early infancy may result in subsequent abusive parenting.
In a recent comprehensive review of behavioral pathology in primates,
Capitanio (1986) presented as a general principle evidence for a
phylogenetic trend regarding the degree to which social behaviors are

affected by privation and deprivation experiences. In general, such effects are maximal among Old World monkeys and apes, compared to prosimians and New World monkeys. By inference such effects would be even greater in *Homo sapiens*. It is perhaps worthwhile here to briefly review the, by now, extensively documented effects of early separation experiences on the physiology and behavior of young monkeys, with a view to examining the mechanisms underlying, and the possible long-term effects of, such early experience.

The Consequences of Early Separation

Research on the behavioral effects of separation from mother in monkey infants dates from the 1960s, arising essentially independently in the laboratories of Harlow (Seay, Hansen, and Harlow, 1962), Hinde (Hinde, Spencer-Booth, and Bruce, 1966), and Kaufman (Kaufman and Rosenblum, 1967). This work was in large part a response to, and a way to independently evaluate, certain early psychoanalytic ideas and observations. The latter included Bowlby's ideas about attachment based upon children's reaction to separation from their parents (Bowlby, 1960) and Spitz's description of anaclitic depression and hospitalism in infants deprived of proper mothering (Spitz, 1946). The nonhuman primate research found that infant monkeys, when separated from their mothers, exhibited behavioral changes very similar to those described by Spitz and Bowlby in human children (see Reite and Short, 1983, for review). Subsequent work extended studies of separation to examination of the physiological, hormonal, and immunological accompaniments of separation. Pigtail (*M. nemestrina*) monkey infants separated from their mothers were found to exhibit impairment in the regulation of body temperature, heart rate and rhythm, and sleep patterns (Reite, Short, Seiler, and Pauley, 1981). Short-lived increases in cortisol secretion were found to accompany maternal separation in both squirrel (*Saimiri sciureus*) (Coe, Mendoza, Smotherman, and Levine, 1978) and rhesus (*M. mulatta*) monkeys (Gunnar, Gonzalez, Goodlin, and Levine, 1981). Evidence of impaired immunological function were observed to accompany peer separation in pigtail infants (Reite, Harbeck, and Hoffman, 1981), and mother–infant separation in bonnet (*M. radiata*) monkeys (Laudenslager, Reite, and Harbeck, 1982). The sum total of such observations suggests that the disruption of early attachment relationships may have significant physiological as well as behavioral consequences. The mechanisms remain to be elucidated and may include removal of the mother as a physiological (e.g., nutrition, temperature, respiration) regulator (as has been demonstrated to occur in separated rat pups by Hofer [1981]), as well as loss of the mother representing the disruption of an attachment bond.

The effects of early maternal separation have been demonstrated to be of long duration. Hinde and colleagues have found evidence of behavioral alteration in rhesus monkeys up to 24 months after a maternal separation in infancy (Spencer-Booth and Hinde, 1971), and we have found subtle behavioral changes including evidence of fewer social preferences and fewer contact preferences with other animals, up to 3.5 to 6 years following a maternal separation in infancy (Capitanio, Weissberg, and Reite, 1985; Capitanio and Reite, 1984). Recently we described evidence of altered immunological function in pigtail monkeys, now 4–7 years of age, who had been previously separated in infancy (Laudenslager, Capitanio, and Reite, 1985).

Thus the weight of the evidence suggests that, in nonhuman primates, an early separation from mother (or, possibly, a peer in the absence of a mother) may result in widespread behavioral and physiological consequences, some of which may endure for years. Such observations, combined with the so far primarily anecdotal evidence that early separations may also contribute to later abusive parenting in some animals, raise the possibility that the consequences of early separation, or, perhaps more generally, disturbances in being parented, may so skew expected behavioral and/or physiological development so as to interfere with the expression of normal parenting behavior at a later date. And to the extent that such later parenting has a biological basis, the aberrant early experience can be interpreted as producing physiological effects that interfere with subsequent physiological maturation and/or normal physiological behavioral interactions.

Data supporting such an interpretation can be found in studies on surrogate- and isolate-reared monkeys. An inanimate surrogate provides an opportunity for a monkey to display an attachment but in no way could be considered a proper parent. Squirrel monkeys raised on an inanimate surrogate, who are subsequently separated from the surrogate for a few days, fail to display the increase in plasma cortisol levels that is observed in mother-reared monkeys experiencing comparable separations (Hennessy, Kaplan, Mendoza, Lowe, and Levine, 1979). Similar findings have been obtained in other monkey species where the dependent measures have been heart rate, body temperature, and/or sleep patterns (Capitanio, unpublished data; Reite and Short, 1978; Reite, Short, Kaufman, Stynes, and Pauley, 1978). Second, monkeys reared with inanimate surrogates who are subjected to psychological stressors (e.g., being placed alone in a novel room; observing the capture of a companion) do not demonstrate the degree of responsiveness (in cortisol and heart rate) observed in monkeys who were reared with either conspecific or nonconspecific, but animate, mothers (Mason, 1978; Meyer, Novak, Bowman, and Harlow, 1975). Third, limited evidence suggests alterations in cortisol levels in non-rehabilitated isolate-reared monkey adolescents (Sackett, Bowman, Meyer, Tripp, and Grady, 1973). Finally, isolate-reared monkeys, who have been housed in social groups for over a year and who did not differ behaviorally from socially reared animals under baseline conditions, were found to show long-term alterations in behavioral and neurochemical systems in response to amphetamine challenge (Kraemer, Ebert, Lake, and McKinney, 1984).

Cortisol, a hormone produced by the adrenal cortex, is excreted in response to many types of stressors. Cortisol, both endogenous and exogenous, can act to suppress the immune response, and indeed is used therapeutically in this manner in patients with autoimmune disorders or in those that have received organ transplants, etc. Several studies have demonstrated that the acute response to separation in young monkeys may include increased cortisol secretion, and in such cases it might be expected that such increased cortisol excretion might effect changes in immune function including decreased lymphocyte response to mitogen stimulation. Other data suggest that increases in cortisol are likely not the only, or even major, explanation for the alterations in immune function, however. This issue is discussed in more detail in Laudenslager and Reite (1984).

In humans, data also support the notion of altered physiological functioning among children who have received less than adequate mothering. Tennes (1982) demonstrated that the quality of a child's relationship to its mother was related to the child's urinary cortisol excretion during a 1-hour separation. Infants classified as exhibiting an "avoidant" relationship with their mothers showed low cortisol responsiveness in contrast to infants displaying a "secure" relationship. Moreover, the rank correlations between these cortisol levels and those observed on control days, either at the same age or 2 years later, were high and significant. Interestingly, mothers of avoidant infants tend to show an aversion to close physical contact with their babies (Ainsworth et al., 1978), and avoidant infants are disproportionately represented in samples of abused/neglected children (Gaensbauer and Harmon, 1982). Finally, in infants with the nonorganic failure-to-thrive syndrome, a number of abnormalities in physiological functioning have been found, including disturbances in sleep, growth hormone responses to insulin-induced hypoglycemia and levels of somatomedin, ACTH, cortisol, and T_4 (see discussion in MacCarthy, 1981).

Together these results suggest that the receipt of abnormal or disturbed parenting can result in alterations in physiological functioning. While it is unclear what the exact nature of the relationship is between the behavior and physiology, many of these data suggest the physiological disturbances may be persistent. It is unclear how many humans who have experienced abnormal parental care (e.g., separations, abuse, neglect, emotionally or physically unavailable parents) later become competent parents themselves. It is clear, however, that one of the most consistent correlates of abusive/neglectful parental behavior is the receipt of such care when young. Thus there is considerable circumstantial evidence that for both human and nonhuman primates, early experiences that are associated with abusive/neglectful parenting are also associated with altered responsiveness in physiological (especially endocrine) systems. This altered responsiveness, in turn, may itself be a consequence of the parent having received similar parental care when young.

Granted then, experiential issues may rank high in their effects on the adequacy of maternal behavior. As has been pointed out earlier, however, it is also likely that maternal (or parenting) behavior is strongly rooted in the biology of the organism. In the next several sections we will examine the evidence in support of the notion that there is a biological basis for maternal behavior. In addition, as discussed previously, considerable evidence supports a strong relationship between disturbance in early mother–infant attachment as predisposing to subsequent abuse. Emerging evidence supports the concept that there may be a significant neurobiological contribution to the attachment behavioral system. Subsequent sections will address these issues as well.

BIOLOGICAL CONTRIBUTIONS TO MATERNAL BEHAVIOR

Hormonal

Few question the notion that maternal behavior in nonprimate mammals or in nonmammals has a strong biological component. In fact, in these groups, a more salient question might be, what, if any, is the role of experience? But our concern here is with primates, especially human primates, where experience has been clearly implicated as important, and the interesting question is, where does biology fit?

In a recent review of the biological basis of maternal behavior, we have reiterated that a distinction must be made between mechanisms underlying the onset of maternal behavior and those that relate to the maintenance of maternal behavior (Capitanio et al., 1985). At least for nonprimate mammals, considerable evidence implicates biological factors in the former, but not the latter, process (Rosenblatt and Siegel, 1981). As might be expected, the majority of work has also been done on rodents; essentially nothing has been published to date addressing these issues in primates.

In rats, the onset of maternal behavior seems to depend in large part upon both hormonal and CNS active peptide mechanisms. Estrogen appears to be a most important hormone underlying the onset of maternal behavior. The onset of its action near parturition may be related to the withdrawal of progesterone inhibition of estrogen due to diminishing progesterone levels later in pregnancy. Exactly how estrogen exerts its effect is largely unknown. Recent data, however, involving intracerebroventricularly (ICV) administered peptides offer a possible explanation. Pedersen, Ascher, Monroe, and Prange (1982) found the ICV administration of oxytocin in estrogen-pretreated ovariectomized virgin female rats resulted in the rapid (usually within 1 hour) onset of maternal behavior. These findings suggest that certain CNS peptides may be active in the initiation of maternal behavior. What appears to be important is the levels of central oxytocin, not circulating or peripheral levels. The interrelationship of estrogen and oxytocin in the initiation of maternal behavior may be based upon estrogen causing a proliferation of oxytocin receptors in specific brain regions (e.g., limbic areas), thus priming these areas to be more receptive to the neuromodulatory and/or neurotransmitter actions of centrally released oxytocin. Such a relationship has been described between estrogen and oxytocin receptors on uterine muscle (Soloff, 1975). Whether this might also be true for CNS regions remains to be determined.

Very few data are available in this area for primates, human or nonhuman. In one study by Holman and Goy (1980), 90% of adult multiparous rhesus females were observed to show maternal behavior immediately to unfamiliar test infants, regardless of whether the females were intact breeders, ovariectomized (at least 19 months earlier), or postmenopausal. By comparison, intact nulliparous females did not display maternal behavior. These authors concluded that hormonal state was unimportant in the display of maternal behavior by multiparous monkeys, but rather that "a learning or imprinting-like process of mothering seems to occur, therefore, around parturition in first-time mothers" (1980:355). A possible mechanism to effect such a seemingly permanent behavioral change induced by a specific experience may be found in recent work reported by Hatton and Ellisman (1982) who found that female rats who had reared young at some time in their lives display apparently permanent alterations in postsynaptic receptor sites on magnocellular (probably oxytocin-producing) neurons in the paraventricular nucleus of the hypothalamus. Overall, however, the lack of sufficient experimental data from species-relevant paradigms precludes any definitive statements at this time about what effects hormonal state may play on the initiation of maternal behavior in primates.

Neuroanatomical

While the relationships between hormonal (or neuropeptide) status and maternal behavior in primates is far from clear, considerable data exist suggesting specific neuroanatomical loci may be important in effecting, maintaining, and otherwise regulating maternal behavior.

During the course of brain lesion studies in monkeys several decades ago, several interesting observations were made on the effect of such lesions on maternal behavior. These were incidental, indeed almost accidental, observations at the time, for mothering was not the major focus of the studies. Nonetheless they are both interesting and relevant to our current considerations. Thompson and Walker (1950) reported a study on behavioral differences observed in 11 rhesus monkeys following bilateral ablations of the medial surface of the temporal lobe. One female subject had given birth to a female infant 6 weeks prior to the surgery and was described as being a very solicitious and protective mother. Following the lesion surgery this animal was described as follows:

> The monkey with a baby . . . showed what can be called a perverted maternal instinct. The signs of affection and devotion towards her youngster were supplanted by indifference and annoyance. If the baby sought the protection of her mother she was often rebuffed, slapped or bitten. This was so serious that the infant's head became a mass of bruises and sores. The mother no longer made any effort to prevent the observer picking up and taking away her baby—in fact she seemed to be quite indifferent to the performance (Thompson and Walker, 1950:447).

Another related and again almost incidental observation was that of Klüver (1950) who described the apparent loss of maternal behavior in a female Java monkey following an experimental CNS lesion. In his discussion of a paper on another topic, Klüver stated:

> I should like to speak about a baby monkey. . . .The baby I am now referring to had a rather remarkable mother: namely, a Java monkey in which the connections between the temporal and the frontal lobes had been severed bilaterally without removing any cerebral tissue. Three years after the operation this monkey delivered a normal baby and within the next two years had two more pregnancies at term. In all three instances the baby was found lying on the floor of the cage. The mother made no attempt to pick it up and definitely refused it even when offered. She showed no excitement when the baby was finally removed. There was, therefore, a complete absence of maternal behavior (1950:226–227).

While in these cases the effects of the lesion on maternal behavior were peripheral to the central purposes of the research, there followed a few studies in which the effects of lesions on maternal behavior were directly addressed. In the first published study specifically addressing the issue of the effect of brain lesions on maternal behavior, Bucher, Myers, and Southwick (1970) bilaterally ablated anterior temporal cortex from two adult female rhesus monkeys, both with 5-week-old infants, and compared their mothering behavior to two sham-operated rhesus mothers, also with 5-week-old infants. Postoperatively the operated mothers exhibited a loss of protective retrieval of their infants in threatening situations, although they tolerated their infants' contact and nursing. This study clearly implicated neuroanatomical lesions as resulting in impaired maternal behavior. It was not clear, however, as Bucher pointed out, whether the effect was anything more than the mother's failure to recognize the infant as her offspring as part of the general impairment in object recognition noted with bilateral anterior temporal lesions (and the better known Klüver–Bucy syndrome).

Franzen and Myers (1973) also described rhesus mothers who had sustained bilateral temporal or anterior–frontal ablations and who demonstrated marked deficits in maternal behavior, generally ignoring their infants and failing to retrieve them when threatened. Control animals who underwent ablation of cingulate or visual association cortex did not suffer similar impairment in maternal behavior. Interestingly, mothers who sustained anterior temporal lesions tended to behave more aggressively toward their infants, pushing them away and actively punishing them, while prefrontally lesioned mothers tended more toward passive acceptance of their infant, with failure of protectiveness.

Subsequently, Myers, Swett, and Miller (1973) reported a dramatic loss of maternal behavior in two rhesus females who underwent bilateral resections of all prefrontal cortex (including orbitofrontal cortex) lying anterior to the frontal eye fields. According to these authors: "Following surgery, these animals consistently neglected their offspring, failed to defend them under circumstances of threat, and were often abusive and punishing when their infants attempted approach" (1973:268). It seems likely that the aberrant mothering behavior noted in these studies may have been part of a larger lesion-induced deficit in social attachment generally, of which mother–infant attachment is but one facet, as will be discussed in more detail in the following section.

The Concept of Attachment and Its Relationship to Child Abuse

General Considerations

Primate offspring tend to be few in number, develop slowly, and require a major parenting investment for their optimal growth and development (and thus reproductive success). Proper growth and development of young primates, human and nonhuman, requires as well an adequate species-typical social environment in which to develop as an infant and child and in which to operate as an adult. In this regard the issue of social attachment and social affiliative behaviors is most important, and this is an area about which there are some relevant primate data. While there may be considerable disagreement about "attachment" as a construct, few would argue that the bond between primate mother and infant is a very important component of maternal behavior and plays a significant role in the infant's development.

In fact, the importance of social attachments to the normal development and integrative functioning of members of our, and closely related, species has become obvious on several levels over the past several decades. The presence of social attachments appears to be related to improved physical health and well being (Berkman and Syme, 1979). Premature or inappropriate sudden disruption of attachment bonds, in addition to being subjectively painful, may lead to psychological disturbances, physiological disorganization, and ill health (Laudensager and Reite, 1984, see also section on consequences of early separation). Disturbances in attachment per se may result in skewed affective development and impaired parenting, including child abuse. Klein and Stern, examining the relationship between low birth weight and child abuse, suggested that "it appears likely that the enforced separation so commonly practiced in premature units contributes to abnormal maternal child relationships, including rejection, neglect, and finally, battering" (1971:17–18). To the extent that the process of attachment involves an increasing attunement and adjustment of each individual to the needs, feelings, etc., of the other, other evidence suggests that deficiencies in these abilities appear to characterize at least some forms of child abuse/neglect (Haynes, Cutler, Gray, O'Keefe, and Kempe, 1983 detailed in the next section). DeLozier (1982) has also implicated disturbances in early attachment as a significant etiological factor in subsequent child abuse and neglect. And, as summarized earlier, data from several primate laboratories support the idea that disturbances in early mother–infant attachment may be related to increased risk for subsequent infant abuse.

The question of what attachment really is (i.e., how you define it and measure it) has drawn increasing attention in the recent past, especially from those interested in studying mother–infant bonding in human and nonhuman mammals and early social–emotional development in human infants. Conceptually, attachment has been viewed from the standpoint of learning theory (Cairns, 1972), from an evolutionary perspective (Bowlby, 1969; Klaus, Trause, and Kennell, 1975; Ainsworth, 1963; 1964, 1973), from the standpoint of classical conditioning (Hoffman and Ratner, 1973), and from the viewpoint of the opponent process theory of motivation (Hoffman and Soloman, 1974). These issues and viewpoints have been reviewed by Rajecki, Lamb, and Obmascher (1978).

There is by now rather extensive evidence that social attachment

and social affiliative behavior is related in an important way to the function of certain limbic and frontal cortical areas. Steklis and Kling in an
unpublished study (quoted in Steklis and Kling, 1985) found that anterior temporal ablations performed in infant rhesus and vervet monkeys led to the operated animals being described as grooming less,
huddling less, and spending more time alone, apparently not attached
to other monkeys. These effects were greatest after the animals had
reached approximately 2 years of age. Similarly, prefrontal cortical
ablations in older animals may lead to deficits in social affiliative behaviors (Franzen and Myers, 1973). Such deficits are not seen in infants
sustaining these ablations, but the question is open as to whether they
would have appeared later (as seems likely the case) had the operated
infants been followed into adulthood. There is evidence that apparent
functional sparing after frontal cortical ablation in infancy is not permanent but rather is tied to the maturational schedule of this brain
region (Steklis and Kling, 1985).

Studies of the effects of regional ablations of specific brain regions
on such behaviors in older monkeys (where the question of developmental and maturational influences is not so prominent) tend to be
clearer. In their recent review, Steklis and Kling state: "From the studies
done to date on the influence of localized brain lesions on social behavior in juvenile or adult animals, it appears that the integrity of three
brain areas, namely the amygdala, temporal pole and orbital frontal
cortex are critical to the maintenance of affiliative interactions and social
bonds" (1985:16). In fact, the lesion studies described earlier as adversely influencing maternal behavior may well be another facet of the
neuroanatomical basis of social attachment generally.

We have as yet little knowledge of the effect of such lesions on similar
social and affiliative behaviors in human beings. It is unfortunate that
appropriate studies were not undertaken several decades ago when
there occurred, in one sense, an experiment in nature in which psychosurgical procedures involving frontal lobe areas were quite popular.
First conceived by Egas Moniz of Lisbon in 1936, the next several decades saw thousands of psychosurgical procedures performed for multiple reasons, although usually for treatment of disabling mental disorders. Characteristic sequelae of most procedures included an
impairment in social function, often described as a certain crudeness,
lack of awareness of social niceties, and diminished capacity to form
social relationships. Unfortunately most outcome studies involved formal tests of mental function and cognitive ability popular at the time
and did not concentrate on finer points of sociability. The data base
was also skewed, of course, by the fact that in many if not most cases
the preexisting illness (e.g., serious psychotic illness) had already been
responsible for major decrements in social functioning.

The overall weight of the evidence does support the notion, however, that certain limbic regions are important to the proper development, regulation, and expression of social attachment and affiliative behavior. The implication of such data for our improved understanding of facets of child abuse are probably substantial. What is needed is a method to noninvasively assess the functioning of these regions in intact individuals.

Attachment as Psychobiological Synchrony

The construct of attachment being a type of psychobiological synchrony between individuals is currently emerging as an attractive hypotheses and has been well articulated by Field (1985). An early proponent of this view of attachment was John Bowlby, who stated his views as follows:

> Until the mid-1950's only one view of the nature and origin of affectional bonds was prevalent, and on this matter, if on few others, psychoanalysts and learning theorists were at one. Bonds between individuals develop, it was held, because an individual discovers that, in order to reduce certain drives, e.g., for food in infancy and for sex in adult life, another human being is necessary. This type of theory postulates two kinds of drive, primary drives and secondary ones, and categorizes food and sex as primary and "dependency" (as the first bonding has unfortunately often been termed) as secondary. As Anna Freud puts it, it is a cupboard love theory of human relations (1973:40–41).

Reviewing data from studies in psychology, ethology, and human infant development, Bowlby then proposed it would be an improvement to consider attachment behavior from a different vantage point, specifically:

> Instead, the behavior I have been describing [attachment behavior] can be conceived best, I believe, in terms of a set of control systems—systems that are activated by certain conditions, for example, isolation or alarm, that when active mediate one or more of those forms of behavior that I am classifying as attachment behavior, and that are inactivated again when the attachment figure is in sight or grasp. To describe fully what I have in mind would take me far beyond the allotted space. Suffice it to say that the kind of apparatus I am proposing is conceived as analogous to the kinds of apparatus that physiologists believe responsible for maintaining body temperature at a certain point or blood sugar at a certain level (1973:50).

Here then is a clear statement postulating metaphorically that attachment is a behavioral system underlying in some way the establishment and/or maintenance of certain aspects of organismic homeostasis. Such a theory of attachment offers the advantage that it is empirically testable, and it is independent of imputed purpose. There now exist considerable suggestive, although not conclusive, data from both animal and human studies relevant to such a consideration of attachment.

We must conceptually separate "attachment" as a construct used to describe certain close social bonds (e.g., parent–offspring, peer–peer, and certain adult bonds) from other more basic aspects of the mother–infant relationship having to do with ensuring the physiological regulation, indeed survival, of the infant. It seems likely, however, that the latter serves as a prototype, an anlage, of the former, and it might be reasonable to expect a certain commonality of function and mechanisms. Relevant to this issue are a series of elegant studies by Myron Hofer, using infant rats as subjects, which have demonstrated the important and multifaceted manner in which the mother serves as an early important source of behavioral and physiological regulation. This body of work (e.g. Hofer, 1981; Hofer and Shair, 1982) has demonstrated that the mother has multiple regulatory influences, nutritional, thermoregulatory, behavioral, and others, that serve as important control systems for many aspects of the pups' behavior, sleep–wake state regulation, regulation of autonomic cardiovascular balance, thermoregulation, etc. The physiological changes found in rat pups subsequent to separation from the mother were thought to be due in large part to the withdrawal of these regulatory influences.

While few would agree that rat pups and their mothers are "attached," as the term is used in primates, the complex interplay of regulatory influences these studies have demonstrated may well form an important part of the biological foundation of social attachment as found in primates. It may well be that the social attachment bonds seen in primate mothers and infants have such early behavioral and physiological regulatory interplay as their foundation, and that older primates, who become "attached" to each other, have as a major component of their attachment a certain interindividual synchrony based upon a derivative of such early mother–infant regulatory interaction.

Sander and his colleagues (1970, 1982) have presented considerable data on the important role played by the mother and the early mother–infant relationship in providing a source of synchronization of behavioral and physiological rhythmicity in human infants, including the organization of sleep and wakefulness patterns and demonstrated interactional synchronization of neonatal movements to adult speech (Condon and Sander, 1974). Brazelton, Koslowski, and Main (1974) and Stern (1974) suggested that gaze and gaze aversion may be important regulators of arousal between mothers and their infants, and the relationship between gaze behavior and arousal level (as measured by heart rate) was subsequently confirmed by Field (1982). Brazelton *et al.* (1974) described the complex pattern of social interactions between mothers and infants in which rules for interactions are constantly altered by each member of the dyad, requiring sensitivity to the nuances of social behavior. They concluded that "this interdependency of rhythms seemed to be at the root of their 'attachment' as well as communication" (p. 74). Lester, Hoffman, and Brazelton (1982) found evidence that synchrony of social interactions between mothers and infants increases in magnitude and complexity as the infant becomes more mature.

Certainly mothers contribute in a very direct way to the physiological regulation of their infants, providing timing of the sleep, wake, and feeding cycles, amount and content of nutrition, overseeing thermoregulation, and the like. Young primates also exhibit evidence of close peer social attachment bonds; in such cases the direct forms of regulation seen with mothers and infants are not so apparent. We have recently collected what we believe to be relevant data on the issue of physiological synchrony in a pair of peer-reared pigtail monkey infants who lived together and appeared closely attached to each other. Separated from their natural mothers at birth, these two infants were placed together when they were 24 and 48 hours old, respectively, and subsequently reared together. At about 7 months of age, they were implanted with multichannel biotelemetry systems (Pauley and Reite, 1981). Following recovery from surgery the implanted telemetry units were turned on and physiological data [heart rate (HR), body temperature (BT), EEG patterns] were recorded simultaneously from both infants 24 hours a day. Recordings were made during 5 days of baseline, 11 of 17 days during which the animals were separated from each other, and for 3 days of reunion. HR and BT both demonstrated a significant circadian rhythmicity. We thus computed the best fitting 24-hour cosine describing the circadian periodicity, subtracted it out, and then computed a Pearson correlation coefficient on the residuals between the two animals' HR and BT data for each day. The resulting correlation coefficients ranged from .35 to .75 during baseline, tended to fall during separation, although still remaining above 0.2, and increased again during reunion. A sign test revealed that the correlation coefficients for HR were significantly greater during baseline than for the corresponding first 5 days of separation. Although no such trend was apparent for BT, the range of correlations was much greater during separation than during either baseline or reunion. Finally, both measures demonstrated increasing correlation during reunion, to levels (by the fifth day) that were well within the range of baseline levels (see Reite and Capitanio, 1985, for details). While these are clearly pilot data, we believe these results support the hypothesis that the two animals' physiological systems were synchronized as a result of their having lived with each other and having developed a strong attachment for each other.

Thus there is considerable evidence from several different areas supporting the notion that a major component of early mother–infant attachment is the development of mutual synchrony in the behavioral and biological rhythmicity of attached organisms. In fact, the impaired development of attachment, as so defined, has been implicated in nonorganic failure-to-thrive children. This syndrome, characterized by (1) disordered infant–caregiver interactions, (2) growth failure due to inadequate caloric intake without organic etiology, and (3) occurrence within the first years of life, has received increasing interest in the recent past. Mothers of children diagnosed as having nonorganic failure-to-thrive have been characterized as misinterpreting or failing to recognize their infant's cues resulting in benign neglect and incoordination between their actions and the cues of their infants (Haynes et al., 1983). Might this represent a fundamental defect in the attachment system, with wider implications for abuse generally? This idea is attractive and at least superficially seems consistent with the data from the early experience research described previously—certainly isolation and inanimate surrogate-rearing would not permit the species-typical development of psychobiological synchrony that may be associated with social attachment.

What is not yet clear is to what extent such disturbances in early mother–infant attachment relationships can be seen as resulting from aberrant early experience on the part of the mother, such that subsequent trouble in being a mother is in a sense a type of learned behavioral pathology, or whether aberrant early experience previously received by the mother as an infant may contribute to altered physiological and/or hormonal activity and/or responsivity that manifests itself later as disturbed maternal behavior. Also important is whether there may be any type of genotype that may preferentially select for vulnerability to disturbances in these areas.

WHERE DO WE GO FROM HERE?

The implications of the data presented in this chapter are severalfold. In this section we will discuss those issues, with the goal of suggesting how such data might influence the manner in which we look at abuse, and more specifically, can we develop specific testable hypotheses that can be empirically evaluated?

The data on abusive parenting in nonhuman primates demonstrate that certain environmental influences that seemingly influence abuse in human cultures are probably not species-specific. The implications of this observation are that such environmental influences, therefore, do not act through mechanisms that are culture- or species-specific. Their influence is more likely at a fundamentally different level, one shared by higher primates generally. The evocation of sociobiological mechanisms, such as has been done in the past by Bakan (1971), Lenington (1981), Lightcap *et al.* (1982), and others, is perhaps not unreasonable. The major implications of such an approach would appear to be in the area of prediction and modification on a large scale that is, certain environmental stresses or family conditions will likely be followed by increased incidence of abusive and/or neglectful parenting behavior. The elimination of such environmental stresses, an increased awareness of at-risk family situations, will likely be followed by decreases in abusive behavior. A major and as yet unanswered question is which individuals are at highest risk for having their parenting behavior adversely affected by such environmental conditions. The ability to answer that question would be of significant value in terms of cost-effective prediction and prevention.

The data demonstrating that primate parenting may be significantly skewed by aberrant early experience, possibly by altering the physiological state of the animal, through, perhaps, alterations in psychobiological synchrony between mother and infant, suggest similar mechanisms should be sought in humans. Considerable data already suggest important commonalities. Major issues include which individuals will be affected in which way by which experiences. Clearly individual differences are significant. Such individual differences may be rooted in both biological and psychosocial realms. What is required is the separation of these various issues as clearly as possible, formulating specific hypothetical interactions, and devising experiments to empirically evaluate each—not an easy task, but one in which a measure of success would be of great value.

This leads us to the final major issue, that is, to what extent is parenting behavior in primates biologically determined? For example, are CNS active peptides involved in maternal (or parenting) behavior? Can such be measured, and to what extent are individual differences in parenting behavior correlated with individual differences in the metabolism of such neurochemicals? To what extent might neuroanatomical differences be reflected in differences in parenting behavior? What, if any, is the role of synchrony in mother–infant attachment, and what might be the long-term consequences of variation in such a process? The relevance of such considerations for prediction of at-risk individuals, and, possibly, the development of rational therapeutic intervention, are obvious. Can altered physiology resulting from aberrant early experience be modified by specific subsequent therapeutic intervention? We only sketch these issues broadly here. The types of experiments required to answer such questions are obvious, and should, we believe, be performed.

Summary

Child abuse has been receiving increasing attention in the recent past, yet with few exceptions the problem has been viewed from an essentially parochial viewpoint which is time, species and cultural limited. Child abuse is a complicated symptom complex with a similar outcome (the abused child) likely resulting from the complex interplay of a number of separable and identifiable causal factors, or etiological agents. It is necessary to examine the problem from a number of vantage points including the historical, cross-cultural, comparative, and psychobiological.

This chapter presents evidence pointing out certain similarities, from an ecological and environmental standpoint, in infant and "child" abuse in human and nonhuman primates. Experimental data is presented suggesting how effective parenting is influenced by specific kinds of alterations in early experience. Finally, evidence is presented suggesting that certain behavioral systems thought to be important for effective parenting are likely determined to a significant degree by biological substrates.

Examination of data from nonhuman primates indicates similarities between infant and child abuse in human and in nonhuman primates. One common thread running through the primate literature is that the incidence of abusive behavior on the part of adults is increased by various forms of social and/or environmental stressors which are also frequently implicated in increasing the risk of child abuse in human populations. A second major theme in the comparative primate data is that aberrant experience in early infancy may result in subsequent skewed behavioral development, including abnormal parenting. Important among these experiences are early separation experiences. Separation experiences (i.e., the disruption of attachment bonds) result in disturbances in behavioral, physiological, and immunological function in nonhuman primates, and probably humans as well. Similarly, there is evidence suggesting that the receipt of abnormal or disturbed parenting can result in alterations in physiological functioning.

Biological contributions to maternal behavior are reviewed in both rodents and nonhuman primates. Substantial evidence is presented suggesting that attachment behaviors have a strong neurobiological substrate, including neuroanatomical localization in portions of the limbic system. Evidence is reviewed supporting the notion that attachment, in fact, represents a type of psychobiological synchrony between attached individuals, and some data supporting this concept obtained from nonhuman primates is presented. The implication of such data for improved understanding of child abuse are probably substantial.

Based upon such aforementioned data, a number of suggestions are made for future research directions.

REFERENCES

Ainsworth, M. D. The development of mother–infant interaction among the Ganda. In B. M. Foss, Ed., Determinants of infant behavior II. New York: Wiley, 1963, pp. 67–112.

Ainsworth, M. D. Patterns of attachment behaviors shown by the infant in interaction with his mother. Merrill-Palmer Quarterly, 1964, 10:51–58.

Ainsworth, M. D. The development of infant–mother attachment. In B. M. Caldwell and H. N. Ricciuti, Eds., Review of child developmental research, Vol. 3. Chicago, IL: University of Chicago Press, 1973, pp. 1–94.

Ainsworth, M. D., Blehar, M. L., Waters, E., and Wall, W. Patterns of attachment. Hillsdale, NJ: Erlbaum, 1978.

Bakan, D. Slaughter of the innocents. San Francisco, CA: Jossey-Bass, 1971.

Berkman, L. F., and Syme, S. L. Social networks, host resistance and mortality: A nine-year follow-up study of Alameda County residents. American Journal of Epidemiology, 1979, 109:186–204.

Bowlby, J. Grief and mourning in infancy and early childhood. Psychoanalytic Study of the Child, 1960, 15:9–52.

Bowlby, J. Attachment and loss, Vol. I. NY: Basic Books, 1969.

Bowlby, J. Affectional bonds: Their nature and origin. In R. S. Weiss Loneliness, the experience of emotional and social isolation. Cambridge, MA: MIT Press, 1973, pp. 38–52.

Brazelton, T. B., Koslowski, B., and Main, M. The origins of reciprocity: The early mother–infant interaction. In M. Lewis and L. A. Rosenblum, Eds., The effect of the infant on its caregiver. NY: John Wiley and Sons, Inc., 1974, pp. 49–76.

Bucher, K., Myers, R. E., and Southwick, C. Anterior temporal cortex and maternal behavior in monkeys. Neurology, 1970, 20:415.

Caine, N. G., and Reite, M. Infant abuse in captive pigtailed macaques: Relevance to human child abuse. In M. Reite and N. G. Caine, Eds., Child abuse: The nonhuman primate data. NY: Alan Liss, 1983, pp. 19–28.

Cairns, R. B. Attachment and dependency: A psychobiological and social-learning synthesis. In J. L. Gewirtz, Ed., Attachment and dependency. Washington, D.C.: V.H. Winston & Sons, 1972, pp. 29–80.

Capitanio, J. P. Behavioral Pathology. In G. Mitchell and J. Erwin, Eds., Comparative primate biology, Vol. 22: Behavior conservation and ecology. NY: Alan Liss, 1986, pp. 411–454.

Capitanio, J. P., and Reite, M. The roles of early separation experience and prior familiarity in social relations of pigtail macaques: A descriptive multivariate study. Primates, 1984, 25:475–484.

Capitanio, J. P., Weissberg, M., and Reite, M. Biology of maternal behavior: Recent findings and implications. In M. Reite and T. Field, Eds., The psychobiology of attachment. NY: Academic Press, 1985.

Clarke, M. R. Infant-killing and infant disappearance following male takeovers in a group of free-ranging howling monkeys (Allouatta palliata) in Costa Rica. American Journal of Primatology, 1983, 5:241–247.

Coe, C. L., Mendoza, S. P., Smotherman, W. P., and Levine, S. Mother–infant attachment in the squirrel monkey: Adrenal response to separation. Behavioral Biology, 1978, 22:256–263.

Condon, W. S., and Sander, L. W. Neonate movement is synchronized with adult speech: Interactional participation and language acquisition. *Science,* 1974, *183*:99–101.

Davenport, R. K. Some behavioral disturbances of great apes in captivity. *In* D. A. Hamburg and E. R. McCown, Eds., *The great apes.* Menlo Park, CA: Benjamin Cummings, 1979, pp. 341–357.

DeLozier, P. P. Attachment theory and child abuse. *In* C. M. Parkes and J. Stevenson-Hinde, Eds., *The place of attachment in human behavior.* NY: Basic Books, 1982, pp. 95–117.

Erwin, J. Primate infant abuse: Communication and conflict. *In* M. Reite and N. G. Caine, Eds., *Child abuse: The nonhuman primate data.* NY: Alan Liss, 1983, pp. 79–102.

Field, T. Affective displays of high risk infants during early interactions. *In* T. Field and A. Fogel, Eds., *Emotion and early interaction.* Hillsdale, NJ: Erlbaum, 1982, pp. 101–125.

Field, T. Attachment as psychobiological attunement: Being on the same wavelength. *In* M. Reite and T. Field, Eds., *The psychobiology of attachment.* NY: Academic Press, 1985.

Franzen, E. A., and Myers, R. E. Neural control of social behavior: Prefrontal and anterior temporal cortex. *Neuropsychologia,* 1973, *11*:141–157.

Gaensbauer, T. J., and Harmon, R. J. Attachment behavior in abused/neglected and premature infants. *In* R. N. Emde and R. J. Harmon, Eds., *The development of attachment and affiliative systems.* NY: Plenum Press, 1982, pp. 263–279.

Gunnar, M. R., Gonzalez, C. A., Goodlin, B. L., and Levine, S. Behavioral and pituitary–adrenal responses during a prolonged separation period in infant rhesus monkeys. *Psychoneuroendocrinology,* 1981, 6:65–75.

Harlow, H. F., and Harlow, M. K. The effects of rearing conditions on behavior. *Bulletin of the Menninger Clinic,* 1962, 26:213–224.

Hatton, J. D., and Ellisman, M. H. A restructuring of hypothalamic synapses is associated with motherhood. *Journal of Neuroscience,* 1982, 2:704–707.

Haynes, C. F., Cutler, C., Gray, J., O'Keefe, K., and Kempe, R. S. Nonorganic failure to thrive: Decision for placement and videotaped evaluations. *Child Abuse and Neglect,* 1983, 7:309–319.

Hennessy, M. B., Kaplan, J. N., Mendoza, S. P., Lowe, E. L., and Levine, S. Separation distress and attachment in surrogate-reared squirrel monkeys. *Physiology and Behavior,* 1979, 23:1017–1023.

Hinde, R. A., Spencer-Booth, Y., and Bruce, M. Effects of 6-day maternal deprivation on rhesus monkey infants. *Nature (London),* 1966, *210*:1021–1023.

Hofer, M. A. Toward a developmental basis for disease predisposition: The effects of early maternal separation on brain, behavior and cardiovascular system. *In* H. Weiner, M. A. Hofer, and A. J. Stunkard, Eds., *Brain, behavior and bodily disease.* NY: Raven Press, 1981, pp. 209–228.

Hofer, M. A., and Shair, H. Control of sleep–wake states in the infant rat by features of the mother–infant relationship. *Developmental Psychobiology,* 1982, *15*:229–243.

Hoffman, H. S., and Ratner, A. M. Effects of stimulus and environmental familiarity on visual imprinting in newly hatched ducklings. *Journal of Comparative and Physiological Psychology,* 1973, 85:11–19.

Hoffman, H. S., and Solomon, R. L. An opponent-process theory of motivation: III. Some affective dynamics in imprinting. *Learning and Motivation,* 1974, 5:149–164.

Holman, S. D., and Goy, R. W. Behavioral and mammary responses of adult female rhesus to strange infants. *Hormones and Behavior,* 1980, *14*(4):348–357.

Horenstein, D. The dynamics and treatment of child abuse: Can primate research provide the answers? *Journal of Clinical Psychology,* 1977, *33*:563–565.

Hrdy, S. B. Infanticide as a primate reproductive strategy. *American Scientist,* 1977, *65*(1):40–49.

Kaufman, I. C., and Rosenblum, L. A. The reaction to separation in infant monkeys: Anaclitic depression and conservation-withdrawal. *Psychosomatic Medicine,* 1967, *29*:649–675.

Klaus, M. H., Trause, M. A., and Kennell, J. H. Does human maternal behavior after delivery show a characteristic pattern? In *Parent–infant Interaction,* CIBA Foundation Symposium 33 Amsterdam: Elsevier, 1975, pp. 69–85.

Klein, M., and Stern, L. Low birth weight and the battered child syndrome. *American Journal of Diseases of Children,* 1971, *122*:15–18.

Klüver, H. Discussion of "Cybernetics. Circular causal and feedback mechanisms in biological and social systems." *Transactions Seventh Conference.* Josiah Macy, Jr. Foundation. New York, 1950, pp. 226–228.

Kraemer, G. W., Ebert, M. H., Lake, C. R., and McKinney, W. T. Hypersensitivity to *d*-amphetamine several years after early social deprivation in rhesus monkeys. *Psychopharmacology,* 1984, *82*:266–271.

Laudenslager, M. L., Capitanio, J. P., and Reite, M. L. Some possible consequences of early separation on subsequent immune function. *American Journal of Psychiatry,* 1985, *142*:862–864.

Laudenslager, M. L., and Reite, M. Losses and separations: Immunological consequences and health implications. In P. Shaver, Ed., *Review of personality and social psychology,* vol. 5, *Special issue on emotions, relationships and health.* Beverly Hills, CA: Sage, 1984, pp. 285–311.

Laudenslager, M. L., Reite, M., and Harbeck, R. Suppressed immune response in infant monkeys associated with maternal separation. *Behavioral and Neural Biology,* 1982, *36*:40–48.

Lealman, G. T., Haigh, D., Phillips, J. M., Stone, J., and Ord-Smith, C. Prediction and prevention of child abuse—an empty hope? *Lancet,* 1983, *1*(8339):1423–1424.

Lenington, S. Child abuse: The limits of sociobiology. *Ethology and Sociobiology,* 1981, *2*:17–29.

Lester, B. M., Hoffman, J., and Brazelton, T. B. Spectral analysis of mother–infant interaction in term and preterm infants. Paper presented to the meeting of the I.C.I.S., Austin, Texas, March 1982.

Lightcap, J. L., Kurland, J. A., and Burgess, R. L. Child abuse: A test of some predictions from evolutionary theory. *Ethology and Sociobiology,* 1982, *3*:61–67.

MacCarthy, D. The effects of emotional disturbance and deprivation on somatic growth. In J. A. David and J. Dobbing, Eds., *Scientific foundations of paediatrics.* London: Heinemann, 1981, pp. 54–73.

Maple, T. L., and Warren-Leubecker, A. Variability in the parental conduct of captive great apes and some generalizations to humankind. In M. Reite and N. G. Caine, Eds., *Child abuse: The nonhuman primate data.* NY: Alan Liss, 1983, pp. 119–137.

Mason, W. A. Social experience and primate cognitive development. In G. M. Burghardt and M. Bekoff, Eds., *The Development of Behavior.* NY: Garland, 1978, pp. 233–251.

Meyer, J. S., Novak, M. A., Bowman, R. E., and Harlow, H. F. Behavioral and hormonal effects of attachment object separations in surrogate–peer-reared and mother-reared infant rhesus monkeys. *Developmental Psychobiology*, 1975, 8:425–435.

Myers, R. E., Swett, C., and Miller, M. Loss of social group affinity following prefrontal lesions in free-ranging macaques. *Brain Research*, 1973, 64:257–269.

Nadler, R. D. Child abuse: Evidence from nonhuman primates. *Developmental Psychobiology*, 1980, 13:507–512.

Nadler, R. D. Experiential influences on infant abuse of gorillas and some other nonhuman primates. In M. Reite and N. G. Caine, Eds., *Child abuse: The nonhuman primate data.* NY: Alan Liss, 1983, pp. 139–149.

Pauley, J. D., and Reite, M. A microminiature hybrid multi-channel implantable biotelemetry system. *Biotelemetry and Patient Monitoring*, 1981, 8:163–172.

Pedersen, C. A., Ascher, J. A., Monroe, Y. L., and Prange, A. J., Jr. Oxytocin induces maternal behavior in virgin female rats. *Science*, 1982, 216:648–650.

Plimpton, E., and Rosenblum, L. The ecological context of infant maltreatment in primates. In M. Reite and N. G. Caine, Eds., *Child abuse: The nonhuman primate data.* NY: Alan Liss, 1983, pp. 103–117.

Rajecki, D. W., Lamb, M. E., and Obmascher, P. Toward a general theory of infantile attachment: A comparative review of aspects of the social bond. *The Behavioral and Brain Sciences*, 1978, 3:417–464.

Reite, M., and Caine, N. G. *Child abuse: The nonhuman primate data.* NY: Alan Liss, 1983.

Reite, M., and Capitanio, J. P. On the nature of social separation and social attachment. In M. Reite and T. Field, Eds., *The psychobiology of attachment.* NY: Academic Press, 1985.

Reite, M., Harbeck, R., and Hoffman, A. Altered cellular immune response following peer separation. *Life Sciences*, 1981, 19:1133–1136.

Reite, M., and Short, R. Nocturnal sleep in separated monkey infants. *Archives General Psychiatry*, 1978, 35:1247–1253.

Reite, M., and Short, R. Maternal separation studies: Rationale and methodological considerations. In K. A. Miczek, Ed., *Primate ethopharmacology: Models for neuropsychiatric disorders.* NY: Alan Liss, 1983, pp. 219–253.

Reite, M., Short, R., Kaufman, I. C., Stynes, A. J., and Pauley, J. D. Heart rate and body temperature in separated monkey infants. *Biological Psychiatry*, 1978, 13(1):91–105.

Reite, M., Short, R., Seiler, C., and Pauley, J. D. Attachment, loss, and depression. *Journal of Child Psychology and Psychiatry*, 1981, 22:141–169.

Rogers, C. M., and Davenport, R. K. Chimpanzee maternal behavior. In G. H. Bourne, Ed., *The chimpanzee*, Vol. 3. Basel: Karger, 1970, pp. 361–368.

Rosenblatt, J. S., and Siegel, H. I. Factors governing the onset and maintenance of maternal behavior among nonprimate mammals: The role of hormonal and nonhormonal factors. In D. Gubernick and P. Klopter, Eds., *Parental care in mammals.* New York: Plenum Press, 1981, pp. 13–76.

Ruppenthal, G. C., Arling, G. L., Harlow, H. F., Sackett, G. P., and Suomi, S. J. A ten-year perspective of motherless-mother monkey behavior. *Journal of Abnormal Psychology*, 1976, 85:341–349.

Sackett, G. P., Bowman, R. E., Meyer, J. S., Tripp, R. L., and Grady, S. S. Adrenocortical and behavioral reactions by differentially raised rhesus monkeys. *Physiological Psychology*, 1973, 1:209–212.

Sander, L. W., Chappell, P. F., and Snyder, P. A. An investigation of change in the infant–caregiver system over the first week of life. In R. N. Emde and R. J. Harmon, Eds., *The development of attachment and affiliative systems.* NY: Plenum, 1982, pp. 119–136.

Sander, L. W., Stechler, G., Burns, P., and Julia, H. Early mother–infant interaction and 24-hour patterns of activity and sleep. *Journal of the Academy of Child Psychiatry*, 1970, 9:103–123.

Schapiro, S. J., and Mitchell, G. Infant-directed abuse in a seminatural environment: Precipitating factors. *In* M. Reite and N. G. Caine, Eds., *Child abuse: The nonhuman primate data*. NY: Alan Liss, 1983, pp. 29–48.

Seay, B. M., Hansen, E. W., and Harlow, H. F. Mother–infant separations in monkeys. *Journal of Child Psychology and Psychiatry*, 1962, 3:123–132.

Soloff, M. S. Uterine receptor for oxytocin: Effects of estrogen. *Biochemical and Biophysical Research Communications*, 1975, 65(1):205–212.

Spencer-Booth, Y., and Hinde, R. A. Effects of brief separations from mothers during infancy on behavior of rhesus monkeys 6–24 months later. *Journal of Child Psychology and Psychiatry*, 1971, 12:157–172.

Spitz, R. A. Anaclitic depression. *Psychoanalytic Study of the Child*, 1946, 2:313–342.

Steklis, H., and Kling, A. Neurobiology of affiliative behavior in non-human primates. *In* M. Reite and T. Field, Eds., *The psychobiology of attachment*. NY: Academic Press, 1985.

Stern, D. Mother and infant at play: The dyadic interaction involving facial, vocal and gaze behaviors. *In* M. Lewis and L. A. Rosenblum, Eds., *The effect of the infant on its caregiver*. NY: Wiley, 1974, pp. 187–213.

Suomi, S. J., and Ripp, C. A history of motherless mother monkey mothering at the University of Wisconsin Primate Laboratory. *In* M. Reite and N. G. Caine, Eds., *Child abuse: The nonhuman primate data*. NY: Alan Liss, 1983, pp. 49–78.

Tennes, K. The role of hormones in mother–infant transactions. *In* R. N. Emde and R. J. Harmon, Eds., *The development of attachment and affiliative systems*. NY: Plenum, 1982, pp. 75–80.

Thompson, A. F., and Walker, A. E. Behavioral alterations following lesions of the medial surface of the temporal lobe. *Folia Psychiatrica, Neurologica et Neurochirurgica Neerlandica*, 1950, 53:444–452.

EXTERNAL AND INTERNAL INFLUENCES ON AGGRESSION IN CAPTIVE GROUP-LIVING MONKEYS*

Euclid O. Smith
Larry D. Byrd

chapter

7

Infant nonhuman primates, particularly Old World monkeys and apes, typically interact with a number of different types of conspecifics on a daily basis. The interactants range from mothers and matrilineally related kin to unrelated adult females and males. In addition, a variety of different behavior patterns can occur. An infant can be the object of extremely solicitous and nurturing behavior, and, in a matter of seconds, the same infant can become the object of a murderous attack. Moreover, a wide range of behavioral actions is possible from most of the members of a group. In order to render the task of describing the various interactions between infants and other group members more manageable, this contribution will be restricted to interactions between infants and mothers, infants and adult males, and infants and nonmaternal females.

MOTHERS

The primate literature abounds with studies of mothers and infants. Indeed, the one area of nonhuman primate behavior that has long been the focus of study of many primatologists is mother–infant relations. In recent years, a clearer picture of the complexity of mother–infant relations has emerged through the application of behavioral–ecology theory to questions of behavioral interactions. The detailed work of Jeanne Altmann (1980) and Nancy Nicolson (1982) has provided a be-

*This research was supported by U.S. Public Health Service grants DA-02128 and RR-00165 from the Division of Research Resources to the Yerkes Primate Research Center. The Yerkes Center is fully accredited by the American Association for Accreditation of Laboratory Animal Care.

ginning toward understanding the complex effects of social and ecological variables on patterns of infant development and independence.

Among the range of potential social interactions between mothers and infants, the vast majority are nurturing and solicitous. However, one should not be too quick to dismiss mothers as a source of aggression toward their own infants. Aggressive behavior by mothers toward their offspring has been studied relatively infrequently when compared to other aspects of the mother–infant relationship. Aggression has typically been studied in the context of the weaning process in captive animals (Jensen, Bobbitt, and Gordon, 1967, 1969; Kaufman and Rosenblum, 1969; Negayama, 1981). However, Troisi, D'Amato, Fuccillo, and Scucchi (1982) reported murderous abuse of an infant by its wild-born Japanese macaque mother housed in a captive group, and Carpenter (1942) reported that 8–10 rhesus mothers killed their infants while in transit from India to Cayo Santiago.

Abusive behavior by monkey mothers toward infants has frequently been observed during studies of the effects of social isolation and separation (Ruppenthal, Arling, Harlow, Sackett, and Suomi, 1976; Suomi and Ripp, 1983). A review of laboratory studies of the effects of social isolation and separation on maternal behavior can be summarized as follows. Most reports indicate that infant neglect or abuse by macaque mothers has occurred when the mother was socially incompetent as a result of (a) inadequate early social experience, (b) solitary housing, or (c) living in an unstable social group.

Recently, interest and attention has been focused on nonhuman primates in the search for a greater understanding of the biosocial bases of child abuse (Caine and Reite, 1983a; Suomi and Ripp, 1983). It has generally been concluded that mothers that were raised under laboratory conditions and were abused as infants tend to be abusive themselves. This is particularly true for mothers that also showed external manifestations of depressive behavior, social withdrawal, etc. (Caine and Reite, 1983b). Furthermore, field observers have noted mothers that act inappropriately or exhibit varying levels of maternal competence (Altmann, 1980).

The findings suggest that mothers are capable of aggressive acts toward their offspring and that these acts would be predicted only to the extent that they represent a disagreement between mother and offspring over termination, or at least reduction, in parental investment (Trivers, 1972).

ADULT MALES

For many species of Old World monkeys, in particular, cercopithecines, resident females and their offspring form the stable core of a social group (Wrangham, 1980). Adult males are typically immigrants who were born elsewhere (Packer, 1979). Given this model, application of evolutionary biology predicts very different types of behavior between mothers and adult males toward infants.

On the one hand, males should be protective and solicitous of the infants they have sired. In fact, many researchers have observed parental behavior by adult males under both laboratory and field conditions [see Redican and Taub (1981) and Taub (1984) for a review]. Adult male Japanese macaques have been reported to adopt infants and to serve as their primary providers (Alexander, 1970; Hasegawa and Hiraiwa, 1980; Itani, 1959; Wolfe, 1981). Although death is the most probable outcome if a male adopts an unweaned infant (DeVore, 1963; Hamilton, Busse, and Smith, 1982; Hasegawa and Hiraiwa, 1980; Rhine, Norton, Roertgen, and Klein, 1980), Berman (1982) reported that an 11-week-old orphan was cared for by four adult males on Cayo Santiago with no adverse consequences. The successful rearing of this infant was probably due to the food-rich and predator-free environment on Cayo Santiago, the persistent care by four unrelated adult males and a sister, which eventually led to a foster parent–infant relationship, and continuous interaction with peers.

Adult males do have the potential for positive affinitive behavior toward infants under certain circumstances. Indeed, adult males that are armed with strong, powerful canine teeth and heavy musculature have the potential to inflict serious wounds on infants. The most dramatic aggressive behavior that can be directed toward an infant results in death or infanticide. Infanticide has been observed or suspected in a wide variety of nonhuman primates, including colobine and cercopithecine Old World monkeys, the great apes, and a single genus of New World monkeys [see Hrdy (1977, 1979) and Hausfater and Hrdy (1984) for an extensive review]. As Sarah Hrdy (1977) noted, it is likely that several different categories of infanticide have developed for very different evolutionary reasons. Hrdy (1977) and Hausfater and Hrdy (1984) suggested that male infanticidal behavior, especially in nonhuman primates, can be explained as a result of sexual selection. For infanticide based on sexual selection, competition over breeding opportunities rather than over ecological resources seems to be the issue. Typically, infanticide occurs when a male from outside the troop usurps the social position of a resident male. However, resident males have been reported to engage in infanticide after changing from a nonbreeding to a breeding status (Busse and Gordon, 1983; Leland, Struhsaker, and Butynski, 1984; Wolf, 1980, cited in Hausfater and Hrdy, 1984). In either case, the male assumed a new status in a breeding situation in which he had previously been excluded and in which he was not the probable father of any infants. Often, related individuals protect the infant against a potentially infanticidal male (Collins, Busse, and Goodall, 1984; Crockett and Sekulic, 1984; Fossey, 1984; Leland et al., 1984).

Adult males may aggress against infants or at least put infants in a state of high potential risk in other, sometimes more subtle, ways. Itani (1959) first suggested that provisioned adult male Japanese macaques (Macaca fuscata) might use an infant to aid them in their social relations. He noted that at least one adult male used an infant as a passport in order to gain access to the central part of the troop. Kummer (1967) also described males using infants in their social interactions. He reported that subadult males would pick up an infant during fights with adult males. Deag and Crook (1971) observed extensive infant-carrying by adult male Barbary macaques (Macaca sylvanus) and coined the term "agonistic buffering." The concept of agonistic buffering has been applied to gelada baboons (Theropithecus gelada) (Bernstein, 1975; Dunbar and Dunbar, 1975), Japanese macaques (Macaca fuscata) (Kurland, 1977), chacma baboons (Papio anubis) (Popp, 1978; Seyfarth, 1978), and yellow baboons (Papio cynocephalus) (Shopland, 1982; Stein, 1981). Packer (1980) noted that infants are at some risk during these encounters. He observed one infant who was wounded severely while being carried during an intermale fight and suggested that three other deaths may have resulted similarly. Shopland (1982) reported the fatal injury of an infant who was used as an "agonistic buffer" in an intergroup encounter of yellow baboons. Stein (1981), however, noted that during nearly 1000 agonistic episodes involving adult male–infant interactions in yellow baboons, no infant received detectable physical injuries.

These observations of nonhuman primates suggest that unrelated adult males may pose a serious threat to young infants, and these males may be responsible for a significant proportion of aggressive behaviors received by immatures. Aggression may be directed toward the immature either directly or as a consequence of other types of interactions.

FEMALES OTHER THAN MOTHERS

Among Old World monkeys, females other than mothers often direct considerable attention toward young conspecifics. This behavior has been called aunting, allo, or play-mothering [for reviews, see Hrdy (1976) and Spencer-Booth (1970)]. It is important to realize that these interactions are often positive and affinitive, and, in extreme cases, can lead to the successful adoption of an orphaned infant (Berman, 1982; Boggess, 1976; Jay, 1965; Marsden and Vessey, 1968). Of course, infants may be "at risk" from the actions of nonmothers. There are reports of females kidnapping unweaned infants and keeping them until they died of starvation or dehydration (Bourliere, Hunkeler, and Bertrand, 1970; McKenna, 1979; Quaitt, 1979).

Perhaps the most extreme examples of violence by nonmothers against immatures can be found in Goodall's (1977, 1983) accounts of infanticide and cannibalism by an adult female chimpanzee and her daughter. Goodall observed three instances and reported eight other possible instances of infanticidal attacks by these two females. Fossey (1984) also noted circumstantial evidence of infanticide and cannibalism by an adult female mountain gorilla (*Gorilla gorilla berengei*) and her daughter. Although cannibalism was not observed, Carpenter (1942) has reported that adult females killed infants during the first year following the release of 350 rhesus monkeys on Cayo Santiago.

Silk and Boyd (1983), Silk, Clark-Wheatley, Rodman, and Samuels (1982), and Silk, Samuels, and Rodman (1981) also observed aggression by adult females toward infants and juveniles. Indeed, daughters of low-ranking mothers were the victims of harassment and aggression significantly more often than were sons of low-ranking females. Harassment and aggression against young females by other females in the group may begin prenatally through preferential attacks upon mothers pregnant with daughters (Sackett, 1981).

CAPTIVE GROUP STUDIES

Given the diversity of social interactions among nonhuman primates, it was important to determine whether drug effects observed in individual, isolated subjects would generalize to a social setting. Others have reported that *d*-amphetamine can increase aggressive behavior in group-living nonhuman primates (Bellarosa, Bedford, and Wilson, 1980; Haber, 1979). Our research has focused on aggressive and affiliative behaviors in captive, group-living monkeys. Although we recognize that studying primates under field conditions provides an opportunity to answer important questions relating to behavior and ecology, the study of captive, group-living, nonhuman primates allows a measure of control and observability that is often lacking in field observations. Studies of the behavioral effects of psychoactive agents have traditionally emphasized isolated animal preparations, an approach that has provided orderly, systematic data. Experiments with isolated, individual, animals have been useful in characterizing the behavioral effects of drugs and in predicting their effects on human behavior. We have developed a paradigm for studying drug effects on behavior within a social setting, an approach that can determine the generality of effects observed in experiments with individual animals. Experiments were conducted that involved the acute administration of a range of doses of *d*-amphetamine to adult male stumptail macaques living in the study group.

The subjects for these experiments lived within a group of 39 stumptail macaques (*Macaca arctoides*) housed in a 28.4 × 32.7 m outdoor enclosure at the Yerkes Regional Primate Research Center Field Station. Details of the housing conditions can be found in Smith and Byrd (1983). For the various experiments described here, subjects were typically observed during 15-minute focal-animal samples (Altmann, 1974). A group-scan observational technique was also used that involved recording the number of individuals engaged in several classes of behavior (e.g., aggression, submission, affiliation, general social activity, play, sexual behavior, and self-directed or solitary behavior) at 1-minute time intervals. This technique does not allow the precision or detail of the focal-animal technique, but it does permit the collection of group-interaction profiles (Smith and Byrd, 1983). Data were collected using a microprocessor-based data-collection device and were computer analyzed (Smith and Begeman, 1980). The drug administration protocol has been described in Smith and Byrd (1983) and will not be discussed in detail here except to note that the procedure does not involve the use of physical restraint and that the negative effects of handling are avoided. Blank, Gordon, and Wilson (1983) have reported the absence of elevated serum cortisol levels using a similar procedure.

Hierarchical dominance rankings of the males in the group have been determined weekly since the animals were initially released into the outdoor enclosure in December 1979. The positions of the five male subjects within the dominance hierarchy ranged from the highest- to the lowest-ranking. The dominance positions of individual animals were determined and verified based on the outcome of agonistic encounters among members of the group under baseline or nondrug conditions. An independent measure of dominance ranking was also obtained that involved scoring priority of access to a preferred food item (pieces of fruit). Correlations between rankings based on the outcome of agonistic encounters and displacement over preferred food items were high (r_s = 0.96).

Given that aggressive behavior is only one of an array of potential behaviors, we also decided to study changes in affiliative behavior. In order to study changes in aggressive and affiliative behaviors as a consequence of *d*-amphetamine administration, the drug was dissolved in sterile normal saline (0.9%) and injected intramuscularly in a volume of less than 1.0 ml. Sodium chloride solution (0.9%) served as a control (placebo) injection. Except for the highest dose (0.56 mg/kg) studied in monkey M-13 and the lowest dose (0.003 mg/kg) studied in monkey M-18, each dose was studied three times in each subject in a mixed, unsystematic order.

Mean hourly rates of occurrence of affiliative and aggressive behaviors were determined for each subject following drug or saline
administration based on observations during a period 90–180 minutes
postinjection (see Figure 7.1). This time period had been determined
previously to encompass the period of maximum effect. Under saline
or control conditions, affiliative behavior initiated by each of the five

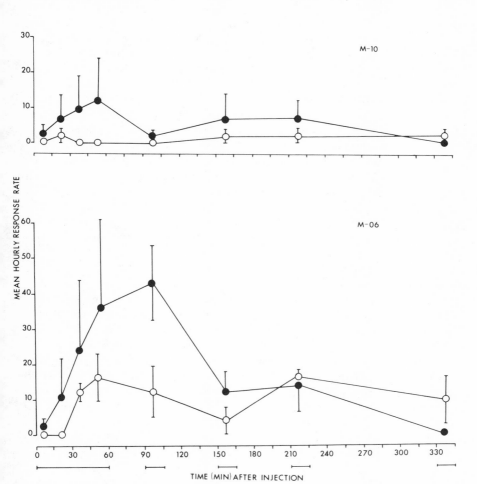

FIGURE 7.1. Time-course effects of 0.1 mg/kg d-amphetamine on self-aggressive
behavior in monkeys M-10 (top) and M-06 (bottom). Each data point
is the mean ± SEM based on three administrations of the drug
(filled circles) or saline (unfilled circles). Line segments beneath
the X-axis indicate time periods during which subjects were observed and data were obtained. (Reprinted by permission from the
Journal of the Experimental Analysis of Behavior.)

subjects was characterized by rates ranging between 20–50 occurrences per hour (see Figure 7.2). The highest-ranking subject (M-13) in the dominance hierarchy had a low control rate of affiliative behavior, and the lowest-ranking subjects (M-18 and M-24) had relatively high control rates. Following administration of d-amphetamine, four of the five subjects showed a dose-related decrease in rate of affiliative behavior. Moreover, the initiation of affiliative behavior was affected similarly in high- and low-ranking animals, and there was no discernible differential effect among those monkeys. When affiliative behavior was subjected to a more detailed analysis, the most pronounced change was evident in decreased rates of grooming, the most common type of affiliative behavior.

In contrast to the monotonically depressive effect of d-amphetamine on affiliative behavior, the drug markedly increased the rate of aggressive behavior in the same subjects (see Figure 7.3). d-Amphetamine increased the rate of aggressive behavior initiated by the highest- and the lowest-ranking animals and had little or no effect in the two mid-ranking subjects at the doses studied. The largest increase was observed in monkey M-13, the highest-ranking animal in the group. Rate of aggression in that monkey increased in direct relation to increases in dose, and at the highest dose studied (0.56 mg/kg), rate increased more than 30 times the saline values. d-Amphetamine also increased the rate of aggressive behavior initiated by monkeys M-18 and M-24, the two lowest-ranking subjects in the group, with a dose of 0.003 mg/kg having no effect and intermediate doses (0.01–0.03 mg/kg) increasing rate two- to eightfold over rates observed in the absence of the drug. A dose of 0.3 mg/kg produced decreases in rate in the two low-ranking monkeys, and the resulting dose-effect curves conformed to inverted U-shaped functions. There was no change in the rate of aggressive behavior over the same range of doses of d-amphetamine (0.01–0.3 mg/kg) in the two mid-ranking subjects in the group. Their behavioral rates remained within the range of rates observed in the absence of the drug (i.e., when saline was administered). The results of this experiment have been described in Smith and Byrd (1984).

The data showed that d-amphetamine can have qualitatively contrasting effects on different classes of naturally occurring behavior in individual monkeys comprising part of a large, heterogeneous social group (see Figure 7.4). d-Amphetamine decreased affiliative behavior to as little as 30% of saline control values, and the effect was monotonic and dose-dependent. In contrast, comparable doses of d-amphetamine increased aggression in the same subjects that exhibited marked decreases in affiliative behavior. The decrease in affiliative behavior observed in the present study is consistent with earlier reports of amphetamine's effects on the behavior of members of social groups.

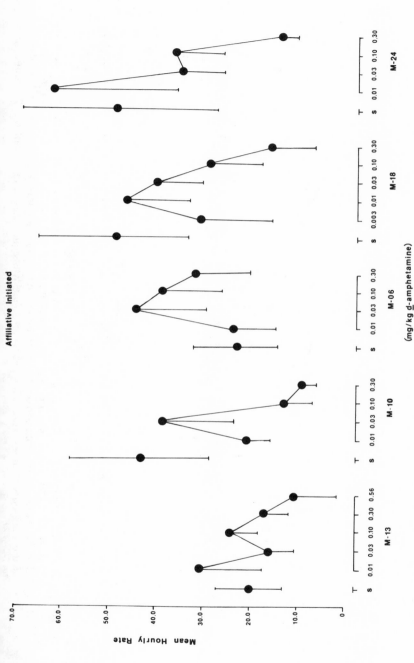

FIGURE 7.2. Effect of *d*-amphetamine on rate of affiliative behavior in five adult male stumptail macaques. Each data point is the mean ± SEM based on three administrations (except that the highest dose for monkey M-13 and the lowest dose for monkey M-18 are based on only one administration). Data points to the left of the dose-effect curves were obtained when saline was administered as a control. (Reprinted by permission from *Pharmacology Biochemistry & Behavior*.)

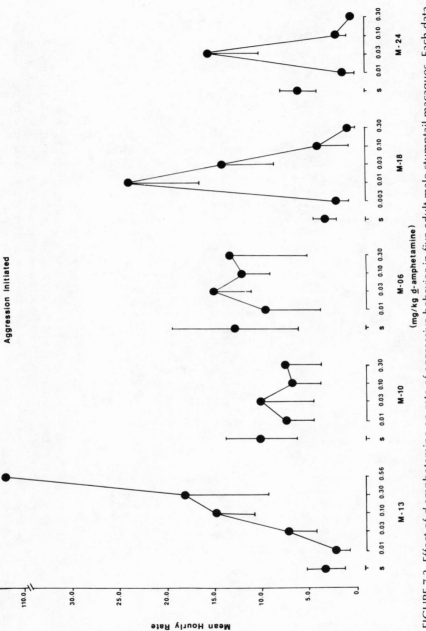

FIGURE 7.3. Effect of *d*-amphetamine on rate of aggressive behavior in five adult male stumptail macaques. Each data point is the mean ± SEM based on three administrations (except that the highest dose for monkey M-13 and the lowest dose for monkey M-18 are based on only one administration). Data points to the left of the dose-effect curves were obtained when saline was administered as a control. (Reprinted from *Pharmacology Biochemistry & Behavior.*)

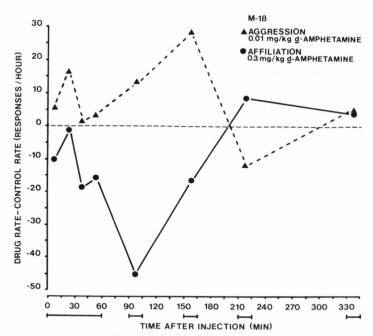

FIGURE 7.4. Time-course effect of 0.01 mg/kg d-amphetamine on aggressive
behavior (triangles) and effect of 0.3 mg/kg d-amphetamine on
affiliative behavior (circles) in monkey M-18. Data points are mean
differences (drug rate – control rate) on three administrations of
the drug. (Reprinted by permission from *Pharmacology Biochemistry & Behavior.*)

Kjellberg and Randrup (1972), Miller and Geiger (1976), and Scraggs
and Ridley (1978) reported dose-dependent decreases in social grooming, a major component of affiliative behavior, following the administration of d-amphetamine. The uniformity and generality of the reports
indicating decreases in affiliative behavior as a consequence of amphetamine administration compel one to regard this effect as characteristic of a number of primate species, especially when constituted as
social groups. The basis of the differential effect of amphetamine on
affiliative behavior is unclear, however.

Given the relatively uniform decrease in the initiation of affiliative
behavior following d-amphetamine administration in the present study,
the qualitatively dissimilar effect on aggression in the same subjects
was striking. The high- and low-ranking subjects exhibited pronounced,
dose-related increases in aggressive behavior at doses that either decreased affiliation or had no effect. In the two low-ranking subjects,

the dose-effect curves described an inverted U-shaped function characteristic of the effect typically obtained with this drug on operant behavior maintained under certain types of reinforcement schedules (Dews and Wenger, 1977; McMillan, 1969). Moreover, the range of doses having behavioral effects in the present study was quite similar to the range others have found to have effects on conditioned behavior in various species of nonhuman primates (Byrd, 1982; Kelleher and Morse, 1968; McKearney, 1968).

In addition to the qualitatively different effects of d-amphetamine on affiliative and aggressive behaviors, the present study provides additional evidence that the effects of this drug are a function of processes evolving out of group dynamics, for example, interactions between one animal and others occupying the same environment or the dominance hierarchy characteristic of a group. d-Amphetamine produced marked increases in rate of aggression in the high- and low-ranking subjects but did not cause similar change in the behavior of mid-ranking subjects. Moreover, the dose-effect curve for the highest-ranking member of the group was shifted to the right more than 1 log unit relative to the other subjects that showed increased responding. These differences in effects suggest that the hierarchical or dominance position of an individual subject in a group may serve as a determinant of the way in which a drug such as d-amphetamine can alter ongoing behavior characteristic of that individual. This hypothesis is supported by other reports that various psychoactive drugs can act selectively to alter the behavior of individual members of a group (Crowley, Stynes, Hydinger, and Kaufman, 1974; Haber, 1979; Miczek, Woolley, Schlisserman, and Hiroyuki, 1981).

The preceding results have been based on observations of individual male monkeys under treatment and nontreatment conditions. Additional information on the effects of drugs on the behavior of individuals can be obtained from an analysis of the data characterizing activities of the group as a whole. This technique allows comparison of the number of individuals in the group engaged in a given activity under different conditions. Figure 7.5 shows the proportion of total group members engaged in play behavior per scan sample expressed as a percentage change from saline conditions when each of five adult males received various doses of d-amphetamine. A sensitive indicator of normal social relations in most heterogeneous nonhuman primate groups or, for that matter, among most social mammals is the expression of play (Fagen, 1981). As can be seen in Figure 7.5, play behavior for the group decreased as a function of the drug dose administered to the highest-ranking male in the group (M-13). When the behavior of the alpha animal was altered, the typical expression of play behavior in the group was also altered and suppressed in a dose-dependent manner.

GROUP PLAY BEHAVIOR

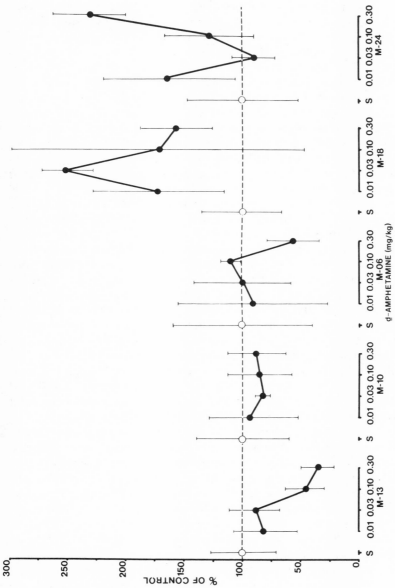

FIGURE 7.5. Effect of *d*-amphetamine on play behavior of nondrugged group members. Each data point is the mean ± SEM based on three administrations expressed as a percentage of control.

In contrast, similar drug administration to the lowest-ranking male (M-18) actually increased play behavior in the group. The result reinforces our view that alteration of the behavior of one individual in a group can have important effects on other aspects of group dynamics. Drug-treated animals can play an important role in altering stable patterns of ongoing social relations between nondrugged animals in a dose-dependent manner.

Given these contrasting results of the effects of d-amphetamine on the behavior of individual males and on nondrugged animals within the group, we sought to determine whether d-amphetamine would produce changes in the pattern or distribution of aggressive and affiliative behaviors toward specific members of the group. The purpose of the study was to describe the effects of d-amphetamine on the directionality of affiliative and aggressive behaviors and to determine if the recipients of these two classes of behaviors represented special subsets of the larger social group. First, data were analyzed to determine if behavior were directed consistently toward nonadult as compared to adult members of the group and whether d-amphetamine altered the directionality of aggressive and affiliative behaviors. Adults were defined as individuals 4 years of age and older and included those animals that were reproductively mature. Nonadults included monkeys less than 4 years of age. To apply the Chi-square test, the number of aggressive and affiliative interactions expected were determined based on the number of individuals in an age-class and on frequencies of behavioral interactions following saline administration. Mean hourly rates of occurrence of affiliative and aggressive behaviors initiated by male subjects following drug or saline administration were determined for each of five male subjects based on data obtained during preselected postinjection observation periods. Full dose-effect functions describing the results were reported previously (Smith and Byrd, 1984).

Table 7.1 summarizes data for the five male subjects that received d-amphetamine. Although maximum increases in aggressive behavior occurred at different doses for each of the five subjects, d-amphetamine uniformly increased aggressive behavior toward nonadult members of the group and decreased aggressive behavior toward adult monkeys in the group. The significance of the drug-induced changes was reflected in the results of the Chi-square tests, as shown in Table 7.1. The greatest redirection of aggressive behavior occurred in the three mid- and low-ranking animals, where values of $p \leq .001$ were obtained.

When the data were analyzed in a similar manner for maximum decreases in affiliative behavior, a contrasting pattern resulted (Table 7.1). Three subjects decreased affiliative behavior toward nonadult animals in the group and increased affiliative behavior toward adults, and two subjects showed an opposite effect. The significance of the changes

TABLE 7.1. Effects of d-Amphetamine on Aggressive or Affiliative Behaviors Initiated by Each of Five Adult Males toward Adult vs. Nonadult Members of the Group

Subject	d-Amphetamine dose (mg/kg)		Nonadult	Adult	χ^2	$p\leq$
Aggressive behaviors						
M-13	0.56	Expected	45.9 ↑	118.1 ↓	0.50	.50
		Observed	50.0	114.0		
M-10	0.03	Expected	17.1 ↑	39.3 ↓	1.37	.30
		Observed	21.0	35.0		
M-06	0.03	Expected	32.3 ↑	53.6 ↓	16.12	.001
		Observed	50.0	35.0		
M-24	0.03	Expected	3.1 ↑	35.5 ↓	123.88	.001
		Observed	22.0	17.0		
M-18	0.01	Expected	26.9 ↑	70.1 ↓	21.40	.001
		Observed	47.0	49.0		
Affiliative behaviors						
M-13	0.56	Expected	6.3 ↓	30.7 ↑	7.58	.01
		Observed	0.0	37.0		
M-10	0.30	Expected	25.2 ↓	58.8 ↑	2.94	.10
		Observed	18.0	66.0		
M-06	0.30	Expected	15.2 ↑	110.5 ↓	3.27	.10
		Observed	22.0	105.0		
M-24	0.30	Expected	6.0 ↑	54.6 ↓	6.80	.01
		Observed	12.0	48.0		
M-18	0.30	Expected	9.7 ↓	78.3 ↑	1.57	.25
		Observed	6.0	82.0		

in recipients of affiliation yielded values of $p \leq .01$ for two of the five subjects when evaluated by Chi-square tests. However, none of the changes in affiliative behavior was so large as the changes in recipients of aggressive behavior.

To determine whether the recipients of aggressive or affiliative behavior could be differentiated on the basis of matrilineally defined, genetic relationship to the aggressor, data were examined for those drug-treated monkeys whose genealogy was known. Subjects for the genealogical analysis were monkeys M-18 and M-24, two adult males that were born into the group and the only two adult males for which exact genealogy was known. Other group members were classified as kin-related or nonkin-related based on matrilineal records. Using rates of affiliative and aggressive behaviors under saline conditions and relative numbers of kin versus nonkin individuals in the group, expected rates of behavior for monkeys M-18 and M-24 were derived as shown in Table 7.2. Following administration of d-amphetamine, both monkeys showed an increase in rate of aggressive behavior toward matrilineally kin-related animals and a decrease in aggression toward nonkin individuals.

d-Amphetamine also produced a significant change in recipients of affiliative behavior following the administration of 0.30 mg/kg d-amphetamine. Statistically significant results were obtained for both subjects indicating significant departures from expected values, but the effects were opposite in direction (Table 7.2). Monkey M-18 increased affiliative behaviors toward nonkin and monkey M-24 increased affiliative behaviors toward kin-related individuals.

The data presented here show that d-amphetamine can have pronounced effects on the expression of aggression and affiliation among animals living in a large, heterogeneous social group. When compared to the pattern of aggression and affiliation under baseline, nondrug conditions, significant changes in rates and in objects or recipients of the behaviors were found for both classes of behavior following administration of the drug.

Although previous research has revealed much regarding the effects of d-amphetamine on the behavior of individuals comprising various types of groupings (Miczek, 1983), none has involved a group that yielded the type of analysis presented here. When the objects or recipients of aggressive behaviors were analyzed by age, for example, an unequivocal pattern based on age was revealed. Aggression directed toward young animals in the group increased for all five subjects following d-amphetamine administration. Moreover, the magnitude of the effect was inversely related to dominance position of the subjects in the group, with the highest-ranking male showing the smallest effect and the low-ranking males the largest effect. Differences in the statistical significance of the effects relative to dominance positions of the subjects

TABLE 7.2. Effects of d-Amphetamine on Aggressive and Affiliative Behaviors Initiated by Two Adult Males toward Kin vs. Nonkin Members of the Group

Subject	d-Amphetamine dose (mg/kg)		Kin	Nonkin	χ^2	$p \leqslant$
Aggressive behaviors initiated						
M-18	0.01	Expected	6.72 ↑	89.28 ↓	13.78	.001
		Observed	16.00	80.00		
M-24	0.03	Expected	8.58 ↑	30.42 ↓	1.75	.20
		Observed	12.00	27.00		
Affiliative behaviors initiated						
M-18	0.30	Expected	26.40 ↓	61.60 ↑	12.83	.01
		Observed	11.00	77.00		
M-24	0.30	Expected	23.40 ↑	36.60 ↓	4.05	.05
		Observed	31.00	29.00		

indicated further that the magnitude of the effects might be due, in part, to the social position of each subject. These data are consistent with other reports showing that the behavioral effects of various drugs may be a function of the dominance position of the drug-treated subject. Wilson, Bailey, and Bedford (1983) reported that d-amphetamine decreased food retrieval in high-ranking subjects and increased food retrieval in lower ranking subjects. In other food competition tests, Bellarosa et al. (1980), Grove, Wilson, and Bedford (1977), and Lovell, Bedford, Grove, and Wilson (1980) found increased food capture by subordinate animals when either the entire group or only the dominant animal was administered d-amphetamine. In other studies, Haber, Barchas, and Barchas (1977) and Haber, Berger, and Barchas (1979) reported that d-amphetamine administration increased submissive behavior in low-ranking animals. Finally, Schlemmer and Davis (1981) found rank-mediated changes in behavior following chronic d-amphetamine administration in small groups of stumptail macaques.

Changes in the directionality of affiliative behavior following drug administration were less uniform among the five subjects. Three of the subjects decreased and two increased the frequency of affiliative behavior directed toward young animals in the group. A possible basis for this difference in effect among the five subjects was not readily apparent. The two subjects that increased affiliative behavior toward nonadult members of the group were in the low–middle positions of the dominance hierarchy, but there was little else to indicate that the dominance position of the subject was a major determinant of the drug effect on affiliation. Indeed, we reported previously that d-amphetamine decreased affiliation uniformly and independently of dominance position in the group (Smith and Byrd, 1984).

Of substantial interest in the present experiment were data showing that kin-related animals were more likely than nonkin-related animals to be targets of aggressive behaviors following d-amphetamine administration. Kinship groups have been shown to form strong interactional subunits for all primate species where kinship relations among members of a social group were known (Chagnon, 1975; Koyama, 1970; Nash, 1976; Chepko-Sade and Sade, 1979; van Lawick-Goodall, 1967). This fact has been well documented by behavioral primatologists, but a detailed analysis of drug-induced behavioral changes in group-living animals with a known network of genealogical relations has not been reported. Although this phenomenon might normally be explained by greater spatial proximity to kin versus nonkin, proximity did not account for the results when the data were corrected for a greater absolute number of nonkin animals. Furthermore, drug versus nondrug comparisons were made against the saline control rate. The data were convincing in that both of the subjects with known genealogical histories exhibited the same pattern of increased aggression toward kin members of the group. That d-amphetamine had opposite effects on affiliation for the same two subjects indicates that there are likely other complex variables regulating the expression of affiliation in a socially living primate.

These findings are suggestive of a phenomenon that might have relevance for studies of child abuse and neglect. Based on studies of aggressive behavior in nonhuman primates, one would predict that individuals should aggress least against, and assist in fights with, those individuals that are related to them. To some extent, these predictions have been supported for rhesus macaques (Kaplan, 1977, 1978), pigtail macaques (Massey, 1977), and Japanese macaques (Kurland, 1977). It is of considerable interest that administration of d-amphetamine increases aggressive behavior against not only immature individuals, but kin-related individuals as well. Unfortunately, due to the small sample size in the present study, the orthogonal comparison of kin-related young versus nonkin-related young could not be made.

Although these results were obtained in a single captive group, they are at least suggestive that a psychoactive substance may modulate in a direct manner the expression of aggressive behavior toward a particular class of individuals. Given available data on the number of male child abusers and on the abuse rate of d-amphetamine, we might be able to make some tentative predictions on the extent to which our animal model may pertain to the human conditions.

Based on a survey by the National Center on Child Abuse and Neglect, Burgdorf (1980), cited in Gelles (1982), notes that there were 351,100 cases of child abuse in 1979. Data provided by the American Humane Association, cited in Lenington (1981), indicate that males were responsible for 39.4% of the 139,580 cases of child abuse reported in 1979. Although these estimates differ by more than a factor of two and illustrate the difficulty in obtaining accurate data, they do give some indication of the extent of child abuse.

The 1982 Household Survey of Drug Abuse, conducted by the National Institute on Drug Abuse, provides information on the nonmedical use of amphetamine. Included in this survey were data indicating lifetime prevalence of the use of psychoactive substances. In a sample of 4100 individuals, 18 years of age or older, 9.7% indicated that they had used amphetamine for nonmedical purposes on at least one occasion. Since data on gender of respondent were not available, males will be assumed to have accounted for one-half the sample, which is probably an underestimate. Based on a population of more than 75 million males aged 18 years or older in the United States in 1979, this means that approximately 3.7 million individuals had used amphetamine at least once.

To the extent that our nonhuman primate model pertains, it may be of interest to compare these observations. Males who are known to abuse amphetamine at least once constitute approximately 5% of the United States population, and 0.2% of the adult males in this country account for the reported cases of child abuse. Based on probability alone, therefore, one would expect that our model might be applicable to approximately 6600 individuals, or about 5% of the total cases of child abuse. Moreover, it is possible that our model has yielded significant results at two different levels. First, we have shown that following the acute administration of *d*-amphetamine, important patterns of behavior can be disrupted and even altered in a consistent manner. Consistent with these results, individuals have been shown to aggress against kin-related individuals at a disproportionately high rate. However, the general increase in aggressive behavior by adult males toward youngsters should signal the potential for biological fathers as well as stepfathers to engage in child-abusive behavior. Johnson (1974) and Gil (1970) noted that stepparents were significantly more likely than biological parents to abuse children. Second, and of more clinical relevance, when our data are applied to the United States population, there are a substantial number of cases to which our research and findings might pertain.

In conclusion, it is only through careful observations and experimentation that we can begin to understand the complex interrelationship between biology and behavior. Our results demonstrate the importance of developing appropriate animal models for studying and understanding complex human behavior patterns.

SUMMARY

The use of animal models to further our understanding of human behavior is significant only insofar as the experimental results have some generalizing properties. The experimental alteration of the behavior of individual, group-living, nonhuman primates has provided the opportunity to understand better the group dynamics of behavioral interactions. This chapter reports on experimentally induced changes in patterns of aggressive behavior by the acute administration of *d*-amphetamine to adult male stumptail monkeys (*Macaca arctoides*). Each subject that received *d*-amphetamine increased aggressive behavior toward nonadult and decreased aggression toward adult animals in the group. Moreover, where matrilineal relationships were known, *d*-amphetamine increased aggression toward matrilineal kin and decreased aggression toward nonkin animals. These results suggest that *d*-amphetamine not only selectively alters the types of behavior exhibited

by individuals, but also alters normal patterns of ongoing social interactions.

ACKNOWLEDGMENTS

The authors thank P. Peffer, S. Martin, F. Kiernan, and P. Plant for
assistance in preparation of the manuscript.

REFERENCES

Alexander, B. K. Parental behavior of adult male Japanese monkeys. *Behaviour*, 1970, *36*:270–285.

Altmann, J. Observational study of behavior: Sampling methods. *Behaviour*,
1974, *49*:227–265.

Altmann, J. *Baboon mothers and infants.* Cambridge, MA: Harvard University
Press, 1980.

Bellarosa, A., Bedford, J. A., and Wilson, M. C. Sociopharmacology of *d*-
amphetamine in *Macaca arctoides*. *Pharmacology Biochemistry & Behavior*, 1980,
13:221–228.

Berman, C. M. The social development of an orphaned rhesus infant on
Cayo Santiago: Male care, foster mother–orphan interaction and peer interaction. *American Journal of Primatology*, 1982, *3*:131–141.

Bernstein, I. S. Activity patterns in a gelada monkey group. *Folia Primatologica*, 1975, *23*:50–71.

Blank, M. S., Gordon, T. P., and Wilson, M. C. Effects of capture and veni-
puncture on serum levels of prolactin, growth hormone and cortisol in outdoor
compound-housed female rhesus monkeys (*Macaca mulatta*). *Acta Endocri-
nologica*, 1983, *102*:190–195.

Boggess, J. E. The social behavior of the Himalayan langur (*Presbytis entellus*)
in the Nepal Himalaya. Unpublished Ph.D. dissertation, University of California,
Berkeley, 1976.

Bourliere, F., Hunkeler, C., and Bertrand, M. Ecology and behavior of Lowe's
guenon (*Cercopithecus campbelli* Lowei) in the Ivory Coast. *In* J. R. Napier
and P. H. Napier, Eds., *Old World monkeys.* NY: Academic Press, 1970, pp.
297–350.

Busse, C. D., and Gordon, T. P. Attacks on neonates by a male mangabey
(*Cercocebus atys*). *American Journal of Primatology*, 1983, *5*:345–356.

Byrd, L. D. Comparison of the behavioral effects of phencyclidine, ketamine,
d-amphetamine and morphine in the squirrel monkey. *Journal of Pharmacology
and Experimental Therapeutics*, 1982, *220*:139–144.

Caine, N., and Reite, M., Eds. *Child abuse: The nonhuman primate data.*
NY: Alan Liss, 1983.(a)

Caine, N., and Reite, M. Infant abuse in captive pig-tailed macaques: Relevance to human child abuse. *In* N. Caine and M. Reite (Eds.), *Child abuse:
The nonhuman primate data.* NY: Alan Liss, 1983, pp. 19–27.(b)

Carpenter, C. R. Societies of monkeys and apes. *Biological Symposia*, 1942,
8:177–204.

Chagnon, N. A. Genealogy, solidarity, and relatedness: Limits to group size
and patterns of fissioning in an expanding population. *Yearbook of Physical
Anthropology*, 1975, *19*:95–110.

Chepko-Sade, B. D., and Sade, D. S. Patterns of group splitting within ma-trilineal kinship groups: A study of social group structure in *Macaca mulatta* (Cercopithecidae: Primates). *Behavioral Ecology and Sociobiology*, 1979, *5*:67–86.

Collins, D. A., Busse, C. D., and Goodall, J. Infanticide in two populations of savanna baboons. *In* G. Hausfater and S. B. Hrdy, Eds., *Infanticide: Comparative and evolutionary perspectives*. NY: Aldine, 1984, pp. 193–215.

Crockett, C. M., and Sekulic, R. Infanticide in red howler monkeys (*Alouatta seniculus*). *In* G. Hausfater and S. B. Hrdy, Eds., *Infanticide: Comparative and evolutionary perspectives*. NY: Aldine, 1984, pp. 173–191.

Crowley, T. J., Stynes, A. J., Hydinger, M., and Kaufman, I. C. Ethanol, methamphetamine, pentobarbital, morphine, and monkey social behavior. *Archives of General Psychiatry*, 1974, *31*:829–838.

Deag, J. M., and Crook, J. H. Social behavior and "agonistic buffering" in the wild barbary macaque *Macaca sylvana* L. *Folia Primatologica*, 1971, *15*:183–200.

DeVore, I. Mother–infant relations in free-ranging baboons. *In* H. Rheingold, Ed., *Maternal behavior in mammals*. NY: Wiley, 1963, pp. 305–335.

Dews, P. B., and Wenger, G. R. Rate-dependency of the behavioral effects of amphetamine. *In* T. Thompson and P.B. Dews, Eds., *Advances in behavioral pharmacology*, vol. 1. NY: Academic Press, 1977, pp. 167–227.

Dunbar, R., and Dunbar, P. *Social dynamics of gelada baboons (Contributions to primatology*, vol. 6). Basel: S. Karger, 1975.

Fagen, R. *Animal play behavior*. New York: Oxford University Press, 1981.

Fossey, D. Infanticide in mountain gorillas (*Gorilla gorilla beringei*) with comparative notes on chimpanzees. *In* G. Hausfater and S. B. Hrdy, Eds., *Infanticide: Comparative and evolutionary perspectives*. NY: Aldine, 1984, pp. 217–235.

Gelles, R. J. Child abuse in the context of violence in the family and society. Paper presented at the Conference on Research Issues in Child Abuse, Oxford, England, November 25–27, 1982.

Gil, D. G. *Violence against children*. Cambridge, MA: Harvard University Press, 1970.

Goodall, J. Infant killing and cannibalism in free-living chimpanzees. *Folia Primatologica*, 1977, *28*:259–282.

Goodall, J. Population dynamics during a 15-year period in one community of free-living chimpanzees in the Gombe National Park, Tanzania. *Zeitschrift für Tierpsychologie*, 1983, *61*:1–60.

Grove, L., Wilson, M., and Bedford, J. Effects of diazepam and *d*-amphetamine on food competition in rhesus monkey. *The Pharmacologist*, 1977, *19*:228.

Haber, S. N. The effects of amphetamine on social and individual behavior of rhesus macaques. Unpublished Ph.D. dissertation, Stanford University, Stanford, 1979.

Haber, S. N., Barchas, P. R., and Barchas, J. D. Effects of amphetamine on social behaviors of rhesus macaques: an animal model of paranoia. *In* I. Hanin and E. Usdin, Eds., *Animal models in psychiatry and neurology*. Elmsford, NY: Pergamon Press, 1977, pp. 107–115.

Haber, S. N., Berger, P. A., and Barchas, P. R. The effects of amphetamine on agonistic behaviors in nonhuman primates. *In* E. Usdin, I. J. Kopin, and J. D. Barchas, Eds., *Catecholamines: Basic and clinical frontiers*. Elmsford, NY: Pergamon Press, 1979, pp. 1702–1704.

Hamilton, W. J. III, Busse, C., and Smith, K. S. Adoption of infant orphan chacma baboons. *Animal Behaviour*, 1982, *30*:29–34.

Hasegawa, T., and Hiraiwa, M. Social interactions of orphans observed in a free-ranging troop of Japanese monkeys. *Folia Primatologica*, 1980, *33*:129–158.

Hausfater, G., and Hrdy, S. B. Eds. *Infanticide: Comparative and evolutionary perspectives*. NY: Aldine, 1984.

Hrdy, S. B. Care and exploitation of nonhuman primate infants by conspecifics other than the mother. *In* J. S. Rosenblatt, R. A. Hinde, E. Shaw, and C. Beer, Eds., *Advances in the study of behavior*, vol. 6. NY: Academic Press, 1976, pp. 101–158.

Hrdy, S. B. *The langurs of Abu: Female and male strategies of reproduction.* Cambridge, MA: Harvard University Press, 1977.

Hrdy, S. B. Infanticide among animals: A review, classification and examination of the implications for the reproductive strategies of females. *Ethology and Sociobiology*, 1979, *1*:13–40.

Itani, J. Paternal care in the wild Japanese monkey, *Macaca fuscata*. *Primates*, 1959, *2*:61–94.

Jay, P. C. The common langur of North India. *In* I. DeVore, Ed., *Primate behavior: Field studies of monkeys and apes*. NY: Holt, Rinehart and Winston, 1965, pp. 197–249.

Jensen, G. D., Bobbitt, R. A., and Gordon, B. N. Development of mutual independence in mother–infant pigtailed monkeys. *In* S. A. Altmann, Ed., *Social communication among primates*. Chicago, IL: University of Chicago Press, 1967, pp. 43–53.

Jensen, G. D., Bobbitt, R. A., and Gordon, B. N. Studies of mother–infant interactions in monkeys (*Macaca nemestrina*): Hitting behavior. *In* C. R. Carpenter, Ed., *Proceedings of the 2nd International Congress of Primatology: Behavior*, vol. 1. Basel: S. Karger, 1969, pp. 186–193.

Johnson, C. L. *Child abuse in the southeast*. Athens, GA: Regional Institute of Social Welfare Research, University of Georgia, 1974.

Kaplan, J. R. Patterns of fight interference in free-ranging rhesus monkeys. *American Journal of Physical Anthropology*, 1977, *47*:279–288.

Kaplan, J. R. Fight interference and altruism in rhesus monkeys. *American Journal of Physical Anthropology*, 1978, *49*:241–249.

Kaufman, I. C., and Rosenblum, L. A. The waning of the mother–infant bond in two species of macaques. *In* B. M. Foss, Ed., *Determinants of infant behavior*, vol. 4. London: Methuen, 1969, pp. 41–59.

Kelleher, R. T., and Morse, W. H. Determinants of the specificity of behavioral effects of drugs. *Ergebnisse der Physiologie, Biologischen Chemie und Experimentellen Pharmakologie*, 1968, *60*:1–56.

Kjellberg, B., and Randrup, A. Changes in social behaviour in pairs of vervet monkeys (*Cercopithecus*) produced by single, low doses of amphetamine. *Psychopharmacologia*, 1972, *26*:127.

Koyama, N. Changes in dominance rank and division of a wild Japanese monkey troop in Arashiyama. *Primates*, 1970, *11*:335–390.

Kummer, H. Tripartite relations in hamadryas baboons. *In* S.A. Altmann, Ed., *Social communication among primates*. Chicago, IL: University of Chicago Press, 1967, pp. 63–71.

Kurland, J. A. *Kin selection in the Japanese monkey*. Basel: S. Karger, 1977.

Leland, L., Struhsaker, T. T., and Butynski, T. M. Infanticide by adult males in three primate species of Kibale Forest, Uganda: A test of hypotheses. *In* G.

Hausfater and S. B. Hrdy, Eds., *Infanticide: Comparative and evolutionary perspectives*. NY: Aldine, 1984, pp. 151–172.

Lenington, S. Child abuse: The limits of sociobiology. *Ethology and Sociobiology*, 1981, 2:17–29.

Lovell, D. K., Bedford, J. A., Grove, L., and Wilson, M. C. Effects of d-amphetamine and diazepam on paired and grouped primate food competition. *Pharmacology Biochemistry and Behavior*, 1980, 13:177–181.

McKearney, J. W. Maintenance of responding under a fixed-interval schedule of electric shock presentation. *Science*, 1968, 160:1249–1251.

McKenna, J. J. The evolution of allomothering behavior among colobine monkeys: Function and opportunism in evolution. *American Anthropologist*, 1979, 81:818–840.

McMillan, D. E. Effects of d-amphetamine on performance under several parameters of multiple fixed-ratio, fixed-interval schedules. *Journal of Pharmacology and Experimental Therapeutics*, 1969, 167:26–33.

Marsden, H. M., and Vessey, S. H. Adoption of an infant green monkey within a social group. *Communications in Behavioral Biology*, Part A, 1968, 2:275–279.

Massey, A. Agonistic aids and kinship in a group of pigtail macaques. *Behavioral Ecology and Sociobiology*, 1977, 231–40.

Miczek, K. A., Ed. *Ethopharmacology: Primate models of neuropsychiatric disorders*. New York: Alan R. Liss, 1983.

Miczek, K. A., Woolley, J., Schlisserman, S., and Hiroyuki, Y. Analysis of amphetamine effects on agonistic and affiliative behavior in squirrel monkeys (*Saimiri sciureus*). *Pharmacology Biochemistry and Behavior*, 1981, 14:103–107.

Miller, M. H., and Geiger, E. Dose effects of amphetamine on macaque social behavior: Reversal by haloperidol. *Research Communications in Psychology, Psychiatry and Behavior*, 1976, 1:125–142.

Nash, L. T. Troop fission in free-ranging baboons in Gombe Stream National Park, Tanzania. *American Journal of Physical Anthropology*, 1976, 44:63–77.

Negayama, K. Maternal aggression to its offspring in Japanese monkeys. *Journal of Human Evolution*, 1981, 10:523–527.

Nicolson, N. Weaning and the development of independence in olive baboons. Unpublished Ph.D. dissertation, Harvard University, Cambridge, 1982.

Packer, C. Inter-troop transfer and inbreeding avoidance in *Papio anubis*. *Animal Behaviour*, 1979, 27:1–36.

Packer, C. Male care and exploitation of infants in *Papio anubis*. *Animal Behaviour*, 1980, 28:512–520.

Popp, J. L. Male baboons and evolutionary principles. Unpublished Ph.D. dissertation, Harvard University, Cambridge, 1978.

Quaitt, D. Aunts and mothers: Adaptive implications of allomaternal behavior. *American Anthropologist*, 1979, 81:310–319.

Redican, W. K., and Taub, D. M. Male parental care in monkeys and apes. *In* M. E. Lamb, Ed., *The role of the father in child development*. NY: Wiley, 1981, pp. 203–258.

Rhine, R. J., Norton, G. W., Roertgen, W. J., and Klein, H. D. The brief survival of free-ranging baboon infants (*Papio cynocephalus*) after separation from their mothers. *International Journal of Primatology*, 1980, 1:401–409.

Ruppenthal, G. C., Arling, G. L., Harlow, H. F., Sackett, G. P., and Suomi, S. J. A 10-year perspective of motherless mother monkey behavior. *Journal of Abnormal Psychology*, 1976, 85:341–349.

Sackett, G. P. Receiving severe aggression correlates with fetal gender in pregnant pigtailed monkeys. *Developmental Psychobiology*, 1981, *14*:267–272.

Schlemmer, R. F., Jr., and Davis, J. M. LSD-induced behavioral changes in selected members of a primate social colony. *Federation Proceedings*, 1981, *40*:306.

Scraggs, P. R., and Ridley, R. M. Behavioural effects of amphetamine in a small primate: Relative potencies of the *d*- and *l*-isomers. *Psychopharmacology*, 1978, *59*:243–245.

Seyfarth, R. M. Social relationships among adult male and female baboons. II. Behaviour throughout the female reproductive cycle. *Behaviour*, 1978, *64*:227–247.

Shopland, J.M . An intergroup encounter with fatal consequences in yellow baboons (Papio cyncocephalus). *American Journal of Primatology*, 1982, *3*:263–266.

Silk, J. B., and Boyd, R. Female cooperation, competition, and mate choice in matrilineal macaque groups. *In* S. K. Wasser, Ed., *Social behavior of female vertebrates*. NY: Academic Press, 1983, pp. 315–347.

Silk, J. B., Clark-Wheatley, C. B., Rodman, P. S., and Samuels, A. Differential reproductive success and facultative adjustment of sex ratios among captive female bonnet macaques (*Macaca radiata*). *Animal Behaviour*, 1982, *29*:1106–1120.

Silk, J. B., Samuels, A., and Rodman, P. S. The influence of kinship, rank, and sex upon affiliation and aggression among adult female and immature bonnet macaques (*Macaca radiata*). *Behaviour*, 1981, *78*:112–137.

Smith, E. O., and Begeman, M. L. BORES: Behavior observation recording and editing system. *Behavior Research Methods and Instrumentation*, 1980, *12*:1–7.

Smith, E. O., and Byrd, L. D. Studying the behavioral effects of drugs in group-living nonhuman primats. *In* K. A. Miczek, Ed., *Ethopharmacology: Primate models of neuropsychiatric disorders*. NY: Alan Liss, 1983, pp. 1–31.

Smith, E. O., and Byrd, L. D. Contrasting effects of *d*-amphetamine on affiliation and aggression in monkeys. *Pharmacology Biochemistry and Behavior*, 1984, *20*:255–260.

Spencer-Booth, Y. The relationship between mammalian young and conspecifics other than mothers and peers: a review. *In* D. S. Lehrman, R. A. Hinde, and E. Shaw, Eds., *Advances in the study of behaviour*, vol. 3. NY: Academic Press, 1970, pp. 120–180.

Stein, D. M. The nature and function of social interactions between infant and adult male yellow baboons (*Papio cynocephalus*). Unpublished Ph.D. dissertation, University of Chicago, Chicago, 1981.

Suomi, S.J., and Ripp, C. A history of motherless mother monkey mothering at the University of Wisconsin Primate Laboratory. *In* N. Caine and M. Reite, Eds., *Child abuse: The nonhuman primate data*. NY: Alan Liss, 1983, pp. 49–78.

Taub, D. M., Ed., *Primate paternalism*. NY: Van Nostrand Reinhold, 1984.

Trivers, R. L. Parental investment and sexual selection. *In* B. G. Campbell, Ed., *Sexual selection and the descent of man*. Chicago, IL: Aldine, 1972, pp. 136–179.

Troisi, A., D'Amato., Fuccillo, R., and Scucchi, S. Infant abuse by a wild-born group-living Japanese macaque mother. *Journal of Abnormal Psychology*, 1980, *91*:451–456.

van Lawick-Goodall, J. Mother-offspring relationships in free-ranging chimpanzees. *In* D. Morris, Ed., *Primate ethology*. Chicago, IL: Aldine, 1967, pp. 287–346.

Wilson, M. C., Bailey, L., and Bedford, J. A. Effects of subacute administration of amphetamine on food competition in primates. *In* K. A. Miczek, Ed., *Ethopharmacology: Primate models of neuropsychiatric disorders.* NY: Alan Liss, 1983, pp. 293–305.

Wolfe, L. D. A case of male adoption in a troop of Japanese monkeys (*Macaca fuscata fuscata*). *In* A. B. Chiarelli and R. S. Corruccini, Eds., *Primate behavior and sociobiology.* Berlin: Springer-Verlag, 1981, pp. 156–160.

Wrangham, R. W. An ecological model of female-bonded primate groups. *Behaviour,* 1980, 75:262–300.

CHILDREN AS HOMICIDE VICTIMS*

Martin Daly
Margo Wilson

This chapter and the one that follows present the results of research that was inspired by taking an evolutionary theoretical ("sociobiological") view of the human animal. These two presentations made up the final session of the Social Science Research Council conference "Biosocial Perspectives on Child Abuse," and when it came our turn to speak, we were in a bit of a quandary. It was clear from discussions over the previous few days that several of the conference participants, although at least mildly interested in evolutionary ideas, also profoundly misunderstood them. The papers we had prepared were long on data and short on theory. We realized that we would have to reallocate some of our time, to at least try to clarify what sociobiology is, and (just as important) what it is not. The presentation provoked some discussion, and the editors suggested we incorporate our arguments here. Hence the discourse that forms the first part of this chapter.

A QUICK INTRODUCTION TO SOCIOBIOLOGY (ESPECIALLY FOR SOCIAL SCIENTISTS WHO CONSIDER THEMSELVES INFORMED SKEPTICS)

Organisms are complex adaptive machines. Once this was the most powerful argument for the existence of gods, but Darwin destroyed that argument by discovering a natural force that creates adaptation automatically. He called it natural selection.

Only two coherent theoretical alternatives have been offered to ex-

*Research reported here received financial support from the Harry Frank Guggenheim Foundation and the Natural Sciences & Engineering Research Council of Canada.

plain why organisms are adaptively constructed. There's the theory proposed by Darwin, and there's the one preferred by Jerry Falwell *et al*. The creationist theory has no empirical implications (what*ever* turns up must be God's will) and it is not worth wasting our time on. Darwin's theory that evolution occurs as a result of natural selection is demonstrably true in particular cases, logically necessary in general, and is as close to certain knowledge as anything in science. (Not to deny that there are many details to work out.) If anyone has come up with a third alternative, it has not been made generally known.

Some behavioral scientists seem to imagine that "learning" constitutes a third explanation for adaptation, a sort of ontogenetic alternative to natural selection. Evolutionary explanations of phenomena are suspiciously regarded as "nativist" (not to mention sexist, racist, and thoroughly reactionary). This naive view is so widespread that it is sometimes hard to convince people that one is even serious in maintaining that sociobiology carries no brief for "nature" contra "nurture" (let alone that your average sociobiologist, like your average academic, tends to be rather left-wing!). Yet, to propose "learning" as an alternative to an evolutionary explanation is categorical nonsense, confusing the simultaneously valid questions of ontogenetic process and natural selective history. Developmental mechanisms, including learning, are *themselves* products of natural selection. Why are reinforcement mechanisms organized in such a way as to produce adaptive outcomes? The only available answers invoke either natural selection or divine intervention. There is nothing in the conceptual framework of sociobiology that denigrates learning (although many sociobiologists have paid it less attention than they should). Neither does the discipline in any way require that the phenomena under study be "innate" rather than "acquired" (if indeed this distinction has any meaning), although sociobiologists have often been as confused as their critics on this issue.

So what is sociobiology about? Gould and Lewontin's (1979) label, "an adaptationist program," is apt (although intended as a slight). To be an adaptationist is to look at species-characteristic attributes and to ask what they are *for*—what is the utility of this structure? This sounds dangerously teleological to the well-trained experimental psychologist, but the concept of natural selection provides a rationale for the expectation that the properties of organisms have "purpose." Advances in medical science are absolutely predicated on this point of view— you open up an organism and you discover something new, the liver, let's say, and you wonder "what is it?" Which means "what does it do?" Which means "what is it for?" Which is precisely the right question to ask! Likewise in zoology: a narwhal's tusks may be for fighting and they may be for digging mollusks, but we had better proceed on the assumption that they have some function if we hope to generate some testable hypotheses.

This adaptationist approach is not very controversial when applied to morphology, but even there it has been attacked by Gould and Lewontin (1979). Their pet example is the human chin, and it will suffice to illustrate their point. Our chin is a peculiar structure among the primates, and one might indeed ask "what is it for?" Gould and Lewontin assert that the chin has no purpose at all but must be understood as an epiphenomenal byproduct of other functional (i.e., naturally selected) changes in the growth patterns of facial bones. Whether they are correct in this particular case, the general point is well taken: sometimes one can certainly waste time and effort in seeking functional significance of a trait that has none. (The redness of the blood is another popular example, less controversial than the chin.) But what's the lesson? That Harvey should not, after all, have wondered what the heart is for? There are, in fact, ground rules for evaluating adaptationist hypotheses and rejecting them when they fail. Sociobiologists generally follow Williams (1966) in arguing that the best criteria for evaluating proposed functions are "design" criteria: the more detailed (and hence unlikely to arise by chance) is the "fit" between the attributes under study and their hypothesized function, the more confidence we have in the hypothesis. This is the logic by which paleontologists are confident that pterodactyls were flying reptiles and ichthyosaurs were aquatic. We apply the same logic to modern adaptations, too, including behavioral ones.

Sociobiology is adaptationism applied to social behavior. And if it is sometimes problematic to apply this perspective to morphology, it can be even more so with behavior, which is not, after all, so neatly "structural" and measurable. But of course all behavioral scientists face problems of measurement and of the identification of behavioral units. Somehow we all cope. We may indeed partition behavior into inappropriate units with no functional integrity and stumble for a while up a blind alley. Alternatives are limited; more holistic approaches have their charm, but advances seem usually to involve analysis. Sociobiologists stand accused of fractionating the organism into traits and then trying to study their adaptive significances separately, but again this seems to be a problem faced by all behavioral scientists.

To return to characterizing sociobiology. In recent years, there have been two "hot" approaches in animal behavior, attracting most of the bright young students and most of the ink. The approaches are really the same: if you happen to be studying social behavior, it is called "sociobiology," and if you happen to be studying anything else, it is called "behavioral ecology." Both involve the application of adaptationist theory to the study of behavior. Both proceed from the proposition that the behavioral control mechanisms of organisms are products of natural selection and ask: given what we know about how selection works, what behavioral outcomes ought to follow? Also characteristic of sociobiology/behavioral ecology is the assumption that adaptive function must ultimately translate into reproductive success, also known as "fitness." This idea seems particularly alien to nonbiologists, but it is simple and essential. The idea is that there are immediate utilities to the things that we organisms do—staying fed, warm, and out of danger—but these functions only have utility in an evolutionary sense insofar as they ultimately contribute to reproduction. Mere survival is no criterion of success; what selection favors is traits that contribute to the long-term survival of the trait-bearer's genetic materials.

Many people would trace the origins of "sociobiology" to W.D. Hamilton's (1964) elaboration of reproductive success ("Darwinian fitness") into the concept of "inclusive fitness." Hamilton pointed out that selection does not operate merely through organisms' success in personal reproduction but through their success in maximizing gene copies, whether in descendant relatives or collateral kin. Hamilton thus solved a number of thorny problems at a stroke, but his contribution is probably not all that essential for getting the general drift of what most sociobiologists are up to. They are generating and testing theoretical ideas about how behavior affects fitness and how natural selection would be expected to have operated upon the mechanisms controlling behavior.

A common misapprehension is that sociobiology is "a theory." We even hear the complaint that sociobiology is "not falsifiable." Sociobiology is in fact a field, full of competing theories, and you might as well complain that sociology is "not falsifiable"! Specific theories are devised within the adaptationist framework and tested daily. There are competing theories within sociobiology that cannot be simultaneously true, and people are engaged in trying to decide which of them has to be chucked out. That's what the whole research enterprise is about. How will variations in the certainty of paternity affect the parental and courtship behavior of males? Will a different frequency of inbreeding make resource-sharing more or less profitable? What resolution is to be expected when the fitness interests of parent and offspring conflict? Do females choose mates for good genes or material benefits or indeed at all? Theoretical models proliferate, compete, get shot down, get improved. Sociobiology has become the dominant framework in animal behavior because it works as a scientific paradigm. It is gaining converts among botanists because it works for them, too. It would only make sense to suppose that it would not work for social scientists, if we were also to suppose that the human psyche has not been shaped by natural selection.

A popular, though inane, slogan among sociobiology's critics is "genetic determinism." If "determinism" is a meaningful accusation at all, then it must be leveled at all scientific approaches to the study of behavior. As scientists, we are committed to the belief that the phenomena we study have knowable causes. We chip away at "unexplained variance" within our various paradigms, trying to better understand what makes our subjects do what they do. If we seem to be making progress in this "deterministic" enterprise, we may become concerned about the implications for the concepts of free will and personal responsibility. If this is a dilemma, it is a dilemma for us all. (Consider Skinner, 1971.) Those who accuse sociobiologists of "determinism" commonly go on to attribute causality to social and economic factors (which, ironically, are also the favorite proximate causes invoked by sociobiologists), but they do not explain what makes their own causal theories "nondeterministic." The ineptness of this critique has been pointed out by several professional philosophers; it would not even warrant discussion had it not been vigorously advanced by some eloquent writers who should know better.

The issue of the role of "genes" in sociobiology is more interesting and less clear. Our view, probably a minority one within the field, is that sociobiology is in fact hardly more "genetic" than any other specialty within the life sciences. Sociobiologists are fond of talking about genes, but they are not particularly interested in how genes act in development or indeed in anything else that goes on in your average genetics department. The main role that the gene plays in sociobiological theories is not that of a causal agent, but that of a *currency:* Fitness is measured, in principle, as success in genetic replication. A secondary role that the gene plays is as a hypothetical entity in thought experiments: we imagine some simple genetical variation underlying the variation in a trait merely in order to trace out how natural selection would be expected to operate upon that trait. This means that some sociobiologists *are* interested in some models of theoretical population genetics, but most sociobiological research remains concerned with adaptationist questions that are no more explicitly genetic than the adaptationist questions of functional morphology.

As psychologists, we are excited about the potential of sociobiological ideas as metatheory. We would argue that the entire social scientific enterprise is concerned with the characterization of human nature. How could Darwin's more encompassing theory of organismic nature—so heuristic in so many areas of the life sciences, and unquestionably correct in its basics—how could it not be relevant to the task? When you take an evolutionary theoretical view of the organism, you assume that the elements of psyche must have adaptive function as the elements of morphology do, and this suggests hypotheses about how motivational systems might be organized. Psychologists, in fact, do this already, subtly assuming efficient design (adaptive function) as they pursue questions of how eating is controlled or how retinal information is processed. What the sociobiological perspective adds is the reminder that all function is ultimately reproductive. The studies described in this and the next chapter were inspired by this view. We think the results are impressive, and that they are testimony to the utility of the perspective.

CHILD HOMICIDE

The killing of children presents an intriguing challenge to sociobiologists. Many cases are perpetrated by the parents of the victim. If motivational systems have evolved by natural selection, we should expect their normal functioning to be effectively nepotistic; in particular, parental psychology must surely have evolved to contribute to offspring welfare. How then to explain the destruction of one's own children?

Of course, human parental solicitude is not without its costs. Indeed, it involves such an enormous commitment of effort—effort that might have earned better fitness returns elsewhere—that we cannot reasonably expect the evolved mechanisms of parental motivation to be indiscriminate. Rather, parents are expected to behave as if they "value" particular offspring in proportion to those offspring's prospects for contributing to parental fitness. As Alexander (1979) has argued, we may expect natural selection to "refine" the motivational mechanisms of parents "as if in response to three hypothetical cost–benefit questions":

- How certain is the putative link of parenthood?
- How capable is the youngster of utilizing parental investments to enhance its own fitness prospects?
- What alternative uses might parental resources be put to?

Parents may be expected to "assess" offspring quality, circumstantial predictors of offspring success, and alternative investment channels (e.g., the needs of siblings or the potential use of available resources to secure additional matings) before committing themselves to raising costly young. If any of these considerations dictate cutting bait, an adaptive decision-making mechanism should be such as to so decide early so as to waste as little parental effort as possible.

Daly and Wilson (1984) examined ethnographers' accounts of the circumstances in which infanticide is said to occur (and, in almost every case, to be condoned) in a standard sample of 60 societies. The great majority of circumstances in which infanticide is allegedly prescribed or tolerated correspond to circumstances in which the child's expected contribution to maternal fitness is low, either because of poor phenotypic quality of the baby itself or because of maternal overburdening. Most of the remaining circumstances involved the knowledge or suspicion of inappropriate paternity, often with the infanticide clearly coerced by the husband. Only 15 of 112 described circumstances of infanticide had no transparent link to one or another of Alexander's "cost–benefit questions," and in only 3 could it be plausibly argued that the actors damaged their fitness in the pursuit of other goals. In virtually all cases where there was information, the infanticidal decision was made and carried out within hours of the birth.

In the modern west, infanticide under any circumstance is criminalized (although generally not treated so severely as other homicides). Nevertheless, cases occur, and records of such cases can be used to test predictions about the variables likely to be associated with infanticidal inclinations (Daly and Wilson, 1984). We predicted, for example, that infanticidal mothers should be relatively young, because, other things being equal, parental willingness to invest in present offspring should increase as the parent's future reproductive potential ("residual reproductive value") declines (see, e.g., Pugesek, 1981). In Canada, we indeed find infanticidal mothers to be substantially younger than new mothers in the population-at-large (Table 8.1). We also anticipated that infanticidal mothers should be significantly more often unmarried than mothers in general, arguing that, as in the ethnographic sample, lack of paternal support damages the child's prospects, thus contributing to maternal despair and disinclination to embark on the possibly lost cause of rearing the child. This hypothesis was also clearly supported (Table 8.2).

TABLE 8.1. Age of Infanticidal Mothers in Canada, 1974–1983, in Comparison to the Age Distribution Expected If Risk of Infanticide Were Unrelated to Maternal Age

Age of the mother (years)	Proportion of mothers in population-at-large	Infanticidal mothers	
		Observed	Expected
<21	.141	39	12.1
21–25	.353	26	30.4
26–30	.338	13	29.1
31–35	.133	5	11.4
>35	.035	3	3.0

$X^2_{4df} = 72.9, p < .0001.$

TABLE 8.2. Marital Status of Infanticidal Mothers versus All New Mothers in
          Canada, 1977–1982.

| Marital | Population-at-large | | Infanticidal mothers | |
status	N	(%)	N	(%)
Legally married	1,862,886	(87.3)	22	(40)
Unmarried	271,384	(12.7)	33	(60)

$p < 10^{-15}$, binomial test.

Unfortunately, the available information on motives and victim characteristics in such cases is crude, and we are not able to assess the
statistical contributions of deformity, inappropriate paternity, and other
attributes that have been implicated as provocations to infanticide in
the ethnographic record.

DIFFERENTIAL VALUATION OF OFFSPRING BY AGE

According to orthodox sociobiological theory, parental psychology
should have evolved to "value" offspring increasingly as the offspring
mature. This is because the offspring's expected fitness (hence, contribution to parental fitness) increases as maturity approaches, primarily
by simple virtue of having survived thus far. Tests of this theory that
confront parents with the choice of investing in older versus younger
offspring are made difficult by the differential needs of the offspring
(i.e., differential capacity to utilize like parental investments); the theory
has been tested and elegantly supported, however, in studies examining
how much risk parents will accept in order to defend equally helpless
nestbound young of different ages (e.g., Pressley, 1981; Patterson, Petrinovich, and James, 1980). Human parental bereavement also matches
theoretical expectation: The death of a child is increasingly painful the
older the child (Littlefield, 1984).

This theoretical model can be used to generate some predictions
about parentally instigated homicides. One is that parents confronted
with a perceived life-or-death choice will sacrifice the younger to save
the older. In our infanticide review, we encountered 11 societies in
which infants were killed when born too soon after a sibling for the
mother to be able to rear both. There were no cases in which the typical
or prescribed solution to such a dilemma was reported to be the killing
of the older. (Indeed, such a report would hardly be credible, and we
invite readers to take a moment to consider why. We believe that the
answer lies in our apprehension of human emotions which seem so
basic we assume them universal, and which also happen to correspond
to Darwinian predictions.)

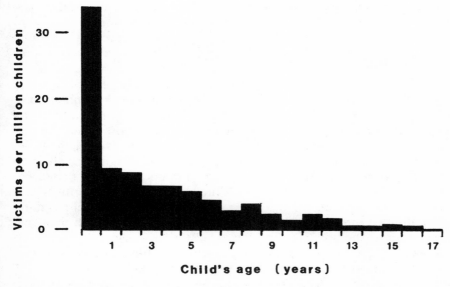

FIGURE 8.1. Homicides by natural parents per million children in the population-
at-large, Canada, 1974–1983.

This model also leads to the expectation that a youngster's risk of
homicide at the hands of its parents will be a monotonic declining
function of age. We predict this because the parent is expected to value
the child increasingly, and therefore to be increasingly inhibited by
that valuation from the use of dangerous tactics in conflict with the
child. The data in Figure 8.1 strongly support this prediction. There is
a huge decline in the risk of parental homicide between infants and 1-
year-old children (and this change is probably underestimated here,
since infants are the only age group in which an appreciable number
of undetected parentally instigated deaths is at all likely). But of special
interest in the present context is the continuing decline throughout
childhood. Risk of homicide at the hands of nonrelatives, by contrast,
is low and approximately constant until the age of 13, and then begins
to rise precipitously. Teenagers are highly conflictual creatures, but
their parents are pushed to a fatal response remarkably rarely.

PARENTS WHO KILL OLDER CHILDREN

Infanticide *by the mother* has been treated in most societies as either
no crime at all or else a distinct and lesser crime than other child homicides. This fact illustrates judicial and societal acknowledgment that

infanticide is generally committed "more in sorrow than in anger." The newborn is seldom reckoned an altogether autonomous person with full and equal right of protection, but more as the vehicle of parental purposes. The older the victim, however, the more likely it becomes that parental homicide will be viewed as malevolent and culpable.

Canadian homicide data support the view that parental killings of older children are indeed a somewhat different matter from infanticides. When mothers killed infants, the victims had been born to them at a mean age of 22.7, whereas older victims had been born at a mean maternal age of 24.4, a significant difference. But like the risk of infanticide, the risk of maternal homicide at an older age is still higher for children born to younger mothers (Table 8.3). Of mothers killing older children, 65% were legally married at the time (including 87% of 15 mothers who killed more than one child) compared to 40% of infanticidal mothers.

Killing of older children appears to be associated with maternal depression. The homicidal mother at least occasionally sees her action as altruistic, as for example when a suicidal mother takes a loved child with her in order to rescue that child from a cruel world. Only 2.3% of 86 infanticidal mothers committed suicide (and this is surely an overestimate, since, again, it is infanticides among which a significant incidence of undetected cases is likely). By contrast, 19.6% of women who killed their own children older than 1 year of age committed suicide. The two infanticidal mothers who did commit suicide were significantly older (mean age = 29.5 years) than those who did not (mean age = 22.5). Infanticide, then, is primarily the recourse of young women who want to live but who cannot presently cope with a baby. Among the women who killed older children, the suicidal mothers also killed children born to them at a significantly older age (mean = 26.3 years)

TABLE 8.3. Ages of Mothers Who Killed Own Children over One Year of Age (and Less than 17) in Canada, 1974–1983, in Comparison to the Age Distribution Expected If Risk Were Unrelated to Maternal Age at the Child's Birth

Age of mother at birth of child (years)	Proportion of mothers in population-at-large	Mothers killing children older than one year	
		Observed	Expected
<21	.141	32	15.9
21–25	.353	37	39.9
26–30	.338	31	38.2
31–35	.133	11	15.0
>35	.035	2	4.0

$X^2_{4df} = 19.9$, $p < .001$.

than the nonsuicidal (mean = 23.9). Also noteworthy is the fact that 37% of maternal infanticides versus 63% of maternal homicides of older children were attributed by the reporting agency to "mental illness or retardation."

Fathers exhibit some similar patterns to mothers. Those who killed infants, for example, were younger (mean = 26.3 years) than new fathers generally, and those who killed older children were somewhat older (mean age at child's birth = 29.4 years) than those who killed infants. Homicidal fathers were much likelier to commit suicide than homicidal mothers: 15.3% of those killing infants and 50.7% of those killing older children. (But of course men are generally much likelier than women to commit suicide.) Like the mothers, infanticidal fathers who committed suicide were significantly older (mean age = 30.5 years) than those who did not (mean = 25.8). Likewise, there was a significant difference in the paternal age at which an older child victim had been born between suicidal (mean = 31.1 years) and nonsuicidal (mean = 26.7) homicidal fathers.

Perhaps the most interesting difference between male and female killers of own children is illustrated in Table 8.4: It is not rare for a man to destroy his wife and children, whereas a corresponding act of familicide by the wife is almost unheard of. Some women kill their children, and other women, for other reasons, kill their husbands. But familicide (often but by no means always followed by suicide) is a peculiarly male crime, which we suggest is linked to men's proprietary attitudes toward women and their reproductive potential (see Daly, Wilson, and Weghorst, 1982).

HOMICIDES BY SUBSTITUTE PARENTS

The first of Alexander's "cost–benefit questions" concerned the reality of the parent–offspring link. This is surely the most obvious dimension of parental discrimination. Wilson and Daly (this volume, Chapter 9) consider at length the theory and the evidence concerning risks to children with substitute parents. Here we wish simply to record

Table 8.4. Spousal and Parental Homicides in Canada, 1974–1983[a]

Sex of offender	Spouse and one or more children	One or more children and not spouse	Spouse but no children
Female	0	160	248
Male	27	103	785

[a]Table entries are numbers of offenders.

their considerable overrepresentation among child homicides. Of 43 Canadian 1-year-olds killed by persons *in loco parentis* to them between 1974 and 1983, 11 (25.6%) were killed by substitute parents; the expected value, if substitute and natural parents presented equal risks, would be well below 1%, since such young children very rarely have a substitute parent (Daly and Wilson, 1985). In a study of all homicides in Detroit in 1972, we found seven cases where children of preschool age had been killed by their "parents"; stepfathers were involved in four (Daly and Wilson, 1982). Similarly, Scott (1973) reported that 15 of 29 British "fathers" who killed children under 5 years of age were in fact substitute fathers of their victims. There is no evidence on what proportion of the remaining cases might involve putative fathers who are not (or who think they are not) the actual fathers, but there is reason to hypothesize that that proportion may be considerable (Daly *et al.*, 1982).

SOCIOBIOLOGY AND PSYCHOLOGY OF HOMICIDE

In taking an adaptationist approach to the study of homicide, it is not necessary to suppose that homicide per se has generally positive fitness consequences for its perpetrators, nor indeed that it ever did in times past. Homicide is a rare, extreme manifestation of human passions and conflicts of interest. Adaptation is surely to be sought at the more abstract levels of those "passions" and "interests" and in their less extreme, more typical behavioral consequences. In predicting that teen-age mothers, for example, will be likelier to kill or abuse their babies than 30-year-olds, we do not maintain that they advance their fitness by infanticide, and still less by abuse. We do maintain, however, that there are good theoretical reasons to expect human psychology to have evolved such that a 30-year-old woman will feel a more selfless love toward her baby than will a 17-year-old, all else equal. Predictable variation in the intensity of maternal love may be adaptive even though certain manifestations of that variation are not.

When we are moved by passions that do not seem to *have* any adaptive functions, then others are likely to see us as deranged. It is interesting to note the varying prevalence of Canadian homicide cases attributed by the reporting agency to "mental illness or retardation." Only 5% of all Canadian homicides with adult victims during 1974–1983 were attributed to this cause, compared to 37% of parental homicides (and 8% of nonparental killings of persons under 18). This "mental inadequacy" cause was imputed to 37% of mothers and 16% of fathers who killed infants, 63% of mothers and 22% of fathers who killed older children. As we have remarked of an earlier similar comparison (Daly and Wilson, 1984):

If these figures can be taken at face value, the implication would seem to be that a loss of reason is more often characteristic of those who kill children than those who kill adults, of those who kill own as opposed to others' children, of those who kill their older children as opposed to their infants, of homicidal mothers than of homicidal fathers. All of these contrasts are readily predicted on sociobiological grounds, if one interprets "loss of reason" as a breakdown of adaptive function, that is to say a collapse (for whatever reason) of a normal, species-characteristic recognition of where one's self-interest lies.

Homicides provide outstanding archival materials for testing theoretically derived hypotheses about human passions and conflicts of interest. People express all sorts of concerns and values, and they may or may not believe their own words, but homicide is drastic action, with a resultant validity that all self-reports lack. Moreover, because homicide is taken so seriously, the data are less contaminated by reporting biases than are records of any lesser sort of conflict. Though homicides are often maladaptive overreactions—disasters for the offenders as well as the victims—they are highly revealing of what people care most profoundly about. These deep human concerns must surely have an adaptive logic as a result of our natural selective history. The immense potential that evolutionary ("sociobiological") theory holds for psychologists is just beginning to be appreciated.

SUMMARY

Why should parents, whose normal relationship to their children is beneficent, ever be moved to kill them? Our review of a standard sample of 60 ethnographies reveals that the circumstances in which infanticide is prescribed or tolerated correspond to circumstances in which the child's potential contribution to maternal fitness is low. Data on a large sample of parental homicides in Canada provide detailed support for several theoretically derived predictions: that risk will be a monotonic declining function of child's age; that infanticide risk will be a declining function of maternal age; that the probability of suicide by the homicidal parent will increase with the age of the child victim; that substitute parents will be much likelier to kill than natural parents. The potential utility of evolutionary ("sociobiological") theory for social scientists is considered.

ACKNOWLEDGMENTS

We thank Joanne Lacroix, Craig McKie, Bryan Reingold, and Bob Blais of Statistics Canada for help and access to data.

REFERENCES

Alexander, R.D. *Darwinism and human affairs*. Seattle, WA: University of Washington Press, 1979.

Daly, M., and Wilson, M. Homicide and kinship. *American Anthropologist*, 1982, *84:*372–378.

Daly, M., and Wilson, M. A sociobiological analysis of human infanticide. *In* G. Hausfater and S.B. Hrdy, Eds., *Infanticide: Comparative and evolutionary perspectives*. NY: Aldine, 1984.

Daly, M., and Wilson, M. Child abuse and other risks of not living with both parents. *Ethology and Sociobiology*, 1985, 6:197–210.

Daly, M., Wilson, M., and Weghorst, S.J. Male sexual jealousy. *Ethology and Sociobiology*, 1982, *3:*11–27.

Gould, S.J., and Lewontin, R.C. The spandrels of San Marco and the Panglossian paradigm: A critique of the adaptationist program. *Proceedings of the Royal Society of London*, 1979, *205:*581–598.

Hamilton, W.D. The genetical evolution of social behaviour. I and II. *Journal of Theoretical Biology*, 1964, *7:*1–52.

Littlefield, C. When a child dies: A sociobiological perspective on parental bereavement. Unpublished Ph.D. thesis, York University, 1984.

Patterson, T.L., Petrinovich, L., and James, D.K. Reproductive value and appropriateness of response to predators by white-crowned sparrows. *Behavioral Ecology and Sociobiology*, 1980, *7:*227–231.

Pressley, P.H. Parental effort and the evolution of nest-guarding tactics in the threespine stickleback, *Gasterosteus aculeatus* L. *Evolution*, 1981, *35:*282–295.

Pugesek, B.H. Increased reproductive effort with age in the California gull (*Larus californicus*). *Science*, 1981, *212:*822–823.

Scott, P.D. Fatal battered baby cases. *Medicine, Science, and the Law*, 1973, *13:*197–206.

Skinner, B.F. *Beyond freedom and dignity*. NY: Knopf, 1971.

Williams, G.C. *Adaptation and natural selection*. Princeton, NJ: Princeton University Press, 1966.

RISK OF MALTREATMENT OF CHILDREN LIVING WITH STEPPARENTS*

Margo Wilson
Martin Daly

chapter

9

Stepparents have rather a poor reputation. Webster's unabridged dictionary defines "stepmother" as follows: "1. The wife of one's father by a subsequent marriage. 2. One that fails to give proper care or attention." The "step" root comes from an Old English word meaning "to deprive or bereave" (Gove, 1976) and evidently retains its negative connotations today. Ganong and Coleman (1983), for example, gave American undergraduates a semantic differential task in which they were called upon to rate "brother," "cousin," "mother," "nephew," and so forth on a variety of evaluative scales; "stepmother" and "stepfather" were rated worst.

Many social scientists have expressed concern that the sorry reputation of stepparents may cause them some problems. Authors too numerous to list have cited the "myth of the cruel stepparent" as an impediment to successful familial reconstitution (more often than not adding the ritual phrase "in our society"). Jacobson (1979) argues that we denigrate stepparents as a "defense" against facing the possibility that our own marriages may fail, and that denigration and ostracism lead to poor "self-images" for people in stepfamilies. Ganong and Coleman (1983) worry that the "negative stereotypes" of "cruel" stepparents and "abused" stepchildren might sometimes become a "self-fulfilling prophecy."

The negative characterization of stepparents is by no means peculiar to our culture. The folklorist who consults Thompson's (1955) massive *Motif-Index of Folk Literature* will encounter such pithy synopses as: "Evil stepmother orders stepdaughter to be killed. Irish myth," and

*The research on which this chapter is based has been supported by grants from Health & Welfare Canada and the Harry Frank Guggenheim Foundation.

"Evil stepmother works stepdaughter to death in absence of merchant husband. India." Stepfathers are conveniently classified as either "cruel" or "lustful." From Eskimos to Indonesians, through dozens of tales, the stepparent is the villain of every piece.

That the "stereotyping" of stepparents might have some basis in fact is an hypothesis hardly contemplated by social scientists (although the widespread concern with the damage done by "myths" implicitly acknowledges the difficulties attending steprelationships). Where there's so much smoke, one might do well to check whether there is a fire! In this chapter, we intend to show that there are strong reasons, both theoretical and empirical, to conclude that stepparents indeed constitute a substantial threat to children.

DARWINIAN PSYCHOLOGY OF PARENTHOOD

People, like other organisms, have evolved by natural selection. We may therefore expect their most basic and characteristic traits to be adaptive. Adaptive has a special meaning in evolutionary biology: A trait is adaptive if it tends to contribute to "fitness," that is, to the relative proliferation of the trait-bearer's genotype, and maladaptive if it tends to contribute to the relative proliferation of alternative genotypes. Traits are therefore expected to have been shaped by selection such that their typical consequences in normal environments are the production of genetic relatives (reproduction) and contribution to the welfare of those relatives (nepotism). More proximal goals like eating, breathing, and copulating are valued only because the achievement of these goals has been contributory to fitness. This Darwinian perspective, and its relevance to the motivational and developmental levels of analysis at which psychologists usually operate, is discussed more fully in the preceding chapter (Daly and Wilson, this volume, Chapter 8).

Parental behavior is a sphere of activity whose links to fitness are direct and obvious. Certain animals characteristically invest a large proportion of their available time and energy in the nurturing of individual offspring of prolonged dependency. In such animals, selection should have favored a parental psychology that is discriminative, investing preferentially where the effort promises best to contribute to parental fitness. Parental solicitude is thus predicted to be a complex function of numerous variables, including characteristics of the child, of the parent, and of the situation (see Daly and Wilson, 1980, and this volume, Chapter 8). Taking this "adaptationist" or "sociobiological" view of parental and other motives has proven extremely fruitful for students of animal behavior and holds great promise for the social sciences (see Daly and Wilson, this volume, Chapter 8). Homo sapiens is, of course, an intensely parental animal, and there is considerable evidence that human parental decision making, like that of other creatures, is sensitive to variables indicative of the child's potential to contribute to parental fitness (Daly and Wilson, 1980, 1981a, 1984).

The view of parental behavior that is currently prevalent in the social sciences is altogether different. Parenthood is typically considered a "role." This metaphor (sometimes inflated to the status of a "theory") nicely captures the abrupt behavioral changes that occur as one switches between parental and other social interactions, and it is also useful in directing attention to the social learning necessary for competent parenting. It is positively misleading, however, in its implication of arbitrary substitutability. A role is something that any competent actor who has studied the part can step into, whereas parent–offspring bonds are individualized and cannot be established at will. Indeed, the concept of "roles" utterly fails to capture the motivational and emotional aspects of parenthood. Parents care profoundly, often selflessly, about their children, a fact with immense behavioral consequences about which "role theory" is mute.

In most dyadic relationships, reciprocity is carefully monitored by both parties, and imbalances are resented as exploitative. Parental altruism is unique among personalized social relationships in that the flow of phenotypic benefits is prolongedly, cumulatively, and ungrudgingly unbalanced. A Darwinian perspective suggests why this should be so: Organisms have evolved to expend their very lives enhancing the fitness prospects of their descendents. That is the ultimate "self-interest" of which more immediate perceptions of personal welfare are tokens.

SUBSTITUTE PARENTS IN DARWINIAN PERSPECTIVE

Parental investment is a valuable resource, and natural selection must operate continuously against its being dispensed ineffectually. We therefore expect evolved mechanisms of parental psychology to be such as to direct solicitude discriminatively toward one's own young. Examples from the animal kingdom abound: While nursing her own kid, a nanny goat attacks a strange kid who attempts to suckle; a male mouse kills pups that he could not have sired, while sparing those that he might have; a gull cannibalizes an unrelated chick while brooding her own. Where we do find indiscriminate parents, as for example in rodent mothers who tolerate experimental cross-fostering, the natural situation is typically one in which immobile young are sequestered in isolated nests, so that there is little danger of nurturing unrelated pups by mistake; offspring recognition and discriminative solicitude typically appear, moreover, at just that stage of the young's developing mobility at which mixups become an imminent risk (see, e.g., Daly and Wilson, 1980; Holmes and Sherman, 1982).

All experience suggests that human parental solicitude, like that of other creatures, is discriminative with respect to the child's identity. The ultimate test of Abraham was not whether he would sacrifice just *any* available baby; it was whether he would sacrifice his *son*. The wise King Solomon knew that the natural mother would be more distressed at the imminent bisection of her baby than would the imposter. Why are these tales even intelligible to us, when they lie so far outside our experience? The answer, of course, is that their meaning resides in the cross-culturally universal phenomenon of individualized parental love.

What, then, of the party who steps into a "parental" relationship with a child not his or her own? With all the good will in the world, the substitute parent is likely to find the situation difficult. Child-specific parental love is the emotional mechanism that permits people to tolerate—even to rejoice in—the prolonged, expensive, unreciprocated exercise of parental altruism. Substitute parents are less likely than natural parents to experience those emotional rewards that make the costs of parenthood tolerable. Thus, for example, Duberman (1975) found that only 53% of stepfathers and 25% of stepmothers could claim to feel "parental feeling" toward their stepchildren and still fewer to "love" them. This is not to deny that parental love can be activated (more or less fully) within a fictive parent–offspring bond. (It can, after all, be activated with surprising intensity toward a nonhuman pet!) But whether a successful approximation of parental love can be established in any given case is by no means certain.

One relevant consideration in predicting the success of artificial parent–offspring relations must surely be the initial strength of the substitute parent's *wish* to simulate a genuine parental love. And therein lies an important reason to discriminate step from adoptive relationships. Adoptions by "strangers" (that is to say by unrelated couples, as distinct from adoptions by stepparents or by biological relatives) are primarily the recourse of childless couples, who are strongly motivated to simulate a natural family experience and who have been carefully screened by adoption agencies. While the adoptive couple may not be in perfect agreement about the desirability of adopting, there is at least no exploitation of one partner's efforts for the other's fitness benefit. And if the adoption proves unsatisfactory, or if the marriage fails, the couple can return the child, which happens more often than is generally realized (e.g., Kadushin and Seidl, 1971; Carroll, 1985). For all these reasons, we would not especially anticipate that failures of parental solicitude should produce a major risk of child maltreatment within adoptions. It is interesting, however, that adoptive children may fare relatively poorly when natural children are subsequently born to the adopting couple, a result that has led some professionals to counsel against adoption by childless couples until infertility is definitely established (e.g., Kraus, 1978).

Stepparenthood presents itself, *a priori,* as a much more dangerous circumstance. Whereas the adoptive couple specifically desires to establish a fictive parent–offspring relationship, the stepparent will usually have entered into such a relationship incidentally to the establishment of a desired mateship. The child must often enter into the prospective stepparent's marital decision as a cost, not a benefit. (Indeed there is evidence that custody of young children reduces a divorced woman's remarriage prospects; e.g., Becker, Landes, and Michael [1977]. It is of course conceivable that divorced mothers are less *inclined* to remarry than childless divorcees, rather than that the latter make more attractive marital candidates. However, one might just as readily have anticipated that motherhood and its attendant financial demands would *increase* the divorcee's desire to remarry.)

There is abundant evidence that the stepparental experience is unsatisfying, and we need not go to dysfunctional families in therapy in order to find it. Perkins and Kahan (1979), for example, found that all parties in stepfather households were much more dissatisfied with family relationships than their counterparts in natural-father households, even within a volunteer sample of families judged to be unanimously functioning "successfully." Nadler (1976) found that stepmothers had more conflict with their stepchildren than natural mothers, regardless of whether the children were permanently or only occasionally coresident. Stepmothers, whether full- or part-time, experienced more "anxiety, depression and anger regarding family relationships" than natural mothers. Indeed, the extensive literature on stepparenting, ranging from empirical surveys to exhortative pop psychology, is almost entirely concerned with coping (e.g., Cherlin, 1978; Duberman, 1975; Einstein, 1982; Fast and Cain, 1966; Giles-Sims, 1984; Goetting, 1982; Jacobson, 1979; Johnson, 1980; Kompara, 1980; Messinger and Walker, 1981; Mills, 1984; Moss and Moss, 1975; Nelson and Nelson, 1982; Papernow, 1984; Turnbull and Turnbull, 1983; Visher and Visher, 1978, 1979). Many of these authors have become convinced that steprelationships are *invariably* conflictual, and that the conflict is best controlled by abandoning efforts to simulate a natural parent–offspring relationship.

The prevalent view of stepparenthood within the social sciences is that it too is a "role," only partly overlapping that of natural parenthood. The undeniable tensions of steprelationships are then attributed to role "ambiguity" and "newness" (e.g., Cherlin, 1978; Kompara, 1980; Giles-Sims, 1984). Stress is alleged to be the product of uncertain and conflicting expectations about what a stepparent can and should do; stepparenthood will remain stressful until "society" defines the role more clearly. We doubt that this view would survive empirical tests of its implications, but its proponents have attempted none. One clear implication is that there is a greater societal consensus about what fathers ought to do around the house than there is about what stepfathers ought to do. Another implication must be that the difficulties attending steprelationships will fade away as the subject is more widely discussed and the "ill-defined new role" becomes better articulated.

There is a commonsense alternative hypothesis about why some "roles" seem easy and "well-defined," whereas others are difficult and "ambiguous." It is simply that the former match our inclinations, whereas the latter defy them. Stepparents do not find their roles less satisfying and more conflictual than natural parents because they do not *know* what they are supposed to do. Their problem is that they do not *want* to do what they feel obliged to do, namely to make a substantial investment of "parental" effort without receiving the usual emotional rewards. Role theorists would have it that "role ambiguity" is the cause of conflict within stephouseholds, but surely, it is better interpreted as a *manifestation* thereof. *People are in conflict when their interests are different and are served by rival courses of action.*

Evolutionary theory identifies the bedrock of organismal self-interest as fitness, and this view provides a theory of family conflict. Couples will perceive themselves to be in conflict whenever their fitness interests are nonconsonant. Children of the marriage create harmony because they are common fitness vehicles for husband and wife, and thus facilitate spousal consensus on the crucial question of how the family's resources should be allocated. Children from former mateships, especially but not only if coresident with the remarried couple, are a source of spousal conflict. (See Daly, Wilson, and Weghorst, 1982, concerning the implications of evolutionary theory for spousal conflict in sexual matters.)

The evidence on steprelationships and family conflict is strongly supportive of this theory. Clingempeel (1981), for example, studied two groups of stepfather–natural-mother families differing in whether the husband had noncustodial own children in a previous marriage; the present marriage was less successful for both parties if he did. According to Becker et al. (1977), the presence of children of the present marriage lowers the divorce rate for first and subsequent marriages alike, but the presence of children of former marriages raises it. Messinger (1976) asked remarried people with children from former marriages to rank the areas of "overt conflict" in each of their marriages. For the failed first marriages, children and money were hardly mentioned as areas of conflict, but they ranked at the top of the list for the remarriages. Remarried people are not poorer than first marrieds; it is instead clear from Messinger's report that financial conflict arose over the delicate issue of the man's degree of investment in his wife's children (Messinger, 1976). Finally there is some evidence that the presence of stepchildren substantially elevates the risk of spousal homicide (Lundsgaarde, 1977; Daly and Wilson, 1982).

STEPPARENTS AND CHILD ABUSE

Several years ago, on the basis of the above considerations, we reviewed the burgeoning literature on child abuse to see what evidence existed on the maltreatment of children living with stepparents. We were surprised to find that the question had hardly been addressed. Gil (1970) had remarked that 22% of a large sample of American victims lived in natural-parent-plus-stepparent households, and other samples also included what seemed to be a heavy representation of substitute parents. But no one had tackled the epidemiological questions of victimization rates and relative risk. Just how much higher was the risk of becoming an abuse victim in a stepparent home as compared to a natural-parent home?

In attempting to answer that question for the United States, we soon discovered that there was no satisfactory information on the incidences of substitute parent situations in the population-at-large or in specified subpopulations. The census bureau distinguished only "one-parent" and "two-parent" families, conflating natural, step, and adoptive parents. However, the senior demographer of the census bureau, Paul Glick, had published some widely cited estimates, claiming that 9.4% of American children under 18 lived with a stepparent in 1970, 10.0% in 1975, and 10.2% in 1978 (e.g., Glick, 1979). These estimates are almost certainly too high because of the way they were based on simplifying assumptions known to be false (Daly and Wilson, 1981a); nevertheless, we adopted them, since they were conservative for our purposes, overestimating the populational incidence of stephouseholds so that we should be in no danger of overestimating the victimization rates therein. Using data on the household circumstances of validated child abuse cases reported to the American Humane Association in 29 states with compulsory reporting schemes, the victimization rates shown in Figure 9.1 were arrived at.

More recently, we have conducted a more intensive epidemiological study of household compositions and risks to children in Hamilton, Ontario, a mid-sized Canadian city (Daly and Wilson, 1985). The Canadian census bureau, like its American counterpart, does not distinguish step from natural parents, so this time we surveyed the population-at-large. At the same time, we collected information on the household circumstances of child abuse victims from the local children's aid societies, as well as information on some other criterion groups discussed further in the section, "Other Risks to Stepchildren". Figure 9.2 presents relevant victimization rates from this study.

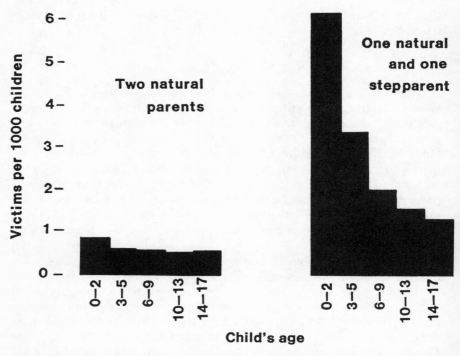

FIGURE 9.1. Child abuse cases validated by the American Humane Association in 1976 expressed as rates per thousand like-aged children in the reporting areas. (Modified from Wilson *et al.*, 1980.)

The differences in abuse rate between step- and natural-parent homes are dramatic. But are they to be taken at face value? One concern is that the effect may be exaggerated by biases in detection or reporting. It is at least possible that stronger evidence of child maltreatment might be required to induce a suspicious neighbor, teacher, or child care professional to report a natural parent than to report a stepparent. Were this so, such reporting biases would be expected to diminish as the maltreatment becomes increasingly severe and unequivocal. So if substitute parent overrepresentation were an artifact of reporting (or detection) bias, then we should expect such overrepresentation to shrink with increasing severity of maltreatment. Just the opposite is the case, as illustrated in Table 9.1: substitute parents were cohabitants of the victim in 15% of all maltreatment cases validated by the American Humane Association in 1976, in 25% of those including nonaccidental injury to the child, and in 43% of fatal cases. Other examples of the great overrepresentation of stepparents in cases of child fatality are noted in the preceding chapter of this volume (Chapter 8).

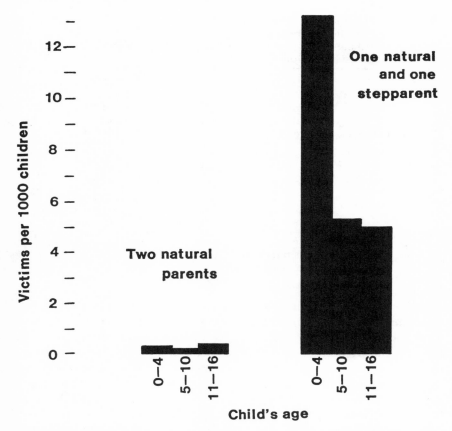

FIGURE 9.2. Child abuse cases handled by the children's aid societies of Hamilton–Wentworth expressed as rates per thousand like-aged children in the region. (Modified from Daly and Wilson, 1985.)

It is our impression that reporting biases might operate more strongly
against single mothers than against stepparents. But be that as it may,
the pattern in Table 9.1 must surely imply that *stepparents really are
greatly overrepresented in the most destructive cases of child maltreatment.* If reporting biases do inflate stepparent representation under
the less severe abuse criteria, then the apparent tendency for stepparent
overrepresentation to increase as severity of abuse increases must be
all the stronger.

Children living with single mothers experience a risk of abuse that
is substantially elevated over that in two natural-parent households,
although less than in natural-parent–stepparent households (Wilson,
Daly, and Weghorst, 1980, 1983; Daly and Wilson, 1985). This does not

TABLE 9.1. Percentages of the United States Population-at-Large in 1976 and of Child Maltreatment Cases of Varying Degrees of Severity Validated by the American Humane Association in That Year, by Household Type

| | | Maltreatment cases | | |
Household type	Population-at-large (weighted[a])	All cases of abuse and/or neglect (N = 87,789)	Physical abuse only (N = 26,779)	Fatal cases (N = 276)
Two natural parents	71	43	46	35
Natural mother or father alone	17	42	29	22
One or more substitute parents	12	15	25	43
	100	100	100	100

[a]Population-at-large percentages are weighted by age in proportion to the age distribution of maltreatment cases in order to provide "expected" values for maltreatment cases.

necessarily mean that the single mother is *herself* more likely than her stably married counterpart to abuse the children. In our Hamilton study, for example, one of the reporting agencies provided information on the abusing person(s); among 13 abused children living with single mothers, a male was the identified perpetrator in 11 cases. Only two of these were putative natural fathers of the victims. Thus the threat to children with single mothers seems to be largely the same threat as that to stepchildren: men other than their fathers.

In addition to our victimization rate estimates, there is plenty of other evidence of an elevated risk of abuse when there are stepparents. Fergusson, Fleming, and O'Neill (1972) compared two groups of children admitted to New Zealand hospitals: those with injuries apparently inflicted deliberately and those with injuries apparently accidental. 20% of the former group lived with a stepparent versus 9% of the latter (9% is still almost certainly excessive compared to the population-at-large; see Fergusson, Horwood, and Shannon, 1984). Daly and Wilson (1981b) studied a sample of cases in London, Ontario, in which police, accompanied by a "family crisis" caseworker, had been called to private homes to intervene in disputes. Confining attention to calls involving a focal juvenile, we compared cases in which there was evidence that the juvenile had been physically abused with cases in which there was no such evidence. Of the former, 48% were stepparent households versus 21% (still decidedly excessive) of the latter. The last example comes from a major study of a cohort of several thousand children born during one week in 1970 in Great Britain. Wadsworth, Burnell, Taylor, and

Butler (1983) reported on accident risk within the first 5 years of life in relation to household type. Accident rates were similar in single-parent and stepparent households, both substantially exceeding that occurring in two natural-parent households; the more suspicious category of *head* injuries occurred at a significantly higher rate in stepparent than in either single-parent or two natural-parent households.

SOME POSSIBLE CONFOUNDS

Still the conclusion that stepparents imperil children could be hasty. Could stepparenthood be an incidental correlate of some other variable that is the cause of elevated abuse risk?

An obvious candidate for such a confound is poverty. Divorce rates in America are higher among the poor, and one might therefore suppose that steprelationships will be more prevalent, too. Countervailing tendencies, however, are that men's remarriage prospects after divorce are positively associated with income (Becker et al., 1977) and that childlessness decreases with income (Daly and Wilson, 1983). It is impossible to surmise from such statistics whether the incidence of steprelationships is positively or negatively associated with socioeconomic status. Survey evidence is required. Sweet (1974) found no correlation between family income and the proportion of children in two-parent American households who were stepchildren, but Burchinal (1964) found stepparental relationships to be quite strongly associated with low occupational status. The issue appears to have been settled by Bachrach's (1983) report on a national probability sample of American mothers (coincidentally conducted in 1976, the very year represented in Figure 9.1). The income distributions of natural-parent and stepparent families are virtually identical; single-parent families are much poorer and adoptive families much more affluent. So the effect in Figure 9.1 is not due to a confound with poverty. The same can be said of the Canadian data in Figure 9.2. In that study, we tested for associations between household composition and socioeconomic status by comparing the frequency distributions of household types in high- versus low-income census tracts. Children living in low-income areas were more likely to live with a single parent than were those in high-income areas, but they were not more likely to live with a stepparent (Daly and Wilson, 1985). So it seems clear that in neither study is there any substantial confound between poverty and steprelationships. And even if such a confound were pronounced, it would not explain away certain patterns in the American Humane Association maltreatment data: whereas poverty and single parenthood were both much more strongly predictive of child neglect than of physical abuse, the reverse was true for stepparenthood (Wilson, Daly, and Weghorst, 1980).

In our Hamilton study, it was possible to test for certain other possible confounds (Daly and Wilson, 1985). Maternal age at the child's birth, for example, was a strong predictor of abuse risk (as predicted on evolutionary theoretical grounds), and children living with stepfathers indeed tended to have been born to younger mothers than children living with two natural parents. However, this confound could account for only a small proportion (13%) of the overrepresentation of stepparent homes among abuse victims. Family size was another predictor of abuse risk: children living with one or two siblings were at lower risk than those living with either none or more than two. The family size distributions of stepparent and natural-parent homes were indiscriminable, however, eliminating this factor as a potential cause of high risk in stephouseholds.

Giles-Sims and Finkelhor (1984) suggest still another possible confound: perhaps children are disproportionately abused in stepparent households simply because adults with a generally violent disposition are likelier to experience marital break-ups and to then find themselves in reconstituted families. Such a confound may exist, but as an explanation of stepparental abuse, this hypothesis (and any other that invokes transsituational personality characteristics of abusers) collapses in the face of evidence that *abusive stepparents are discriminative*. Lightcap, Kurland, and Burgess (1982), for example, in an observational study of identified abusive families in rural Pennsylvania, found that abusive parents with both natural and stepchildren in the same house invariably abused only the stepchildren. Similarly, in the abuse sample in our Hamilton study, there were 10 households that included both children of the present marriage and stepchildren. Only the stepchildren were abused in 9 of these 10 households, while a 2-year-old stepchild and an infant of the present marriage were both deserted in the exceptional case. There were no households in which the child of the present marriage was abused while the stepchild was spared, which should be equally prevalent under the null hypothesis that stepparents are an indiscriminately violent lot.

RELATIVE RISK FROM STEP- VERSUS NATURAL PARENTS DECLINES WITH AGE

Stepparent situations characterize a larger proportion of abused children than would be expected from their prevalence in the population-at-large. This is true for every age group in both the American and Canadian data. Nevertheless, the extent to which stephouseholds are overrepresented is variable—not just between the two studies and between abuse criteria (e.g., Table 9.1), but also between age groups within a study. It appears that stepparent households are especially risky (by comparison to natural-parent households) for the youngest children (Table 9.2). One possible interpretation of this trend is that "parental" obligation to a child not one's own may be especially likely to provoke resentment when the anticipated costs of that obligation are maximal, since young children will make the greatest, most prolonged demands.

The trend in Table 9.2 is of particular interest because it is often maintained that the friction in steprelationships derives *primarily* from the child's nonacceptance of the stepparent rather than the reverse. There is no question that children often resist parental remarriage plans, reject the stepparent, and fervently wish that their natural parents will be reconciled (e.g., Papernow, 1984; Wallerstein, 1984). Indeed, we would argue that children's extreme dislike of discord between their natural parents and their alarm at the prospect of parental remarriage reflect a remarkably astute assessment of their own best interests, and may even be adaptive emotional responses that have been specifically favored in our natural selective history. But whether this speculation is correct or not, it is difficult to imagine that the child's rejection of the stepparent is the primary stimulus to abuse when the relative risk from step- versus natural parents is maximal with *infants!* Overt conflict may be most conspicuous between adolescents and new stepparents, but at least with an adolescent, the stepparent is not being pressured to invest years of parental effort. Instead, both parties can look forward to the stepchild's imminent departure from the home. Early departure is an option that stepchildren indeed exercise (e.g., Flinn, 1983; Rankin, 1983; Daly and Wilson, 1985). In this context, it is interesting that despite overt, tempestuous conflicts, the relative risk of abuse from stepparents as opposed to natural parents is minimal for adolescents.

TABLE 9.2. Relative Risk of Child Abuse in Natural-Parent Plus Stepparent versus Two Natural-Parent Households, by Child's Age[a]

United States 1976		Hamilton, Ontario, 1983	
Child's age (year)	Relative risk	Child's age (years)	Relative risk
0–2	6.9	0–4	40.1
3–5	5.1	5–10	19.4
6–9	3.3	11–17	9.8
10–13	3.0		
14–17	2.2		

[a]Table entries are the ratios of abuse rate (frequency of cases/frequency of household type in population) in stepparent households over abuse rate in natural-parent households.

OTHER RISKS TO STEPCHILDREN

Besides the risk of physical maltreatment, it might be expected that stepchildren would show elevated risks for other negative outcomes, and there is some supportive evidence. Fortes (1933) and others have noted the prevalence of children with stepparents among "delinquents." Burchinal (1964) reported elevated rates of school absenteeism. Wadsworth *et al.* (1983) found an elevated risk of accident. In our Hamilton study, we assessed the rates of police apprehension for children in various household types (Daly and Wilson, 1985) and noted elevated rates of apprehension for both running away and criminal offenses for children from stepparent homes, as opposed to two natural-parent homes.

An interesting aspect of these studies emerges when the comparisons are extended to include single-mother households: "Broken homes" are generally hazardous for children, but the hazards do not always vary similarly between household types. In the American Humane Association data, child "neglect" occurred at a higher rate in single-parent homes than in stephouseholds, but this pattern was reversed where the child had been physically abused (Wilson *et al.*, 1980). In the British cohort study, "accidents" were comparably elevated over the two natural-parent situation in both stepparent and single-parent homes, but the rate of head injuries was more elevated in stepparent households (Wadsworth *et al.*, 1983). Rates of apprehension for criminal offenses were higher for children with single mothers than for stepchildren in our Hamilton study, but the reverse was true for abuse risk (Daly and Wilson, 1985). Throughout these studies, it appears that economic and supervisory disadvantages put children of single mothers at risk, but that the risks in stephouseholds have an additional, more sinister element. Stepchildren are not merely disadvantaged. They are physically endangered.

CONCLUDING REMARKS

Investigators of child maltreatment and family relations have virtually ignored the potential for violence in stephouseholds. We suspect that this omission is more than an oversight. There is a distinctly defensive tone to the literature on stepparents, and some authors have even troubled to defend the thesis that having a stepparent is "not inevitably detrimental." Well, of course not! A single success story makes that point. (Abe Lincoln was raised by a devoted stepmother.)

On the one hand, preschoolers in Hamilton living with one natural and one stepparent in 1983 were 40 times as likely to become child abuse statistics as like-aged children living with two natural parents, and that is an alarming fact. On the other hand, these victims still represent only a tiny proportion of stepchildren, most of whom thrive.

Many professionals, legitimately concerned to help stepparents, seem to feel that the dissemination of such information as that in Figures 9.1 and 9.2 does the struggling stepparent a disservice by validating and perpetuating the "myth." We take the view that ignorance is hardly ever preferable to knowledge, and that the genuine risks to children in stephouseholds will not be swept away by denying them.

Social scientists often mistake evolutionary theory for a doctrine of despair. Giles-Sims and Finkelhor (1984), for example, characterize the theory as arguing "that abuse of stepchildren is ultimately caused by an evolutionary process that favors expending resources on natural children over stepchildren" and consider this view pessimistic, because "if the ultimate cause is biologically inherited, it is hard to affect change by altering present conditions." This argument betrays a profound incomprehension of evolutionary thought. For one thing, every act and attribute of living creatures necessarily has both "ultimate" (evolutionary) and more proximate causes. For another, an "inherited" trait may be easily changed by environmental manipulation; consider phenylketonuria. But most importantly, the theory in question does *not* maintain that abusive tendencies are "inherited," which would mean (if anything) that variations in parental caretaking are due to genetic differences between individuals; in fact, the theory maintains precisely the opposite, namely that *abusive versus nonabusive behavior is situationally determined.*

Far from being a doctrine of despair, the evolutionary perspective raises a host of empirical questions, only a few of which are touched upon here. We believe it may have therapeutic utility as well. This chapter has probably made the stepparent seem rather a villain, but that has not been our intention. One could as readily portray stepparents as *victims:* their naturally nepotistic efforts are exploited by nonrelatives and they are made to feel guilty when they resent the fact! Evolutionary theory identifies fundamental conflicts of interest within the stepfamily, conflicts that are unlikely to evaporate when people are advised to model their relationships on those of blood relatives with spontaneous commonalities of interest. Therapists in the trenches have apprehended the futility of pretending to be a biological family already, and an evolutionary perspective could help them clarify what is at issue. The welfare of offspring (a token of their probability of eventual fitness) is reward enough for altruistic natural parents, but not for nonrelatives. Substitute parents are likely to feel exploited and resentful unless they have contractual guarantees of more proximal reciprocities. We believe that the articulation of this perspective might help some struggling stepfamilies acknowledge their conflicts and negotiate solutions to them.

SUMMARY

Children living with one natural parent and one stepparent are much likelier to be physically abused or killed than children living with two natural parents. This phenomenon cannot plausibly be attributed to reporting biases, nor to socioeconomic differences between step- and natural-parent families. The relative risk from step- vs. natural parents declines with the child's age. The risks in step-households are qualitatively different from those in single-parent households, suggesting that stepchildren are not merely "disadvantaged," but imperiled. These and other aspects of steprelationships support a Darwinian theory of family conflict.

ACKNOWLEDGMENTS

We appreciate the cooperation and assistance of the Children's Aid Society and the Catholic Children's Aid Society of Hamilton–Wentworth, of the Hamilton–Wentworth Regional Police, and of the American Humane Association.

REFERENCES

Bachrach, C.A. Children in families: Characteristics of biological, step-, and adopted children. *Journal of Marriage and the Family*, 1983, *45*:171–179.

Becker, G.S., Landes, E.M., and Michael, R.T. An economic analysis of marital instability. *Journal of Political Economy*, 1977, *85*:1141–1187.

Burchinal, L.G. Characteristics of adolescents from unbroken, broken and reconstituted families. *Journal of Marriage and the Family*, 1964, *26*:44–51.

Carroll, E.N. Abrogation of adoption by adoptive parents. *Family Law Quarterly*, 1985, *19*:155–177.

Cherlin, A. Remarriage as an incomplete institution. *American Journal of Sociology*, 1978, *84*:634–650.

Clingempeel, W.G. Quasi-kin relationships and marital quality in stepfather families. *Journal of Personality and Social Psychology*, 1981, *41*:890–901.

Daly, M., and Wilson, M.I. Discriminative parental solicitude: A biological perspective. *Journal of Marriage and the Family*, 1980, *42*:277–288.

Daly, M., and Wilson, M. Abuse and neglect of children in evolutionary perspective. In R. D. Alexander and D. W. Tinkle, Eds., *Natural selection and social behavior: New research and theory*. NY: Chiron Press, 1981.(a)

Daly, M., and Wilson, M. Child maltreatment from a sociobiological perspective. *New Directions for Child Development*, 1981, *11*:93–112.(b)

Daly, M., and Wilson, M.I. Homicide and kinship. *American Anthropologist*, 1982, *84*:372–378.

Daly, M., and Wilson, M. *Sex evolution and behavior. Adaptations for reproduction*, 2d edition. Boston: Willard Grant Press, 1983.

Daly, M., and Wilson, M. A sociobiological analysis of human infanticide. *In* G. Hausfater and S. B. Hrdy, Eds., *Infanticide: Comparative and evolutionary perspectives.* NY: Aldine, 1984.

Daly, M., and Wilson, M. Children as homicide victims. *In* R. Gelles and J. Lancaster, Eds., *Child abuse and neglect: Biosocial perspectives.* NY: Aldine, 1987.

Daly, M., and Wilson, M. Child abuse and other risks of not living with both parents. *Ethology and Sociobiology,* 1985, *6:*197–210.

Daly, M., Wilson, M.I., and Weghorst, S.J. Male sexual jealousy. *Ethology and Sociobiology,* 1982, *3:*11–27.

Duberman, L. *The reconstituted family: A study of remarried couples and their children.* Chicago: Nelson-Hall, 1975.

Einstein, E. *The stepfamily.* New York: Macmillan, 1982.

Fast, I., and Cain, A.C. The stepparent role: Potential for disturbances in family functioning. *American Journal of Orthopsychiatry,* 1966, *36:*485–491.

Fergusson, D.M., Fleming, J., and O'Neill, D.P. *Child abuse in New Zealand.* Wellington: Government of New Zealand Printer, 1972.

Fergusson, D.M., Horwood, L.J., and Shannon, F.T. A proportional hazards model of family breakdown. *Journal of Marriage and the Family,* 1984, *46:*539–549.

Flinn, M.V. *Resources, mating and kinship: The behavioral ecology of a Trinidadian village.* Ph.D. dissertation, Northwestern University, 1983.

Fortes, M. Notes on juvenile delinquency: II. Step-parenthood and delinquency. *Sociological Review,* 1933, *25:*153–158.

Ganong, L.H., and Coleman, M. Stepparent: A pejorative term? *Psychological Reports,* 1983, *52:*919–922.

Gil, D. *Violence against children.* Cambridge: Harvard University Press, 1970.

Giles-Sims, J. The stepparent role. Expectations, behavior and sanctions. *Journal of family Issues,* 1984, *5:*116–130.

Giles-Sims, J., and Finkelhor, D. Child abuse in stepfamilies. *Family Relations,* 1984, *33:*407–413.

Glick, P.C. Children of divorced parents in demographic perspective. *Journal of Social Issues,* 1979, *35:*170–182.

Goetting, A. The six stations of remarriage: Developmental tasks of remarriage after divorce. *Family Relations,* 1982, *31:*213–222.

Gove, P.B., Ed. *Webster's 3rd new international dictionary of the English language, unabridged.* Springfield, Mass: G. & C. Merriam Co., 1976.

Holmes, W.G., and Sherman, P.W. The ontogeny of kin recognition in two species of ground squirrels. *American Zoologist,* 1982, *22:*491–517.

Jacobson, D.S. Stepfamilies: Myths and realities. *Social Work,* 1979, *24:*202–207.

Johnson, H.C. Working with stepfamilies: Principles of practice. *Social Work,* 1980, *25:*304–308.

Kadushin, A., and Seidl, F.W. Adoption failure: A social work postmortem. *Social Work,* 1971, *16:*32–38.

Kompara, D.R. Difficulties in the socialization process of step-parenting. *Family Relations,* 1980, *29:*69–73.

Kraus, J. Family structure as a factor in the adjustment of adopted children. *British Journal of Social Work,* 1978, *8:*327–337.

Lightcap, J.L., Kurland, J.A., and Burgess, R.L. Child abuse: A test of some predictions from evolutionary theory. *Ethology and Sociobiology,* 1982, *3:*61–67.

Lundsgaarde, H.P. *Murder in space city.* New York: Oxford University Press, 1977.

Messinger, L. Remarriage between divorced people with children from previous marriages: A proposal for preparation for remarriage. *Journal of Marriage and the Family*, 1976, *2*:193–199.

Messinger, L., and Walker, K.N. From marriage breakdown to remarriage: Parental tasks and therapeutic guidelines. *American Journal of Orthopsychiatry*, 1981, *51*:429–438.

Mills, D.M. A model for stepfamily development. *Family Relations*, 1984, *33*:365–372.

Moss, S.Z., and Moss, M.S. Surrogate mother–child relationships. *American Journal of Orthopsychiatry*, 1975, *45*:382–390.

Nadler, J.H. The psychological stress of the stepmother. Ph.D. dissertation. California School of professional Psychology. *Dissertation Abstracts* B: 5367, 1976.

Nelson, M., and Nelson, G.K. Problems of equity in the reconstituted family: A social exchange analysis. *Family Relations*, 1982, *31*:223–231.

Papernow, P.L. The stepfamily cycle: An experimental model of stepfamily development. *Family Relations*, 1984, *33*:355–363.

Perkins, T.F., and Kahan, J.P. An empirical comparison of natural-father and stepfather family systems. *Family Process*, 1979, *18*:175–183.

Rankin, J.H. The family context of delinquency. *Social Problems*, 1983, *30*:466–479.

Sweet, J.A. *The family living arrangements of children*. Working Paper 74-28. University of Wisconsin Center for Demography and Ecology, Madison, 1974.

Thompson, S. *Motif-index of folk literature*. (Revised edition in 6 volumes.) Bloomington: Indiana University Press, 1955.

Turnbull, S.K., and Turnbull, J.M. To dream the impossible dream: An agenda for discussion with stepparents. *Family Relations*, 1983, *32*:227–230.

Visher, E.B., and Visher, J.S. Common problems of stepparents and their spouses. *American Journal of Orthopsychiatry*, 1978, *48*:252–262.

Visher, E.B., and Visher, J.S. *Stepfamilies: A guide to working with stepparents and stepchildren*. New York: Brunner/Mazel, 1979.

Wadsworth, J., Burnell, I., Taylor, B., and Butler, N. Family type and accidents in preschool children. *Journal of Epidemiology and Community Health*, 1983, *37*:100–104.

Wallerstein, J.S. Children of divorce: Preliminary report of a ten-year follow-up of young children. *American Journal of Orthopsychiatry*, 1984, *54*:444–458.

Wilson, M.I., Daly, M., and Weghorst, S.J. Household composition and the risk of child abuse and neglect. *Journal of Biosocial Science*, 1980, *12*:333–340.

Wilson, M.I., Daly, M., and Weghorst, S.J. Differential maltreatment of girls and boys. *Victimology*, 1983, *6*:249–261.

TIME, PLACE, AND PARENTAL AWARENESS: A COGNITIVE–DEVELOPMENTAL PERSPECTIVE ON FAMILY ADAPTATION AND PARENTAL CARE

Carolyn Moore Newberger

This chapter considers the application of cognitive–developmental theory to the study of parental understanding of children and the parental role and evidence that supports a relationship between parental awareness and parental care. A cognitive–developmental analysis of parental thinking and of this role in child rearing raises many questions that are relevant to this volume. The parental awareness construct was developed from interviews with twentieth-century American parents. Does the thinking of these parents represent the way parents think about children and child rearing in different cultures or during different historical times? Stated another way, as the search for biosocial constructs to help explain parental functioning continues, can the parental awareness construct be considered as representing a fundamental and universal "truth" about the nature and development of parental understanding of children and child rearing? And if one accepts the notion of a developmental progression of parental awareness, is it reasonable to assume that what is cognitively more "mature" on this scale of parental cognitive reasoning is also "better," or that what is considered "adaptive" here and now is also "adaptive" for other people or during other times? What can be said about the meaning and function of parental awareness across cultures and historical time? Before these questions are considered, let's turn to cognitive–developmental theory and to the research that has sought to define the nature and development of parental awareness.

THE COGNITIVE-DEVELOPMENTAL MODEL FOR THE STUDY OF HUMAN RELATIONSHIPS

The study of parental awareness began with a series of clinical interviews with parents at a pediatric hospital in a major eastern city.

Among the parents interviewed were several who had clinical histories of having abused a child in their care. What was striking about the abusive parents, in contrast with the parents who were not (as far as that fact could be known) was their tendency to talk about their children in terms of their children's effect on them rather than the effect of their own actions on their children. These parents appeared to view their children from an egocentric perspective, much as younger children are described in the social–cognitive developmental literature as understanding others only in terms of their own perspectives, rather than in terms of the perspectives of others. This suggested that perhaps one could apply a social–cognitive developmental analysis to adults' as well as to children's thinking about others in relation to the self, and specifically to parents' understanding of their children.

The theoretical basis for this work derives from studies by Piaget and his followers of developmental stages and changes in children's understanding of the physical and social world. Piaget (1952, 1963) applies biological concepts to the study of children's thinking. His central proposition is that the course of development is lawful, and that there is a universal and coherent pattern of cognitive development. As with physical structures in biology, Piaget emphasizes that cognitive structures progress from the simple to the complex, from the rigid to the flexible, and that this progression unfolds through a sequence of transformations of cognitive structures into increasingly complex and differentiated wholes.

In his writings, Piaget describes how the process of coming to know the world for a child proceeds through successive stages, with each stage operating as a cognitive blueprint for structuring information perceived about the world into organized systems for acting in the world. Each successive stage is not simply an aggregate of new information on top of old, but is a qualitatively different, as well as a more comprehensive and differentiated way, of understanding experience. At less mature stages, the individual can take into account only limited aspects of experience and can think about that experience in limited ways. As the developing individual moves into more mature stages of thinking, a more comprehensive range of information can be acknowledged and utilized. Thinking becomes increasingly flexible as solutions to problems can be considered from various perspectives and with greater depth.

Stage change comes about through the interaction of the child's internal cognitive structures and experience with the external environment. As children mature biologically, their cognitive structures are challenged by their increasing ability to differentiate new features of the environment and to perceive discrepancies between how they expect the world to operate and how they perceive it as operating. The external environment, in turn, must provide the stimulation that will challenge the child's cognitive structures. The perceived discrepancy between the child's expectations and the child's experience requires an adjustment on the part of the child. Such adjustments are the substance of cognitive stage change. Internal cognitive structures must accommodate to the new information so that a balance, or equilibrium, is achieved between expectations and perceptions. An active child and a stimulating environment generates stage change and leads to an increasingly better match between the child's world view and the adult-expected world view.

The operations by which children construct their understanding of the physical world are thought to underlie their understanding of the social or interpersonal world as well. Piaget (1932–1950) and Kohlberg (1969) identify a developmental progression of cognitive stages of interpersonal understanding. Piaget defines two age-related stages, heteronomous and autonomous, which describe a developmental reorganization of how children think about moral issues. Children at the heteronomous stage judge acts in terms of their consequences. Children at the autonomous stage consider intention when judging the goodness or badness of an act. Kohlberg analyzed responses to hypothetical moral dilemmas where one person's needs or interests conflict with another's. Respondents are asked to resolve the dilemmas and to justify their choices. Kohlberg identified six age-related stages of thinking about the moral issues raised by these dilemmas. He found that younger children resolved the situations egocentrically, or in terms of their own self-interests were the dilemmas to apply to them. Older children were more likely to resolve the dilemmas in terms of more abstract ideas about individual rights and fairness.

Kohlberg defines morality in terms of justice or rules or principles of fairness. Within his framework, as children develop "moral judgment," they free themselves from the constraints of self-interest and personal ties and move toward an ability to consider everyone equally within a framework of universal principles of social justice. In her book *In a Different Voice: Psychological Theory and Women's Development* (1982), Carol Gilligan argues that Kohlberg's theory of moral development fails to consider a different facet of moral development, the morality of care. There is currently considerable controversy over her claims of sex differences in moral judgment and of systematic bias against women in the development of psychological theory. Her identification of a complementary facet of moral orientation that focuses on the connections of people to each other in the course of everyday life has, however, provided an important moral perspective. She identifies a developmental path that reflects a deepening awareness of others as persons with particular needs that may require differences in response.

Kohlberg has emphasized that role-taking, or the ability to be aware of the perspectives of others, is the basic structure underlying moral judgment as he has defined it, and Selman (1971a) has empirically confirmed this assertion. It makes logical sense that role-taking would underlie a morality of care as well. The concept of role-taking was introduced by George Herbert Mead in 1934 with his thesis that the basis for social development and activity lies in the growing ability of the individual to take the role of others and to see him or herself as other see him or her, while progressively widening the scope of human involvement (Mead, 1934). Later thinkers (Feffer, 1970; Flavell, 1968; Selman, 1971b) have identified a developmental sequence of social perspective-taking and argue that the ability to take the point of view of another is the central process of social development. The common developmental perspective-taking path identified across investigations in this field proceeds from egocentrism, where the individual understands others in terms of his or her own needs and experiences; to a conventional perspective, in which the individual views the other in terms of conventional views or norms; to other-oriented perspectives in which others can be understood in terms of their own needs and experiences, and oneself viewed as others see one.

COGNITIVE STRUCTURE IN ORDINARY RELATIONSHIPS: APPLICATION TO PARENTHOOD

An underlying perspective-taking orientation can be argued to be reflected in ordinary interpersonal interactions, including parent–child interactions. Several investigators have attempted to identify and describe levels of interpersonal awareness in particular relationship contexts, such as children's friendships (Selman, 1980; Bigelow, 1977), group relationships (Selman, Jaquette, and Lavin, 1977), and social and occupational roles (Damon, 1976; Furth, 1977). Through these research efforts, a picture of the developmental progression of children's awareness of others in a variety of social contexts is being constructed.

In order to study the nature and development of parents' awareness of their children's experience, it is hypothesized that the model of stage sequence in children's social awareness might also be applied to the study of adult awareness in adult relationships, such as marriage, adult friendship, work relationships, and, of course, the parent–child relationship. It was also of concern to bring the study of interpersonal awareness from the abstract to the particular; from the study of abstract concepts of hypothetical relationships, to the study of perceptions of individuals with whom one is intimately tied.

As applied to parenthood, it is hypothesized that cognitive structure would be revealed in how parents reason about their children's experiences and about the effects of experience on the child, and in how they think about maintaining fairness or justice and assuming responsibility in the parental role. Parental awareness can be thought of as an organized knowledge system with which the parent makes sense out of the child's actions and responses and formulates policies to guide parental action. A parent might not necessarily be formally aware of this knowledge system, but when probing parents' reasons why they believe or act as they do, the underlying cognitive structure is revealed. At successive stages of parental awareness, parents would theoretically move from self- to child-oriented perspectives through which to understand the child and the child's world.

Constructing a Measure of Parental Awareness

The first step in the construction of a developmental measure of parental awareness was to outline logically a hypothetical progression of levels of awareness of the child from a parental point of view. But in order to define the parameters of the parental awareness construct, it was necessary to move beyond clinical impressions and logical analysis and construct an interview that would permit data to be systematically collected and analyzed and the construct empirically tested.

The format of a semistructured reflective interview was chosen because it permits a standard set of questions to be asked, but it also provides flexibility so that parents' answers can be clarified and the reasons for their opinions and beliefs can be probed. In order to construct the interview, a set of eight issues, or tasks of understanding, was identified around which questions could be drawn. These issues fall roughly into three dimensions of the social world of parent-with-child: (1) a perspective-taking dimension: reflected in reasoning about the child's subjective experience and the availability of the growing child to environmental and psychological experience; (2) a justice dimension: reflected in reasoning about the resolution of conflicting claims between and among family members and about the socialization of the child; and (3) a care dimension: reflected in reasoning about the child's needs and about parental responsibility to nurture the child and to engender emotional ties. At least two questions are asked about each issue.

The interview has two sections, a series of personal questions about the parent's own child and child-rearing practices and hypothetical dilemmas presenting situations of conflict between parent and child. Examples of personal questions include, "What do children need most from their parents? How do you know what they need? How do you meet those needs?" and "What do you rely on most to get your children to do what you feel they should do and to stop doing what you feel they shouldn't do? How does it work? Why do you think it works that way?" The dilemmas deal with issues of authority, trust and communication, resolving conflicting needs, and understanding the child's subjective experience. For example, the "Working Mother Dilemma" presents a conflict between a bored and frustrated housewife who needs the stimulation and self-esteem a job will give her, and a 10-year-old daughter who wants her mother home when she comes home from school. Resolving conflict and meeting needs are the central issues of this dilemma.

Fifty-one white and black parents, both fathers and mothers, representing a cross-section of economic levels (Hollingshead [1965] levels 1–5), family sizes, and children's ages were administered the parental-awareness interview. Forty-two subjects were recruited from outpatient clinics at a major pediatric hospital, and eight from a suburban middle-class community near Boston.

The Nature of Parental Awareness

An analysis of interview responses revealed that parental conceptions could be ordered into four qualitatively different and increasingly comprehensive and psychologically oriented levels. These levels are described briefly below.

• Level 1: Egoistic (Self-) Orientation. The basis for parental activity and for understanding of the child is the child's actions in relation to the parent's needs. Child care tasks and parenting are seen as being carried out in response to external cues that effect the parent's emotional and physical comfort or that offer approval to the parent. Intentions of the child are recognized, but as a projection of parental feelings, and are not separated from actions. The organizing principle is achieving what the parent wants, and the object of socialization of the child is to maximize parental comfort.

• Level 2: Conventional (Norms) Orientation. The basis for parental activity and for understanding of the child is the child's actions and inferred intentions in relation to preconceived, externally derived expectations. The child is conceived as having internal states and needs that must be acknowledged, but the parent conceives of the child's subjective reality in a stereotypical way. The child is not seen as unique but as a member of the class of "children," and the parent draws upon tradition, "authority," or conventional wisdom, rather than solely upon the self, to inform expectations and practices. The parent and the child are understood to have well-defined roles which it is their responsibility to fulfill. The parent–child relationship is conceived as mutual fulfillment of role obligations.

• Level 3: Individualistic (Child) Orientation. Each child is recognized to have unique as well as universally shared qualities and is understood in terms of his or her subjective reality. The parent tries to understand the child's world from the child's particular point of view and conceptualizes the parent–child relationship as exchange of feelings and sharing of perspectives, rather than only as the fulfillment of role obligations.

• Level 4: Analytic (Systems) Orientation. The parent can view the relationship between parent and child as a mutual and reciprocal system and understands the child as a complex psychological self-system. The parent can conceive that motives underlying a child's actions may reflect simultaneous and conflicted feelings. The parent can also recognize that there may be ambivalence in his or her own feelings and actions as a parent yet he still loves and cares for the child. Individuals and relationships are understood not only in terms of their stable elements but also as a continual process of growth and change. The parent–child relationship is built not only on shared feelings but also on shared acceptance of each other's faults and frailties as well as virtues and each other's separateness as well as closeness (Newberger and Cook, 1983).

From the interview material, a scoring manual was constructed, adapting the organization and scoring procedures developed by Selman (1980). The manual has now been extensively used by independent investigators with interrater reliabilities ranging from .88 to .96 (Newberger and Cook, 1983).

In the following examples, taken from the parental awareness manual, a sense of the character of parental responses is provided with some discussion of the reasons why they represent the logic of parental reasoning at the assigned level.

Level 1
HOW DOES SOMEONE KNOW IF THEY ARE A GOOD PARENT?

By the way that the kids act when they are grown up, so other people would say that the mother taught them right and put respect on them when they were small.

WHY DO YOU THINK CHILDREN SHOULD BE DISCIPLINED?

It can be embarrassing if you are out in a crowd or something, or the child has a tantrum over something small.

HOW DO YOU KNOW IF YOU'RE A GOOD PARENT?

You try to bring your child up right, and if your child refuses to listen, I don't feel that any parent should feel, "What did I do wrong?" The parent should be easy-going, but they should put the laws down so that their child doesn't walk all over them. I will not stand a child walking over me, because I feel that I am doing my best, and if this child thinks he is going to come in and start hassling

me and pushing me around when I am trying to bring him up right,
I won't tolerate it. And I feel that the child should also have respect
for its parent. If the parent can show respect for them, why can't
a child show respect for a parent?

All three of these parents understand the parental role as making
the child behave as the parent wishes. The parent reasoning at Level
1 orients to personal comfort and understands the child by projecting
his or her own feelings and experiences on the child. The parent's
orientation to self can take the form of preoccupation about what others
will think of the parent when they look at the child, as in the first two
examples. One can also see in the last example a characteristic orientation toward judging parental action in terms of parental intention
rather than in terms of the effect of parental action on the child's development or well-being.

Level 2
HOW HAVE YOU LEARNED TO BE A PARENT; WHAT HAS BEEN THE MOST
IMPORTANT INFLUENCE?
I would have to say religion. I believe in God, that He expects
certain things of a parent. That He entrusted me with another life,
and I have to do the best that I can to take care of it. It is my
responsibility to sacrifice and to do what I must to make sure that
the child is happy in life.

As the preceding example illustrates, the parent's orientation at Level
2 shifts from an egoistic concern for personal comfort and approval to
conformity to external standards and values. An orientation to "doing
ones duty" and to maintaining the valued social order for its own sake
is implicit in the Level 2 focus on traditional or cultural definitions and
prescriptions for what is normal, correct, and responsible, as the following examples further illustrate.

WHAT DO YOU FEEL IS THE MOST IMPORTANT GOAL OF RAISING A CHILD?
I think you want to make them a good moral individual. I am very
religious myself. A lot of kids, it is very difficult when they get to
a certain age to get them to go to church, but I want them to have
a good moral feel of God, and I hope they get to heaven someday.
I bring them up to someday get to heaven.
WHAT DO YOU MEAN BY A GOOD, MORAL INDIVIDUAL?
I mean somebody that wouldn't take anything that didn't belong
to them, that wouldn't steal, that would help people. Make sure
they go to church and make sure they know a little about their

religion. And if you see something and it's not yours, you leave it there and that's it.

At Level 2, the focus shifts from a parent-bound to a more abstract societal or cultural perspective. In these examples, religion provides that perspective. For other parents it may be family or neighborhood values, or child-rearing authorities. What is important is that the parent can step outside the relationship and view it from a third-person perspective, the perspective of the norms and standards of the tradition or culture that the parent embraces. In contrast with the Level 1 focus on parental intention, the focus at Level 2 is on the continuance of the standards and values that the parent embraces.

Level 3

WHAT DO YOU THINK CHILDREN NEED MOST FROM THEIR PARENTS?

Love and time and they need to have their needs considered, that they can't be happy with the things that we want to make them happy. You have to look at them, and if they don't tell you, you have to ask them. You have to try to find out what they want and what is going on in their heads. If I feel that I have lost touch with where he is at, I will sit down and talk and say, "What is happening?" and, "Is everything alright?" . . . And if there is anything wrong he lets me know and we just talk about it and we try to reach an opinion.

WHAT HAS BEEN THE MOST IMPORTANT INFLUENCE ON YOU AS A PARENT?

My son. Before with other kids, I never paid that much attention to them, but now I find that I respect children more because I have my own and see how it is for them.

WHAT DO YOU MEAN?

I know a lot more now than I did before. I understand better how kids feel, what they need from their parents. And Jason kind of showed me how to be his father. Not just what to do for him, but he made me aware that he had feelings, and what they were. And because I love him so much, I just try to respect those feelings.

A major shift from a Level 2 to a Level 3 orientation is from a reliance on external sources to "teach" the parent to a focus on the child as the principle "authority" about that child. One finds a new orientation to the child as a unique and separate individual. This implies a mutuality in the parent–child relationship that was not conceptualized at Levels 1 or 2 and a shift from fixed values and standards toward which all children should be directed to a more flexibly negotiated relationship in which the child's developing preferences and values are acknowledged, even when they might conflict with those of the parent.

Level 4

HOW DO YOU KNOW IF YOU ARE A GOOD PARENT?

That's a hard question because there are two people involved. You don't parent all by yourself and then look at the product and say how good I was. You parent with a child. You're in it together. So we are both responsible, and yet neither are entirely responsible. And I have learned over the years that Rose is not me. That the symptoms of behavior may be the same, but they come from different backgrounds, because I am different from what she is, and my parents from her environment. So while the pattern of behavior may be the same, the moodiness stems from a different post and is neither as severe as mine was, or as light as mine was. It is different. So being a good parent is a difficult question because I am not the only one who has to answer it. The best I can do is tell you that I try to be continually aware that we are different people. I allow her that and I expect her to allow me that, too.

Parental reasoning at Level 4 reveals an understanding of persons, relationships, and roles as embedded in systems with their own processes of growth and evolution. For this parent that means that "knowing" her child or "knowing" how good a parent she is is a process that is never complete, that unfolds over time, as two separate and different people evolve apart and together.

CAN PARENTAL AWARENESS BE DEVELOPED? THE INTERACTIONIST PERSPECTIVE

The parental awareness paradigm provides a method for clarifying the distinctiveness of different parents' "way of making sense of child rearing." The analyses of individual interviews reveal that parental reasoning tends to be quite consistent, with an average of about 75% of parents' responses falling into one level and about 21% into an adjacent level. It is also a model of development. Previous studies exploring the development of parental conceptions in childhood and in parents with differing years of parental experience support the hypothesis that the parental awareness construct represents a developmental process (Newberger, 1980).

The application of a developmental analysis to adult functioning raises many questions. A developmental researcher might argue that all adults should be capable of mature interpersonal conceptions. Why, then, would any adult function at a developmentally immature level? This question might best be addressed by reflecting on the view of the nature of human change presented by structural–developmental theorists.

Structural–developmental psychology offers an oranismic–interactive model of human change. Human development is understood as deriving from neither biological development nor from environmental influences alone. Such a model assumes an active organism interacting with the social and physical environment (Havighurst, 1973). Experience must interact with a receptive organism in order for development to take place. A child who is not developmentally ready to perform the mental operations necessary to understand another's psychological perspectives will not do so, even if the other's feelings are carefully explained. A child who lives in a family where no one explains their feelings or their reasons for their action might have more difficulty understanding other's subjective experience as different from his or her own than other children of the same age until the child is in a social environment where subjective experience is shared. Development, therefore, is described as age-related but not age-defined.

Normal development assumes that the biologically developing child will engage with an environment with stimuli adequate to facilitate the orderly progression of increasingly comprehensive mental structures in a variety of realms of physical and social experience. But variations both in the internal development of the child and in the experiences offered by the environment will produce different rates of development in different children. Diverse individuals may reach chronological maturity having achieved varying levels of cognitive maturity, and a single individual may organize his or her thinking at different levels for differing realms of social experience.

Kohlberg (1973) observes that the development of moral judgment continues in adulthood, and Loevinger (1966) finds that levels of ego development, although developmental, also describe the qualitatively different ways that adults organize their understanding and their action. Although children develop through a sequence of levels or stages, different individuals equilibrate in adulthood at varying levels of cognitive or ego organization, depending on the level of maturity to which he or she is assumed (on the basis of the measures used to make that assumption) to have progressed. Cognitive equilibration, however, at any point in the life cycle, need not suggest the end point of development. New experiences that challenge the adequacy of existing structures should be able, at least hypothetically, to stimulate development at any age or from any level, including the "highest" levels. Although cognitive–developmental sequences have "highest levels," authors of cognitive sequences would be presumptuous to assume that they have defined all that there is to growth.

The next challenge of this work is to learn how to promote growth in parental understanding, and how to facilitate the application of that understanding in flexible and appropriate ways. A recent intervention study suggests in a preliminary way that the development of parental awareness can be facilitated. Sandy (1982) found a significant increase in parental awareness levels following a 12-week parent education program that combined group discussion of child-rearing dilemmas with didactic presentation of child development information ($p<.03$). When reinterviewed 4 months following the completion of the program, further significant gains were found ($p<.05$). A process of development appears to have been initiated during the intervention that continued in the absence of further intervention. No changes were found over the same interval in a comparison group.

PARENTAL AWARENESS AND PARENTAL BEHAVIOR: EVIDENCE FOR A RELATIONSHIP

A basic assumption of a developmental analysis is that the developmental level at which an individual organizes his or her awareness of people, relationships, and roles will bear a relationship to behavior. This assumption has been tested in a preliminary way in two small controlled studies of parents with protective service histories for abuse or severe neglect (Newberger and Cook, 1983).

In the first study, eight parents with histories of having abused a child in their care were identified in a large, urban, pediatric hospital. They were matched with eight parents without a known history of having abused a child on social class, race, family size, and age of the oldest child. In seven of the eight matched pairs, the parent identified as abusive scored lower on the parental awareness scale than the matched counterpart. A t-test for correlated observations (Winer, 1971) indicates that the difference between the groups is highly significant ($t=5.20$, $p<.01$, two-tailed).

This study was replicated on a sample of 16 parents selected from a home-based intervention project for developmentally delayed children in rural Maine. Eight of the parents had protective service histories of severe neglect. As with the urban sample, they were matched, case-by-case, with the other eight parents on race, social class, age of oldest child, and family size, but to control for effects of the child on parental awareness, they were also matched on sex of the child and type and extent of developmental delay using the Alpern–Boll Developmental Profile (Alpern and Boll, 1972). In six of the eight pairs the mother with a history of neglect scored lower than the comparison mother. A t-test for correlated observations was significant at the $p<.05$ level ($t=2.22$, one-tailed).

Further evidence for a relationship between parental awareness and behavior is currently being sought by several investigators. Preliminary analyses of an observational study of adolescent parents in St. Louis, Missouri, supported by a grant from the National Institute of Mental

Health, is revealing strong significant relationships between parental awareness scores and the behavior of these young mothers toward their children, as well as between parental awareness scores and children's responsiveness to parental attention (Flick, 1984).

PARENTAL AWARENESS AND PARENTAL BEHAVIOR: LIMITATIONS TO THE RELATIONSHIP IN STUDY SAMPLES

Evidence for a relationship between parental conceptions and parental behavior is emerging in recent research. This might lead to the conclusion that parental conceptions are a cause of child abuse. Caution must be taken when making such assertions. It is important to note that three of the 16 parents with protective service histories reported in our studies had conceptions scored at higher levels than their matched comparison parents. And many parents in these and other investigations of parental awareness have been scored at lower levels of awareness yet do not have a known history of abusive or neglectful parenting. There is no necessary and direct relationship between parental understanding and parental action. Rather, parental awareness must be considered as one of many aspects of parental experience, such as social supports, parental mental health, and life stresses, which may contribute to the quality of the relationship between parent and child. The use of interview methods also carry their own limitations. For example, it is not known whether for some parents with limited verbal abilities, an implicit awareness may exist that simply may not be expressed on interview. Clearly it is necessary to move beyond verbal measures for assessing parental understanding.

When using a "labeled" group to study behavior, the validity of the label as a proxy for behavior must also be considered. Differences between populations labeled as abusive and comparison populations may reflect other factors that contribute to the assignment of the label that are not directly related to the behavior the labels are assumed to represent. For example, a recent study by Hampton and Newberger (1985) demonstrates that social class and race are more important determinants of whether an inflicted injury will be reported as abuse than severity of injury. Matching on social class and race only partially corrects the problem in bias in assigning the abuse or neglect label. It seems reasonable to assume that how a parent talks about his or her child to a physician or a social worker in a hospital emergency room will contribute to the decision whether or not to identify and/or report a case as child abuse or neglect. Studies of parental awareness and parent–child interactions in nonclinical populations, such as the St. Louis study, are absolutely necessary if more about the parental reasoning–parental action relationship is to be learned.

We must also be careful not to be labelers ourselves and to assume that parents whose conceptions fall into what are hypothesized to be more mature levels of parental awareness are "better" parents who love their children more than parents whose reasoning is scored at less mature levels. We found concerned, loving parents reasoning at all levels of awareness, coping as best they could with a variety of life experiences. One impoverished black father described the pull of the streets that had drawn him into serious trouble with the law, and with clear love for his little boy, explained how he had to "lay down" very strict and unnegotiable rules, because the temptations are so great, and the price for succumbing to the temptations is so high. One cannot say whether a more individualistic and psychologically oriented awareness would be better for this family, with their own particular realities, but this father displayed as much love and concern as any parent in the study.

A more individualized perspective, however, would not mean that strict rules could not be established where appropriate. As individuals attain the capacity to comprehend another in a more differentiated and other-oriented way, they do not lose the perspective of self or the perspective of societal norms and standards. Rather, each level incorporates the structures of preceding levels into its own structure. Social–cognitive development can be understood as an expanding circle rather than as a series of steps, where the attainment of each new step means that the previous step is left behind. Theoretically, parents at more "mature" levels have available a greater and more flexible range of choices and can apply these choices appropriately.

But do parents whose reasoning falls into the individualized or analytic levels apply flexibly the greater range of choices theoretically available to them? Do they make "better" parents? A second vignette demonstrates the danger of making those assumptions. This vignette does not derive from a parent interviewed for one of our studies, but rather from the author's opportunity to observe, at a picnic, an interaction between a 12-year-old boy and his psychiatrist father. The boy was behaving very rudely, refusing to eat, throwing his food on the ground, and swearing at his parents. The father said to the boy, "You feel angry, don't you?", and persisted in trying to interpret the child's feelings rather than to enforce standards of behavior. The boy's behavior became more and more angry and disruptive until the family finally left the picnic. Rather than "laying down the law" and requiring his son to behave appropriately or to leave the group, this parent seemed immobilized by his orientation to the child's psychological issues.

Although he appears highly sensitive to his children's individual emotional functioning and development, one could argue that this father was really not "tuning in" to his son but was failing to recognize the child's needs for firm rules at that moment. In other words, he was "tuning out" by "tuning in." Although his reasoning was not assessed with the parental awareness measure, it is probable that he would have scored at the individualized or analytic levels. What he perhaps lacked was the personal wisdom and flexibility to match his "awareness" with the child's needs. Or perhaps he was worried that he would look like an insensitive parent if he took a more authoritarian stance with his child. Is this, then, a conventional or even an egoistic level of awareness masquerading as an individualized perspective? Or is this more simply an example of the importance of considering noncognitive as well as cognitive factors in explaining parental behavior?

PARENTAL AWARENESS, ADAPTATION, AND ABUSE: HISTORICAL AND CULTURAL PERSPECTIVES

Within the limited frame of urban and rural United States in the late twentieth century, preliminary evidence is unfolding that suggests that, in general, parents with more mature levels of parental awareness are more responsive to their children and less likely to have been identified as abusive or neglectful. It seems reasonable to assume that these parents are, in some important ways, providing a parental context that is more adaptive than parents who are not able to take their child's perspective. Another way of stating it is that a more individualized parental orientation will better equip the child for physical and emotional survival. Child abuse and neglect certainly compromise physical and emotional survival in a very basic way, and one could argue that being able to take the child's perspective would inhibit parental behavior which might harm the child and would be reflected in greater parental sensitivity to the child's needs in general.

But can we support the argument that parental awareness of the child's perspective is in general more adaptive to a "good" outcome than an egocentric or a conventional orientation? And how shall adaptation be defined? Evolutionary biologists define adaptation in terms of enhancing opportunities for reproductive success. We tend to think of enhancing opportunities as facilitating the physical, intellectual, and psychological well-being of the child in order to maximize opportunities for economic success, which is linked to attracting a high quality mate, which in turn is linked with reproductive success or producing high quality children. Such a pathway to reproductive success is hardly universal. In nonhuman species, reproductive success of families and of individuals can be achieved through a variety of means, including infanticide (Hausfater and Hrdy, 1984). What is adaptive for one individual is clearly not always adaptive for another, even within the same family. In human societies, what is adaptive may also be variously defined, and how or whether more "mature" parental awareness contributes to adaptation and to the better care of children is not always clear. Within a context of plentiful resources and from the point of view of the individual child, the developmental sequence of parental awareness levels appears logically to move in the direction of adaptation. The more a parent is able to orient to the child's needs and perspectives, the more likely it would seem that the parent would be able to provide what the child needs to develop into an adult capable of economic and reproductive success. But examples of seemingly insensitive or cruel parental practices from other cultures and historical contexts introduce a more complex and paradoxical picture.

In circumstances of limited resources, reproductive success of a family group may best be served by investing in the offspring most likely to achieve success, often to the detriment of more vulnerable offspring. In Chapter 4 of this volume, Johansson describes the practice in seventeenth- and eighteenth-century Japan of "weeding out" children. The sacrifice of some children enabled a high degree of investment in those children permitted to survive. From an evolutionary perspective, sacrificing the weak and strengthening the strong may be a more adaptive strategy to maximize a family's chances that its gene pool will survive than struggling to sustain many children with limited resources. But this is a biological rationale that may or may not carry with it the element of reasoning and justification tapped by the parental awareness paradigm. Does the practice of "weeding out" demonstrate this culture's lack of sensitivity to the needs and well-being of children, or does it demonstrate its sensitivity? One could argue that infanticide is the most extreme form of child abuse, yet in a context of limited resources with few other means to limit the size of families, some form of infanticide may be necessary both for the personal survival of individuals and for the survival of the community. In this context, infanticide could be interpreted as compatible with a level of parental awareness of the highest order, in which recognition of the embeddedness of children in broader relationships and survival systems forces parents (individually or collectively) to make choices that we find unthinkable.

One of the paradoxes illuminated by the foregoing example is the paradox of parental investment and family size. An individualized level of parental awareness requires by definition separate attention to and recognition of each child. In the author's data, there is the suggestion of an inverse relationship between parental awareness level and the number of children in the family (Newberger, 1977). Although the association does not reach significance, the sample is small ($N = 35$), and it is possible that with a larger sample, a statistically significant relationship would be seen. (Of course, even if this relationship does not exist by chance, it might be explained by other factors that are common both to larger family size and to lower levels of parental awareness, such as lower levels of educational attainment.) The question remains, however, whether an individualized or analytic level of parental awareness requires, independent of material resources, a limited number of children. A number of children above a certain, as yet unknown, threshold may overwhelm parental capacity to develop or to express an individualized perspective. Yet most of the strategies to limit children (birth control, abortion, infanticide) are considered by various people to be abusive or worse.

Johansson's description of child care practices of premodern Catholic and Protestant families offers some further insights into the issue of parental awareness, parental care, and adaptation. Both groups, operating within Christian principles which prohibit infanticide, demonstrate solutions to the dilemma of parental cognitive (as well as economic and emotional) resources strained by large numbers of births. The Catholic families practiced a philosophy of "God's Will," in which children were considered in God's care and left largely unsupervised. The resultant high "accidental" death rate in effect performed the "weeding out" that limited family size. If one could apply the parental awareness paradigm to a culture, one might argue that the "neglect" or lack of attention to their children's ability to protect themselves from environmental hazards indicates that as a group, these parents did not utilize an individualized level of parental awareness when caring for their children. On the other hand, the "acts of God" may have allowed them to invest more intensely in those children who survived.

Johansson points out that the Protestants, in contrast, had a much lower childhood mortality rate and subsequently larger families, but a very different orientation to child rearing. Protestant parents approached their children as clay to be molded to the standards and expectations of their culture, and their child rearing patterns could be characterized as "conventional" on the Parental Awareness Scale. What they characterized as "parental stewardship" had the function of supporting the survival of greater numbers of children and also of limiting the personal parental choices an individualized perspective requires. In this context, high levels of survival and a "conventional" orientation to parenthood can be seen as parts of the same whole. Parental investment is intense, but it is oriented toward shaping the child to the parent's and the community's expectations, not toward the idiosyncratic needs of the individual child. One could argue that a more "mature" individualized orientation would be less adaptive in this setting, in part because parental investment must be distributed among a large number of children, in part because a more individualized orientation might hinder the child's ability to "fit in" and be successful in this community. "Awareness" and "adaptation" are not always parallel.

Korbin (this volume, Chapter 3), states that idiosyncratic departure from cultural norms is the most fruitful domain in which to examine child abuse cross-culturally. One of the limitations of that view is that deviations in the direction of greater sensitivity to the child may be viewed in one culture as abusive, for example as neglectful of a child's moral growth, and in another as more sensitive. Another limitation is that patterns of child rearing might be both culturally accepted and genuinely harmful, not just to individual children, but also to the course of human history. Several thinkers have argued that patterns of child rearing derived from the Protestant ethic have been, in fact, an historically grounded and culturally accepted form of child abuse that have created incalculable harm (Greven, 1977; Miller, 1984).

When examining culturally syntonic parental practices and the implicit parental cognitive orientations implied by those practices, it is difficult to remove the question of what is "adaptive" from the time, the place, and the circumstances of that culture. Clearly, what is considered cognitively "mature" in that segment of our culture that we are able to study, and what may indeed represent a more developmentally advanced level of cognitive functioning, may not be universally "adaptive." On the other hand, culturally accepted practices that contribute to human intolerance and cruelty must be acknowledged, because with human awareness comes the possibility for choice and for change.

REFERENCES

Alpern, G., and Boll, T. *Alpern–Boll developmental profile*. Indianapolis, IN: Developmental Publications, 1972.

Bigelow, B. Children's friendship expectations: A cognitive–developmental study. *Child Development, 1977, 48*: 246–253.

Damon, W. Some thoughts on the nature of children's social development. *In* J. Mayer, Ed., *Reflections on values education*. Waterloo, Canada: Laurier Press, 1976.

Feffer, M. A developmental analysis of interpersonal behavior. *Psychological Review, 1970, 77*: 197–214.

Flavell, J. *The development of role-taking and communication skills in children*. NY: Wiley, 1968.

Flick, L. Personal communication. St. Louis, Missouri, 1984.

Furth, H. Young children's understanding of society. *In* H. McGurk, Ed., *Social development*. Amsterdam: North Holland, 1977.

Gilligan, C. *In a different voice*. Cambridge, MA: Harvard University Press, 1982.

Greven, P. *The Protestant temperament: Patterns of child-rearing, religious experience, and the self in early America*. NY: Knopf, 1977.

Hampton, R. L., and Newberger, E. H. Child abuse incidence and reporting by hospitals: Significance of severity, class, and race. *American Journal of Public Health*, 1985, *75*: 56–60.

Hausfater, G., and Hrdy, S., Eds. *Infanticide: Comparative and evolutionary perspectives*. NY: Aldine, 1984.

Havighurst, R. J. History of developmental psychology: Socialization and personality development through the life span. *In* P. B. Baltes and K. W. Schaie, Eds., *Life-span developmental psychology.* NY: Academic Press, 1973.

Hollingshead, A. *Two-factor index of social position.* New Haven, CT: Yale University Press, 1965.

Kohlberg, L. Stage and sequence: The cognitive–developmental approach to socialization. *In* D. Goslin, Ed., *Handbook of socialization theory and research.* NY: Rand McNally, 1969.

Kohlberg, L. Continuities in childhood and adult moral development revisited. *In* P. B. Baltes and K. W. Schaie, Eds., *Life-span developmental psychology.* NY: Academic Press, 1973.

Loevinger, J. The meaning and measurement of ego development. *American Psychologist,* 1966, *21*: 195–206.

Mead, G. H. Mind, self and society. Chicago, IL: University of Chicago Press, 1934.

Miller, A. *For your own good: Hidden cruelty in child-rearing and the roots of violence.* NY: Farrar, Straus, Giroux, 1984.

Newberger, C. Parental conceptions of children and childrearing: A structural–developmental analysis. Unpublished doctoral dissertation, Harvard University, 1977.

Newberger, C. The cognitive structure of parenthood: The development of a descriptive measure. *In* R. Selman and R. Yando, Eds., *New directions for child development: Clinical–developmental research.* San Francisco, CA: Jossey-Bass, 1980.

Newberger, C., and Cook, S. Parental awareness and child abuse: A cognitive–developmental analysis of urban and rural samples. *American Journal of Orthopsychiatry,* 1983, *53*: 512–524.

Piaget, J. *The moral judgement of the child.* NY: Harcourt Brace, 1932/1950.

Piaget, J. *The origins of intelligence in children.* NY: Norton, 1952/1963.

Sandy, L. Teaching child development principles to parents: A cognitive–developmental approach. Unpublished doctoral dissertation, Boston University, 1982.

Selman, R. The relation of role-taking ability to the development of moral judgement in children. *Child Development,* 1971, *42*: 79–91 (a).

Selman, R. Taking another's perspective: Role-taking development in early childhood. *Child Development,* 1971, *42*: 1721–1734 (b).

Selman, R. *The growth of interpersonal understanding: Developmental and clinical analyses.* NY: Academic Press, 1980.

Selman, R., Jaquette, D., and Lavin, D. Interpersonal awareness in children: Toward an integration of developmental and clinical child psychology. *American Journal of Orthopsychiatry,* 1977, *47*: 264–274.

OUTCOMES AND CONSEQUENCES
OF MALTREATMENT

part

IV

INTERGENERATIONAL CONTINUITY OF ABUSE*

Byron Egeland
Deborah Jacobvitz
Kathleen Papatola

Over the past 20 years considerable effort has been made to understand the causes and consequences of child abuse. This effort, along with clinical case study, has resulted in a number of theories and models of child abuse. Despite differing viewpoints and inconsistent research findings one can conclude that child abuse is highly complex and does not lend itself to a simple explanation or theory. Few empirical systematic studies have investigated the antecedents and consequences of abusive parent–child relationships. If we are to develop effective prevention and intervention strategies, systematic investigations identifying antecedents of child maltreatment are needed.

Much of the child abuse research has been retrospective in nature. As a result, cause and effect relationships have often been erroneously concluded from significant differences between abusers and non-abusers. By starting with the final outcome and tracing backward, the chain of events may appear inevitable (Kaufman and Zigler, in press). However, when following events prospectively, or forward in time, it becomes evident that numerous pathways for each event are possible. For example, one conclusion drawn from such retrospective research is that poverty is a cause of abuse. An important question remains unanswered: Why do some poor parents abuse their children whereas the majority do not? The strength of the relationship between poverty and abuse weakens when examined prospectively. Numerous other examples exist. According to retrospective studies abused children have been found to be born premature compared to a control group (Frei-

*Research for this chapter was supported in part by grants from the National Center on Child Abuse and Neglect, the Administration for Children, Youth, and Families (DHEW 90-C-424) and Maternal and Child Health and Crippled Children Services (DHEW MC-R-27041601).

drich and Boriskin, 1976). Such findings have been used to argue that the child causes his/her own abuse. An equally plausible explanation is that abusing parents mistreat their children during pregnancy by not receiving proper medical care or not taking care of themselves resulting in a higher likelihood that the child will be premature. In a prospective study of a group of parents at risk for abuse, Egeland and Vaughn (1981) found that looking forward, the relationship between prematurity and abuse did not exist. Abuse among children born prematurely was not any greater than among a group of full-term babies. While retrospective data has been useful in generating hypotheses and ideas, we must be extremely cautious in concluding cause and effect relationships from the results of such research.

Psychologists and other professionals interested in the antecedents of parental behavior have noted the transmission of a number of parenting behaviors across generations (Ricks, 1985). Although no prospective studies have been conducted in the area of child abuse, many professionals have found that parents who abuse their children were abused as children (Delozier, 1982). Based on clinical, retrospective data, Steele and Pollack (1968) report that abusing parents were abused and they hypothesize that abusing one's child is linked with the parent's treatment during childhood. Bowlby (1982) noted that, "of the many types of psychological disturbances resulting from maternal deprivation, the effects on one's ability to nurture and parent are potentially the most serious" (p. 675).

Contemporary attachment theory provides a framework for exploring the importance of early care in predicting later parenting patterns. Based on a recent summary by Martha Erickson (1984), we will present an overview of attachment theory. A critical developmental issue in the first 12–18 months of life is the establishment of what Erikson (1963) describes as a sense of basic trust. Bowlby (1969, 1980) and Ainsworth (1973) describes the nature of the caregiver–infant relationship and its importance to later development. Their attachment theory views human development within an evolutionary context and proposes that infants are predisposed to form an attachment to the caregiver, that the infant has a repertoire of attachment behaviors (e.g., sucking, crying, smiling, grasping) which facilitates this relationship, and that this attachment relationship serves a biological function, primarily the protection of the infant from harm. Although their attachment theory draws heavily from psychoanalytic theory it departs from the early psychoanalytic view that all motivation derives from one or two basic sources (e.g., tension reduction, according to Freud's early postulation), and that love and attachment are secondary motives. Likewise, attachment theory differs from the contention of social learning theorists (Bandura and Walters, 1963) that love and attachment arise secondarily as a result of their association with a primary drive such as hunger. This theory contends and extensive evidence supports that love and attachment are part of a primary motive system possessed by primates as a result of their unique evolution.

While attachment behaviors are present at birth, the attachment relationship is not. Attachment develops over time, during the first year of the infant's life, and is contingent upon repeated interactions with the caregiver as well as certain cognitive developments with the infant. Major cognitive developmental tasks in the first few months of life are the differentiation of self from others and the acquisition of the schema of object permanence (Piaget, 1952). The development of such a relationship between the infant and the caregiver is dependent upon these developments. The child must recognize that the caregiver is a separate entity and that the caregiver exists even when he or she is not within the infant's sight. It is this gradual development over time that distinguishes attachment in humans from the more immediate bonding in other species (e.g., imprinting in ducks).

For the attached infant, separation from the attachment figure is the occasion for anxiety. Once again this differs somewhat from early psychoanalytic theory and from social learning theory which views separation anxiety as a secondary motive. Attachment theory or ethological/evolutionary theory contends, instead, that separation anxiety is a primary instinctual system. Primate existence depends upon organized group living; thus this special instinctual system has evolved among primates, who foster close social bonds by making separation from others the precipitator of anxiety. This anxiety first serves as the motive for closeness between caregiver and child, a closeness that is essential for survival. This theoretical view differs from the traditional psychoanalytic and social-learning belief that there is a basic antagonism between a child's natural behavioral inclinations and societal constraints. Attachment theory implies, instead, a basic compatibility between child and society: a disposition to become socialized develops naturally in infants reared in an environment similar to the environment in which the species adapted (Stayton, Hogan, and Ainsworth, 1971).

In developing autonomous functioning during the second year of life, the infant faces the task of separating from the caregiver without threatening the established bond. The manner in which caregivers respond to their infant's increasing capacity for coping and behavior regulation influences the infant's development of autonomous functioning (Mahler, Pine, and Bergman, 1975; Sander, 1975; Matas, Arend, and Sroufe, 1978). A healthy attachment relationship is characterized by a balance of attachment behavior and exploration. In the presence of an attachment figure the infant engages in healthy growth that promotes exploration of the environment while periodically maintaining contact with the caregiver through a touch, a smile, or a vocalization. When distressed the infant accepts comfort from the attachment figure. With a caregiver who meets the infant's needs in a consistent, predictable fashion and provides a secure base from which the infant can test his or her new skills and explore the world, the infant should develop a feeling of security and trust (Ainsworth, Blehar, Waters, and Wall, 1978). As securely attached children become older a sense of security and trust facilitates independent functioning.

Compared to children with a history of a secure attachment, children with a history of an anxious attachment either avoid their caregiver or are in constant conflict with their caregiver. Anxiously attached children tend to hover near their caregiver rather than independently explore their environment during toddlerhood (Matas, Arend, and Sroufe, 1978) and were more dependent on their teacher in the nursery school (Sroufe, Fox, and Pancake, 1983). Our data (Egeland and Sroufe, 1981) as well as other research (Main, 1983) indicate that abused children tend to be anxiously attached.

Through this early primary relationship or attachment the infant forms representational models of others and self, models that not only strongly influence the way in which a child relates to others but also, determine the child's expectations regarding self and attachment figures. The child who has formed a secure attachment is "likely to possess a representational model of attachment figures as being available, responsive and helpful, and a complimentary model of him/herself as at least a potentially loveable and valuable person" (Bowlby, 1980, p. 242). The securely attached child with positive expectations of him/herself and others is more likely to enter into other loving and trusting relationships. In contrast, infants whose needs have not been met consistently, infants whose attachment figure responded inadequately or inappropriately to their behavior, come to expect that care is not available or dependable. Their representational model, of the attachment figure as being unavailable, unresponsive and un-loveable, is what they bring to the caregiving relationship when they become parents.

The relationship between the parents early history of care and their own caregiving patterns as adults is the subject of the present investigation. In this chapter, we will examine the relation between caregiving in the first and second generation for mothers who are part of a large, prospective, longitudinal study of high-risk parents and their children. Systematic research into the effects of childhood experiences on the way parents treat their children is only beginning, however, as Bowlby (1982) has pointed out, it seems likely to be one of the most fruitful of all fields for further research.

BACKGROUND

Starting in 1975, we enrolled 267 mothers who were in their last trimester of pregnancy at the Minneapolis Public Health Clinics. They were considered at risk for caretaking problems due to lower SES and a number of other factors, such as age (mean, 20 years; range, 12–32). Of the mothers, 62% were unwed at the time of the birth of their child, 86% of the pregnancies were unplanned, and 33% were not prepared for the arrival of their child, which means that they had not obtained the necessary equipment to care for the baby or made arrangements for a place for the baby to sleep. Their lives were chaotic and disruptive. For example, over the first 30 months of their child's life, 88% of the mothers moved an average of four times. Many experienced a high number of stressful life events and lacked support from husband/boyfriend, family, and friends.

Within this high-risk sample we identified 44 cases of maltreatment that included physical abuse ($N=24$), neglect ($N=19$), as well as hostile/rejecting ($N=19$), and psychologically unavailable ($N=19$) patterns of caretaking. There is considerable overlap among the groups; for example, all but four of the children in the hostile/rejecting group were also physically abused. In addition to the 44 mothers who maltreated their child, there was a borderline group in which maltreatment was suspect but not certain. These parents could not be classified as maltreating nor could they be placed in the adequate care group. There was evidence that they were maltreating their child; however, this could not be substantiated. The "other" problem group consisted of mothers who for one reason or another were not the primary caregiver for their child. One mother in this group traveled with the circus and saw very little of her child; others had basically abandoned their child for other reasons.

Behaviors of mothers in the physically abusive group ranged from frequent and intense spanking in disciplining their children to unprovoked angry outbursts resulting in serious injuries, such as severe cigarette burns. In many cases, bruises or cuts were observed or serious injuries were reported in clinic files. In all instances, the abuse was seen as potentially physically damaging to the child.

Mothers in the hostile/verbally abusive group chronically found fault with their children and criticized them in an extremely harsh fashion. Whereas many physically abusive mothers were not constantly hostile or rejecting (but rather prone to violent, unprovoked outbursts), mothers in this group constantly berated and harassed their children.

The mothers in the psychologically unavailable group were unresponsive to their children and, in many cases, passively rejected them.

These mothers appeared detached and uninvolved with their children, interacting with them only when necessary. In general, they were withdrawn, displayed flat affect, and seemed depressed. There was no indication that these mothers derived any pleasure or satisfaction from their relationship with their children nor did they react with sympathy or concern when their child was distressed.

Mothers in the neglect group were irresponsible or incompetent in managing day-to-day child-care activities. They failed to provide for the necessary health or physical care of the children and did little to protect them from possible dangers in the home. While these mothers sometimes expressed interest in their children's well being, they lacked the skill, knowledge, or understanding to provide consistent, adequate care.

Mothers in all maltreatment groups were identified on the basis of information obtained from observations of mother and infant in the home 7 and 10 days postpartum and when the infant was 3, 6, and 12 months of age. During each of these visits, a Child Care Rating Scale (Egeland and Deinard, 1975) was completed, and the mother was asked questions regarding her caregiving skills, feelings toward the infant, disciplinary practices, etc. In addition, observational data and other information were collected systematically during mothers' visits to the Maternal and Infant Care Clinic and to our laboratory when their infants were 9, 12, 18, and 24 months old. The validity of our staff's identification of maltreating mothers was supported by some additional information. All mothers in the physical abuse group had been under the care of child protection or were referred to child protection by someone outside of our project. Most of the mothers in the neglect group were under the care of the public health nurse or child protection worker.

Observers independently rated mothers and infants at 12 and 18 months in a situation requiring that the mother set limits for her child and at 24 months in a problem-solving task. These ratings supported the classification of mothers in the hostile/verbal abuse and the psychologically unavailable groups.

Independent of identifying mothers who were maltreating their children, we determined the quality of care the mother received as a child. At the time of the 48- and 54-month assessment, mothers ($N = 181$) were asked a series of questions about their childhood and family situation including whether or not they were raised by a relative or placed in a foster home. They were asked about how they were disciplined and whether or not they were beaten and physically abused, sexually molested, or neglected.

On the basis of the responses the mothers were divided into two groups: (1) not abused and (2) abused groups. Women in the nonabused group were further divided into those who were emotionally supported and the remainder of the sample. The mothers who were emotionally supported as children ($N = 35$) described their families as loving, concerned, and encouraging. Most importantly, they expressed a sense of emotional security distinguishing them from other women in the sample. "I always knew that no matter what I did my parents would be there" was a common, almost universal statement from women in this group. Women who did not report any abuse but did not describe their families as loving or emotionally supportive were placed in a "control" group ($N = 79$).

The abused group included women who experienced one or more of the following forms of abuse: (1) physical; (2) sexual; (3) foster home placement; and (4) neglect. The physical abuse group consisted of women who reported clear incidences of severe maltreatment during childhood ($N = 47$). These women were burned with irons, scalded with hot water, thrown into walls and radiators, and hit repeatedly with belts, switches, and electrical cords. These women were not only beaten daily or weekly, but their bodies were also frequently marked (i.e., bruises, scars, or internal trauma manifested by broken bones, subdural hematoma, internal bleeding, and previously undetected fractures at various stages of healing). Women beaten only once or twice were included in the group if they reported physical injuries such as broken bones, burns, or lacerations sometimes requiring hospitalization or leaving scars. The sexual abuse group included women reporting sexual intercourse by an older relative (usually their father, stepfather, or brother) during their childhood ($N = 13$). These women did not receive any emotional support at the time of the abuse; the incident was either kept secret or when reported, the child was not believed. Some of the mothers in the sexual abuse group were also in the physical abuse group.

A group of mothers placed in a foster or group home for more than 1 year during their childhood were identified ($N = 20$). The reasons for being raised out of their own homes were court-ordered, child-initiated, or due to circumstances beyond control, such as the mother's death or hospitalization.

Finally, the neglect group included mothers who reported their primary caregiver's failure to provide for basic physical needs (food, clothing, or shelter). In some cases, the child received inadequate clothing and shelter for weather conditions or was locked outside her dwelling for lengthy time periods during cold winter months ($N = 8$). There was overlap among all of the maltreatment groups. In cases where there was overlap the mother was included in each maltreatment group, which explains why there were more than 181 total cases reported in Tables 11.1 and 11.2.

TABLE 11.1. Relations of Patterns of Caretaking from First to Second Generation

Mother caretaking history: First generation	Patterns of caretaking: Second generation									
	Maltreatment		Other problems		Borderline		Adequate care		Totals	
	Males	Females	Males	Females	Males	Females	Males	Females	Males	Females
Severe physical abuse	10 (38%)	6 (28%)	2 (8%)	1 (5%)	4 (15%)	10 (48%)	10 (39%)	4 (19%)	26	21
	16 (34%)		3 (6%)		14 (30%)		14 (30%)		47	
Emotionally supportive	1 (5%)	0 (0%)	0 (0%)	0 (0%)	11 (58%)	3 (19%)	7 (37%)	13 (81%)	19	16
	1 (3%)		0 (0%)		14 (40%)		20 (57%)		35	
Control (remainder of people)	6 (15%)	1 (3%)	4 (10%)	3 (8%)	14 (34%)	10 (26%)	17 (41%)	24 (63%)	41	38
	7 (9%)		7 (9%)		24 (30%)		41 (52%)		79	

262

TABLE 11.2. Relations of Patterns of Caretaking from First to Second Generation

Mother caretaking history: First generation	Patterns of caretaking: Second generation									
	Maltreatment		Other problems		Borderline		Adequate care		Totals	
	Males	Females	Males	Females	Males	Females	Males	Females	Males	Females
Sexual abuse	5 (56%)	1 (25%)	1 (11%)	1 (25%)	2 (22%)	2 (50%)	1 (11%)	0 (0%)	9	4
	6 (46%)		2 (15%)		4 (31%)		1 (8%)		13	
Foster home placement	6 (43%)	1 (17%)	1 (7%)	1 (17%)	3 (21%)	3 (50%)	4 (29%)	1 (17%)	14	6
	7 (35%)		2 (10%)		6 (30%)		5 (25%)		20	
Neglect	3 (75%)	0 (0%)	0 (0%)	0 (0%)	1 (25%)	2 (50%)	0 (0%)	2 (50%)	4	4
	3 (38%)		0 (0%)		3 (37%)		2 (25%)		8	

Relation of Parental Abuse across Generations

Our data strongly support the notion of intergenerational continuity of abuse. As can be seen from Table 11.1, a large proportion (70%) of the 47 mothers who were abused were currently mistreating their children. Altogether 33 mistreated their children, of which 16 were clear-cut abuse cases, 3 were being taken care of by someone other than the mother and 14 were providing borderline care (i.e., were suspected of maltreating their child).

Of the mothers who were judged to have had emotionally supportive parents, only 1 was currently maltreating her child, 1 was not the primary caretaker, and 14 were borderline abusers. For the remainder of the mothers who were judged not to have been abused or emotionally supported in childhood (control), 9% were maltreating their children, 30% were in the borderline group, and 52% were providing adequate care.

The cross-generational effects of severe physical abuse were basically not related to the sex of the mother's child, however, there was a sex-of-child effect for emotional support. Approximately equal proportions of mothers who were abused were abusing their child regardless of the child's sex. For mothers with a history of receiving emotional support from their parents, there was a sex difference in the quality of care they provided their own children. There was greater continuity of emotionally supportive parenting for mothers of girls. Of the mothers who were emotionally supported as a child and whose child is a girl, 81% were providing adequate care. For the mothers in the emotionally supported group who have boys, only 37% were providing adequate care.

Cross-generational effects appear to vary depending on the type of caregiving studied and the sex of the offspring in the second generation. As indicated previously, most mothers (70%) who were abused as children maltreated their children regardless of the sex of the child. Cross-generational effects were not so large for mothers who were emotionally supported as a child. Continuity across this parenting dimension depended upon the sex of the mother's child. Mothers in this poverty sample tended not to provide adequate care for their boys even though they had a history of having received emotional support from their parents.

Discontinuity of Emotionally Supportive Caretaking

What is the explanation for the relatively high incidence of borderline maltreatment in the second generation for mothers who were judged to have emotionally supportive parents? Only one mother in this group abused her child; however, a number (40%) were in the borderline abuse group. We have shown that continuity of child abuse in the first and second generations was high. However, our data also show that the intergenerational explanation does not account for all abuse cases, particularly for the control group. This may be due to the limitations of relying on retrospective reports to determine the mother's relationship history. One explanation for the high incidence of borderline maltreatment in the emotionally supportive group and maltreatment in the control group is that these mothers may have been abused as children but were unable or unwilling to report it to the interviewer. We have no way of knowing the accuracy of mother's recall of her childhood. Perhaps the mothers have forgotten or choose to lie about their childhood. It is easy to understand how mothers distort their recollections of having been abused as a child (Ricks, 1985). Main and Goldwyn (1984) noted that the accuracy and extent of recall of childhood experiences is related to the quality of the childhood experienced.

A more plausible explanation for the smaller degree of continuity for the emotionally supportive and control groups has to do with the high-risk nature of our sample and the fact that they live in poverty. It is likely that the life stress, chaos, and disruption the mothers experience is a major cause of abuse. In earlier investigations, we found life stress to be an antecedent of abuse, particularly in combination with lack of social support and certain characteristics of the mother (Egeland, Breitenbucher, and Rosenberg, 1980). Despite having been raised by emotionally supportive parents, our mothers are at greater risk for maltreating their children due to living in impoverished conditions. A preliminary analysis of our life stress data indicates that mothers who were emotionally supported as children but have not provided adequate care for their child (borderline group) had higher stressful life event and anxiety scores during the preschool period compared to the emotionally supported mothers who were providing adequate care. At least, for some mothers, life stress and poverty are the antecedents of parental abuse even for those who were raised by emotionally supportive parents.

RELATION OF SEXUAL ABUSE, NEGLECT, AND FOSTER HOME PLACEMENT ACROSS GENERATIONS

The cross-generational relation between a mother having been sexually abused by her parents and maltreatment is very high (see Table 11.2). As children, 13 mothers reported having been sexually abused by a family member. Of these mothers, 12 maltreated their children: 6 were clear-cut abuse cases, 2 were having other problems, and 4 were in the borderline maltreatment group. Only 1 mother who had a history of having been sexually abused provided adequate care for her child.

Surprisingly, of all the mothers interviewed about their family of origin, only 8 were judged to have been neglected in childhood (the mothers who were neglected were also physically abused). Most mothers reported that their fathers worked and the family always had enough food, clothes, adequate shelter, and medical care. The relation between a history of neglect and maltreatment in the next generation was very high. Of the 8 mothers who were neglected as children, 6 maltreated their children; 3 were cases of severe maltreatment, 3 were in the borderline care group, and 2 were providing adequate care (see Table 11.2).

Placement in a foster home in the first generation was highly related to maltreatment in the second generation (see Table 11.2). However, one must be careful not to conclude that a history of foster home placement causes maltreatment in the next generation. Most of the mothers were placed in foster homes because of having been abused. It is most likely that the poor quality care that led to foster placement was more related to the maltreatment in the next generation than out-of-home placement.

EXAMINING THE EXCEPTIONS TO INTERGENERATIONAL CONTINUITY

In the last section of this chapter, we will attempt to understand the phenomena of intergenerational continuity of caregiving behavior as it pertains to parental abuse, neglect, and other forms of maltreatment. Our data suggest that parents who were abused as children were clearly at risk for abusing their own children. Of the mothers who were abused, 70% maltreated their children. Developing means for breaking this cycle would be a big step toward eliminating the problem of abuse. Before this can be accomplished, we need to have a better understanding of how abuse in one generation is carried to the next. One approach to understanding this phenomena is to study the exceptions to continuity, particularly cases in which abuse in the first generation is followed by adequate care in the second generation.

We studied these exceptions by comparing the case histories of mothers who were abused in childhood and abusing their children with mothers who were abused but provided adequate care for their children. For the sake of brevity, we will refer to these groups as the continuity and exceptions groups, respectively. The files of those showing continuity of maltreatment across generations were compared to those showing exceptions. These case studies were based on extensive interviews of the mother when assessments were made at 12, 18, 24, 30, 42, 48, and 54 months. The ideas and conclusions presented in this section are clearly subjective. They were based on clinical impressions which require further study and empirical testing before definite conclusions can be made. Despite the clinical nature of these data, a number of interesting ideas emerged contributing to understanding continuity (and lack of) of parental abuse across generations.

A major variable seemed to be the severity of the abuse the mother experienced as a child. The more severe the treatment the greater the likelihood of the mother continuing the pattern of maltreatment with her own children. The five most "mild cases" of abuse in the physical abuse group were mothers who did not abuse their own children.

One mother reported that although her mother was not very interested in raising a child, she did provide for all of her child's physical needs. In this case, the only instance of physical discipline occurred when the mother was 10 years old. She had left the neighborhood without notifying her mother and was spanked hard enough to leave severe bruises requiring medical attention. Another mother described her parents as supportive and reliable—always concerned with providing for the children's needs first and then their own. There was one instance of physical punishment when she was growing up. She had wandered away from the family and was found near a creek where there had been a recent drowning. She was spanked severely with a belt and badly bruised; prior to that she had only had her "butt paddled."

The five mildest cases of abused mothers who were not abusing their children had other characteristics in common. All five of these women married the father of their babies. Four of these remained married through the preschool years, and all reported that the father shared in the caretaking. In the relationship that dissolved, custody of the two children was given to the father. All of the less severely abused mothers lived in homes they owned and relied on the father as the primary means of support, although some of the mothers also worked. They were very "middle class" and were upwardly mobile. Four of the five mothers in this group came from intact families themselves. They reported family activities and involvement as they were growing up and considered their parents' methods of discipline as fair and warranted by the situation. Thus, for a subset of mothers who we judged were abused as children but were not abusing, the "milder" abuse they received as a child is a major factor in accounting for the exception to intergenerational parental abuse. The less-severe-form-of-abuse mother received, along with a supportive husband, adequate living conditions and an awareness of her own caretaking history made the abused mother less at risk for abusing her own children.

An examination of the case histories of mothers who were more severely abused as children yielded some interesting hypotheses.

Case #1

DB is an example of a mother who was more severely abused as a child. She was hit repeatedly with a fly swatter leaving red welts; she describes her mother as critical and hostile. In contrast to her mother, DB described her relationship with her father as very loving. "There was no love in our house except between my dad and me." Throughout her life she felt closer to her father than her mother.

When her first born was 18 months old, DB was asked: "Do you believe you are raising your child in the same way you were raised?" DB responded, "No, my parents were constantly fighting and there was no show of affection . . . I want my child to grow up living in a relaxed atmosphere." Throughout the 5 years of interviews DB demonstrated a consciousness and concern regarding child rearing. At the 18- and 24-month interviews, DB claims she had difficulties disciplining her child. She left that task to her husband. She understands her own strengths and weaknesses regarding child-rearing skills, and she sees the relationship between her own child-rearing history and the care she provides her child. She reported that her daughter respected her father's discipline, which involved verbal reprimands or discussions, more than her own. At the 48-month interview, she read the book, *Dare to Discipline*, apparently trying to gain insight regarding discipline since her own mother did not provide an adequate model. Although DB does not abuse her child, patterns apparent in her early relationship with her parents are repeated with her husband and firstborn child. DB reports on a number of occasions that her daughter, "has a preference for her father."

Unlike other mothers who repeat the abuse of their childhood, DB has a model of a loving relationship along with the abusive one. Her heightened awareness of her history of abuse and her self-consciousness regarding child rearing may help her draw upon the supportive model in raising her daughter. Furthermore, she has a loving relationship with her husband, who provided both emotional support for her and helps her to control her daughter's behavior more appropriately.

Case #2

VF comes from one of the most severely abusive backgrounds in our sample. There were 10 children in her family of origin, and as each child neared adolescence they were systematically signed over to the state and placed in foster homes. The father was a passive man who seemed to want to help the children but did not know how to go about it. The mother beat the children frequently, using a belt or a broom, and once threw a hot iron at VF, leaving scars that she still has. VF had never been to a doctor or dentist prior to age 11 (she did not know what they were), at which time she was made a ward of the state. Prior to that, her mother had frequently threatened to "get rid of her," and since that was the worst thing she could imagine happening, she denied the beatings when the school nurse inquired about her bruises. When her mother finally called in the authorities to take her (they had a minor argument), VF felt relief. VF (age 11) was taken to the local jail where she spent 6 days awaiting a hearing. At the hearing, her mother gave up custody of her and she neither saw nor spoke to her parents for the next 8 or 9 years. She spent 2½ years in her first foster home, followed by placement two more homes. In the third home, VF took some pills to get high, but it was interpreted as a suicide attempt. Because the county had no vacancies in adolescent treatment centers, she was sent to a hospital in Wisconsin that treated adult chemical dependents. Although the other patients stayed for 1 to 3 months, VF remained for 2 years. She received a great deal of help and support from the other patients along with ongoing psychotherapy. Her next placement was a residential treatment center in northern Minnesota where she remained for 2 years until she was ready for a group home in Minneapolis. At age 18, she moved into an apartment with another girl, and shortly thereafter she became pregnant by a black man (VF is white) who was in town on business. VF never told him about the pregnancy but was determined to keep and raise the baby as her own. When the baby was almost 1 year old, VF met another man whom she eventually married. They have had three more children and purchased a home in a rural area. Both VF and her husband are hardworking, deriving most of their support from each other and being very committed to their family. VF has visited with her parents a number of times in recent years and seems accepting of the fact that she cannot change her past but is really determined to change the future for her children. VF seems particularly aware of her past, and she talked about it with great emotion. This was in contrast to many mothers in the continuity group who discussed their history of abuse with little detail and no emotion. It seems that VF learned enough from therapy to be aware of her own child-rearing history and how it might affect the child care she provides her own children. With the support she receives from her husband and the help he provides in child care, she is able to provide adequate care to her children.

Case #3

DM suffered from extreme abuse by her father until she was 10 years old, at which time her parents separated. In a family of five children, she felt that she was not abused quite so badly as her siblings, since she learned to stay out of his way as much as possible. Still she was beaten, thrown across the room, slapped so hard that her lip was split (because she would not kiss him), and suffered a fractured skull when he pushed her down a hill on a sled without telling her how to steer it. He beat one of her sisters with a telephone, broke another one's arm, etc.

DM left home at 16 but did not have her first child until she was 23. She was married to the father of the baby, who was very supportive both financially and emotionally. She has always had a difficult relationship with her first child but she found it much easier to interact with her second one. As a result, her husband took on more and more of the responsibility for the oldest one, and he developed an exceptionally close relationship with the child. When the parents finally separated, the husband kept both children. DM saw a counselor off and on for about 2 years after the first child was born. She also attended Alanon for a while, and her husband had started seeing a psychiatrist for depression before the separation. As in Case 2, DM was very aware of her history of having been abused, and she speaks of her abuse with great emotion.

CONCLUSION

Mothers who were severely abused as children but have not abused their children had a number of characteristics in common. They had one parent (or foster parent) who provided some love and support, they were currently living in more stable home situations, and they had husbands who were emotionally supportive and who were involved in caring for their children. A stable home situation, intact family, and supportive husband, who is the father of the child, appear to be major factors in accounting for the exceptions to the intergenerational continuity of parental abuse. The severity of parental abuse experienced by mother in childhood also seems to be an important factor.

The data suggest that early relationship histories have a powerful influence on the parents' subsequent relationship with their children. Although there were caregivers who did not abuse their children (the "exception group"), 70% of those parents with abusive childhood histories maltreat their children. Observations of current child abuse were gathered independent of parents' reports. Thus, the high incidence of an abusive relationship history among parents who abuse their children cannot be explained by defensive reporting, that is, parents exaggerating their past victimization to justify or explain their current abusive patterns.

One way to interpret intergenerational continuity is within contemporary attachment theory. As discussed earlier, the early infant–caregiver attachment relationship provides a prototype of later relationships and intergenerational continuity is caused through an individual's expectation regarding the self and attachment figure. Bowlby notes (1980) that there is a strong causal relationship between an individual's experience with his/her parents and his/her later capacity to make affectionate bonds. Children who have not been properly nurtured will have difficulty as adults nurturing their offspring.

Even though many abused children avoid their caregiver (Egeland and Sroufe, 1981; Main, 1983), they do not gain independence or function in an autonomous fashion. Abused children tend to be dependent on their caregiver, and as they grow up, will likely remain highly dependent on others. As a consequence, as an adult these children may have difficulty meeting their needs through a stable, supportive relationship with a partner. Consistent with clinical reports that abused victims are more socially isolated (Kempe and Kempe, 1978; Garbarino, 1975), in the present study, parents with abusive childhood histories who abuse their children were significantly less likely to have stable and supportive relationships. Due to their own histories of maltreatment these parents may withdraw and avoid making themselves available and vulnerable to a mate.

During childhood, withdrawal and detachment may help the maltreated child adaptively cope with the unique circumstances in which he or she lives. Main (1983) observed the behavior of 12- to 18-month-old infants placed in an unfamiliar setting who experience a brief separation from their attachment figure. Upon reunion with their caregiver, infants whose primary attachment figure habitually rejects them (in contrast to infants with a history of sensitive and responsive caregiving) avoid contact. These anxiously attached infants habitually play with toys rather than seek comfort and support. Bowlby (1980) elaborates the survival advantage of this response, "in doing so he is effectively excluding any sensory inflow that would elicit his attachment behavior and thus avoiding any risk at being rebuffed and becoming distressed and disorganized; in addition he is avoiding any risk of eliciting hostile behavior from his mother. Yet he remains in her vicinity . . . the chances being that, should risk of danger become high, she would then protect him" (p. 73).

While withdrawal and detachment may be adaptive during childhood, these coping behaviors may become maladaptive (in the sense of compromising emotional growth and development) when they persist into adulthood. Consistent with the abuse literature, parents with histories of abusive and rejecting caregiving in our sample were more emotionally isolated than nonabused parents, withdrawing and avoiding intimate, supportive relationships with a partner. The representational model they had constructed based on their early experiences is one of rejection and unresponsiveness.

Once established, representational models of the attachment figure are difficult to change. The pain experienced by these parents who were abused as children does not seem to prevent them from reenacting the abuse with their own children. The model a child constructs is based on the child's experience that best fits the reality experienced by the child at an early age. They are built by defensively excluding information (Bowlby, 1980). New relationships formed by the individual are assimilated into existing models. From birth, infants are bombarded with massive amounts of sensory data. Having a limited capacity to process information they selectively attend to only a portion of the information in their environment. Infants organize their experiences and expand the amount of information they can process by organizing incoming input into meaningful units developing an internal structure or scheme to process future information. Learning involves attending to information that is consistent with or slightly departs from their existing structures. However, new experiences which deviate too greatly from existing structures and thus cannot be assimilated into them are selectively not attended. The excluded information is characterized by not making sense or not being understandable to the person (Sullivan, 1953). For example, later experiences of love from a male or friend may not make sense to parents with a history of abusive relationships. They have developed expectations of relationships from their past experiences and may distrust the affection shown by another, perhaps even embuing their partner or friend with ill motives. Since individuals do not integrate later experiences that are too incompatible with their existing representational models, the established models of their attachment figure as being unavailable and unloveable are difficult to change (Bowlby, 1980).

Mothers who were abused and are abusing spoke in generalities about their history of abuse. Their recall was vague, and they lacked understanding of the relation between their caregiving history and the care they provided their child. The abuse in their childhood appeared to be somewhat repressed, and they did not seem to associate the affect (emotion) and cognitions (memories) from this period. It is an example of what Sullivan (1953) refers to as "splitting." The process of "splitting" may provide one explanation for parents' adaptation to the traumatic experience of having been abused as a child.

In contrast to mothers in the continuity group, mothers able to break the abusive cycle had an awareness of their past history of having been abused. Many mothers in the exception group were in therapy as adolescents or young adults, which may explain why they were so aware of having been abused by their own parents. They spoke of their own abuse with much emotion. These mothers were often quite verbal about the way they intended to raise their own children. They recognized the effects parental abuse had on them, and they were determined not to repeat this abuse with their own children. By being conscious and aware of their own history of having been abused and understanding how this may affect the way they take care of their own children appears to be a major determinant in breaking the cycle of intergenerational parental abuse.

Anecdotal data used to compare continuity and exception groups provide support for this hypothesis. As indicated earlier in the discussion of the case studies of mothers who were abused as children and abused their children, these mothers talked about abuse in an unemotional fashion, and their recall of specific experiences was poor. Mothers who were exceptions to intergenerational continuity recalled their childhood experiences in greater detail and with much emotion. The experience of having been abused was very much a part of their reality.

For Sullivan (1953) the dissassociative process of splitting is a defense used to cope with experiences that arouse anxiety. Anxiety is connected with feelings of helplessness initially experienced during separation from the caregiver. Abandonment and loss of love threaten the infant whose survival depends upon the protection, comfort, and nurturance of a caregiver. Breger (1974) explains "as a general rule, we might expect that those factors in a child's actual situation which make him feel helpless, which make him feel the victim of forces he can do little to effect, will reinforce dissociation. Being abandoned, treated with inconsistent love and abuse all contribute to the child's sense of helplessness" (p. 216).

Dissociation provides a means for resolving conflicts the child cannot cope with in reality. For example, an abused child in a relatively powerless position outwardly complies to the adults demands, yet, inwardly creates fantasies of conquering or retaliating against the abusive parent. Abused victims defend against their anxiety by splitting themselves off from reality and avoid acknowledging and confronting these hurtful experiences. As a result, having been abused does not enable parents to empathize with their own children and refrain from abusing them. From an information processing view, these early models of an unloving and abusive parent become overlearned and applied automatically and without awareness.

Bowlby (1973) emphasizes that parents pressure their children not only to comply with their wishes but also to view them in a favorable light. Acknowledging the maltreatment may contradict the parents wishes contributing to the abused victim's dissociation of the anxiety, pain, and anger associated with the abuse. Pretending and creating fantasies may be adaptive during childhood, thus enabling children to wait until adolescence or adulthood when they are in a position of more equal stature and can outwardly defend themselves. Often, however, rather than active mastery over the conflict, these patterns of retreating into fantasies persist, compromising the individual's growth. Dissociation during childhood provides patterns and means of later dealing with pain, anxiety, and conflict during adolescence and adulthood (Breger, 1974).

The reason individuals become fixated with these disassociative solutions rather than attempting to cope with the anxiety-arousing experience directly may have to do with the tremendous psychological hurt associated with the abuse. Breger explained that "excessive anxiety has become connected with the original motivation for the dissociation and that attempts to reopen the area to nondissociative reality testing rearouses anxiety" (p. 218). Thus fixation results from the lack of reality testing associated with dissociation.

Abused victims defend against their anxiety by splitting themselves off from the reality instead of "owning" and confronting these painful experiences. Opening up the dissociation or confronting the pain associated with earlier abuse rearouses anxiety. Consequently, the model built of the attachment figure as unloving and unavailable may be defensively excluded from awareness, banned from review and revision. Unable to integrate maltreatment with more kindly and favorable treatment, the child comes to view the parent/caregiver as either "good" or "bad." In the absence of understanding the psychological complexity of their parental relationship, these early models of an abusive parent persist.

One way to repress and dissociate oneself from unpleasant affect is to rationalize or justify abusive history. Kreindler (1976) reports that abused individuals compared to those who were not abused have lower self-esteem. The individual's self-concept (e.g., estimation of self-worth) emerges from the infant and toddler's relationship to the attachment figure (Sullivan, 1953). Infants organize their behavior around this primary relationship, and ill treatment communicates a sense of unworthiness to the infant. Furthermore, the parental pressure for the child to view the parent's treatment in a favorable light furthers the child's low self-esteem. Abused victims may hold themselves responsible and deserving of harsh treatment. Believing themselves unworthy of more supportive and loving care, the victim internalizes the maltreatment.

Like representational models, once established, the self-concept proves difficult to change. Experiences contrary to the self-concept are characterized by not being understandable and, consequently, are disregarded (see Epstein, 1973). Abused individuals may create relationships that further validate their low self-opinion by maltreating their child or their partner or by reenacting the victim role with a mate. This, in turn, perpetuates the abusive cycle. Victimizing others as well as invoking ill treatment from another prevents abused individuals from receiving the necessary emotional support and contributes to their social isolation. With overwhelming unmet needs, parents unrealistically turn to their children to help them. When the child cannot comply, the parents become enraged and frustrated, venting anger by physically or emotionally abusing the child.

REFERENCES

Ainsworth, M. D. S. The development of infant-mothers attachment. *In* B. M. Caldwell and H. N. Riccinti, Eds., *Review of child development research,* Vol. 3. Chicago, IL: University of Chicago Press, 1973.

Ainsworth, M. D. S., Blehar, M., Waters, E., and Wall, S. *Patterns of attachment.* Hillsdale, NJ: Lawrence Erlbaum, 1978.

Bandura, A., and Walters, R. H. *Social learning and personality development.* NY: Holt, Rinehart & Winston, 1963.

Belsky, J. Three theoretical models of child abuse: A critical review. *International Journal of Child Abuse and Neglect,* 1978, 2: 37–49.

Bowlby, J. *Attachment and loss. Vol. I: Attachment.* NY: Basic Books, 1969.

Bowlby, J. *Attachment and loss. Vol. II: Separation: Anxiety and anger.* NY: Basic Books, 1973.

Bowlby, J. *Attachment and loss. Vol. III: Loss, sadness and depression.* NY: Basic Books, 1980.

Bowlby, J. Attachment and loss: Retrospect and prospect. *American Journal of Orthopsychiatry, 1982,* 4(52): October.

Breger, L. *From instinct to identity.* Englewood Cliffs, NJ: Prentice Hall, 1974.

Brunquell, D., Crichton, L., and Egeland, B. Maternal personality and attitude in disturbances of child-rearing. *Journal of Orthopsychiatry,* 1981, *51:* 680–691.

Delozier, P. Attachment theory and child abuse. *In* C. Parkes and J. Steven-Hinde, Eds., *The place of attachment in human behavior.* NY: Basic Books, 1982.

Egeland, B., and Deinard, A. Child care rating scale. Unpublished test, University of Minnesota, 1975.

Egeland, B., and Erickson, M. F. Psychologically unavailable caregiving: The effects on development of young children and the implications for intervention. *In* M. Brassard and S. Hart, Eds., *Psychological maltreatment of children and youth.* NY: Pergamon Press, 1984.

Egeland, B., and Sroufe, L. A. Developmental sequelae of maltreatment in infancy. *In* R. Rizley and D. Cicchetti, Eds., *New directions for child development: Developmental perspectives in child maltreatment.* San Francisco, CA: Jossey Bass, 1981.

Egeland, B., and Vaughn, B. Failure of "bond formation" as a cause of abuse, neglect, and maltreatment. *American Journal of Orthopsychiatry,* 1981, *51:* 78–84.

Egeland, B., Breitenbucher, M., and Rosenberg, D. Prospective study of the significance of life stress in the etiology of child abuse. *Journal of Consulting and Clinical Psychology,* 1980, *48*(2): 195–205.

Epstein, S. The self-concept revisited, or a theory of a theory, *American Psychologist,* 1973, *28:* 404–416.

Erickson, M. F. *Developmental antecedents of individual differences in compliance in young children.* Doctoral dissertation, University of Minnesota, September, 1984.

Friedrich, W. H., and Boriskin, J. A. The role of the child in abuse: A review of the literature. *American Journal of Orthopsychiatry,* 1976, *46:* 580–590.

Garbarino, J., and Stocking, S. H. *Supporting families and protecting children.* San Francisco, CA: Jossey-Bass, 1980.

Helfer, R. E., and Pollock, C. B. The battered child syndrome. *Advances in Pediatrics,* 1968, *15:* 9–27.

Kempe, R. S., and Kempe, C. H. *Child abuse.* Cambridge, MA: Harvard University Press, 1978.

Kreindler, S. Psychiatric treatment for the abusing parent and the abused child. *Canadian Psychiatric Association Journal,* 1976, *21:* 275–279.

Mahler, M., Pine, F., and Bergman, A. *The psychological birth of the human infant.* NY: Basic Books, 1975.

Main, M. Analysis of a peculiar form of reunion behavior seen in some day care children: It's history and sequelae in children who are home-reared. *In* R. Webb, Ed., *Social development in childhood: Daycare programs and research.* Baltimore, MD: Johns Hopkins University Press, 1983.

Main, M., and Goldwyn, R. Predicting rejection of her infant from mother's representation of her own experience: implications for the abused-abusing intergenerational cycle. *Child Abuse and Neglect,* 1984, *8:* 203–217.

Matas, L., Arend, R., and Sroufe, L. A. Continuity of adaptation in the second year: The relationship between quality of attachment and later competence. *Child Development,* 1978, *49:* 547–556.

Papatola, K. J. The effects of ontogenic microsystem and mesosystem variables on the outcome of child abuse. Unpublished Ph.D. dissertation, Columbia University, New York, 1983.

Piaget, J. *The origins of intelligence in children.* NY: International Universities Press, 1952.

Ricks, M. The social inheritance of parenting: Attachment across generations. *In* I. Bretherton and E. Waters, Eds., *New directions for attachment research.* Monograph of the Society for Research in Child Development, 1985.

Sander, L. Infant and caretaking environment. *In* E. J. Anthony, Ed., *Explorations in child psychiatry.* NY: Plenum, 1975.

Sroufe, L. A., and Fleeson, J. Attachment and the construction of relationships. *In* W. Hartup and Z. Rubin, Eds., *Relationships and development.* Hillsdale, NJ: Erlbaum, in press.

Sroufe, L. A., Fox, N. E., and Pancake, V. R. Attachment and dependency in developmental perspective. *Child Development,* 1983, *54:* 1615–1627.

Stayton, D., Hogan, R., and Ainsworth, M. Infant obedience and maternal behavior: The origins of socialization reconsidered. *Child Development,* 1971, *42:* 1057–1069.

Steele, B. F., and Pollock, C. B. A psychiatric study of parents who abuse infants and small children. *In* R. E. Helfer and C. H. Kempe, Eds., *The battered child.* Chicago, IL: University of Chicago Press, 1968.

Sullivan, H. S. *The interpersonal theory of psychiatry.* NY: Norton, 1953.

THE SEQUELAE OF CHILD MALTREATMENT*

Dante Cicchetti,
Vicki Carlson
Karen G. Braunwald
J. Lawrence Aber

chapter

12

While interest, efforts, and funding in the area of child maltreatment research have grown rapidly in the past two decades, research has yet to provide a fully accurate understanding of the etiology, intergenerational transmission, and consequences of child maltreatment. The Harvard Child Maltreatment Project (HCMP) was initiated in 1979 in an effort to integrate the rich history of child maltreatment research with current theoretical and empirical advances in developmental psychopathology. This chapter describes the historical context, guiding assumptions, and recent findings of the HCMP.

HISTORY OF RESEARCH ON THE DEVELOPMENTAL SEQUELAE OF CHILD MALTREATMENT

A major focus of recent research in the area of child maltreatment has been on the etiology of the phenomenon (Belsky, 1980; Cicchetti, Taraldson, and Egeland, 1978; Parke and Collmer, 1975; Zigler, 1980). While research on etiology is important in order to develop parent treatment programs and major preventive techniques, it is equally important to document the ways in which maltreated children may be impaired by their experiences. In a recent review article, Aber and Cicchetti (1984) have described research efforts to date in this area.

*The Harvard Child Maltreatment Project was supported by grants from W. T. Grant Foundation (83089400), the National Center for Child Abuse and Neglect (90-C-1929), and the National Institute of Mental Health (1-R01-MH27960-01). The authors extend their thanks to the project staff, volunteers, and families, as well as to the Massachusetts Department of Social Services and the Massachusetts Society for the Prevention of Cruelty to Children, for making this research possible. They would like to acknowledge the contributions that Ann Churchill and Carol Kottmeier made to this project.

Previous research directed toward examining the socioemotional and cognitive sequelae of child abuse and neglect has led to incomplete or ambiguous portrayals of the effects of maltreatment on a wide range of characteristics (Aber and Cicchetti, 1984). Clinical descriptions of maltreated children (Elmer, 1967; Galdston, 1971; Gray and Kempe, 1976; Green, 1978; Johnson and Morse, 1968; Kempe and Kempe, 1978; Martin and Beezeley, 1977; Morse, Sahler, and Friedman, 1970; Ounsted, Oppenheimer, and Lindsay, 1974; Rolston, 1971; Terr, 1970) have enumerated a variety of emotional, social, and cognitive disturbances including lack of responsivity, inappropriate affect, inhibition, anhedonia, extreme withdrawal, aggressivity, lack of impulse control, low frustration tolerance, school learning problems, and impaired interpersonal interactions. Some clinical studies have included assessments of IQ and language skills in maltreated children by employing product-oriented, standardized psychometric measures (Elmer, 1977; Martin, 1976). While these descriptions provide a picture of the range of clinical features characterizing children who have been maltreated, they are only descriptive and do not allow for an understanding of the processes by which these symptoms become manifest. In addition, they are based on varying methods of data collection that were employed by a variety of professional personnel and that were collected in diverse settings, including homes, schools, day-care centers, and hospitals. Various definitions of maltreatment were used, and criteria for inclusion in the maltreatment category were often not operationally defined.

The majority of available research has employed a cross-sectional design (Aragona and Eyberg, 1981; Reidy, 1977; Relich, Giblin, Starr, and Agronow, 1980). While these studies constituted an advance over mere clinical descriptions, they were replete with methodological flaws, including the lack of appropriate control groups, confounding socio-economic backgrounds of the subjects under investigation with mal-treatment history, small sample size, developmentally inappropriate assessment techniques, wide variations in the ages of the subjects, and lack of independent "blind" raters. Perhaps most importantly, there has been a disregard for operationally defined criteria for describing the types of maltreatment experienced.

Follow-up investigations of the effects of maltreatment on subsequent development were typically more methodologically advanced than cross-sectional studies. Perhaps most significantly, they allow the documentation of the enduring sequelae of maltreatment. While several follow-up studies have been reported, the two most important studies were conducted by Kent (1976) and Elmer (1977). Kent's study represented a significant advance because it evaluated the effects of different types of maltreatment on more than one domain of development. In addition, Kent demonstrated that maltreatment's consequences may not be static. The findings are important for issues of intervention since the positive changes in many of the children at follow-up may have been related to treatment efforts such as foster care. However, because no study can include a maltreatment comparison group for which no intervention occurred (for obvious ethical reasons), it is impossible to disentangle the relative contributions of treatment and age effects. While this design limitation was unavoidable, there were other methodological errors that could have been prevented. The validity of the diagnostic groups and of the benefits of intervention were questionable because ratings were not made by blind or independent raters. In addition, Kent did not use assessment criteria that were sensitive to the different ages of the children included in the sample.

Elmer's (1977) study examined the long-term effects of physical abuse by measuring physical, cognitive, and language development in three groups of children at age 8. All of the children were of low SES. One comparison group consisted of accident victims, and the second comparison group was composed of noninjured children. The maltreated group and the accident group had both experienced injuries prior to age 1. In general, Elmer did not find differences among the groups in any of the areas that were investigated. This study may be criticized for a number of reasons. First, it employed outcome measures that do not represent the salient developmental tasks of the age period under investigation (see later in this chapter). The measures failed to include assessment of the socioemotional domain that may be more vulnerable to the impact of maltreatment than the cognitive and linguistic domains. Second, the failure to find differences among the groups may have been due to the prevalence of general disorganization and stressors that characterized all of these low SES children's home experiences. Third, ambiguous distinctions between "abuse" and "accident" groups may have resulted in substantial overlap between the two groups and point to the need for operationally defined inclusion and exclusion criteria in any classification system. Fourth, given the study's focus on physical abuse, in a low SES population at risk for other forms of maltreatment (e.g., emotional abuse and neglect), there may have been other undetected forms of maltreatment in the early experiences of children in all three groups.

There are several important empirical investigations that have focused on theoretically meaningful, stage-specific tasks of social, emotional, and cognitive development of maltreated children during infancy and early childhood. The design of these studies avoided many of the methodological flaws criticized previously and, therefore, allow more definitive conclusions to be drawn. George and Main (1979, 1980) investigated the organization of attachment behavior in physically abused and matched control children, and they clearly documented anomalies in the development of the attachment and social interaction systems in physically abused children. Abnormalities in the development of affective communication between infants and caregivers have been studied by Gaensbauer and his colleagues (Gaensbauer, Mrazek, and Harmon, 1980; Gaensbauer and Sands, 1979). Their work represents a significant advance in both methodology and theory in that they adopted a broader perspective on the study of development in maltreated children. Most notably, in a design guided by developmental theory, they assessed the stage-salient affective communication between infant and caregiver, and they recognized the underlying continuity of adaptive processes that contribute to successful interactive patterns.

The work of Egeland and Sroufe and their colleagues has contributed to our understanding of the consequences of child maltreatment upon social, emotional, and cognitive development. In their prospective study, they identified over 200 children who were at risk for developmental delay or pathology due to poverty, limitations in parental knowledge about child care, lack of education, and mothers' young age. Their developmentally salient outcome measures included behavior during feeding and mother/infant freeplay situations at 3 and 6 months, the Bayley Scales of Infant Development at 9, 12, and 24 months, the "Strange Situation" paradigm for assessing quality of attachment at 12 and 18 months, and a tool use/problem-solving paradigm to assess a toddler's emerging autonomy, independent exploration of the environment, and ability to cope with frustration at 24 months (Matas, Arend, and Sroufe, 1978).

Egeland and Sroufe (1981b) identified four groups of maltreated children based on several sources of information. These included home observations, maternal interviews about child-care skills and discipline techniques, laboratory observations, and welfare, hospital, and public health clinic case records. The four groups that emerged were defined by maternal behaviors and attitudes and included physical abuse, hostile/verbal abuse, psychological unavailability, and neglect. Despite their endeavors to advance diagnostic clarity by seeking information from multiple sources, Egeland and Sroufe did not clearly specify the criteria by which children were separated into the four groups.

Extremely interesting patterns of results emerged from Egeland and Sroufe's analyses. For example, there was a markedly higher percentage of insecure attachments at 18 months of age in the physically abused group than in the control group. At 24 months, the physically abused children showed more anger, frustration, and noncompliance in mother–child teaching situations than did controls. None of the 12-month-old infants who were securely attached to psychologically unavailable mothers maintained this classification when assessed at 18 months. In contrast, there was a slight increase in the percentage of secure attachments across this period in the control group. In a comparison of the Bayley Scale of Developmental Quotients determined at 9 and 24 months, there was a significant decline in scores among children of psychologically unavailable mothers as compared to control children.

In summary, this brief, selected review of available research on the social, emotional, and cognitive development in maltreated children serves to highlight some of the methodological and theoretical advances that have been made. Further contributions to our understanding of the sequelae of child maltreatment will be possible when the problems of previous work are taken into account in the design of subsequent research endeavors.

The Organizational Perspective of Development

The theoretical orientation providing the underlying framework for the HCMP is the organizational perspective (Cicchetti and Sroufe, 1978; Sroufe, 1979a, b). This increasingly accepted approach to development considers relationships among behavioral systems, consequences of advances and lags in the functioning of one system for the functioning of other behavioral systems, and the consequences of earlier adaptations for later adaptation (Cicchetti and Schneider-Rosen, 1986). In short, a holistic picture of behavior and development is sought, in which change in the integration and organization of competencies in the social, emotional, cognitive, and linguistic domains is investigated, rather than there being an emphasis on cataloguing the capacities themselves.

Within the organizational perspective, development is depicted as a series of behavioral reorganizations around a set of developmental tasks or issues. Table 12.1 provides the outline of stage-salient issues during the first 12 years of life. These issues are not to be viewed as hurdles associated with any one age; each task remains important to the child's continuing adaptation, although it decreases in salience relative to other newly emerging tasks. For example, while the formation of a secure attachment relationship is the stage-salient task of the first year of life, emotional connections to others remain important across the life span.

Within an organizational–developmental perspective, the specific pattern of behavior manifested in one situation at a particular developmental level cannot be expected to recur in the exact form in either the same or other contexts at later developmental periods. Rather, with development, behaviors are expected to undergo transfor-

TABLE 12.1. Stage-Salient Issues According to the Organizational Perspective

General developmental issue	Approximate age			
	0–12 months	12–30 months	30 months–7 years	7–12 years
Attachment	Modulation of arousal Physiological regulation Formation of secure attachment relationship with primary caregiver Differentiation and integration of emotional reactions	Differentiation of persons Awareness of self as distinct entity Exploration of environment		
Autonomy		Regulation and control of emotional reactions Problem-solving, pride and mastery motivation Capacity to delay gratification and to tolerate frustration Awareness of standards Development of language and communicative skills	Development of sense of efficacy and pride Awareness of social roles Ego-resiliency and ego control Sex-role development Integration into peer groups and social support networks Development of emotional bonds with peers	

Establishing peer relationships

Hierarchical integration of attachment, autonomy and peer relationships

Role-taking
Empathy and prosocial behavior
Capacity to take initiative
Self-regulation
Development of criteria for evaluating one's performance
Hierarchization of plans

Hierarchization of social networks and multiple attachment figures
Formation of feelings of volition and agency of the self
Awareness of and ability to express multiple emotions
Internalization of standards of right and wrong and development of morality
Capacity to assume responsibilities and to accomplish tasks
Awareness of internal psychological processes

283

mation, hierarchical integration, and reorganization (Werner and Kaplan, 1963). Instead of seeking stability of behavioral expression across time, the organizational viewpoint requires coherence of patterns of behavioral organization or adaptation, such that early adaptation is related to later adaptation in a lawful fashion. Within this framework, continuity refers to the prediction that competence in dealing with one developmental issue (e.g., the formation of a secure attachment relationship) will be related to competence with respect to subsequent issues (e.g., successful integration into and mastery of the peer world) as long as the quality of the child's care/environmental support remains stable.

THE HARVARD CHILD MALTREATMENT PROJECT

Besides the changing zeitgeist in the focus of research and theoretical inquiry in developmental psychology, the ascendance of the discipline of developmental psychopathology (Cicchetti, 1984) contributed to the increased interest in the developmental sequelae of child maltreatment. Developmental psychopathology brings a developmental perspective to bear on the study of psychopathology and argues that the study of psychopathology from a developmental framework could greatly enhance our knowledge of normal development (Cicchetti and Schneider-Rosen, 1986; A. Freud, 1965; Rutter and Garmezy, 1983; Sroufe and Rutter, 1984; Werner and Kaplan, 1963).

Buoyed by the upsurgent interest in developmental psychopathology, we launched the HCMP. The guiding assumption in the design of this longitudinal study was that child maltreatment is a complex, heterogeneous phenomenon, with a variety of different manifestations, etiologies, and developmental sequelae. The scientific perspective with which we approached the problem can best be described as empirical and broad based, drawing on the best theories and measurement techniques from a variety of disciplines—developmental psychology and psychopathology, descriptive and experimental psychopathology, sociology, epidemiology, applied behavioral analysis, and personality assessment.

In a recent review of research on the impact of child maltreatment on the social and emotional domains of child development, Aber and Cicchetti (1984) laid out their prescriptions for future research programs in this important area. Those prescriptions included using: theoretically guided designs including age- and stage-salient measurements utilizing the state-of-the-art measurement techniques developed by researchers on normal development; employing multiple measures of each construct; longitudinally tracking development over time to observe the process of development as well as its products; clear definition and measurement of the types of maltreatment being studied; use of carefully matched control groups; and insistence on the use of interviewers, testers, and raters all blind to the maltreatment status of subjects. The principles outlined previously are those that have guided the design and implementation of the HCMP.

The HCMP is a longitudinal study of child maltreatment in the Boston and Greater Boston area. The study, initially funded by the National Center on Child Abuse and Neglect, is currently supported by the National Institute of Mental Health and the W. T. Grant Foundation. Maltreating families were recruited through the Department of Social Services of the Commonwealth of Massachusetts and the Massachusetts Society for the Prevention of Cruelty to Children, the state's largest private provider of protective services.

In the 6-year history of the project, over 300 families have been recruited to the study, and developmental assessments of nearly 400 children from these families have been conducted. Approximately 130 families have received protective services for issues of child abuse and/ or neglect from the agencies previously described. A second group of approximately 130 families are comparison families who were recruited in a manner designed to create a group that would closely match the demographic characteristics of the families in protective services. Control groups have often been omitted from previous research on child maltreatment. Therefore, it was a major goal of this research effort to include an appropriate control group, both for general design reasons and for an additional substantive reason, the disentangling of consequences of maltreatment from the consequences of being from a low SES. National incidence studies of maltreatment indicate that there are higher levels of reported abuse and neglect in those from a lower SES than from a higher SES. Pelton (1978, 1981) has argued that this difference in incidence rate is not an artifact of reporting bias but is the real result of the many stresses of poverty that lead to increased levels of abuse and neglect. Garbarino (1976) has listed demographic variables that can be used as accurate predictors of levels of reported maltreatment. On the other hand, Newberger (1983), Daniel, Hampton, and Newberger (in press), Gelles (1983), and others argue that belonging to a low SES itself makes a family more at risk of being reported to a protective service agency. For these reasons, the creation of a very carefully matched comparison group was given special attention. Within the HCMP, the maltreatment group and therefore the comparison group are characterized by relatively low education and income levels. Most families are receiving AFDC and are single-parent households. Overall the families in our maltreatment group and in the matched comparison group have characteristics very similar to the statewide demographic characteristics of the Department of Social Services Protective Services population with one exception. Our population has a smaller minority group representation than that of protective service families in the inner Boston area. Our sample is racially representative of the Greater Boston area.

In addition to the demographically matched comparison group we have a second comparison group, a middle SES group of about 35 families. These are families characterized by higher education, income, and other resource levels, families essentially like those who make up study samples in most university-based child-development research efforts.

An additional small group of 12 families is included as a pilot study for the generation of hypotheses relevant to the intergenerational transmission of maltreatment issue. In each of these families the mother experienced serious forms of maltreatment while she was growing up, yet none of these women has gone on to maltreat her own children. We believe that by studying the families of these survivors, we can gain insights into the ways of breaking the all too familiar cycle of abuse.

The primary caregivers in the study's families have been interviewed on a wide range of topics ranging from the characteristics of their households and neighborhoods, to their early experiences, current beliefs and practices regarding child rearing. The issues covered were selected to cover the ontogenic, or individual, level; the microsystem, or family, level; and the exosystem, or community, level of analysis (Belsky, 1980).

The children included in the study were initially between 1 and 8 years of age. They are being followed in laboratory-based developmental assessments in a cross-sectional/longitudinal design called a convergence design (Bell, 1968). Each child is followed for 1–3 years. The specifics of the time design vary with the age of the child. The developmental assessments cover the cognitive, social, social–cognitive, emotional, and linguistic domains. The research protocol is designed to allow us to describe the organizational integration of behavior with a special focus on stage salient aspects of development. These include the development of a secure attachment relationship in infancy, the development of self-concept and autonomy during toddlerhood, the emergence of the social ability to relate to nonfamilial caregivers during the preschool and early school years, and mastery of the peer world during the elementary school years (see Table 12.1). In order to study this latter issue we have followed the children to their school settings during the past year and to our own camp setting during the summer months.

Another area that we have explored in the process of doing this research is that of definition of types of maltreatment. Giovannoni and Becerra (1979) have described the ways in which professionals and lay persons evaluate the seriousness and relevant treatment and punishment implications of maltreatment, yet we have yet to document empirically the developmental consequences of the many acts and conditions of mistreatment that come under the umbrella term of maltreatment. In an effort to add to our understanding in this area, we have taken care to document the specific ways in which the children in the study were maltreated. We collected two sets of variables from the social workers assigned to the families in the study. The first set of variables was that of legally documented and investigated filings of abuse and neglect reports to the Department of Social Services. The second set of variables came from interviews with those social workers in which they indicated specific types of maltreatment experienced by each child in the family, using Giovannoni and Becerra's (1979) checklist of maltreatment issues. By employing these two types of information, the legal filings, and the ratings of the workers who know the families best, we have created summary variables for use in the studies of child outcome described in this chapter.

ILLUSTRATIVE FINDINGS

In the following section, we provide two examples of our research on the development of maltreated children. The first focuses on the quality of attachment during infancy, the second upon dependency and effectance motivation in 4- to 8-year-old children.

The Development of Attachment

Since the advent of Bowlby's (1969) seminal exposition on attachment theory, there has been general assent among developmental psychologists that the establishment of a secure attachment relationship between an infant and his/her caregiver is one of the primary tasks during the first year of life. Bowlby's is an ethological perspective that has been greatly influenced by psychoanalytic principles (Bretherton, 1985). According to his formulation, the attachment relationship has both a physical and a psychological function. It possesses evolutionary survival value in that the caregiver serves to protect the infant from potential physical harm. A number of diverse infant behaviors, such as smiling, vocalizing, and clinging, promote physical proximity to and contact with the attachment figure. In addition, the relationship has the psychological set-goal of "felt security" that will enable the infant to explore both the social and inanimate worlds (Sroufe and Waters, 1977).

Contemporary elaborations of attachment theory have emphasized this function of the attachment relationship, stressing the enduring affective tie between infant and caregiver (e.g., Ainsworth, 1973; Sroufe

and Waters, 1977). To this end, rather than focusing on individual behaviors emitted by the infant, the organization of the attachment behaviors is considered and the quality of the relationship is seen to be
dependent upon the quality of interaction between the dyad during
the first year of life. Thus, the investigation of infants who have been
maltreated provides the unique opportunity to examine the influence
of the early caregiving environment on subsequent attachment behavior. The chaotic, disorganized environment in which many maltreated
infants are reared and the inconsistent or abusive patterns of care provided for them place maltreated infants at risk for suffering the negative
consequences of "caretaking casualty" (Sameroff and Chandler, 1975)
and may be expected to disrupt the development of the attachment
relationship.

The widely employed "Strange Situation" procedure was developed
by Ainsworth and Wittig (1969) as a means by which to assess the quality
of the attachment relationship. This procedure consists of a standard
series of eight 3-minute episodes during which the infant is exposed
to a series of increasingly stressful events. The infant's responses to a
new room and an unfamiliar female stranger, both in the presence and
the absence of the caregiver, are appraised (see Ainsworth, Blehar,
Waters, and Wall, 1978, for a detailed elaboration of this technique).
In particular, the infant's response to the caregiver in the reunion episodes is especially important for evaluating the quality of the attachment relationship.

Based upon the organization of infant behaviors during the "Strange
Situation," infants are classified into one of three categories. Infants
in Groups A and C are considered to be insecurely attached to the
caregiver and either avoid her (Group A) or manifest angry, resistant
behavior alternating with proximity-seeking or passive behavior (Group
C) upon reunion. In contrast, the securely attached infant (Group B)
uses the caregiver as a secure base from which to explore the environment. If distressed, s/he first approaches the caregiver to seek comfort and then returns to play. If not distressed, the infant greets the
caregiver positively and actively initiates contact. Approximately 70%
of all nonclinical samples of infants are securely attached, while 30%
(20% A, 10% C) are insecurely attached to their primary caregiver (Ainsworth et al., 1978).

Two empirical studies examining the relationship between maltreatment and quality of attachment have been conducted by the HCMP.
The first considered the interaction between affect and cognition, focusing on both security of attachment and the emergence of visual
self-recognition (Schneider-Rosen and Cicchetti, 1984). The sample
consisted of 37 infants, all from families of low SES. Of the infants, 18
had been maltreated while living in their natural homes, while 19 infants
comprised the comparison group. The infants ranged in age from 18

to 20 months. The mother–infant dyads were observed in the Strange Situation procedure, and infants were administered the standard mirror-and-rouge paradigm (Lewis and Brooks-Gunn, 1979) to assess visual self-recognition. It was found that 12 (67%) of the maltreated infants were classified as insecure (Group A = 7, Group C = 5), whereas 6 (33%) were classified as secure. In contrast, 5 (26%) of the 19 matched comparison infants were classified as insecure (Group A = 2, Group C = 3), whereas 14 (74%) were classified as secure. This significant group difference demonstrates the deleterious impact that maltreatment may have upon this developmental task of infancy. However, we did not find a relationship between type of maltreatment and quality of attachment.

An interesting pattern of findings emerged with regard to the interaction between maltreatment, quality of attachment, and visual self-recognition. There were no differences in the number of maltreated and comparison infants who were able to recognize themselves. For the group as a whole, infants who manifested visual self-recognition were significantly more likely to be securely attached to their caregivers. A different pattern of results was revealed, however, when the maltreated and comparison infant groups were analyzed separately. Of the comparison infants who recognized themselves, 90% were classified as secure (Group B). In contrast, there was no significant relationship between visual self-recognition and security of attachment for the maltreated infants. Of those maltreated infants who recognized themselves (N = 5), three were insecurely attached and two were securely attached to their caregivers. These findings suggest that the effects of maltreatment may be sufficiently potent to disrupt the expected relationship between quality of attachment and visual self-recognition. The process by which maltreatment might have such an effect, however, has yet to be determined.

Several longitudinal studies, conducted both at the HCMP (Schneider-Rosen, Braunwald, Carlson, and Cicchetti, 1985) and by Egeland and Sroufe (1981a, 1981b) have demonstrated the instability of attachment classifications of maltreated infants, particularly those who were classified as secure upon initial assessment. In our study, 24 infants (10 maltreated, 14 comparison) were seen with their caregivers in the Strange Situation at both 12 and 18 months of age. Thirty-two infants (16 maltreated, 16 comparison) were seen at both 18 and 24 months of age. Of the 4 maltreated infants who had a secure attachment at 12 months of age, 3 shifted to insecure attachment classification by 18 months (2 A's, 1 C). Likewise, 3 of the 4 securely attached 18-month-old infants developed an insecure attachment relationship by 24 months (2 A's, 1 C). Again there was no relationship between type of maltreatment and quality of attachment.

Schneider-Rosen et al. (1985) have applied Cicchetti and Rizley's

(1981) model of the etiology, transmission, and sequelae of child maltreatment to the formation and stability of the attachment relationship (see Table 12.2). Implicit in the model is the assumption that the quality of attachment represents neither enduring nor transient influences alone, but rather a multiplicity of factors that need to be considered in combination to account for the developmental outcome achieved.

Within this model, there are two broad categories of factors associated with each outcome, secure or insecure attachment relationship: (1) potentiating factors, which increase the likelihood of an insecure attachment relationship; and (2) compensatory factors, which increase the probability of a secure attachment relationship. Each category includes influences that are transient and fluctuating, as well as more enduring, permanent attributes or conditions. For example, potentiating factors include the transient influence of challengers such as stressful life events and more enduring psychological, environmental, or biological vulnerability factors. Similarly, compensatory factors include transient buffers such as a supportive social network, as well as enduring protective factors that may be present in the infant, the caregiver, or the environment. This model highlights an ongoing transaction among parent, child, and environmental influences that serves to support or inhibit the establishment of a secure attachment relationship with the caregiver.

TABLE 12.2. Factors Associated with Qualitative Differences in the Attachment Relationship

| Temporal dimensions | Impact on the attachment system | |
	Potentiating factors	Compensatory factors
Enduring factors	Vulnerability factors: Enduring conditions in the caregiving environment that decrease the harmony of interaction and the quality of care.	Protective factors: Enduring conditions that promote harmonious interaction between the infant and the caregiver and maintain responsive, sensitive, and continuous care.
Transient factors	Challengers: Transient but significant factors that increase the probability of inconsistent or inadequate care being provided for the infant.	Buffers: Transient conditions that protect the infant against experiencing negative consequences that could result from temporary disruptions in quality of care provided.
Outcome	Insecure attachment	Secure attachment

The Effects of Maltreatment on Children's Development in the Preschool and Early School-Age Years

In addition to our research on the effects of maltreatment on infant and toddler development, the HCMP has also collected both cross-sectional and short-term longitudinal data on the impact of maltreatment on the socioemotional and cognitive development of preschool and early school-age children. These studies of older children also have been guided by the organizational perspective on development already described. Thus, in designing our studies of maltreated preschool and early school-age children, we have endeavored to identify and articulate a number of developmental tasks that: (1) are especially salient during the preschool and early school-age years; (2) may be effected by a history of maltreatment; and (3) are also theoretically related to those aspects of the early development of maltreated children upon which our other studies have focused. Two examples of the many such tasks included in our studies are the establishment of relations with novel adults and the development of effectance motivation.

A child's relations with novel adults are especially important for entry to nursery school, kindergarten, or elementary school. Certain child characteristics, like excessive dependency upon, wariness of, or avoidance of novel adults, may interfere with a child's effective entry into school. Previous research by Zigler and his colleagues (Balla and Zigler, 1975; Weaver, Balla, and Zigler, 1971; Yando, Seitz, and Zigler, 1978) indicates that a history of social deprivation leads children to become excessively dependent upon and wary of novel adults. We wished to ascertain whether maltreated preschool and early school-age children were especially dependent upon or wary of novel adults in ways similar to other samples of socially deprived children.

Effectance motivation, the child's motive to deal competently with his/her environment for the intrinsic pleasure of mastery, also is influenced by a child's social history (Harter and Zigler, 1974; Zigler, 1971) and may also influence how the child adapts to the achievement and mastery demands of entry into school (Harter, 1978; Dweck and Elliott, 1983). Zigler (1971), drawing upon Maslow's theory of a hierarchy of motives, has described effectance motivation as a "life fulfilling" rather than "life preserving" need and consequently vulnerable to a history of debilitating life experiences. Thus, we wished to investigate whether maltreated children subordinated effectance motivation to the need to establish secure social relationships with novel adults as do other samples of socially deprived children. Taken together, relations with novel adults and effectance motivation were conceptualized as component parts of the child's larger developmental task of competently adapting to the first major out-of-home environment of the child's life, namely school, and to the larger world that school represents.

292 Outcomes and Consequences

Another developmental domain of special interest in studies of the effects of child maltreatment is cognitive maturity. Children's performance on measures of cognitive maturity (e.g., mental age as measured by standardized intelligence tasks) may be diminished by a history of maltreatment (Baharal, Waterman, and Martin, 1981; Elmer, 1977). One research report raises the possibility that a history of maltreatment may produce an extrinsically oriented social–cognitive style that influences a child's test-taking style in such a way as to lower their scores on IQ-like tests (Baharal et al., 1981; Smetana, Kelly, and Twentyman, 1984). For these reasons, we decided to examine whether maltreated children score lower on tests of cognitive maturity than do appropriately matched comparison children.

Recently the HCMP completed the collection and analysis of data on these three domains of development. Three samples of children comprise the cohort of 191 preschool and early school-age children selected for study. The maltreatment sample consisted of 91 maltreated children and their siblings who were considered to be at risk for maltreatment. There were 70 nonmaltreated children from families receiving Aid for Families with Dependent Children (the sample demographically matched to the maltreated children). Finally a sample of 30 maltreated children from middle SES families were included. The middle SES children were recruited in order to provide not only a contrast to the other two samples on a host of sociodemographic characteristics but also a context for the interpretation of findings on the measures of development. Children in each of the three samples ranged in age from 4.0 to 8.1 years (mean age for each sample = 5.7 years). In addition, each sample included approximately equal numbers of boys and girls. Complete descriptions of the recruitment procedures and sample characteristics are available in Aber (1982) and Aber (submitted).

The data on the three domains of the children's socioemotional and cognitive development were collected during two experimental sessions (held within 2 weeks of each other on average) at our university-based laboratories. These sessions were the first of a series of three phases of data collection planned for each child over a 30-month period. The specific constructs measured included:

- Relations with novel adults: dependency, wariness, interpersonal distance, verbal attention seeking, and imitation
- Effectance motivation: mastery smiles, pictorial curiosity, variability seeking, and level of aspiration
- Cognitive maturity: IQ (derived)

The measures employed in this phase of our study had been successfully employed in previous studies of the effects of social deprivation on children's development. Complete descriptions of the measures and experimental procedures employed in this phase of the study are also available in Aber (1982) and Aber (submitted).

The results of this initial cross-sectional study appear quite interesting. Unlike some past studies of the sequelae of child maltreatment (Elmer, 1977) that were not guided by the theoretical notion of competence at stage-salient tasks, our studies have begun to demonstrate that preschool and early school age children are effected by a history of maltreatment over and above the effects on development of low SES and welfare dependency. More specifically, 4- to 8-year-old children, compared to a well-matched group of nonmaltreated, welfare-dependent children, appear more dependent upon novel adults, more imitative of novel adults, less pictorially curious, and less cognitively mature.

Our confidence in the validity of these findings is increased, in part, because they seem to correspond well with previous findings of the effects of maltreatment on children's early development. The work of Egeland and Sroufe (1981a, b), as well as work from our own laboratory cited previously (Schneider-Rosen et al., 1985) indicate that maltreated children establish a higher percentage of insecure attachment relationships with their primary caregivers than do nonmaltreated children. In Bowlby's and Ainsworth's terms, they are so anxious about the availability and responsiveness of their caregiver that they are unable to utilize their caregiver as a secure base from which to explore their environment. We believe that preschool and early school-age children's relations with novel adults and effectance motivation can be appropriately conceptualized as developmental successors to infants' and toddlers' attachments and exploratory systems of behavior, respectively. To the extent that this is true, with older children as well as with younger children, our project has been investigating whether maltreated children can strike a stage-specific, age-appropriate balance between establishing safe, satisfying relationships with important adults and going out, on the basis of that relationship, to explore and engage in the world in an effective, competent fashion. Data from our studies of preschool and school-age children indicate that maltreated children may be more preoccupied with security issues in their relationships with novel adults (more dependent, more imitative), therefore, less free to be motivated by competency concerns (less pictorially curious). Thus, our work, like that of Baharal et al. (1981) and Smetana et al. (1984) suggest that social–cognitive or social–motivational factors may underlie observed differences in cognitive maturity (in our studies, the equivalent of 9 IQ points) between maltreated and well-matched nonmaltreated children.

Finally, recent work reported by Sroufe (1983) on the relationship between insecurity of attachment in infancy and dependency upon teachers in the preschool years provides further support for our belief that we are beginning to identify an important developmental process that seems to be impaired by a history of maltreatment. While the specific tasks change from infancy to the early school years, the theme of balancing interpersonal connectedness with exploration remains similar. The careful tracing of such themes is the essence of our research strategy on the development of maltreated children.

CONCLUSION

In the past 6 years, the HCMP has made marked progress toward its eventual goal of achieving an integrated picture of the sequelae of child maltreatment. Much groundwork has been laid, including the development of an appropriate assessment strategy, the establishment of a collaborative arrangement with protective service agencies, the recruitment of a large cohort of subjects, and the collection of a substantial amount of empirical data. We have integrated relevant aspects of developmental theory, experimental psychopathology, sociology, and clinical practice. Through this process, we have become convinced of the value of such an approach.

Our initial efforts described herein have proven fruitful. Future goals of the HCMP include: (1) continued analysis of both cross-sectional and longitudinal data; (2) the linking of parent and environmental characteristics to specific developmental outcomes; and (3) expansion of our data collection into nonlaboratory settings (e.g., school and camp). The achievement of these goals will yield knowledge of importance not only to scientific theories of development but also to prevention and treatment efforts on behalf of maltreated children.

REFERENCES

Aber, J. L. The socio-emotional development of maltreated children. Unpublished Ph.D. dissertation, Yale University, 1982.

Aber, J. L. Differentiating the effects of child maltreatment from the consequences of lower-class membership: Research of the socio-emotional development of school-age children. Unpublished manuscript, Barnard College, submitted for publication.

Aber, J. L., and Cicchetti, D. The socio-emotional development of maltreated children: An empirical and theoretical analysis. In H. Fitzgerald, B. Lester, and M. Yogman, Eds., Theory and research in behavioral pediatrics. NY: Plenum, 1984.

Ainsworth, M. D. S. The development of infant–mother attachment. In B. Caldwell and H. Ricciuti, Eds., Review of child development research, vol. 3, Chicago, IL: University of Chicago Press, 1973.

Ainsworth, M. D. S., Blehar, M. C., Waters, E., and Wall, S. Patterns of attachment: A psychological study of the strange situation. Hillsdale, NJ: Erlbaum, 1978.

Ainsworth, M. D. S., and Wittig, B. A. Attachment and exploratory behavior of one year olds in a strange situation. *In* B. M. Foss, Ed., *Determinants of infant behavior*, vol. 4. NY: Wiley, 1969.

Aragona, J. A., and Eyberg, S. M. Neglected children: Mother's report of child behavior problems and observed verbal behavior. *Child Development*, 1981, *52*: 596–602.

Baharal, R. M., Waterman, J., and Martin, H. P. The social cognitive development of abused children. *Journal of Consulting and Clinical Psychology*, 1981, *49*: 508–516.

Balla, D., and Zigler, E. Preinstitutional social deprivation and responsiveness to social reinforcement in institutionalized retarded individuals: A six-year study. *American Journal of Mental Deficiency*, 1975, *80*: 228–230.

Bell, R. Q. Convergence: An accelerated longitudinal approach. *Child Development*, 1968, *24*: 142–145.

Belsky, J. Child maltreatment: An ecological integration. *American Psychologist*, 1980, *35*: 320–335.

Bowlby, J. *Attachment and loss*, vol. 1: *Attachment*. NY: Basic Books, 1969.

Bretherton, I. Attachment theory: Retrospect and prospect. *In* I. Bretherton and E. Waters, Eds., *Growing points in attachment theory and research. Monographs of the Society for Research in Child Development*, 1985, *50*(209).

Cicchetti, D. The emergence of developmental psychopathology. *Child Development*, 1984, *55*: 1–7.

Cicchetti, D., and Rizley, R. Developmental perspectives on the etiology, intergenerational transmission, and sequelae of child maltreatment. *New Directions for Child Development*, 1981, *11*: 31–55.

Cicchetti, D., and Schneider-Rosen, K. An organizational approach to childhood depression. *In* M. Rutter, C. Izard, and P. Read, Eds., *Depression in young people: Clinical and developmental perspectives*. NY: Guilford, 1986.

Cicchetti, D., and Sroufe, L. A. An organizational view of affect: Illustration from the study of Down's syndrome infants. *In* M. Lewis and L. Rosenblum, Eds., *The development of affect*. NY: Plenum, 1978.

Cicchetti, D., Taraldson, B., and Egeland, B. Perspectives in the treatment and understanding of child abuse. *In* A. Goldstein, Ed., *Prescriptions for child mental health and education*. NY: Pergamon Press, 1978.

Daniel, J. H., Hampton, R. L., and Newberger, E. Child abuse and accidents in black families: A controlled comparative study. *American Journal of Orthopsychiatry*, in press.

Dweck, C., and Elliott, E. Achievement motivation. *In* P. Mussen, Ed., *Handbook of child psychology*, vol. 4. NY: Wiley, 1983, pp. 643–691.

Egeland, B., and Sroufe, L. A. Attachment and early maltreatment. *Child Development*, 1981, *52*: 44–52. (a)

Egeland, B., and Sroufe, L. A. Developmental sequelae of maltreatment in infancy. *New Directions for Child Development: Developmental Perspectives on Child Maltreatment*, 1981, *11*: 77–92. (b)

Elmer, E. *Children in jeopardy: A study of abused minors and their families.* Pittsburgh, PA: University of Pittsburgh Press, 1967.

Elmer, E. *Fragile families, troubled children*. Pittsburgh, PA: University of Pittsburgh Press, 1977.

Emde, R., Gaensbauer, T., and Harmon, R. *Emotional expression in infancy: A biobehavioral study*. NY: International Universities Press, 1976.

Freud, A. *Normality and pathology in childhood*. NY: International Universities Press, 1965.

Gaensbauer, T. J., Mrazek, D., and Harmon, R. J. Affective behavior patterns in abused and/or neglected infants. *In* N. Frude, Ed., *The understanding and prevention of child abuse: Psychological approaches.* London: Concord Press, 1980.

Gaensbauer, T. J., and Sands, K. Distorted affective communication in abused/neglected infants and their potential impact on caretakers. *American Journal of Child Psychiatry,* 1979, *18:* 236–250.

Galdston, R. Violence begins at home: The parents' center project for the study and prevention of child abuse. *American Academy of Child Psychiatry,* 1971, *10:* 336–350.

Garbarino, J. A preliminary study of some ecological correlates of child abuse: The impact of socioeconomic stress on mothers. *Child Development,* 1976, *47:* 178–185.

Gelles, R. J. Child abuse and family violence: Implications for medical .professionals. *In* E. H. Newberger, Ed., *Child abuse.* Boston: Little, Brown, 1983.

George, C., and Main, M. Social interactions of young abused children: Approach, avoidance, and aggression. *Child Development,* 1979, *50:* 306–318.

George, C., and Main, M. Abused children: Their rejection of peers and caregivers. *In* T. M. Field, S. Goldberg, D. Stern, and A. M. Sostek, Eds., *High risk infants and children: Adult and peer interactions.* NY: Academic Press, 1980.

Giovannoni, J. M., and Becerra, R. M. *Defining child abuse.* NY: Free Press, 1979.

Gray, J., and Kempe, R. S. The abused child at time of injury. *In* H. P. Martin, Ed., *The abused child: A multidisciplinary approach to developmental issues and treatment.* Cambridge, MA: Ballinger, 1976.

Green, A. H. Psychopathology of abused children. *Journal of the American Academy of Child Psychiatry,* 1978, *17:* 92–103.

Harter, S. Effectance motivation reconsidered: Toward a developmental model. *Human Development,* 1978, *21:* 34–64.

Harter, S., and Zigler, E. The assessment of effectance motivation in normal and retarded children. *Developmental Psychology,* 1974, *10:* 169–180.

Johnson, B., and Morse, H. A. Injured children and their parents. *Children,* 1968, *15:* 147–152.

Kempe, R., and Kempe, C. H. *Child abuse.* Cambridge, MA: Harvard University Press, 1978.

Kent, J. A follow-up study of abused children. *Journal of Pediatric Psychology,* 1976, *1:* 25–31.

Lewis, M., and Brooks-Gunn, J. *Social cognition and the acquisition of self.* NY: Plenum Press, 1979.

Martin, H. P., Ed. *The abused child: A multidisciplinary approach to developmental issues and treatment.* Cambridge, MA: Ballinger, 1976.

Martin, H. P., and Beezeley, P. Behavioral observations of abused children. *Developmental Medicine and Child Neurology,* 1977, *19:* 373–387.

Matas, L., Arend, R., and Sroufe, L. A. Continuity in adaptation in the second year. *Child Development,* 1978, *49:* 547–556.

Morse, C. W., Sahler, O., and Friedman, S. A three year follow-up study of abused and neglected children. *American Journal of Diseases of Children,* 1970, *120:* 439–446.

National Center on Child Abuse and Neglect. *Study findings: National study of incidence and severity of child abuse and neglect.* Washington, D.C. DHHS Publication No (OHDS) 81-3125, September 1981.

Newberger, E. H. *Child abuse.* Boston: Little, Brown, 1983.

Ounstead, C., Oppenheimer, R., and Lindsay, J. Aspects of bonding failure: The psychopathology and psychotherapeutic treatment of families of battered children. *Developmental Medicine and Child Neurology*, 1974, *16*: 447–456.

Parke, R. D., and Collmer, C. W. Child abuse: An interdisciplinary analysis. *In* E. M. Hetherington, Ed., *Review of child development research*, vol. 5. Chicago, IL: University of Chicago Press, 1975, pp. 509–590.

Pelton, L. Child abuse and neglect: The myth of classlessness. *American Journal of Orthopsychiatry*, 1978, *48*: 608–617.

Pelton, L. H. *The social context of child abuse and neglect.* NY: Human Sciences Press, 1981.

Reidy, T. J. The aggressive characteristics of abused and neglected children. *Journal of Clinical Psychology*, 1977, *33*: 1140–1145.

Relich, R., Giblin, R., Starr, R., and Agronow, S. Motor and social behavior in abused and control children: Observations of parent–child interactions. *The Journal of Psychology*, 1980, *106*: 193–204.

Rolston, R. The effect of prior physical abuse on the expression of overt and fantasy aggression behavior in children. *Dissertation Abstracts International*, 1971, *32*: 3016A.

Rutter, M., and Garmezy, N. Developmental psychopathology. *In* P. Mussen, Ed., *Handbook of child psychology.* NY: Wiley, 1983.

Sameroff, A., and Chandler, M. Reproductive risk and the continuum of caretaking casualty. *In* F. Horowitz, Ed., *Review of child development research*, vol. 4. Chicago, IL: University of Chicago Press, 1975.

Schneider-Rosen, K., Braunwald, K., Carlson, V., and Cicchetti, D. Current perspectives in attachment theory: Illustration from the study of maltreated infants. *In* I. Bretherton and E. Waters, Eds., *Growing points in attachment theory and research.* Monographs of the Society for Research in Child Development, 1985, *50* (209).

Schneider-Rosen, K., and Cicchetti, D. The relationship between affect and cognition in maltreated infants: Quality of attachment and the development of self recognition. *Child Development*, 1984, *55*: 648–658.

Smetana, J. G., Kelly, M., and Twentyman, C. T. Abused, neglected, and nonmaltreated children's conceptions of moral and social–conventional transgressions. *Child Development*, 1984, *55*: 277–287.

Sroufe, L. A. The coherence of individual development. *American Psychologist*, 1979, *34*: 834–841. (a)

Sroufe, L. A. Socioemotional development. *In* J. Osofsky, Ed., *Handbook of infant development.* NY: Wiley, 1979. (b)

Sroufe, L. A. Infant–caregiver attachment and patterns of adaptation in preschool: The roots of maladaptation and competence. *In* M. Perlmutter, Ed., *Minnesota symposium in child psychology*, vol. 16. Hillsdale, NJ: Erlbaum, 1983.

Sroufe, L. A., and Rutter, M. The domain of developmental psychopathology. *Child Development*, 1984, *55*: 17–29.

Sroufe, L. A., and Waters, E. Attachment as an organizational construct. *Child Development*, 1977, *48*: 1184–1199.

Terr, L. C. A family study of child abuse. *American Journal of Psychiatry*, 1970, *127*: 125–131.

Vaughn, B., Egeland, B., Sroufe, L. A., and Waters, E. Individual differences in infant–mother attachment at 12 and 18 months: Stability and change in families under stress. *Child Development*, 1979, *50*: 971–975.

Weaver, J., Balla, D., and Zigler, E. Social approach and avoidance tendencies of institutionalized retarded and noninstitutionalized retarded and normal children. *Journal of Experimental Research in Personality*, 1971, *5*: 98–110.

Werner, H., and Kaplan, B. *Symbol formation: An organismic-developmental approach to language and the expression of thought.* NY: Wiley, 1963.

Yando, R., Seitz, V., and Zigler, E. *Imitation: A developmental perspective.* Hillsdale, NJ: Erlbaum, 1978.

Zigler, E. The retarded child as a whole person. *In* H. E. Adams and W. K. Boardman, III, Eds., *Advances in experimental clinical psychology,* vol. 1. NY: Pergamon Press, 1971.

Zigler, E. Controlling child abuse: Do we have the knowledge and or the will? *In* G. Gerbner, C. Ross, and E. Zigler, Eds., *Child abuse: An agenda for action.* NY: Oxford University Press, 1980.

THE CONSEQUENCES OF CHILD MALTREATMENT: BIOSOCIAL AND ECOLOGICAL ISSUES

James Garbarino

chapter

13

THE HUMAN ECOLOGY OF CHILD MALTREATMENT

A complete and unambiguous analysis of the outcomes of child maltreatment is certainly beyond the scope of this analysis and probably the knowledge available to us at this point in the history of scientific inquiry into child abuse and neglect. Most of the research is retrospective (see Egeland, Jacobvitz, and Papatola, Chapter 11, and Cicchetti, Carlson, Braunwald, and Aber, Chapter 12, this volume, for important exceptions), and this limits our ability to detect causal relations. In the case of the link between child abuse and juvenile delinquency, for example, a review indicated that virtually all the available studies were retrospective (Garbarino and Plantz, 1984). Nonetheless, concern about the consequences of child maltreatment is justifiable.

On the one hand, most researchers are convinced that child maltreatment has multiple and often severe consequences. On the other hand, we must acknowledge that the prevalence of specific forms of harm, the mediators of damage, and the processes of influence are not as yet completely clear (to say the least). Speaking of the socioemotional consequences of physical abuse, Egeland and Sroufe (1981) assert: "In the area of socioemotional development, even the obvious is often difficult to demonstrate. . . . Uncovering the developmental consequences of child abuse is a prime example. . . . Yet, no one can doubt that there are consequences of being physically abused" (p. 77).

What are some of those consequences? Even a cursory review of the literature reveals numerous possibilities. These include death, permanent disability, developmental delay, speech and learning problems, impaired attachment relations, self- and other-directed aggression, psychosis (particularly multiple personalities), juvenile delinquency, depression, deficient social skills, and sexual dysfunction. Indeed, it is difficult to identify any problem that has not been linked to child maltreatment on the basis of clinical observation, survey research, or informed speculation.

In a comprehensive review of the consequences of abuse and neglect, Martin (1980) identified three major forms of harm: medical problems (ranging from nutritional deficiencies to hearing loss to brain damage); developmental problems (from mental retardation to language deficiencies to impaired motor skills); psychological problems (encompassing the extremes on most dimensions of personality—for example, being either very shy and inhibited or very aggressive and provocative—as well as general unhappiness, poor attachment, and inadequate peer relations). Martin does attempt to shed some light on the "Dynamics of the Effect of Abusive Environment on Development." He includes the idea that a pattern of transactions develops (cf. Sameroff and Chandler, 1975) in which the damaged child elicits responses that reinforce the damage. For example, brain damage adversely affects personality, a pattern of entrapped parent–child conflict releases a pattern of abuse, mastery languishes, increasingly iatrogenic interventions occur as foster placement occurs then fails. All this is plausible, and the reality of damage appears undeniable. It is the form, severity, prevalence, and duration of harm that remain at issue. It is, therefore, appropriate that we consider a theoretical scheme that may help organize existing knowledge and guide further research and speculation. We find this needed scheme in an ecological perspective.

An Ecological Perspective on the Development of Abused and Neglected Children

If there is one useful aspect of what we may term an ecological perspective on human development (Bronfenbrenner, 1979), it is its characteristic approach to answering the question, "Does X cause Y?" The ecologically sound answer is always, "It depends" (Garbarino and Associates, 1982). Because of its insistence that the course, and indeed the very content, of development derives from the complex interaction of biological and social systems nested hierarchically one within the other, an ecological perspective is particularly well suited to issues like the consequences of child maltreatment that are dominated by the interplay of individual factors, social resources, cultural definition, and public policy. It provides an intellectual home for the general orientation we label a "biosocial perspective" in that it organizes the various nested arrangements of social systems around the developing individual. What is more, it puts to rest the simple nature/nurture dichotomy through its fundamental principle that the relative impact of each varies and depends upon the total context in which it is operating.

In some cases, and in making some comparisons, nature is all important. For example, there are specific genetic conditions and chromosomal abnormalities that produce mental retardation. These genetic factors seem to override normal environmental influences. Even here, however, the level of human functioning that the person develops depends in some measure upon the kind of nurture the organism receives. In the case of PKU (phenylketonuria), for example, special diets can prevent its disastrous consequences for mental development. In general, the risk posed by biological deficits increases or decreases in direct proportion to the willingness and ability of the environment to provide supplementary nurture (a point to which we will return later). Biology is important, but so is society. Our "nature" is as much social as it is biological.

A brief exposition should make this clear. As used here, an ecological perspective on human development focuses on the biological and psychological systems of the individual acting in combination with the social systems of the family, neighborhood, community, and society to generate the ecological niche in which development proceeds. It emphasizes a phenomenologically based formulation of development that is conveyed in the following statement: "The developmental status of the individual is reflected in the substantive variety and structural complexity of the . . . activities which he initiates and maintains in the absence of instigation or direction by others" (Bronfenbrenner, 1979: 55).

The evolutionary foundations of this conception of development themselves warrant note here. If human evolution is significantly distinct it is in the production of a brain that operates in the domain of verbally mediated consciousness—"Mind." It is thus fully appropriate to define individual development in terms of an ever-more sophisticated representation of the world and the competence to act in that world.

Whether sociohistorical change can be encompassed in a similar evolutionary paradigm is open to debate, of course. Nonetheless, the transition from technologically simple and homogenous communities to more technologically complex and heterogenous societies does seem to represent a significant "development," if not uniformly within the historical era (i.e., in the last 3000 years), then certainly when contrasting the historical era with the 90 + % of our evolutionary history as a species that went before it (hereafter referred to as the evolutionary period of human species history). The modern world represents a broader and more complex arena for development; there is more developing to be done in the modern society than there was in the premodern society. This idea is intrinsic to the various histories of childhood produced in the last two decades.

What do we know of the evolutionary background of individual child development? We know that biology does much to establish the probabilities and limits within which the individual synthesizes a representation of the world and the competence to act in that world. Our evolved biology sets an agenda for environmental influences on the organism's growth and development. When nurtured properly (or at least when not insulted beyond the individual's limits of adaptability), the organism's biological script provides that most newborns will turn their heads to suck if touched on the cheek, that 4-month-old infants will respond with a smile to human voices and faces, that 1-year-olds will start walking, that 2-year-olds will start talking, and that 13-year-olds will begin to think abstractly. As the infant moves through the early weeks and months of life, its particular experience plays an ever-increasing role in shaping its behavior and ultimately its character as a person. However, while biological forces lose their domination over specific behaviors (e.g., as some reflexes subside), they continue to influence development by setting the organism's agenda. This agenda constitutes the basic needs, characteristics, and capabilities that make up human nature in general and specific organisms in particular.

The standard aspects of growth and maturation combine with individual differences in constitution and temperament to form the raw materials for child development. And, even in adulthood, biological timetables play a role (although they are much more variable than in childhood). They play a role in shaping the individual's readiness to make use of environmental circumstances. How do we conceptualize these environmental circumstances? We do so through the component parts of an ecological perspective beyond the individual—micro-, meso-, exo-, and macrosystems.

Microsystem

The systems most immediate to the developing individual are microsystems, the actual social–psychological settings in which individuals experience and create day-to-day reality. One of the most important aspects of a microsystem is the existence of relationships that go beyond simple dyads because such $N + 2$ relationships offer the increasing complexity that feeds development. Family, school, and peer group are salient microsystems for most children.

Mesosystem

The interrelations among major settings containing the developing person constitute mesosystems. Mesosystems can exist through links between family and school, peer group and church, and camp and workplace, among others. These links include both actual participation and cognitive representations of those settings. Mesosystem is a heavily phenomenological concept, and it exists to greater or lesser degrees for different individuals, groups, and cultures. In general, the stronger and more diverse the links between settings, the more powerful the influence of the mesosystem on the individual's development.

Exosystem

Exosystems are settings that have a bearing on the individual's development but in which he or she does not actually play a direct role. They include the major microsystems in which institutional decisions are made (e.g., local government and corporate headquarters) and in which key figures in the individual's life (but not the individual him- or herself) are directly active and which, therefore, indirectly influence the individual (e.g., when the workplace influences the worker's behavior at home in the role of parent).

Macrosystem

The meso- and exosystems are set within the broad ideological and institutional patterns of a particular culture or subculture. This is the macrosystem. It is a "blueprint" for the ecology of human development. It reflects a shared assumption of "how things should be done" and of "human nature." It normalizes behavior and provides the foundation for roles and expectations by systematizing cultural axioms.

APPLICATION OF AN ECOLOGICAL PERSPECTIVE

This ecological perspective can aid in efforts to generate hypotheses about causation, about unintended consequences, and about alternative avenues for intervening in social and personal problems. Consider as an illustrative example the relation between early developmental delay and later IQ deficit (one that is relevant to our interest in the outcomes of child maltreatment). Does early delay cause later IQ deficit? According to Willerman, Broman, and Fiedler's (1970) classic study, it depends. Whereas nearly 13% of developmentally delayed 8-month-olds from low SES homes had IQs of 79 or less (a standard indicator of mental retardation) at 4 years of age, only 7% of the middle SES and 2% of the children from high SES families did so. There was no social class effect evident among 4-year-olds who were developmentally advanced at 8 months of age. This model suggests that contextual factors are particularly influential in cases of individuals at high risk. This hypothesis may prove critical in understanding the consequences of child maltreatment because it suggests that the impact of socially and economically impoverished environments may be greatest for the victims of child maltreatment. We can hold it firmly in mind as we proceed to review the consequences of child maltreatment in ecological perspective.

Organism

What role do organismic factors play in mediating the consequences of child maltreatment? One influence may lie in affecting the degree of harm. Clearly some individuals are more vulnerable to harm than others. Garmezy (1977), for example, has argued that "stress-resistant children" (the successor term to "invulnerable children") may overcome the experience of maltreatment, whereas vulnerable children may be developmentally devastated by it. A second organismic difference may be found in effects on the type of harm. Some children are more likely to internalize harm (in the form of somatic complaints, disordered thinking, extreme but unarticulated emotions, etc.), whereas others externalize it (in the form of aggression, delinquent behavior, and the like). Achenbach and Edelbrock's (1979) research on the two-factor structure of problems assessed via the Child Behavior Checklist documents this differentiation.

Finally, evidence derived from observational studies reporting on the role of aversive child behavior in instigating and sustaining patterns of maltreatment implies an active role for the child (Wahler, 1984), perhaps based upon temperamental differences such as those uncovered by Thomas and Chess (1980). Presumably this active role pertains to shaping the consequences of maltreatment as well. Biologically based temperamental factors include differences in rhythmicity, basic activity level, and reactivity. Such temperamental variation (on both the child's and adult's part) affects the degree to which family relationships are harmonious and satisfying. Some children are cuddlers; others seem to be stressed by close physical contact. Some parents (and cultures) make greater demands for regular eating and sleeping habits; some children are better able to meet such demands. The match of parental expectations, values, and temperament with the child's temperament—what has been called the "goodness-of-fit" between child and environment—does much to predict effective socialization (Thomas and Chess, 1980). It implies that parental ability to flexibly adjust to the individual temperament of the child is important. In cases of extreme asynchrony or incompatibility, temperamental differences may markedly increase the risk for child maltreatment and decrease the likelihood of ameliorating it within the family microsystem.

Temperamental differences are part of a more general pattern of interindividual biological variation with implications for family functioning. The child's capabilities and the demands he or she places on the family derive in part from biology. Biological maturation plays a general role in shaping the sequence and character of shifts in cognitive development, for example. Recent evidence suggests that the shift from more concrete to more abstract forms of reasoning in adolescence places special demands on parents—particularly fathers—to readjust their use of power-assertive techniques in discipline (Garbarino, Schellenbach, and Sebes, 1986; Garbarino, Sebes, and Schellenbach, 1984). The onset of puberty may alter the character of family relationships, for example, by reducing the appropriateness and comfortableness of physical intimacy between fathers and daughters.

What are the evolutionary foundations for these three classes of effects? Certainly the vicissitudes of childhood in the evolutionary period of human species' history placed a premium on stress resistance. Of particular interest here is the power of attachment—the primary human relationship. If the evolutionary analysis of children has reached one conclusion it is certainly that parent–infant attachment is fundamentally grounded in development of the species. The very power of this relationship suggests, however, that behavior motivated by it may become extremely costly to the long-term developmental prognosis if attachment is thwarted. Because the human organism is primed to make extreme investments to establish and maintain attachment, the consequences to the child of a parent who impedes this process are likely to be grave. If we view child maltreatment as a threat or impediment to attachment then we should expect that maltreated children will suffer developmentally for their efforts to fulfill the biological script for attachment. This seems consistent with the available evidence (see Chapters 11 and 12, this volume). The attachment relations of maltreated children are distorted, and this distortion correlates with otherwise impaired development. This consequence seems firmly grounded in our evolutionary history as a species.

Microsystem

What role do microsystem factors play in mediating the consequences of child maltreatment? We can break this question into two others. First, what else is going on in the family that may affect the damage done by maltreatment? Second, in what other microsystems does the child participate, and what is going on in those microsystems? As we shall soon see, this second question quickly leads us into a consideration of mesosystem issues.

A study conducted by Hunter and Kilstrom (1979) suggests that the efforts of a nonabusive parent within a family can be very significant in reducing the damage done to the child by an abusive parent. They studied 49 families in which at least one of the parents had been a childhood victim of maltreatment. Those that did not abuse their own (premature) infant within the first year of life (N = 40) either were abused by their fathers but not their mothers or were abused by their mothers but were "rescued" by some other adult (a point we will refer to again in discussing mesosystems). In the nine families that were re-peating the pattern of abuse, the mothers had all been abused by their own mothers and had not been rescued.

Egeland and Sroufe (1981) reinforce this emphasis on the role of the mother and its consequences in the first 3 years of life as a function of whether the mother was involved in psychological and/or physical maltreatment. The general finding seems to be that the incidence of psychosocial damage (e.g., as manifest in "insecure attachment") is greatest when the roles of "abuser" and "primary caregiver" are played by the same person, as is usually the case when the mother is abusive. This highlights the importance of assessing "relationship of the per-petrator to the victim" as a mediating factor in the consequences of maltreatment.

It seems reasonable to expect that different combinations of type and perpetrator of maltreatment will produce different consequences. For example, many students of sexual abuse report that the reaction to the abuse by a noninvolved parent (as well as others) is critical in determining the extent of psychological damage that will result (cf. Fin-kelhor, 1979). Many victims of paternal sexual abuse report that the sense of betrayal they felt when not supported and protected by their mothers was a critical negative influence.

What of nonfamilial microsystems? Little evidence bearing on the role of nonfamilial microsystems in mediating the consequences of maltreatment is available. Few intervention programs deal directly with children (and fewer still have adequate outcome data), because most interventions concentrate their attention on the task of changing the parents (Martin, 1980). This fact, itself, may have an evolutionary foun-dation if we view the lack of investment in abused children as an ev-olutionarily "wise" strategy for decreasing the survival rate for damaged organisms and thereby conserving resources for more promising off-spring.

Perhaps as evidence of our ability to transcend evolutionarily derived imperatives and make an investment in damaged children, some pro-jects do include crisis nurseries, play therapy groups, and other attempts to involve maltreated children in alternative or therapeutic microsys-tems. But at this point we can only hope and assume that these groups reduce the long-term damage to the victim of child maltreatment.

Mesosystem

What role do mesosystems play in mediating the consequences of child maltreatment? Two seem most likely. The first is the degree to which the family microsystem is isolated from other social systems (families, peer groups, religious and civic associations, recreational groups, etc.). The well-documented social isolation and "distancing" of many abusive and neglectful families (Garbarino, 1977; Gaudin and Pollane, 1983; Polansky, Chalmers, Buttenwieser, and Williams, 1981) highlights this factor. In the absence of such family-other mesosystems, there is less likelihood of compensatory socialization or access to what Emlen (1977) calls "protective behaviors." That these are important is suggested by Hunter and Kilstrom's (1979) study of child maltreatment discussed previously. Among their sample of 49 families in which one or both parents had been abused as a child, the childhood experience of being "rescued" by an adult outside the nuclear family figured prominently in whether or not the parents became perpetrators of mal-treatment within a year after the birth of a premature infant. Contemporary presence of adequate social support was also a critical influence—being described as adequate for 73% of the nonrepeaters versus 22% of the repeaters.

The evolutionary basis for these findings seems to lie in the concept of "investment" (Trivers, 1972). In the strictly biological sense, those who have the greatest genetic stake in a particular child are most likely to expend effort and take risks on its behalf. If we permit a social analogy of genetic investment we can add kith to kin as persons beyond the mother–father dyad who have an investment in the child. This suggests that the probability of an abused or neglected child being "rescued" depends largely upon the mother–father–child triad being enmeshed in a social system in which there are multiple individuals with an investment in the child and who are empowered to act on its behalf.

Those who have considered the foundations of the family (kin) and social networks (kith) conclude that the modern era is at odds with the ground rules laid down in the species evolutionary period (van den Berghe, 1979). This is the basis for Alice Rossi's (1977) assessment: "By neglecting the biosocial dimensions of human life . . . society may set the stage for unprecedented stress in the lives of young mothers and an impoverishment of their children" (p. 21).

A second, related mesosystem influence is the degree to which family-other relationships provide ideological support for maltreatment or provide counter values. We must consider whether or not associations outside the immediate family reinforce abusive or neglectful treatment of the child. Straus, Gelles, and Steinmetz (1980) report that where kin are the only or principal association of parents, the result is more rather than less physically abusive treatment of the child when the family is subject to significant social and economic stress. This may reflect a process of ideological congruence within kinships groups regarding the treatment of children. Whether such ideological congruence exacerbates or mitigates the consequences of such abuse is unknown. It is possible that by "normalizing" it such congruence reduces negative developmental consequences. Certainly the results of anthropological studies (cf. Korbin, 1979) add plausibility to this speculation. However, it may well be that some forms of child treatment such as rejection have a negative influence that is "transcultural" (Rohner, 1975), in which case defining it as normal does not significantly diminish the damage inflicted upon the child.

Mesosystem factors appear to be important in formal intervention efforts as well. Whether it be residential institutions (Whittaker, Garbarino, and Associates, 1983), foster care placements (Fanshel and Shinn, 1978), or behavioral modification programs (Wahler, 1984), the power of intervention to produce lasting improvement in the lives of children (including maltreated children) appears to depend upon the degree to which a strongly positive home-intervention program mesosystem is established. Where such a mesosystem is lacking, intrafamilial change extinguishes—perhaps most notably among low-income families not having access to sufficient compensatory resources in their social networks (Wahler, 1984). The evolutionary foundations for this may lie in the aforementioned intrinsically social nature of human beings, their families, and their development—isolated and distancing parents tended to be casualties. The very existence of individual behavior patterns without the reinforcement of a social network seems to fly in the face of our picture of existence in the premodern evolutionary era. As Rossi (1977) suggests, it seems to be our heritage to depend upon continuous social support (in the sense of coupling feedback and nurturance as proposed by Gerald Caplan, 1974). Without such social support (as operationalized in part through mesosystems) individual behavior and family functioning are in jeopardy (Garbarino, 1977).

Exosystem

What role do exosystems play in mediating the consequences of child maltreatment? Put another way, how does institutional policy and practice affect victims of child maltreatment? Efforts to evaluate intervention projects (e.g., Cohn, 1979) suggest that recidivism can be controlled by an intelligently applied mixture of professional expertise and lay helping. The home health visitor approach can even be effective in preventing child maltreatment (Gray and Kaplan, 1980; Olds, Chamberlin, Henderson, and Tatelbaum, 1983). Finally, skilled intensive intervention in times of extreme family crisis (such as is provided by the Homebuilders program) can even avert out-of-home placement (Kinney, Madson, Fleming, and Haapala, 1977). The point of all this is to suggest that policy decisions (exosystem effects) can influence all aspects of child maltreatment by shaping the infrastructure, resources, goods, and configuration of human service delivery systems (Whittaker et al., 1983).

And yet, effective intervention in child maltreatment languishes. Why? What evolutionary speculation suggests itself here? One that has received insufficient attention concerns what social psychologists called "the strain toward cognitive consistency." Simply put, in situations in which humans experience dissonance between their view of the world (including themselves) and their experience of the world (including their own behavior) they will be highly motivated to reduce the dissonance. This may involve changing their behavior or their view— whichever is easier from the point of view of their temperament, history, and analysis of the situation.

Thus, for example, parents who have learned to behave more effectively with their children will tend to think more positively about them, parents who learn to speak more positively about their children will tend to treat those children better, and parents who cannot do anything about changing a situation will tend to organize their thinking about the situation to "rationalize" it as best they can. The research literature dealing with the power, persuasiveness, and apparent universality of the motive to seek cognitive consistency is voluminous.

What is its evolutionary basis? A plausible speculation is that it is an adaptive response to the evolutionary rise of "Mind" noted earlier. As logical consciousness arose we can imagine a growing survival value to the ability to make sense of experience, even if such making sense required shifting beliefs around and changing patterns of behavior. The alternative? Madness and suicide. Without cognitive consistency life would be maddening (or rather, more so than it already is). Interestingly enough, people sometimes lapse into madness because they cannot find a healthy resolution in situations of extreme dissonance. This is the core insight in Gregory Bateson's (1972) theory of the "Double Bind" as the origins of schizophrenia. Make the world make sense! This is the message we inherit.

What relevance does this have to understanding the outcomes of child maltreatment? A clue appears in accounts of the Holocaust, where people were under devastating pressure to make a crazy world make sense. Consider this report by Jozef Zelkowicz (as cited in the *New York Times Magazine*, July 29, 1984: 17) concerning the response of the Lodz Ghetto in Poland in 1942, as 25,000 children and elderly were "resettled" (to death camps):

> Incidentally, the populace's strange reaction to the recent events is noteworthy. There is not the slightest doubt that this was a profound and terrible shock, and yet one must wonder at the indifference shown by those— apart from the ones who were not directly affected and who returned to normal life at once—from whom loved ones had been taken. It would seem that the events of recent days would have immersed the entire population of the ghetto in mourning for a long time to come, and yet, right after the incidents, and even during the resettlement action, the populace

was obsessed with everyday concerns—getting bread, rations, and so forth—and often went from immediate personal tragedy right back into daily life. Is this some sort of numbing of the nerves, an indifference, or a symptom of an illness that manifests itself in atrophied emotional reactions? After losing those nearest to them, people talk constantly about rations, potatoes, soup, etc.! It is beyond comprehension! Why this lack of warmth toward those they loved? Naturally, here and there, there are some mothers weeping in a corner for a child or children shipped from the ghetto, but, as a whole, the mood of the ghetto does not reflect last week's terrible ordeal.

Sad but true! (Jozef Zelkowicz).

Certainly one of the barriers to ameliorating the outcomes of child maltreatment is the fact that the motive to achieve cognitive consonance is strong and strongly expressed at all levels of the human ecology. Parents rationalize their abusive and neglectful treatment of their children just as "the general public" favors quick dramatic action that restores a sense of moral legitimacy to community institutions and, indeed, to society as a whole. This may be why foster care is the leading "solution" to child maltreatment in the public mind. "Business as usual" seems to be an evolutionary message. And it implies that progress in dealing with the consequences of child maltreatment must come spasmodically, as outbursts of public need for moral rationalization are used to achieve concrete institutional change. Interestingly, this same need for cognitive consistency in affected individuals with a strong internal locus of control orientation can produce social leadership, as the affected individual seeks to change society to rationalize their place in it (rather than altering their view of their experience). It also suggests— as many activists have long recognized—that personalizing maltreatment aids in turning the consistency motive toward social change rather than simply internal cognitive reorganization—the easiest solution when personal "investment" is low. Exosystems are crucial, and they are governed by what seems to be an evolutionarily produced process of rationalization.

Masson's (1984) recent critique of Freudian-based psychoanalysis and its handling of sexual abuse illuminates another possible exosystem effect (as well as the power of cognitive dissonance as a factor in clinical and theoretical analysis). By deciding to interpret female reports of sexual abuse as fantasy, the psychoanalytic "community" may well have exacerbated the psychological damage experienced by female victims of sexual abuse. This policy decision and others that punish the victim of sexual abuse—for example, by removing her rather than the offending father from the home or by forcing her to testify in open court— may contribute significantly to the adverse consequences of abuse. Professional helpers often seem to be operating under the domination of cognitive consonance mechanisms.

On the positive side, policy decisions that lead to improved functioning on the part of abusive parents may well increase the parental ability to rehabilitate the child through compensatory caregiving. This presumed exosystem effect is the foundation for most parent treatment programs. It finds support in anecdotal reports from victims and parents alike but has not been subjected to rigorous empirical verification.

Macrosystem

What role do macrosystem factors play in mediating the consequences of child maltreatment? One may speculate that various components of political ideology play a role in macrosystem influences on the consequences of maltreatment. A collectivist, interventionist ideology such as that dominating Chinese institutions may minimize damage by providing for powerful intervention supported across all levels of the human ecology. In contrast, the individualistic, noninterventionist ideology contained in the concept of "family privacy" may maximize damage by permitting the negative patterns begun in the family microsystem to generalize and even become functionally autonomous. With so little systematic cross-cultural evidence regarding intervention in child maltreatment, it seems impossible as yet to subject these speculations to empirical test. What cross-cultural evidence we do have, however, does seem consistent with the hypothesis that the overall level of support (nurturance and feedback) given to parents on an institutionalized basis does translate into differences in the prevalence of child maltreatment (Garbarino and Ebata, 1983; Korbin, 1979).

The power of culture to "normalize" experience is enormous. As Korbin's (1979) anthropological review demonstrates, parental behaviors that would be devastatingly abusive or neglectful in one culture seem nearly or actually benign in another. This leads Korbin to focus on "idiosyncratic" maltreatment—behavior that is outside the realm of acceptable child treatment in a particular culture. As she correctly acknowledges, however, a totally passive acceptance of a culture's criteria for defining idiosyncratic maltreatment is insufficient. Such extreme cultural relativism completely denies the validity of professional expertise which may act in a dialectical relationship with "community norms" to produce historical improvement in the lives of children (cf. Garbarino and Gilliam, 1980: 6).

Indeed, the very concept of child maltreatment is evolutionary in nature. It represents the gap between what is defined as idiosyncratic deviance and what is articulated as a higher order of consciousness about children. Our experience with child maltreatment as a moral phenomenon tells us that simple acceptance of the biologically probable as the psychologically inevitable constitutes a misreading of human potentials and flexibility. The act of recognizing child maltreatment is a triumph of Mind.

Research by Money and Ehrhardt (1972) suggests that androgen levels predict the amount of rough and tumble play in children, both within and across the sexes. Thus, it may be harder to socialize most males to be physically nonaggressive than it is to achieve the same result with most females—harder, but not impossible (Eron, 1980). In the same vein, the greater investment (Trivers, 1972) of females in their infants may make it easier to maintain social arrangements emphasizing maternal child care than paternal child care—easier but not predetermined. These "old" solutions to human experience may be anachronistic, but the value of a sociobiological orientation is that it alerts us to the possibility that some social forms (and particularly family forms) are more in tune with our evolutionary history than others. It certainly tells us that we make our individual and collective choices with respect to social arrangements in counterpoint to our species' traditional answers to these questions. In confronting the consequences of child maltreatment as moral beings we are contending with biological dispositions through social organizations.

By the same token, historical patterns of social evolution (again assuming it is appropriate to use this parallelism) may affect probabilities but not establish inevitabilities. Isaiah Berlin and others have offered up the definitive analysis of the reality of "free will" as a necessary and workable concept for understanding human affairs. What is more, we can recognize that neither biological nor social evolution can be presumed to produce "conclusions" (i.e., organisms and ideologies/institutions) that are valid in the current era. Are our evolutionary predelictions (social and biological) valid? As always, it depends. Donald Campbell highlighted this when he noted that: "The wisdom of any evolutionary process, biological or social, is wisdom about past worlds" (1979: 37).

This emboldens us to authorize efforts to transcend the "natural" inclinations we may have to write off maltreated children as high-risk prospects for future investment, even as we wisely recognize that in doing so we may be engaging some powerful psychological and social forces deeply rooted in our biosocial heritage. But in doing so we are also fulfilling the developmental nature of our heritage to create new, more evolved, and differentiated representations of the world and in then seeking the competence necessary to master them.

SUMMARY

This chapter addresses the consequences of child maltreatment. What effects does maltreatment have on development? What biological and social factors mediate these effects? What are the evolutionary underpinnings of psychological and social responses to child maltreatment—to the perpetrator as well as to the victim? It begins with a bio-social and ecological formulation of how biosocial factors translate into influences on human development. How this framework helps us understand the consequences of child maltreatment is considered next.

Child maltreatment seems a particularly appropriate topic for a bio-social perspective for two reasons. First, concerned academics and practitioners have paid considerable attention to the issue of how "natural" or "unnatural" abuse and neglect are. Is child maltreatment an expectable aspect of parent–child relations, or is it a qualitatively distinct phenomenon? Is it but the extreme form of "normal" behavior, or a different, pathological class of behavior? Second, there is ample evidence to document the existence of complex interactions between individual and social factors in generating and sustaining maltreatment. This evidence demands a biosocial integration that helps sort out that which is inherent in *Homo sapiens* as organisms from that which is inherent in people as cultural creatures.

REFERENCES

Achenbach, T., and Edelbrock, C. The child behavior profile. *Journal of Consulting and Clinical Psychology*, 1979, *47*: 223–233.

Bateson, G. *Steps to an ecology of mind.* NY: Chandler, 1972.

Bronfenbrenner, U. *The ecology of human development.* Cambridge, MA: Harvard University Press, 1979.

Campbell, D. Comments on the sociobiology of ethics and moralizing. *Behavioral Science*, 1979, *24*: 37–45.

Caplan, *Support systems and community health.* NY: Behavioral Publ., 1974.

Cohn, A. Essential elements of successful child abuse and neglect treatment. *Child Abuse and Neglect*, 1979, *3*: 491–496.

Egeland, B., and Sroufe, A. Developmental sequelae of maltreatment in infancy. *In* R. Rizley and D. Cicchetti, Eds., *New directions in child development.* San Francisco, CA: Jossey-Bass, 1981.

Emlen, A. If you care about children, then care about families. Address to the Tennessee Association for Young Children, Nashville, Tennessee, November, 1977.

Eron, L. Prescription for reduction of aggression. *American Psychologist,* 1980, *35*: 244–252.

Fanshel, D., and Shinn, E. *Children in foster care.* NY: Columbia University Press, 1978.

Finkelhor, D. *Sexually victimized children.* NY: Academic Press, 1979.

Garbarino, J. The human ecology of child maltreatment. *Journal of Marriage and the Family*, 1977, *39*: 721–736.

Garbarino, J., and Associates. *Children and families in the social environment.* NY: Aldine, 1982.

Garbarino, J., and Ebata, A. On the significance of ethnic and cultural differences in child maltreatment. *Journal of Marriage and the Family*, 1983, *45*: 773–783.

Garbarino, J., and Gilliam, G. *Understanding abusive families.* Lexington, MA: Lexington Books, 1980.

Garbarino, J., and Plantz, M. Child maltreatment and juvenile delinquency: What are the links? Paper presented to a symposium on Child Abuse and Juvenile Delinquency, Racine, Wisconsin, April 8, 1984.

Garbarino, J., Schellenbach, C., and Sebes, J. *Troubled youth, troubled families.* NY: Aldine, 1986.

Garbarino, J., Sebes, J., and Schellenbach, C. Families at-risk for destructive parent–child relations in adolescence. *Child Development,* 1984, *55:* 174–183.

Garmezy, N. Observations on research with children at risk for child and adult psychopathology. *In* McMillan and Hengo, Eds., *Child psychiatry, treatment, and research.* NY: Brunner/Mazel, 1977.

Gaudin, J., and Pollane, L. Social networks, stress, and child abuse. *Children and Youth Services Review,* 1983, *5:* 91–102.

Gray, J., and Kaplan, B. The lay health visitor program: An eighteen month experience. *In* C. H. Kempe and R. Helfer, Eds., *The battered child.* Chicago, IL: University of Chicago Press, 1980.

Hunter, R., and Kilstrom, N. Breaking the cycle in abusive families. *American Journal of Psychiatry,* 1979, *136:* 1320–1322.

Kinney, S., Madson, B., Fleming, T., and Haapala, D. Homebuilders: Keeping families together. *Journal of Consulting and Clinical Psychology,* 1977, *45:* 667–673.

Korbin, J., Ed. *Child abuse and neglect: Cross-cultural perspectives.* Berkeley, CA: University of California Press, 1979.

Martin, H. The consequences of being abused and neglected: How the child fares. *In* C. H. Kempe and R. Helfer, Eds., *The battered child,* 3rd ed. Chicago, IL: University of Chicago Press, 1980.

Masson, J. *The assault on truth: Freud's suppression of the seduction theory.* NY: Farrar, Straus, and Giroux, 1984.

Money, J., and Ehrhart, A. *Man and woman, boy and girl.* Baltimore, MD: John Hopkins University Press, 1972.

New York Times Magazine. The untold story of the Lodz Ghetto. *New York Times Magazine,* 29 July 1984, 13 ff.

Olds, D., Chamberlin, R., Henderson, C., and Tatelbaum, R. Preventing childrearing dysfunction and high-risk families. Colloquium presentation, Department of Individual and Family Studies, the Pennsylvania State University, University Park, Pennsylvania, May 6, 1983.

Polansky, N., Chalmers, M., Buttenwieser, E., and Williams, D. *Damaged parents.* Chicago, IL: University of Chicago Press, 1981.

Rohner, R. *They love me, they love me not.* New Haven, CT: HRAF Press, 1975.

Rossi, A. A biosocial perspective on parenting. *Daedelus,* 1977, *106:* 1–31.

Sameroff, A., and Chandler, M. Reproductive risk and the continuum of caretaking casualty. *In* F. D. Horowitz, Ed., *Review of child development research.* Chicago, IL: University of Chicago Press, 1975.

Straus, M., Gelles, R., and Steinmetz, S. *Behind closed doors.* NY: Doubleday, 1980.

Thomas and Chess. The dynamics of psychological development. NY: Brunner/Mazel, 1980.

Trivers, R. L. Parental investment and sexual selection. *In* B. Campbell, Ed., *Sexual selection and descent of man, 1871–1971.* Chicago, IL: Aldine, 1972.

Van den Berghe, P. *Human family systems: An evolutionary view.* NY: Elsevier, 1979.

Wahler, R. Problems of maintaining changes in parenting for "insular" disadvantaged families. Paper presented at a seminar on Professional and Lay

Partnerships in Prevention of Unnecessary Out of Home Care, University of North Carolina, Chapel Hill, North Carolina, March 5, 1984.

Whittaker, J., Garbarino, J., and Associates. *Social support networks.* NY: Aldine, 1983.

Willerman, L., Broman, S., and Fiedler, M. Infant development, preschool IQ, and social class. *Child Development,* 1970, *41:* 69–77.

INDEX